AF335585

PN #	Item ID	Alibris ID	Media Type	Title / Author	Seller List Price	Order Date
76523813-32	47218	B083658711	BOOK	Resisting Citizenship Feminist Essays on Politics, Community, and Democracy Ackelsberg, Martha A.	$12.00	Jul, 6 2026

RESISTING CITIZENSHIP

Political participation in America—supposedly the world's strongest democracy—is startlingly low, and many of the civil rights and economic equity initiatives that were instituted in the 1960s and 1970s have been abandoned, as significant proportions of the populace seem to believe that the civil rights battle has been won. However, rates of collective engagement, like community activism, are surprisingly high. In *Resisting Citizenship*, renowned feminist political scientist Martha Ackelsberg argues that community activism may hold important clues to reviving democracy in this time of growing bureaucratization and inequality.

Resisting Citizenship brings together many of Ackelsberg's writings over the past 25 years, combining her own fieldwork and interviews with cutting-edge research and theory on democracy and activism. She explores these efforts in order to draw lessons—and attempt to incorporate knowledge—about current notions of democracy from those who engage in "non-traditional" participation, those who have, in many respects, been relegated to the margins of political life in the United States.

Martha Ackelsberg is Five College Fortieth Anniversary Professor and William R. Kenan, Jr., Professor in the Department of Government and Program for the Study of Women and Gender at Smith College, USA. Her research and teaching interests are in applied democratic theory, urban politics, and feminist theory.

RESISTING CITIZENSHIP

Feminist Essays on Politics, Community, and Democracy

Martha A. Ackelsberg

NEW YORK AND LONDON

First published 2010
by Routledge
270 Madison Ave, New York, NY 10016

Simultaneously published in the UK
by Routledge
2 Park Square, Milton Park, Abingdon, Oxon OX14 4RN

Routledge is an imprint of the Taylor & Francis Group, an informa business

© 2010 Taylor & Francis

Typeset in Baskerville by Taylor & Francis Books
Printed and bound in the United States of America on acid-free paper
by Walsworth Publishing Company, Marceline, MO

Library of Congress Cataloging in Publication Data
Ackelsberg, Martha A.
Resisting citizenship : feminist essays on politics, community and
democracy / Martha A. Ackelsberg.
p. cm.
Includes bibliographical references and index.
1. Women in politics–United States. 2. Political participation–United
States. 3. Feminism–United States. I. Title.
HQ1236.5.U6A22 2009
320.082–dc22
2009003541

ISBN10: 0-415-93518-0 (hbk)
ISBN10: 0-415-93519-9 (pbk)

ISBN13: 978-0-415-93518-0 (hbk)
ISBN13: 978-0-415-93519-7 (pbk)

FOR MY STUDENTS

CONTENTS

CONTENTS

ACKNOWLEDGMENTS

A book that incorporates essays written over decades is indebted to so many friends and colleagues that it would be inconsiderate to the reader to list them all. Those who have helped me think through the ideas in particular essays are named in the acknowledgments to the individual essays. But some people have been so much part of my intellectual journey that I feel a need to thank them more directly.

My first debt is to my co-authors on a number of these essays, Mary Lyndon (Molly) Shanley and Myrna Breitbart, with whom I have had the pleasure and good fortune to share at least some components of our personal, political, and intellectual odysseys over these many years. Their friendships have been invaluable, as has been the opportunity to think through with them ideas about in/equality, anarchism, direct action, feminism, politics and the relationship between activism and the academy that animate these pages.

Molly is also a member of the "Tower Ladies," an informal group of feminist political scientists who meet to read one another's work, talk about teaching, and share our lives and struggles. Over the years, the group has provided invaluable support of the sort that feminist theologian Nelle Morton once termed "hearing one another into speech." I am honored and blessed to have been able to participate in conversations with Amrita Basu, Cathy Cohen, Cynthia Enloe, Mary Katzenstein, Eileen McDonagh, Gwendolyn Mink and Molly Shanley.

Colleagues in the American Political Science Association and, in particular, in the Feminist Political Theory Group of the Western Political Science Association, have offered venues for the presentation and discussion of my work, and opportunities for the sort of challenging interactions that characterize academia at its best. Conversations over many years with Jane Bayes, Marla Brettschneider, Susan J. Carroll, Cynthia Daniels, Irene Diamond, Christine DiStefano, Kathy Ferguson, Janet Flammang, Joyce Gelb, Mary Hawkesworth, Nancy Hirschmann, Jyl Josephson, Jenny Mansbridge, Lori Marso, Kristen Monroe, Carole Pateman, Ann Robbart, Wendy Sarvasy, Anna Marie Smith, Holloway Sparks, Judith Stiehm, Joan Tronto, and the late Iris Marion Young have stimulated my curiosity and helped me to remember for whom it is that I write.

Women's Studies and political science colleagues, both at Smith and elsewhere, have challenged and sustained me in multiple ways. I wish especially to thank Susan Bourque, Darcy Buerkle, Tamar Carroll, Barbara Cruikshank, Donna Divine, Ann Ferguson, Joyce Follet, Velma Garcia, the late Mary Geske, Mickey Glazer, Philip Green, Christina Greer, Jennifer Guglielmo, Vivien Hart, Alice Hearst, Nancy Hewitt, Temma Kaplan, Ira Katznelson, Gary Lehring, Ros Petchesky, Frances Fox Piven, Sherrill Redmon, Revan Schendler, Marilyn Schuster, Susan Van Dyne, and Nancy Whittier. Faculty and student colleagues in Kahn Institute projects at Smith—on "Community Activism" and on "City Life, City Lives"—have provided important communities of support as well as venues for the presentation of work in progress. I am also grateful for the time I spent as a Visiting Fellow at the Walt Whitman Center for the Culture and Politics of Democracy at Rutgers University, and to Smith College for both sabbatical and research support over the years.

An invitation from Nira Yuval-Davis to participate in a conference on gender and citizenship at the University of Greenwich in 1996 prompted me to engage more fully with the issues that have animated the final third of the book. Both she and Verena Stolcke have helped me to move beyond a simply US-focused framework for discussing participation and citizenship. Dennis F. Thompson, Isaac Balbus, and Manfred Halpern, teachers and mentors in graduate school, first modeled for me the scholarly pursuit of questions of democracy and inequality. Philip Green has been a valued friend and critic since I first arrived at Smith. I'm sure it's not coincidental that he was also my predecessor in teaching the course on "problems in democratic thought" that provided a springboard for so much of my—and his—writing on democratic theory and practice.

The women of the National Congress of Neighborhood Women—especially Jan Peterson, LaDoris Payne, Lisel Burns, Marie Cirillo, Linda Duke, Sally Martino Fisher, Christine Noschese, María Rivera, Habiba Soudan, and Ethel Velez—shared their stories with me. More significantly, they remind me that the questions of equality, participation, inclusion and citizenship that animate this book are not of academic interest alone: these women have devoted their lives to making their communities better places for themselves, their friends and neighbors, and the generations to come.

This book would not have come into being were it not for my students at Smith College. Their engagement with issues of democratic participation, equality/inequality, and justice continue to inspire and energize me, even as their questions about both political activism and political theory make teaching both a challenge and (mostly) a joy. The research assistance of Rachel Mioni, Shivani Khatau, Ruth María Cáceres, Brenna Davis, Neema Khatri, and Raquel Manzanares eased the writing of many of the articles that made their way into this book. Raquel, in particular, read through all these essays (and more), providing extensive and valuable feedback that enabled me, finally, to pull this volume into shape. I am deeply in her debt.

My experiences over many years with a variety of groups and organizations have worked themselves into these essays in ways I cannot even begin to name. I am truly grateful to members of all of them for enabling me to participate in our mutual efforts to make the world (or even small parts of it) a better place: Ezrat Nashim, B'not Esh, the New York Havurah, the National Havurah Institute, Havurat Ha-Emek, Havurah Su Kasha, the National Women's Studies Association, the Women's Caucus for Political Science, the Gay, Lesbian, Bisexual, and Transgendered Political Science Caucus, the Northampton Housing Partnership, ARISE for Social Justice, the Food Bank Farm, and Barack Obama's 2008 Campaign for Change.

Finally, Judith Plaskow, my partner in life in all its dimensions, has been with me through all the phases of the creation of this book. Her steady presence, sense of humor, and mantra of "work, thank God for the might of it" sustain me in more ways than I know how to name.

I am grateful to the following publishers for permission to use material previously published:

Chapter 1: "Women's Collaborative Activities and City Life: Politics and Policy," originally published in Janet Flammang, ed., *Political Women: Current Roles in State and Local Politics*, Sage Yearbooks in Women's Policy Studies, Vol. 8 (Beverly Hills, CA: Sage Publications, 1984), pp. 242–59 © Sage Publications.

Chapter 2: "Communities, Resistance, and Women's Activism: Reflections on Democratic Theory," originally published in *Women and the Politics of Empowerment: Perspectives from the Community and the Workplace*, ed. Ann Bookman and Sandra Morgen (Philadelphia, PA: Temple University Press, 1988), pp. 297–313 © Temple University Press.

Chapter 3: "Terrains of Protest: Striking City Women" (with Myrna Breitbart), originally published in *Our Generation*, Vol. 19, No. 1 (Fall 1987), pp. 151–175.

Chapter 4: "Dependency or Mutuality: A Feminist Perspective on Dilemmas of Welfare Policy," originally published in *Rethinking Marxism*, Vol. 7, No. 2 (1994), pp. 73–86 © ASEA 1994.

Chapter 5: "Privacy, Publicity, and Power: A Feminist Rethinking of the Public–Private Distinction," coauthored with Mary Lyndon Shanley, originally published in *Revisioning the Political: Feminist Reconstructions of Traditional Concepts in Western Political Theory*, ed. Nancy Hirschmann and Christine DiStefano (Boulder, CO: Westview Press, 1996), pp. 213–33, © Westview Press.

Chapter 7: "Rethinking Anarchism/Rethinking Power: A Contemporary Feminist Perspective," originally published in *Reconstructing Political Theory: Feminist Perspectives*, ed. Mary Lyndon Shanley and Uma Narayan (Cambridge: Polity Press, 1997), pp. 158–77 © Martha Ackelsberg.

ACKNOWLEDGMENTS

Chapter 9: "Broadening the Study of Women's Participation," originally published in *Women and American Politics: New Questions, New Directions*, edited by Susan J. Carroll (Oxford: Oxford University Press, 2003), pp. 214–35, © Martha Ackelsberg.

Chapter 10: "Women's Community Activism and the Rejection of 'Politics': Some Dilemmas of Popular Democratic Movements," originally published in *Women and Citizenship*, ed. Marilyn Friedman (New York: Oxford University Press, 2005), pp. 67–90, © Oxford University Press.

Chapter 12: "Democracy and (In)Equality: Community Activism and Democracy in a Time of Retrenchment," originally published in *Feminist Studies* 27, No. 2 (Summer 2001), pp. 391–418.

INTRODUCTION

From Resisting the Canon to *Resisting Citizenship*

Many years ago, when I was in the throes of both writing my dissertation and preparing to start teaching, I had a brief exchange with Dennis F. Thompson, my advisor. I remember very clearly writing to him, in the midst of some political upheaval of the early 1970s, that I had had an epiphany: the study of politics was really all about the study of communities. He replied that, while my comment was interesting, most political scientists would say that politics was about the study of power. Shortly thereafter, I discovered *Power and Community*, the groundbreaking anthology by Philip Green and Sanford Levinson, and I remember chuckling over the title. The study of politics, of course, entails exploring both power *and* community; and I now suspect that my insistence on attending to community was, in large part, a product of my own political history, and, in particular, of the state of the country and the world when I was in graduate school in the late 1960s and early 1970s. Since then, my work has focused increasingly on the ways power is experienced and expressed *in and through* community, a perspective that effectively challenged both the political and the intellectual orthodoxy of the time.

As I think back to that period, and reflect on the world, academia, and my own intellectual development over the past 30 years, I see the exchange with Thompson as a kind of touchstone for my journey and that of many of my feminist, would-be progressive, political scientist colleagues. The study of US politics at the time we were in graduate school was surely in a state of flux: Daniel Bell's "end of ideology" framework—arguing that all the major ideological disputes that had divided the country and the academy had been resolved—had barely been replaced intellectually, even though protestors, signaling the rebirth of ideology, were everywhere visible on the streets. The struggles of the Civil Rights movement seemed to have demonstrated both the strengths and the limits of democratic change in the US: schools and public accommodations were slowly being desegregated, but only after years of protest and litigation, and full equality was still but a distant dream. While some of us were challenging—in protest marches, in the classroom, and through our research projects—pluralist paradigms that celebrated a supposedly open and responsive US political system, pluralist and behavioralist perspectives still dominated the discipline.

It was increasingly obvious to us—and to some of our professors—that all was not well in the pluralist universe. As E.E. Schattschneider had so aptly quipped, the "flaw in the pluralist heaven is that the heavenly chorus sings with a strong upper-class accent."[1] Indeed, the pluralist heaven was not really so "heavenly" at all—at least not for the majority of the people actually *living* in the country, who were not, of course, necessarily the majority of those who voted or otherwise exercised political influence. We *knew* that resistance to the authorities—to the dominant *powers*, as well as to the "dominant paradigms"—was taking place then, as it had been for years. But we had little knowledge of how to incorporate that awareness into the disciplinary frameworks we were being taught. Princeton's Politics Department was trying to teach us a *science* of politics: I was assigned to read Thomas Kuhn's *The Structure of Scientific Revolutions* in three of the four classes I took during my first semester in graduate school. But how were we to understand the changes on the street (and on the campus) in which we were taking part?

It was also clear to many of us that formal, electoral, politics was not really the only form "politics" could take. Indeed, if any significant changes were to take place in the US, they would more likely come from non-electoral, direct action of the sort that would socialize conflict by forcing controversial issues onto the agenda, rather than through formal structures. We were living through the last great years of the civil rights revolution, the birth of the women's liberation movement, and the height of the anti-Vietnam War movement; the gay rights movement was just about to break out onto the streets. But the books we were reading and the scholarship we were being trained to undertake rarely focused on the activities of ordinary people, the nameless or the formally-powerless. Even Marx's focus on class struggle—though it did offer a dynamic understanding of social/political life—did not seem fully capable of comprehending the changes that were taking place around us. And, despite the fact that men and women were, at the very least, equally represented in those demonstrations and protests, virtually no one even noticed (I include myself, here) that we had read no women political theorists, that we studied the works of very few female scholars, and that we failed to see that there might be different patterns of engagement for men and for women. How could we, students of politics, *not* have found those times both empowering *and* disconcerting?

I was studying political philosophy—exploring theories of liberalism, representation, power, and democracy—while participating in movements (e.g. the anti-war and early feminist movements) that struggled to bring those values and ideals to life. The women's liberation consciousness-raising group of which I was a part in New York City helped create the New York Women's Health Collective, which confronted the medical establishment on issues of abortion, advocated for "free [and legal] abortion on demand," and offered classes on "women and their bodies"[*sic*] in storefronts in Greenwich Village and the Upper West Side. (We found out later that a similar series was being offered in Boston; that became *Our Bodies, Ourselves*.) We were completely self-taught and constantly having to learn new materials. We struggled hard to adapt, for example, when a group of lesbians pointed out that we had discussed sexuality and reproduction within a completely heterosexual framework. (Although it now seems absurd, it had never occurred to any of us to think about lesbians, or that lesbianism had anything to do with sexuality!) But I rarely had the opportunity to explore in class the connections between these sorts of activities and what I was reading in classic texts. Conversely, the articles and book-length studies we read about local community politics seemed mostly to look at who voted (or didn't); not at the structural relations among voters and non-voters, nor at factors that might have accounted for those patterns.[2] And they rarely asked the broader questions of what such patterns meant for the realities of "democracy" in the US.[3]

It was clear that those who were formally outside the realms of official, electoral, politics could, nevertheless, care deeply about what was (or was not) being done in their name. Some were excluded from voting directly and overtly, by complicated voter registration laws, poll taxes, or voter intimidation; some seemed to separate themselves voluntarily from any formal engagement with political institutions, apparently expressing alienation from a system they did not trust, and over which they felt they had no influence. But when we questioned the then-dominant view that "apathy implies consent," we were told that there was no empirical data to support a contrary perspective.[4]

Nevertheless, the times were beginning to change. Both theoretical and empirical studies raised the possibility that alienation might be as much (or more) a commentary on the US political *system* as it was a reflection of individual/psychological characteristics.[5] The Civil Rights, Women's Liberation, and anti-war movements were producing writings as well as demonstrations, including analyses that took to task not just specific policies and programs, but the very structures of political competition and participation. We could begin to ask, Where should we look to examine "political activity"? What *was* the "stuff" of history or of politics? How broadly should we define the domain of "the political"? Were the educational activities of the Women's Health Collective "political"? Why did we not focus as much attention on those who *challenged* dominant structures of power as on those who upheld them?

In fact, I was learning and theorizing about politics in a number of different contexts, although I did not necessarily recognize that at the time. In my scholarly life, I explored the "possibility of anarchism"—whether, why, and under what circumstances political authority was necessary. My dissertation challenged conventional political/sociological texts by holding them up against writings by anarchist theorists, and used the anarchist movement in Spain during the Spanish Civil War as a case-study of anarchism in power [however oxymoronic that phrase appears to be]. At the same time, I was, myself, deeply engaged in the anti-war movement and the burgeoning women's liberation movement, both of which were enacting versions of the anti-authoritarian, direct-action politics that I was researching. But it was not until I had almost finished writing my dissertation that I recognized that there might be any connection between all the things I was *doing* and what I was *studying*. So deep was the "disconnect" between activism and scholarship that I could not see that I was both enacting and challenging that separation in my own work.[6]

It was to be through my teaching that I first began explicitly to explore the connections and the tensions between the theory and the practice of democracy, between democratic theory and direct action politics, between studies of generalized apathy and experiences of political engagement; and, further, to examine both the presence and the absence of women and members of so-called marginalized groups in the texts we were reading and studies we were undertaking. In courses and seminars on urban politics and political participation and, more recently, on problems of democratic thought and on the politics of wealth and poverty in the United States, I began to draw out these issues for and with my students. In the process, questions of inequality, participation, exclusion, and citizenship came to be the focus of my own research and writing. Hence, the essays in this book, which bring together my efforts over the past two decades to engage in applied political theory that draws on concrete political experience—historical and contemporary, US-based and non-US-based—in order to rethink some central categories of politics, and of democratic theory in particular, from feminist perspectives.

The book is arranged in three parts, although a number of themes—especially challenges to dichotomous understandings of public and private, and of dependence and independence—run through the volume as a whole. The chapters in Part I, "Rethinking Politics/Rethinking Community," take up the question of "power" versus "community" as central organizing concepts for political theorizing, and reflect initial efforts to engage with the then-dominant paradigms in the academic literature on urban politics and on community activism. My insistence on attending to the activities of women—both in their similarities to, and differences from, those of men—is paradigmatic of the early stages of feminist scholarship that asked, "Where are the women?" and "What difference does (or might) gender make?"[7] That women, as well as men, engaged in efforts to improve their communities may now seem obvious; but it was not obvious to much of mainstream political science, at least through the mid-1980s. I have reproduced those essays here (with a few additional references to more recent material) largely to make visible the profound change in frameworks of analysis since those early days. "Women's Collaborative Activities and City Life" and "Communities, Resistance and Women's Activism" also begin to explore how looking at the activities of women leads directly to questioning dichotomies (largely taken for granted within the mainstream literatures), especially understandings of women's versus men's "proper" places, and the distinction between "public" and "private" spaces. "Terrains of Protest" represents one of the fruits of a long-standing collaboration with Myrna Breitbart, who shares my seemingly disparate interests in Spanish anarchism and women's urban activism. In it, we applied some of the frameworks we were developing in the US urban context to examine aspects of anarchist-inspired urban activism in early twentieth-century Barcelona. Our claim that it was precisely the crossing of boundaries—of both geography and prescribed social roles—that led to consciousness change is one that I follow up, to one degree or another, in many of the essays that follow.

Part II, composed of essays written mostly in the mid-1990s, takes up the feminist challenge to dichotomous thinking through a number of case-studies. At a time when feminist activism and scholarship were increasingly attempting to come to terms with the complexity and diversity of the category "woman," these essays challenge both conceptual dichotomies and, at the same time, the assumption that "women" constitute a unitary group. "Dependency or Mutuality"—which I began writing in the midst of major debates about welfare "dependency"—explored dominant discourses of welfare reform and social provision to examine the relationship between presumed "independence" and citizenship. Most discussions of citizenship within liberal polities accepted as a given that citizenship was meant for "independent," self-supporting, individuals. Effectively, only feminists were asking to what degree *anyone* in a complex society was, in fact, truly independent. Particularly in the years when "welfare reform" was central to national political conversations, it seemed important to question many of the assumptions on which those debates hinged. Thus, "Dependency or Mutuality" was meant as an intervention in the debate about how best to reframe the language of welfare reform so as not to ignore or victimize (poor) women, and to recognize the degree to which we are *all inter*dependent. While it focused less on citizenship than on the language of "dependence," it laid the groundwork for the essays that follow. Ultimately, as the essays in the final part make clear, rethinking "independence" becomes critical to any transformative understanding of citizenship that takes account of the ways women and the relatively powerless are (or might better be) incorporated *as* citizens.

"Privacy, Publicity, and Power" had its roots in an effort—as part of a volume on feminist rethinkings of major concepts in political theory—to define the boundaries between public and private. But after exploring a number of different cases that seemed to point to mutually contradictory conclusions, Molly Shanley and I came to believe that there is no one, consistent, way to draw a boundary line; indeed, the effort to do so was mistaken. Instead, we argued, what debates about any proposed boundary do is to make visible the centrality of the presumed dichotomy between public and private to *justifying* exercises of power. In fact, in the following chapter, "Gender, Resistance, and Citizenship," we explore in greater detail the ways efforts to define—and then to challenge—what is appropriate to the domain of politics, and who ought to have access to that arena, often play out in the language of "public" and "private." Further, throughout much of US history, those definitions of would-be boundaries have also been profoundly gendered and racialized. Thus, black women at the turn of the nineteenth–twentieth centuries attempted to *socialize* the issue of lynching, insisting that it was a matter for *public* attention, rather than an activity of "private" citizens. Further, they questioned the effort to *privatize and depoliticize* the sexual mistreatment of black women by white men and to *publicize* and *criminalize* all relations between black men and white women, including those that were consensual. Similarly, the Mothers of the Plaza de Mayo of Argentina refused to accept the disappearances of their children as a matter of "private" sorrow and loss, and publicly enacted their challenge to the ruling Junta. In the process, they developed a more sophisticated political consciousness and helped to spark a broader movement of resistance to the regime. "Rethinking Anarchism/ Rethinking Power" draws out some of the implications of these complexities for our understandings of power more generally. Anarchists, of course, are wary of power; and much of my earlier work had adopted a somewhat uncritical tone toward the anarchist perspective. This final essay of this Part attempts to turn feminist challenges to dichotomous thinking onto anarchist understandings of power, itself.

Essays in the final part revolve around the language of citizenship as both goal and critique, and participate in the recent revival of interest in citizenship claims as a framework for resistance. As Catherine Holland put it, they ask what it would mean to "think about citizenship in terms of action rather than essence … directing our attention toward what it means to *act as* citizens rather than what it means to *be* citizens"[8] (emphasis mine). On the one hand, as a product of, and participant in, the so-called new social movements of the 1960s and 1970s, I have argued that we must recognize, and *value* various forms of resistance, or direct action, as, themselves, important expressions of citizenship.[9] Rather than threatening to undermine democracy, direct action challenges to established authority may well be critical to sustaining it. At the same time, the language of citizenship—the promise of power and participation that it offers—has provided important resources for those who have challenged both dominant authorities and their own exclusions from the official body politic.[10] Nevertheless, while much radical activism has couched itself in the language of citizenship claims, critics have become increasingly wary of that same discourse of citizenship: to be a citizen of a country is, of course, to be considered an *insider*, to be *at home*, but in a context in which others are kept out, as strangers or aliens.[11] Indeed, the very notion of citizenship *implies and entails exclusions*—of those who are not citizens. If it did not, what would be the value of that prize, itself?

I begin Part III, then, by turning directly to an exploration of questions of inclusion and exclusion, pointing out in the process how many of the ambiguities inherent in contemporary discourses of citizenship can be understood in continuity with earlier challenges to the dichotomies of public/private and dependence/independence. The following chapter, "Broadening the Study of Women's Participation," takes up a somewhat different dimension of the challenge to dominant paradigms: the question of what *constitutes* "political participation" and how it should be studied. This essay might well be considered as a companion piece to the first essay in the book—offering further reflections on what we learn from examining the many dimensions of women's community-based activism, and what those lessons might offer in the way of challenges to dominant understandings of the activities of citizenship. It and the chapter that follows represent attempts to explore what Desforges and others refer to as "understanding citizenship as it unfolds 'on the ground,'" by looking at "practices of citizenship as they are enacted in everyday life."[12] Nevertheless, "Women's Community Activism and the Rejection of 'Politics'" may also be read as a sort of *caveat*. Although I have argued that studying women's community-based activism ought to lead us to change our understandings of what constitutes the domain of "politics," it is also the case (as we see in the final chapter, as well) that those who engage in non-electoral forms of engagement do not necessarily see themselves as "political" beings. Ought we, then, to view these activities as challenges to conventional understandings of the practices of citizenship, or as evidence that conventional paradigms contain important truths? What is the significance of the rejection of "politics" by those who may be seen by others as deeply engaged in it?

"Families, Care, and Citizenship" engages with recent feminist work on the politics of care in an effort to broaden even further ideas about what constitute the activities of citizenship. Ruth Lister, drawing on Ken Plummer and others, writes of "intimate citizenship," as "public discourse on the personal life" that can offer a "potential bridge between the personal and the political."[13] Again, we confront the themes of public/private and dependence/independence, and the impossibility of drawing firm and clear lines around any of these supposedly separate and separable domains. The chapter explores some of the ways that care work is not only valuable *as work* but, in addition, ought potentially to be recognized as an activity of citizenship.

Finally, "Democracy and (In)equality" opens up questions of politicization and consciousness-change in a more international/global context. Rather than providing answers, it sets out questions and issues for further exploration, and attempts to locate many of the issues of citizenship, equality, inclusion, and exclusion in a broader framework.

I completed the editing of these essays in the fall of 2008, in the midst of Barack Obama's historic presidential campaign. Thus, it seems fitting that, after a lifetime studying the connections between scholarship and activism, I end this introduction with some reflections on my experience of what I can only describe as "politics as community organizing." Despite my own history of wariness toward electoral politics, I found myself drawn into the campaign as a volunteer. On the one hand, it seemed odd—perhaps even hypocritical—to be engaging in get-out-the-vote activities precisely at a time when I was writing about the limits of what electoral politics can achieve and the importance of expanding our understanding of what constitute political activities. On the other hand, this election felt to me, as it did to so many who had doubted whether the US (or indeed the world!) could ever recover from eight years of the lawlessness of the Bush Administration, like a last-ditch effort to save whatever "democracy" might be left in the United States. So I volunteered, trained at Camp Obama sessions in Brooklyn, NY, and went to suburban Philadelphia for the final two weeks of the campaign.

It was an extraordinary experience; one that I am still attempting to integrate and analyze. As David Carr noted in a column in *The New York Times*,[14] the Obama campaign managed to combine social networking with local organizing to create an astonishingly powerful network. The combination of decentralization and discipline was both inspiring and effective. It was as if the campaign's strategists had yoked anarchist/decentralist processes to conventional electoral politics—and, somehow, the hybrid not only functioned, it flourished.

In the aftermath of the election, I found myself thinking anew about civil rights organizing in the US South, anti-apartheid struggles in South Africa, and freedom movements around the world. I do not mean to suggest that this election campaign was a freedom struggle of the same magnitude; but the organization was of historic proportions, and it marked a watershed and a turning point in US politics. For once, at least, the politics of hate and divisiveness, the fear-mongering, the robocalls, and the disinformation that the McCain campaign threw out in the final weeks of the campaign did not work. All of us who could not allow ourselves to imagine that McCain might win, but who, nevertheless, could not quite believe that Obama would pull it off, suddenly found that all the work, all the hope, all the heart had paid off. What exhilaration. No wonder there were tears *and* laughter, spontaneous celebrations everywhere [one colleague said that the dancing in the streets on the night of November 4 reminded her of the dancing in Berlin the night the Wall fell in 1989]. I wrote at the time that:

> The road ahead will not be easy; but we will finally have in the White House a president who is thoughtful, sober, and intelligent, and to whom we can look for sane and competent leadership in difficult times. It feels like a burden has been lifted, the poisons are working their way out of our system.

Politics is/was, indeed, about both power *and* community; and the power of this campaign came, precisely, from and with the multiple communities (both actual and virtual) it created around the country. Hopes for change in the direction of greater social and economic equality and justice continue to run high, even as the economy seems to be in free fall. It is impossible to know where we will find ourselves—as individuals, as communities, as a nation—in the years ahead. But I cannot help but notice the irony that it was in the midst of a national election campaign—albeit one organized with the sensibilities of a "community organizer"—that so many were able to experience the thrill of communal engagement and the sense of possibility that has long sustained direct-action politics and what I have come to think of as resistant citizenship. *La lucha* [and the analysis of it] *continua*.

I

RETHINKING POLITICS/ RETHINKING COMMUNITY

1

WOMEN'S COLLABORATIVE ACTIVITIES AND CITY LIFE

Politics and Policy

What would it mean for women to be fully participatory citizens of a truly democratic urban political community? What changes in urban policy would follow from the integration of women's activities and behaviors into our understanding of the practice of urban politics?

A number of studies have explored the depoliticization of economic life in the United States over the past 200 years, and the development of a split between "economics" and "politics" in the American political consciousness.[1] Others have examined the implications of that split for urban politics and "the patterning of class" in particular.[2] But despite the sensitivity of these works to issues of class, race, and ethnicity, and their implications for the potential of integrating work life and community life in a democratic polity, all are strangely silent about women, whose concerns have been largely absent from the American political agenda and whose actions have gone virtually unnoticed by students of urban political struggles.

Studies of women's lives and activities—especially those focusing on urban contexts—suggest that women experience their environment in ways that may differ significantly from the ways most men do. Recent research, for example, has documented the prominent, if not predominant, role of women in urban struggles over what have been termed "quality of life" issues (i.e., housing, cost of living, and so on).[3] Similarly, both historians and analysts of the contemporary social scene have noted the significance of social networks, or webs of relationships, in the lives of (urban) women.[4]

This chapter explores the implications of those differences both for our understanding of urban policy and, more broadly, for our notions of democratic citizenship. On one hand, it examines what it might mean to integrate economics and politics, work and community, in a democratic polity which took into account the concerns and behaviors of women, as well as of men. On the other, and more generally, it begins to develop an analysis of the significance of relationships—not only in and for the lives of women, but also as a crucial (if as yet inadequately explored) aspect of democratic citizenship itself.

Avoiding the Workplace–Community Split

Social historians and contemporary urbanologists alike have highlighted one significant characteristic of city spatial structure in the United States: the physical/geographical separation of workplace and residence. Some have focused on patterns of urban growth and their implications for urban political community; others on the consequences of the separation for the class- and race-based segregation of metropolitan areas.[5] Some of the most provocative and suggestive work in this area, however, is that of Ira Katznelson, who explores in detail the connections between the separation of work and community and the development of industrial capitalism, and the specific implications of that separation for the structuring of urban political consciousness in the United States.

Katznelson's focus is on the specifically American response to that separation (characteristic of the development of industrial capitalism)—namely, a "split consciousness" among urban residents who see a "stark division ... between the politics of work and the politics of community."[6] In his view, American workers look to unions, focused at the workplace, to resolve what they see as economic issues; and they look to urban political parties, oriented around ethnicity and territoriality, rather than class, to resolve what they take to be political concerns, and they never really join the two sets of issues. This perspective permeates all aspects of workers' lives, resulting in "a stark split between the ways workers in major industrial cities think, talk, and act when they are at work and when they are away from work in their communities."[7] The political and strategic message of Katznelson's analysis is clear:

> Community-based strategies for social change in the United States cannot succeed unless they pay attention to the country's special pattern of class formation; to the split in the practical consciousness of American workers between the language and practice of a politics of work and those of a politics of community.[8]

Only when urban activists succeed in linking what are perceived as two independent sets of concerns, making clear the dependence of communities on the context set by capitalist relations, can there be significant, transformative, change in urban areas.

While Katznelson's analysis hints at a new understanding of democratic citizenship, others have drawn the links somewhat more directly. Wolin, Piven and Cloward, and Bender all explore the development of the ideological split between economics and politics (or "private" and "public") in American consciousness, although they focus more directly on the consequences of the split for our understandings of democracy. Specifically, Wolin bemoans the shift from a participatory, democratic, and decentralist model of politics and citizenship (in which economic issues were thoroughly integrated), central to the structure and practice of US democracy in the early years of the Republic, to a more passive, remote, inegalitarian, and representative notion of citizenship (which excluded the economy from democratic control), which has come to characterize US politics since the early nineteenth century. His point is that it is not just that the economy has been depoliticized and removed from the realm of meaningful popular control, but that citizenship, as such, has been limited. People have come to develop passive and deferential dispositions toward politics.[9]

Along the same lines, Piven and Cloward argued that the insulation of property and economic policy from popular political control that structured late nineteenth-century politics in the United States "persuaded Americans that the most pressing issues of their daily lives had nothing to do with the democratic rights for which they had fought, and of which they were so proud."[10] Yet Piven and Cloward are far from convinced that the battle has been lost: welfare state policies have undermined that division, even as they represented attempts to protect the context upholding it. In fact, Piven and Cloward later argued, the welfare state has had a "transforming effect on popular understandings of what politics is about. It brought economic issues to the very center of democratic politics."[11] The separation between economics and politics has already been undermined in practice, and we are beginning to see the ideological implications: in American popular consciousness, they argue, there is an increasing recognition of the necessity for greater economic democracy if political democracy is to be a reality.[12] Clearly, in their view, the promise of overcoming the separation (in both ideology and in practice) is the promise of a more democratic political community.

Finally, an article by Thomas Bender argues in yet another vein for the necessity of integrating economic issues into the agenda of politics. He calls for us to reclaim, in a democratic context, the notion of a "moral economy"—to envision a city whose "moral, political, and economic universes of discourse [are] continuous."[13]

These analyses recognize the significance of class and race in structuring the dimensions of American political consciousness and action. And each makes a powerful case for integrating economic and political issues, workplace and community concerns, and for the fundamental significance of such integration for the development of a truly democratic politics. Nevertheless, they read as if all workers—and virtually all urban citizens!—were male.

Since it is the most detailed—and the most suggestive—I focus, here, on Katznelson's analysis. Significantly, he devotes no attention at all to the specific experience of women, either as workers or as city dwellers. Thus, in his discussion of the relationship between suffrage and worker militancy in the nineteenth century, he states,

> Modern industrial society in the United States, with its distinctive patterns of class interaction, was forged in the crucible of democracy.

Workers as citizens did not feel they needed to battle the state, for they were included in its embrace.[14]

Surely, however, the workers he refers to were exclusively male (and white). In a more contemporary vein, he notes (in a passage cited above) that "workers in the major industrial cities think, talk, and act," differently, "when they are at work and when they are away from work in their communities."[15] Again, one has the sense that he is talking about male workers. As more than one feminist critic has pointed out,

> Men see a relatively clear divide between problems of home and problems of work, so this unwritten rule [that workplace issues are separate from "home" issues] seems to be adequate for them. Bills, household budgets, baby-sitters, and another baby on the way are all "individual problems." ... But for women workers, especially for those with children (and whether single or married) that kind of separation is rarely possible.[16]

His analysis, in short, gives no indication either that women workers exist, or that female workers' attitudes, approaches, or experiences might differ from those of men.

Second, although he argues quite persuasively for the need to focus on the social relations of community ("people create a culture which in all its dimensions composes a set of resources for living in society and for affecting the contours of society," p. 1), Katznelson is apparently ignorant of the role women play in developing and maintaining such community. In the absence of any suggestion to the contrary, we are left with the presumption that (like the workers) the actors in the community movements, political machines, and neighborhood associations he describes are all male.[17]

Finally, Katznelson and the others are remarkably oblivious to the growing feminist literature on urban spatial structure and on the significance of the split between workplace and residence for women's experiences of the city. I shall argue that the assumptions about gender roles that apparently underlie these analyses mask the interplay between workplace and community that already exists. Furthermore, they limit our understandings of community itself, and thus have important implications for political action. A new look at the relationship between workplace and community that fully integrates women will lead to a fundamental reconceptualization both of the split and of the nature and possibilities of democratic politics.

Feminist Analyses of Urban Spatial Structure

Feminist attention to the increased numbers of female-headed families, and to the feminization of poverty (i.e., the increased proportion of the poverty-level population composed of women and their dependent children) has made it evident that women, and particularly poor women, are overrepresented in our older central cities.[18] Feminist urbanologists have argued that such over-representation is both "cause and consequence" of the fiscal woes of those cities[19] and is directly related to the separation of workplace and residence that characterizes American urban areas. Marxist-feminist critics, in particular, have argued that the separation needs to be understood not just as a consequence of the demands of capitalist production relations but also as a "product of the patriarchal organization of household production."[20]

Specifically, the overwhelming predominance of single-family detached dwellings in American housing stock; the assumption that a single, nuclear, family will occupy any unit (even within apartment complexes); and the separation of residential areas from workplaces both reflect the social norms of the heterosexually constructed nuclear family and have significant consequences for women within central cities.[21] Sex segregation of the labor market relegates women to relatively low-paid, low-status work, thus reinforcing their dependence on men and/or on the state.[22] The scarcity of affordable housing in suburbs—increasingly where employment opportunities are to be found—assures that even many low-paying jobs will be largely inaccessible to poor women, especially single heads of households.[23] The greater availability of public transportation in central cities has resulted in a growing concentration of women—again, particularly those who are poor heads of households and dependent on public transport—in those cities.[24]

In short, the assumption that the "normal" family is one in which the husband/father is the breadwinner who "supports" a wife and children at home (a constellation that described only approximately 13 percent of "family" units in the United States in 1981) has been central to the development of the spatial and socioeconomic differentiation of urban areas. Yet that same assumption—and its manifestation in social and economic polity—effectively and often severely penalizes those whose lives do not conform to the norm.[25] Policies and practices deriving from this assumption are related to the feminization of poverty.[26] In addition, the operation of race- as well as sex-discrimination in the labor and housing markets assures that the situation of women of color, and, particularly, of those who are heads of households, is even more desperate.[27] In 1981, slightly more than one-third of all families headed by a single woman fell below official US poverty levels; but 52.9 percent of families headed by a black women were poor, and the corresponding figure is slightly higher for families headed by Hispanic women.[28]

In the view of these feminist critics, then, the patterning of urban space—in particular, the physical separation of workplace and home—is a product both of capitalist industrial development and of heterosexual social norms. Beyond that, they make clear that the consequences of spatial segregation fall differently on women than on men. To ignore those consequences is inadequately to understand urban dynamics and to be in danger of developing policies that

17

will contribute to the continued subordination of women. On a theoretical level, for example, it is essential to see residences as workplaces and to recognize the connection between urban spatial structure (including the separation of workplace and residence) and women's exploitation both at home and at work. It means developing urban policies that will overcome women's economic dependence by truly opening up to women the opportunity for equal labor force participation. And the provision of such opportunity, in turn, will require formidable support structures—including child care, housing, and urban spatial arrangements that take children into account—allowing women effective access to those employment possibilities. More generally, it will mean exploding the assumption that everyone lives—or ought to live—in a male-headed nuclear family with a second adult present for support, and then developing housing alternatives and child-care programs for people who do not live in such families.[29]

These critics offer an important corrective to our understanding and analysis of the relationship between urban spatial patterns, intrafamily dynamics, and the treatment of women and men at the workplace. They insist that the spatial patterning of cities derives as much from patriarchal assumptions about household structures and relationships as from the requirements of capitalism. Nevertheless, it is important to note that neither the spatial separation of home and work nor the sexual division of labor are unique to, or definitive of, capitalist urban systems. "Socialist" systems are far from egalitarian with respect to the division of labor; and not all capitalist systems are characterized by the patterns of residential specialization and decentralization these critics deplore.[30]

Although feminist urbanologists offer us a much richer understanding of residence or community, and suggest that the home deserves recognition as a workplace, they still seem to accept, at least on a theoretical level, the distinction between workplace and community. Women are portrayed as disadvantaged in traditional workplaces; and as both exploited in, and also identified with, residential workplaces. The resolution these critics offer is to open up paid work to women on a more equal basis with men, and to recognize the dependence of the entire set of relationships on the exploited domestic labor of women.[31]

It remained for a British analyst, Cynthia Cockburn, to go beyond this formulation and to explore the role of women as crucial links in the relationship between workplace and community, public and private, the state and the household. For, as she argues, women's roles in the household situate them uniquely to experience urban life in such a way as to challenge the very assumption of a dichotomy between workplace and community. Regardless of their status in the paid workforce, women in Western Europe and the United States bear primary responsibility for the nurturing of children (and of adult males!) within the household. It is they who are concerned with the care, education, and nurturance of those who will take their places as adult members of society.[32] But, as Cockburn points out, the responsibility to maintain the household and its members means that women (even those who are not engaged in paid wage-labor) are active in the urban arena considerably beyond the limits of the so-called domestic sphere: for it is women who tend to be those who negotiate with landlords, markets, welfare officers, health-care providers, and the like. It is women who mediate the standards of living for their families, adjust budgets when wages (those paid to them, or to the others with whom they may be living) either increase or decrease, when rents fluctuate, when food prices increase, or when welfare services are cut.[33] Cheryl Gilkes has even characterized the work of black women who struggle to maintain and improve their communities as an occupation in itself.[34]

In other words, because of their place in the sexual division of labor, women experience, in their day-to-day lives, very specific relationships not only with the males to whom they may be related but also with shopkeepers and landlords, with employers (whether directly, as exploited workers; indirectly, through the men who may be the official support of their household; or, even more indirectly, through their own exclusion from the labor market), and with agencies of the state. The context of women's lives and daily activities belies the supposed distinction or separation between public and private, workplace and community, state and household; for women's roles situate them to experience the interpenetration of these spheres. Thus, to understand women as living their lives solely within the realm of reproductive activity (or to treat a so-called sphere of reproduction as somehow distinct from a sphere of production, as many feminist-Marxist analysts do)—even for analytical purposes—is to miss both the complexity of women's lives and the implications of that complexity for the development of women's social and political consciousness.[35]

Specifically, Cockburn's analysis leads us to a number of important observations about political strategy that amplify and modify the analyses of Katznelson and others. First, it does not make sense to speak of struggles at work as separate from struggles in the community, or to describe struggles over community-based issues as somehow political, rather than economic. In Cockburn's words, "struggles around housing or benefits or schools are economic, as well as 'merely' political."[36] Surely, as Cheryl Gilkes[37] (among others) notes, looking at women's activism within black communities, for example, makes clear the interconnections. Second, to recognize the relationship between workplace and household issues would change the nature of workplace struggles as well. In recent years, some workers have extended their efforts in negotiations and strikes to take account of the impact of work rules and policies on home life and on the conditions of work, as well as on wages and hours.[38] In addition, this analysis leads us to explore the specific reasons why women tend, disproportionately, to be in temporary jobs. We need to examine the effects of domestic cutbacks on the relative positions of women within and without the paid labor force.[39]

To acknowledge these interconnections is to challenge the claim that only struggles at the workplace can result in fundamental social change. To focus only on workplace struggles is to ignore a significant proportion of people's own life experience (including the potentially consciousness-changing experiences of exploitation at the hands of landlords, shopkeepers, public employers, and so on) and to exclude all wageless people, and many women, from the possibility of participating effectively in movements for social change.[40] Finally, this perspective points up the particular role of women in urban social movements; for Cockburn claimed that women's involvement in struggle "sprang directly from their experience in the home."[41]

These observations, while exposing some of the limits of a public/private dichotomization, still fail to detail the nature of women's collaborative relationships that underlie many urban social movements. Urban women live in a context of webs of relationships, informal and formal, which structure their patterns of interaction, give meaning and order to their lives, and may well be crucial factors affecting the development of their political consciousness.

Historians of popular protest movements have noted the prominent role of women in many urban movements.[42] Some have suggested that their prominence in these types of activities is a consequence of a specific female consciousness, which derives from women's particular place in the social-sexual division of labor. Temma Kaplan, for example, has argued that as primary caretakers of households and communities—regardless of their status in the paid workforce—women have developed a special sensitivity to quality-of-life issues. Both historically and in our own time, that sensitivity has led them to demonstrate, riot, and demand from the state that it fulfill its proper role in providing adequate urban social services.[43] Similarly, Lawson and associates noted the prominence of women in tenant organizing for better housing, both in the early part of this century and in the contemporary period, in New York City. They suggest that women's "numerical predominance" in tenant organizing is attributable, in part, to "woman's role as homemaker and budget supervisor." In that role, she spends a great deal of time around the home, and is likely to feel, immediately and directly, any "increase in rent or deterioration in services."[44]

Yet they also emphasize the importance of friendship and other networks in contributing both to the development of women's political consciousness and to their availability for mobilization. In their words, "the common activities of women in their building and neighborhood ... all tend to create social ties that can provide a basis for mobilization."[45] Kaplan argues that women met regularly at various communal spots (e.g., markets, water taps, and the like), which became important loci not only for the exchange of gossip, but also for political organizing.[46] Gilkes points out that once black women "are 'out there' and have shown some skill in solving problems shared by other-members of the community, people seek them out."[47] Finally, the activities of such organizations as the National Welfare Rights Organization or the National

Congress of Neighborhood Women—particularly the success of the latter in mobilizing large numbers of working-class women to action on issues such as housing, schools, and social services—provide further evidence of the power of women's networks and their implications for women's participation in urban social movements.[48] If we ignore these specific gender-related experiences of women in urban contexts, we will fail to understand at least some of the sources of women's activity in the community. And political movements which fail to acknowledge and address these differences will also fail effectively to incorporate women or to address issues which are crucial to their day-to-day lives.

As a number of analysts have argued with respect to other aspects of women's lives, women's experience of the city is relational, importantly rooted in webs of association, collaboration, and mutual support.[49] Historians have demonstrated that, throughout US history, women's networks have been crucial, both in providing material support to individual women and their families and in providing the context for broader political activity.[50] Contemporary urban women who develop collaborative relationships with their neighbors around child care, transportation to and from welfare centers, shopping, or the like are also able to call on those networks when their communal lives are threatened.

In addition, these very activities—even if undertaken in defense of what might be seen as narrowly-domestic concerns—often challenge both the supposed distinction between the public and the private spheres and women's own understandings of their place in families and communities. For example, Lois Gibbs and others at Love Canal may have engaged, initially, in protesting the dumping of toxic wastes out of their understanding of their place as protectors of the home. But their experience in organizing changed them fundamentally, broke down the supposed distinction between domestic and public arenas, and challenged the bases of many of their marriages. One of the women activists Cockburn interviewed reported that:

> [W]hen you start getting involved, you find you're not a cabbage any more. You've got a mind and can do things. … I think Tom's realized I'm a human being since I did this [started a tenants' association]. He used to think I had no ideas and opinions of my own. And you grow into it yourself, and believe those things about yourself, in the end.[51]

Collaborative Activities and Democratic Politics

What are the implications of these studies? What might it mean to incorporate these new perspectives and treat women's experience of the city as an important element of our conceptualizations of urban life?

First, taking women's lives seriously requires that, in political analysis, strategy, and policy recommendations alike, we explore the links between state policy, workplace issues, and community/residential issues. One consequence here is to explode the presumed dichotomy between workplace and community, public and private; and, conversely, to explore the connections between familial structures, economic relations, and urban spatial structure—specifically, between employment and housing as they affect women. Some clues as to the potential policy implications of such a perspective might be taken from the experience of the Montreal Citizens Movement, an urban movement that explicitly attempted to link workplace and community issues (specifically housing costs and availability, and control over the quality of the urban environment) and in which women were notably active.[52]

Aside from the obvious advantages to women—who have been the hardest hit by unresponsive urban policies—there would be fiscal advantages, as well, to the cities themselves. As it is now, low wages and lack of access to jobs make women more dependent on public resources—for example, transportation and housing—than are men of similar class and ethnic background. If women's employment options were improved, and if adequate housing were available, they would be able to make more, and more substantial, contributions to the urban tax base. "For these reasons alone urban finances would be improved by increasing women's employment opportunities and pay."[53]

Second, a rethinking of analytical categories to take account of women's experience would add new dimensions to the community side of the picture. It would mean expanding what Katznelson, Kornblum, and others have seen as the relatively limited potential of community-related issues (which, in their view, must of necessity focus on ethnic territorial claims and, therefore, founder on the rocks of particularism and divisiveness) to recognize the ways in which women's organization to improve the community's quality of life has grown out of existing networks, and united people across racial and ethnic lines. The transformative potential of a focus on quality-of-life issues is enormous—even if largely (to date) untapped by mainstream parties and social change movements.

We would need to look, for example, at the ways in which urban spaces are structured. Do the patterns of housing and social services presuppose the universality of heterosexually-constructed nuclear families? Do they take into account the needs of women with children, or of others who do not live in families so constructed? Are there places for children to play? Do policies and programs support, or do they undermine, existing urban networks? Can we devote resources and attention to programs which will support such networks and existing collaborative patterns, rather than ignore their existence and see only patterns of decay?[54] It is important to note that, although Katznelson and Kornblum are aware of the significance of community feeling among the people they studied, and acknowledge the importance of communal networks in sustaining a certain degree of class consciousness, neither examines the ways in which those networks operate. Yet, it is precisely such community-based networks, rooted largely in women's collaborative activities, which provide the context and basis for the class consciousness they so value in those communities. To put it another way, this analysis suggests that we must not only take seriously the actions of women in their communities, but also recognize that what goes on in urban communities, even within the confines of particular households, may have public, political import.

Finally, to integrate the activities and concerns that have traditionally been the province of women into the urban political-economic arena will have fundamental consequences for our understanding of urban democracy itself. Sheldon Wolin articulated a notion of democratic citizenship—one based on the citizen as active participant in collective decision making, rather than as a "bearer of rights"—which can provide a useful starting-point for this discussion:

> A political being is not to be defined as the citizen has been, as an abstract, disconnected bearer of rights, privileges, and immunities, but as a person whose existence is located in a particular place and draws its sustenance from circumscribed relationships: family, friends, church, neighborhood, workplace, community, town, city. These relationships are the sources from which political beings draw power ... and that enable them to act together ... From a democratic perspective, power is not simply force that is generated; it is experience, sensibility, wisdom, even melancholy distilled from the diverse relations and circles we move in.[55]

A number of aspects of this perspective merit attention. First, given Wolin's sensitivity to issues of the origins of power, and the location of power in community, it is particularly striking that he devotes little or no attention to the specific position of women within American political communities. Yet it is precisely such a concern with origins that should alert us to the importance of taking women's specific experience into account when formulating a full understanding of democratic participation and citizenship. Second, he emphasizes the importance of recognizing diversity within a democratic political community. Finally, he suggests that democracies treat people not so much as isolated individuals, but as members of communities. Each of these elements of his definition has important implications for the effective integration of women into a democratic political community in urban areas.

It seems clear that, both historically and in our own day, much of women's political consciousness and activities in urban contexts develop out of their participation in networks of friends and neighbors on a daily basis. Such networks tend to be "spontaneously organized"[56] (in the sense of lacking formal leadership structures), and nonhierarchical. Yet members can be readily mobilized, whether for help on an individual basis or to respond to broader community issues. Many women who become activists on the local (and then supra-local) scene do so not because they have been called out by unions, by political parties, or even by formally structured community organizations. Instead, they respond to the issues which come before them as members of households and, importantly, of the communities (primarily, but not exclusively, of women) in which those households are embedded.

Urban women, that is, do not come to politics as isolated, self-interested individuals. For them, the problem of politics is not—as much traditional democratic theory would have us believe—that of creating an allegiance to something other than the self, but, rather, of finding ways to link the concerns, visions, and perspectives they share with their neighbors to the political system that stands apart from them and seems to control their lives.[57] Studies of women in urban communities suggest that even participatory democratic theorists—those who claim to be the most sensitive to the interconnections between political orientations (e.g., feelings of political efficacy) and social reality—may have put their emphasis on factors that miss the point of many women's experiences. Many urban women seem to have little or no difficulty acknowledging the connections between their concerns and those of others. They do not feel themselves to be in a competitive relationship with their fellow urban residents. Yet there is little theory of (urban) democracy which responds to the reality of their interconnected lives, or which can help them make sense—or political use—of those networks. Instead, we talk of the need to unite workplace and community. But women's lives have done that—and continue to do it—on a daily basis, although perhaps without the consciousness that that is what they are about! In Cockburn's words:

> [W]omen bring a totality, an all-or-nothing feeling to action. It is something of which trade unions and political parties with their hierarchies and agenda know little, and to which they can give little. This totality is not just of the work day but of the whole day, not just of wages but of feelings, not just of economics but of relationships.[58]

The perspective of networks and relationships provides another angle of vision on the question of diversity, as well. Although much liberal democratic theorizing has been pluralistic (if not pluralist) in orientation, insisting that people can unite—e.g., across ethnic or racial lines—on the basis of common interests, or that their ethnic-racial interests can serve as the basis for political organization and pressure (so that conflicting interests can be resolved in the political arena), true diversity almost always appears as a threat to stability. There is no guarantee, of course, that a politics that takes account of women's networks, or that focuses and builds on relationships between people, in general, will be open, nonracist, and nonexclusive. Yet, conceptualizing politics and political behavior around relationships, rather than around interests, provides at least the possibility of a more open, egalitarian perspective.

We return, finally, to the significance of community in a democratic politics. I have tried to suggest that much of the debate about workplace versus community organization, or about the limits of a community focus for social change, has been misplaced. For women, at least, the community—constituted of networks of friends and neighbors—is one locus of the development of whatever we might want to call political consciousness. It is in and through such networks, located at the interface of personal/household concerns and the impact of employer or public policy decisions, that many urban women engage in collaborative activity and begin to experience themselves, and others, as (potential) citizens of a democratic polity. It is precisely in the quintessential urban experience of diversity and difference—differences that, rather than necessarily separating people, provide a context for the development of relationships—that women (and, presumably, men) can come to see themselves as competent social-political actors.

This is not to suggest, of course, that employment discrimination is irrelevant to women, or that there is no need to address the separation of workplace from residence in American urban areas. On the contrary, these concerns are central to the lives of most urban women. But this examination of the situation of women in the city suggests that a simple focus either on employment issues, or on housing—even attending to the interconnections between these concerns—will not be sufficient to contribute, effectively, to integrating women fully into the context of urban political life. Instead, we must change the way we conceptualize that context, both to reflect the realities of women's lives and to make visible the networks and activities that underlie much of what we have taken to be democratic politics.

Acknowledgments

This chapter builds on collaborative work with Myrna M. Breitbart (see Chapter 3). I am grateful to Irene Diamond, Janet Flammang, and Philip Green for helpful comments on earlier drafts.

2

COMMUNITIES, RESISTANCE, AND WOMEN'S ACTIVISM

Reflections on Democratic Theory

Women have been, and continue to be, centrally involved in resistance movements in many workplaces and neighborhoods. Multiple studies document the active role of women in social movements and challenge the conventional view of women as passive members of the polity who live their lives in a private sphere protected (in the case of middle- or upper-class women) or isolated (in the case of working-class women) from the mainstream of "public" life and politics. Not only have women been active in what have been presumed to be the male preserves of work and political life; a closer look at women's lives belies the notion of distinct public and private spheres altogether. Although an ideological split between "public" and "private," community and workplace, may be alive and well in American political ideology—even among feminists—women's activities challenge the existence of the distinction in practice.

In this chapter, I examine the patterns of women's activities and the relationship of activist women to their communities. In the first sections I explore the limits of both American pluralist ideology and of many of the Marxist and neoMarxist critiques of pluralism. I then examine the implications of women's activism for a more comprehensive conception of democratic politics.

Democratic Theory and Democratic Citizenship

Democratic theory (particularly in the "pluralist" form dominant in the contemporary United States) rests on certain assumptions about people, their interests, their relationships with others, and their relationship to the larger polity, each of which must be unraveled before our analysis can proceed. Liberal theories of democracy assume self-interested individuals with clearly felt needs and preferences. Each of these individuals aims to assure the attainment of his or her ends or, in utilitarian terms, the maximization of his or her interests.[1] In theory, a democratic political community treats each of these individuals equally, guaranteeing to all its members the right to pursue their own ends as they see fit, while setting as few constraints as possible on

26

the definition of what those ends might be.[2] Politics—and even community—take on essentially instrumental value: We engage with others primarily for the purpose of achieving our individually chosen ends.

In the above view, interest in politics is not significantly different from interest in any other set of activities: some of us may enjoy softball, others reading, and still others, politics. Those who find fulfillment in attempts to manipulate power engage in what is termed "political life"—voting, lobbying, or even running for elective office. The rest of us (the vast majority) turn our attention to politics only when we feel our interests directly threatened.[3] Apathy or nonparticipation is the normal state. We can assume people's consent to prevailing policies unless they indicate their dissent through action. Since political life is of real interest only to a few, differences in degrees of influence or power within the polity are the result of differences in degrees of participation: the greater influence of some is a direct consequence of their more consistent participation.

Many critics of US democracy have argued that this model is fundamentally flawed, that it limits our understanding of politics and the political process, masks significant levels of discontent, and mystifies the actual exercise of power and influence in the United States.[4] First, political interests are not analogous to an interest in football. Since politics involves decision making about public matters, it is, in fact, of concern to all. When we define politics narrowly, as activities in the electoral political arena, for example, we treat politics as a specialized activity of concern only to a few. This move effectively depoliticizes politics; it prevents many citizens from recognizing that their concerns could be represented on the larger political agenda and convinces them that "politics" is an activity beyond their ken. The seeming apathy that results from such experiences is less a sign of popular consent to the political process (or to the outcome of voting, for example) than of people's frustration with the options available to them and, ultimately, of resignation to their relative powerlessness. Recent experiences with suppression of voting (both in terms of suppressing turnout, and in preventing votes from being counted) in the elections of 2000 and 2004 have further increased overall cynicism about the meaningfulness of "democracy" in the US. While these practices may lead to increased politicization on the part of some, they seem also to have increased resignation and alienation for many more. And campaigning that deliberately shifts the focus of voters away from strongly-felt, material, economic concerns and onto "values" issues can further heighten the sense that "no one is listening out there."

Second, who participates (effectively) in political life is not simply a matter of who happens to be interested in politics. People's perceptions of themselves and their possibilities are very much affected by their position in the social and economic structure of our society, by levels of education, and by a variety of factors that contribute to a sense of "political efficacy"—including efforts on the part of those in power to undermine the development of a sense of efficacy.[5]

Finally, citizens do not meet as equals in a free and open political arena. In any structure of relationships (including pluralist democracy), some interests are perceived as more legitimate than others—and those who articulate them are treated with greater respect. Even beyond that, the resources available to people, whether as individuals or as members of groups, vary greatly. As a consequence, representatives of some interests (especially those of the status quo) have much more ready access to formal structures of political power and influence than others. Even on its own terms, then, the pluralist model is flawed. But, as we shall see, women's experiences of resistance highlight other serious problems with this model.

Democratic Ideology and the Definition of the Political

Crucial to the development of either resistance or resignation is the prevailing societal definition of what constitutes the appropriate subject matter of politics.[6] If what matters most to me is considered not to be appropriate to "politics," I will tend not to participate in (electoral) political activity. Furthermore, in the absence of a community to validate my perceptions, I may well come to see my own concerns as "merely" personal and profess little interest in politics. Many studies provide evidence of these sorts of perceptions—and of their changing through activism. If the activities I undertake in the larger political context are ignored, or their political significance denied, my frustration may well end in resignation and the process of the production of consent. Examples of this phenomenon include the early efforts of women in the United States and Britain to gain the suffrage; civil disorders and unrest on the part of Blacks in this country during the 1960s (characterized by Edward Banfield, for example, as "rioting mainly for fun and profit");[7] and many activities of the contemporary women's movement. As numerous feminist critics have pointed out, prevailing societal expectations that "woman's place is in the home" have contributed both to many women's perception of themselves as apolitical and to the failure of many political analysts to recognize women's activities as political.[8]

What is defined as "political"—that is, as publicly relevant—determines what is available for open discussion, the categories in which people come to understand their experience, and the possibilities they see for resistance. I focus here on two aspects of the structuring of political consciousness in the United States that are particularly problematic when we attempt to understand women's political behavior: the split between public and private, and the relationship between individuals and community(ies). With respect to both of these formulations, much democratic theory posits dichotomous separations that misrepresent the experience of many women and make it difficult for us even to imagine what a truly democratic, participatory polity might look like.

Exploring the "Public–Private Split"

Three arenas of research on the so-called public–private split are of particular interest here. The first, less overtly focused on women, has been the purview of political economists: a concern with the division between economics and politics in American political ideology and its implications for political resistance. The second, a concern with the supposed separation between the public and domestic realms, and the relegation of women primarily to the domestic, has been the focus of many works by feminist social theorists. Finally, urbanologists have explored the separation of public and private space in the structure of urban and suburban life. While the foci of these studies are different, all point to the fact that both in ideology and in the physical structures of our lives Americans tend to divide the world into public and private spheres; and, furthermore, that this division is detrimental both to radical political organizing and to women.

The ideological separation of economics and politics, or workplace and community, is one manifestation of the public–private split (see discussion above, Chapter 1). One effect of this division is the virtual sanctification of "private property" in American political life. More generally, the dichotomizing perspective prevents people from seeing the ways in which their work relationships affect their home and community lives, or the ways in which political decisions (or nondecisions) affect economic relationships. Most important, that perspective helps to sustain the perception that there is nothing citizens can do, either as individuals or as members of communities, to affect the broader context of economic and political relationships in which their daily lives are embedded.[9]

Sexual stereotyping, the designation of separate "public" and "domestic" realms and the relegation of women to the latter, further compound the public–private distinction. In its earliest formulations (with roots in Aristotle's *Politics*), politics was identified with the public, moral world and limited to men; the home, the arena of private morality, was assigned to women. In post-Machiavellian times, politics came to be identified with the amoral, male domain of force; the home became the symbol of purity, morality, and privacy, the domain of women. In this view, women have no proper place in the public sphere; their participation is neither encouraged nor welcomed.[10] When women have acted outside their homes (which, despite this ideology, women have been doing for centuries, whether as workers or as activists), their activities have often been ignored or ridiculed, defined as lying outside the domain of politics properly construed.[11]

The full effect of these ideological separations limits both the agenda of politics and the range of likely participants. On the one hand, the dichotomization weakens the impact of moral issues on politics and excludes what are perceived as private concerns from public discussion. Many women, as a result, have found that the issues of greatest concern to them (safe neighborhoods, decent jobs, day care and education for their children, availability of health care) have been treated as irrelevant, or of secondary significance to politics.

Feminist urbanologists have explored the confluence of these two dichotomies in the spatial separation of workplaces and communities, both in terms of the sources of the division (its roots in patriarchal relationships and in capitalism) and of its consequences for women (the overrepresentation of poor women and children in central cities, with inadequate access to jobs and services).[12] They argue that women are particularly disadvantaged by the separation of workplace from residence and the inadequacy of facilities for the care of young children. As a result of the translation of this dichotomous thinking into social policy, many women do not have the freedom (from child- or other dependent-care responsibilities) necessary to take advantage even of those jobs that do exist.

Each of these schools of analysis points to the ways in which prevailing stereotypes and ideologies about the public–private split limit our conceptions of what constitutes the appropriate subject matter of politics and consequently limit the ability of many people (and, in particular, women, workers, or people of color) effectively to introduce their concerns into the political arena. Conversely, when members of such marginalized groups do take action on their own behalf, its political significance is often ignored or denied, again on the basis of prevailing conceptions of what constitutes appropriate (or legitimate) political action.

Individuality and Community

Although the liberal theory of democracy is rooted in a presumed separation between the public and private realms (designed to protect the individual from the demands or encroachments of others), it also rests on a series of assumptions about the relationship of individuals to their communities. I suggested earlier that liberal democratic theory asserts the priority of the individual, with his or her wants and needs as given; and that the purpose of the political community is to provide the least restrictive environment possible in which each may pursue his or her own ends. Freedom, then, means to be let alone; and politics (and community) take on a purely instrumental value. Finally, citizens will often find themselves in conflict with others over the realization of their interests. (Political) communities stand both as the arenas in which we fight out these conflicts, and, at times, as protagonists in them.

In this theoretical context, the key problem of politics is to overcome at least some of what is perceived as "natural" self-interest and to create allegiance to a community, to something larger than the self. Given their tendency to naturalize self-interest, democratic theorists recognized that a considerable imposition of force, a major transformation of the human psyche, or massive "public education" would be necessary to create community.[13]

However, the individualist premises of the liberal paradigm provide little basis for that community other than "interests," which, in the words of Irene Diamond and Nancy Hartsock, "reduce the human community to an instrumental, arbitrary, and deeply unstable alliance."[14] Further, the methodological individualism implicit in the liberal perspective obscures the extent to which the desire for connection and relationship is a human need, not just a means to achieve individually focused ends.[15] Liberalism denies, that is, that politics is about more than simply meeting individual needs: that it can be, as well, an arena in which people work together with others and find pleasure and fulfillment in mutuality. Finally, in its insistence that all people come to politics equally, as individuals, the liberal paradigm denies people their roots in communities (a fact that particularly denies the social reality of many Black and white working-class women's lives); denies the class, race, and ethnic constitution of communities; and further masks the impact of economic inequality on political participation. In sum, the liberal paradigm tends to homogenize and isolate people in the name of preserving and protecting individuality.[16]

Women's Activism and Democratic Politics

Attention to the many forms of women's activism and resistance highlights the limitations of these dichotomous forms of thinking. As Cynthia Cockburn, Temma Kaplan, Ida Susser, and others have argued (and as I explore in more detail in Chapters 3, 6, and 10 in this volume), even women's traditional household roles may lead them into activities that challenge the very assumption of a dichotomy between public and private, community and workplace. Women in industrial societies bear primary responsibility for the nurturance of both children and adult males within their households. But that responsibility means that women must be active in the urban arena considerably beyond the boundaries of the so-called domestic sphere: They are the ones who negotiate with landlords, markets, welfare officers, health-care providers, and the like. They are the ones who must make the adjustment when wages, prices, or rents fluctuate. Far from being isolated in the home, most working- and middle-class women are forced into relationships with a variety of people and institutions in the so-called public sphere. Women dependent on public assistance, in particular, but others as well, soon come to recognize that the state and other public institutions have an immediate impact on their daily lives. Carrying that recognition one step further, women have joined together with their friends and neighbors to meet their needs and, often, to demand of public institutions that they fulfill their obligations to citizens. As Wendy Luttrell summarizes the situation of women in the community she studied, "[T] heir ability to change roles and to negotiate between the world of politics, community, and families grew directly from those multiple responsibilities [as workers, wives, and mothers]."[17]

Making these sorts of connections is not new for women. Scholars have uncovered a long tradition of women's activism that specifically bridges the community–workplace dichotomy. We now know that women have been leaders and activists in "bread riots" and tenant organizations; that they have participated actively in factory-based strikes that engendered, and depended on, local community support; that they have led struggles for new and better schools.[18] In each of these cases, not only have women crossed the boundaries between the so-called public and domestic arenas, they have also drawn on their relationships with other women (and men) to create networks through which they have engaged in public activity.

Recent work highlights the complexity of this process. On the one hand, gender, racial-ethnic, and class divisions can contribute to the development of feelings of solidarity within homogeneous groups, facilitating radical consciousness and resistance. On the other hand, those same divisions—often exacerbated by dominant social forces and institutions—can serve as barriers to the development of feelings of solidarity across those racial-ethnic or class lines and can impair the growth of resistance.[19]

Despite these complexities, however, attention to women's networks forces us to call into question some of the basic premises of the democratic theory discussed above. For one thing, the existence of these networks suggests that women do not necessarily enter the public arena as "individuals." Networks and community associations develop from women's responses to issues that confront them not as isolated individuals but as members of households, and, more important, as members of the communities in which those households are embedded. The many different groups of women studied by feminist historians, sociologists, and anthropologists who have developed a massive bibliography on women's activism did not come together as isolates, but as women strongly rooted in their class, ethnic, or cultural communities. For most of these women, the "problem of politics" seems less that of creating an allegiance to something *other* than the self—building community out of isolated individuals—than of finding ways to link the concerns, visions, and perspectives they share with their neighbors and coworkers to the "political system" that stands apart from them and seems to control their lives. (I examine this point in Chapter 1, in this volume.)

Moreover, it is not only that women see themselves as members of communities (whether in neighborhoods or at the workplace); they work hard at developing and maintaining the networks and relationships that give life to these communities. As the work of Carol Stack, Cheryl Gilkes, and others makes clear in the case of urban Black communities, Black women play extremely important roles in sustaining one another and their communities, providing services to young and old, male and female.[20] Without those networks, and women's work in and for their communities, neither isolated individuals, nor even isolated families would long survive. Scholars have found similar patterns in white working-class and ethnic communities. And others have discussed, more generally, women's roles as "community-builders."[21] This role is hardly a modern invention, nor is it limited to neighborhood-based communities. Women workers also develop "work cultures" and "work-related networks" that sustain them both in the workplace and outside it.

In addition to providing nurturance and contexts for activism, women's networks can be crucial to the process of consciousness-change. Kathleen McCourt, for example, notes that strong feelings of "community belonging" accompany activism, although it is difficult to determine the direction of causation.[22] Through working with others, and confronting institutions, many women have come to a better understanding of the power relations that affect their lives and of their own abilities—together with others—to have some influence on them. The process, of course, is a dynamic one. Many studies suggest that the development of a changed consciousness is multilayered. On the one hand, participation in campaigns can contribute to refocusing and reshaping women's political analysis, enabling them to forge links between their own experience and that of others (particularly others within their own racial-ethnic class group). On the other hand, racial-ethnic and class divisions can isolate women in homogenous networks and make effective coalition-building very difficult.

Many studies of women's community-based movements note that, although the women often begin with what might appear to be a relatively unsophisticated analysis of the power relations constraining them, their confrontations with specific institutions help them to recognize broader patterns, including the role that assumptions about gender and class may have played in the responses they received. Thus, Sandra Morgen notes that, through their resistance, women health care activists in "Fleetport" developed a new understanding of the relationship among doctors, patients, and the larger socioeconomic context in which both operated—but not before class and racial-ethnic divisions among them threatened to destroy the group.[23]

Similarly, McCourt's study of women in assertive community organizations in Chicago suggests that the more active women "may well be those who are experiencing an expanding realization of the ways in which they … are being mistreated"[24]—even when their organizations are not focused on remedying that mistreatment. Ethnic and class identities can draw women into supportive networks that, in turn, can aid unionization struggles that may involve cross-ethnic organizing.[25] Cheryl Townsend Gilkes's studies of community workers in urban Black communities suggest, even beyond the development of a broader political awareness (which, because of societal racism, is a characteristic shared by Black community members more generally), a developing ability to use the connections they have—especially those crossing the boundaries between Black and white communities—to further "Black interests."[26] In short, community-based activism, itself a product of changed consciousness, can, in turn, generate new knowledge, a renewed commitment to resistance, and new—possibly more effective—strategies of resistance.

To put it another way, for many activist women, the process of coming to political consciousness seems to be a process of *making connections*—between their own lives and those of others, between issues that affect them and their families in the neighborhood or community and those that affect them in the workplace, between the so-called differing spheres of their lives—a process of overcoming precisely the "fragmented consciousness" that, in Ira Katznelson's view, constrains political action in the United States. (Katznelson, of course, argued that it is precisely the tendency of workers to separate workplace and community concerns that is important to the understanding of "American exceptionalism."[27]) In fact, as Ida Susser demonstrates, much of the power of women's activism derives precisely from making those connections—from their perceiving a relationship among state policy, work possibilities, and the availability of social services, and then using whatever resources are available to them (regardless of the "sphere" in which they are located) to provide for their families and communities.[28]

To return, then, to our discussion of democratic theory and politics: Many urban women seem to have little or no difficulty acknowledging the connections between their concerns and those of others—at least within their class- or ethnic-based networks. They may feel themselves to be in a competitive relationship with members of other groups—particularly as politicians or employers attempt to use ethnic, class, or gender divisions to isolate them from one another and hinder the development of resistance. At the same time, however, work-related or community-based networks do provide strong sources of solidarity that can bridge the "community/workplace divide." Most of the working-class women profiled in studies of activism were by no means isolated—either from public life and the world of work or from one another. In Cynthia Cockburn's words:

> Women bring a totality, an all-or-nothing feeling to action. It is something of which trade unions and political parties with their hierarchies and agenda know little, and to which they can give little. This totality is not just of the work day but of the whole day, not just of wages but of feelings, not just of economics but of relationships.[29]

It is in this context that we must undertake a rethinking of the categories of democratic theory. It seems clear from these studies that women's coming to political consciousness (and I suspect that this applies to men as well) may be more a phenomenon of *relationship* and *connection*, than one of recognizing interests in the traditional, individualistic sense. It is in and through networks (located in their neighborhoods, at their workplaces, or at the interface of the "public" and "private" realms) that most women engage in collaborative activity and, through that activity, can begin to experience themselves as confident, competent beings, citizens of a democratic polity. This is not to suggest that political life for women is nonconflictual: multiple historical and sociological studies belie any such claim. Rather it is to point out that when many women engage in political struggles, they do so not as the isolated individuals the pluralist paradigm would lead us to expect but as people rooted in networks and communities.

There is, of course, another aspect to relationships and the feelings of commonality they support. Communities also divide those who experience the commonality from others who do not. Feelings of group identity almost always imply that some are included, and others are excluded. Urban and workplace communities, through which we meet (and, often, struggle with) people and groups unlike ourselves, can be highly conflictual settings. Though they heighten solidarity within groups, they may also increase conflict between groups. As we have seen, resistance movements often suffer from, and sometimes are undermined or destroyed by, the divisions among women that surface (or do not surface!) during these confrontations. Yet, at the same time, we have also seen that those same confrontations can provide contexts for *change*, for the development of cross-ethnic and cross-class coalitions among women, however tentative they may be. Through the diversity they incorporate, cities and many of the workplaces in and near them provide contexts in which the forming of relationships among different groups of people is at least a possibility. It may well be such contexts, then, that facilitate women's and men's seeing themselves as social-political actors in the fullest sense.[30]

In sum, if we take seriously the "relatedness" that seems to characterize the lives of many women, we are forced to see that the vision of isolated individuals that is at the center of much democratic theory is much too starkly drawn. Conversely, the assumption central to the Marxist paradigm that the development of a truly radical consciousness requires the transcendence, or abandonment, of all sources of community feeling other than class (in particular, those feelings based in racial, ethnic, national, or—we might add—sexual identity) is equally flawed. In fact, rather than acting as a "drag" on radical consciousness, communities—and the network of relationships that they nurture and on which they are based—have been, and can be, important contexts for politicization.[31] Political activism—rather than necessarily deriving from and reinforcing antagonistic social relationships among individuals—may more accurately reflect (and reinforce) community and connection.

What are the implications of these findings for the ways in which we think about politics?

To question the reality of dichotomous distinctions in people's activities and relationships is not to deny the power of those dichotomies as political ideology. As all too many studies—and everyday politics—make clear, although many women ignore these supposed boundaries in their daily lives, the ideology of separate public and private spheres still affects both people's perceptions of their situation and their ability to organize in resistance to it. Belief systems—particularly those that define the boundaries of "the political"—structure both what can be conceptualized as a problem and what solutions to that problem fall within the realm of possibility. Institutions such as schools, families, and the media socialize people to perceive a distinction between public and private, politics and economics, that then predisposes them to accept, for example, the legitimacy of management prerogatives in the workplace.[32]

Louis Lamphere and Guillermo Grenier provide an example of a way ideology may constrain resistance. In the case they explored, a management-articulated ideology of participative management prevented workers from building on a sense of commonality with one another. Management was able to use the ideology of democracy effectively to undermine democratic organization in the plant. Ideology functioned to remove from the "political" agenda of the workplace precisely the issues that most concerned the women workers, leaving those issues to be understood, instead, either as individual psychological problems or as matters beyond the bounds of workers' proper influence.[33]

We can see the inhibiting effects of ideology even in more successful organizing contexts. The campaign Sandra Morgen described in Fleetport, for example, had to combat doctors' and health officials' claims that the issues were "medical, not political" (an assertion based on the assumption of a public–private split); that the women in the campaign were not proper judges of what constituted quality medical care; and that their grievances ought to be brought through "appropriate channels" (a claim, meant to enforce a particular definition of what counts as political action). As members of the organization soon learned, the doctors and hospitals had more than just economic and social power on their side. They also defined the agenda. That power to define what is political, rooted in the dichotomizing of public/private and individual/community, can effectively constrain the development of consciousness and limit the range of resistance.[34]

Nevertheless, despite ideological and economic pressures, women have managed to organize in ways that transcend these dichotomies. Their activities point to the need for a new, more comprehensive conceptualization of what politics is about. One clear message is that networks of relationships, and the activism that they support, can be important sources of empowerment. Communities and workplaces can nurture consciousness-change by contextualizing issues, enabling people to recognize that what they may have perceived as their own particular problems are shared and may even be socially structured. Moreover, participation in resistance often engenders a broader consciousness of both the nature and the dimensions of social inequality and of the power of people united to confront and change it.[35] Since the relationship between the development of consciousness and participation in assertive community or workplace organizations is an interactive one, the most effective organizations seem to be those that flow directly from people's own experiences and concerns. Finally, since those concerns do not necessarily respect a division between public and private, it is important that organizations do not assume such a division in their goals and strategies. What this review suggests, in short, is that democratic theorizing ought to address the ways in which people experience connections and the ways in which those connections can be conceptualized as political. New theory must enable people to overcome, conceptually, the boundaries they have already crossed in practice.[36]

Conclusions

The implications of this change of viewpoint for democratic politics are potentially profound. Many years ago, Carole Pateman used a focus on women's experience of rape to explore the limitations of a politics based on liberal-democratic notions of "consent." Since then, many contemporary theorists have called for a new paradigm that would move beyond the individual/community dichotomy inherent in that same liberal tradition.[37]

My own sense is that any new paradigm must take account of—in fact must have as a central focus—the politics of relationship. Such a politics would move beyond liberalism in a number of respects. First, it would treat people as they live, not as isolated individuals but in the complex and multifold contexts of their communities and workplaces. Second, it would recognize that these webs of connection may well entail relationships based in workplace, residential, racial, or ethnic-cultural concerns (or, more likely, a combination of all of them). Rather than assuming these networks to be completely independent of, or necessarily antagonistic to one another, a new paradigm should recognize—and build on—the ways in which they can sustain and nurture their members, allowing people to come to social-political life not as monads, desperate to overcome their isolation, but as *beings in relationships*, concerned with protecting and improving the households, communities, and workplaces in which they live and work. Finally, such a paradigm would recognize that politics is not a narrow range of behaviors undertaken by a few, meant to influence the formal structures of governmental power. Rather, it is precisely that web of activities in which people engage out of concerns generated by their daily lives. For many community-based activist women, political life *is* community life; and politics is attending to the quality of life in households, communities, and workplaces.

This is not to suggest, of course, that all friendship networks necessarily become communities of political resistance, nor that all resistance is empowering. Some communities seem simply to reinforce powerlessness, and failed resistance often leads to increased frustration and even resignation. Nor is it to envision a public life devoid of conflict. But it is to suggest a model of social struggle, rooted in and nourished by ongoing social relationships, to replace the pluralist model of interest-group bargaining, a model that masks both the intensity of the feelings and commitments people bring to political life and the power relationships that structure their interactions.

Unless we change our conceptual framework to incorporate a broader conception of politics, and of who can and does participate in it, much of the radical potential of actions that are already taking place will be lost—even to those who participate in them (I explore "broadening the conception of political participation" in Chapter 9, in this volume). Ideologies do not control behavior, but they do set the categories within which we understand it.

In this respect, attending to "communities" in democratic theorizing offers an important new perspective. Along with Marxists, feminist theorists have criticized democratic theory both for its individualism and for its assumption of a public–private split. Marxists have insisted that this individualism must be transcended, but have articulated an alternative paradigm requiring that people deny connections to any community other than one based on class. Drawing, initially, on the work of Carol Gilligan, many feminist theorists focused their attention on the "women's values" of relationship, connection, and nurturance, suggesting that these, rather than "male values" of competition and achievement, ought to be the basis of our political-social communities and theorizing. But that feminist strategy—which tends to define these values as rooted in biologically-based sex difference, or, at best, in women's capacity to "mother," rather than in the complex social realities of many working-class women's lives—runs the risk of biologistic reductionism, of reinstituting traditional male–female dichotomies in a new guise.[38]

A focus on communities and networks offers us another language, one not necessarily burdened with gender-based connotations. It can provide a way to speak of transformed interpersonal and social relations that does not link them, specifically, to women's domestic roles but allows us to explore the ways in which, in given societies, women have undertaken a disproportionate share of the work of sustaining communities.

There is no reason to assume, after all, that a need for relationship and connection is felt only by women. The extent to which traditional democratic theorists strove to define bases for the creation of a political community is significant evidence to the contrary. The relative neglect with which human connectedness has been treated in that same theoretical tradition is, I would suggest, a reflection more of the way in which men, and male-defined perceptions of experience, have dominated the construction of theory than of any full assessment of the ways in which real human communities operate. Once we integrate women's experiences into those constructions, new possibilities emerge. To do so should allow us to tap more fully into the sources of (women's) political consciousness and to begin to build a democratic polity that is respectful not just of our interests but of the fullness of our relationships and of our integrity as people.

3

TERRAINS OF PROTEST

Striking City Women

(with Myrna Margulies Breitbart)

By 1917, 1918, 1919, people were already more revolutionary. Here, in San Martín, they struck … The women of San Martín (Pueblo Nuevo) were very revolutionary. And when the strikes came, they came. They were the first who got people to go out. People would say, "Here come the women from San Martín, here come the women from San Martín … "

There was a strike of women (in 1918 or 1919) because the cost of living was high. Coal was expensive, bread was expensive. And people demonstrated. They were all women in those demonstrations; there weren't any men. They went out into the streets, and they got others to follow them. "Come on, let's go, come with us," they would say. And in this, even women with hats came out and went on strike with us. And there were also times when women demonstrated for the freedom of prisoners. I wasn't there, but there were lots of women. And do you know how they were received? With a cannonade! Right in the little plaza of Badalona, which isn't very large. With a cannonade! But our strike in Barcelona lasted a long time, three weeks No, not three weeks, seven weeks! Yes, seven weeks in Gràcia, women were on strike.

(Cristina Piera, who was about seventeen years old at the time)[1]

There were times, you know, in Pueblo Nuevo, for example, when there were strikes, and there were *thousands* of women behind those barricades. And we would confront the Guardia Civil. Do you know how we "confronted" them? With salt and pepper: we'd throw it in the eyes of the horses as they advanced! The women were very active.

(Soledad Estorach)[2]

The Barcelona "bread riots" of 1918 were a classic example of widespread participation in "spontaneous" uprisings. They were not organized by unions; in fact, union members (mostly male at the time) had little to do with them. Rather, they were started, supported, and sustained by the women of Barcelona. Many of these women had been affected and influenced by anarchist

39

and other radical propaganda, but most seemed to be acting simply out of a desire to ensure that their families would have food, at reasonable prices.

That the riots and strikes could spread so quickly, paralyzing parts of the city for weeks, seemingly without much prior organization, is testimony to the particular position in the city of the women who participated in them. City life in Barcelona at the time was neighborhood life: many women may have worked in factories,[3] but their primary associations took place in the streets and marketplaces of their neighborhoods. When the time came to strike, therefore, neither advanced organization nor strike committees seemed necessary. The revolutionary women of San Martín simply went into the streets and called on other women to boycott the stores. Word spread rapidly; peer pressure—even across class lines—was strong. There was, in fact, no escaping it. The strikes spread, participation was high, and both male workers and capitalist managers found themselves surprised that these women could so easily disrupt accepted patterns of daily life.

Lawrence Goodwyn observed, of another context, how very difficult it is for citizens of contemporary democratic polities, far removed from mass participatory movements, to envision or understand such phenomena.[4] The tendency is, he says, to ignore, dismiss, or refrain from analyzing decentralist struggles. What is lost in the process, however, is valuable insight into the structuring of social change and of a truly democratic political life. (In 2008, of course, we live in a world where the organizing powers of the web have become almost commonplace. Perhaps we need to think about the ways the decentralized, word-of-mouth organizing that made possible neighborhood— or even city-wide—demonstrations in Barcelona at the beginning of the twentieth century have been replaced by decentralized web-based communication, that made possible the anti-WTO protests in Seattle in November of 1999 and the Obama campaign of 2008.)

While anarchists and some democratic populists assume a relationship between popular participation and radicalization,[5] little attention has been directed to determining what that relationship is. Anarchists discuss the empowerment that derives from active engagement in the issues of one's community, and from knowing that one's personal participation can make a difference in day-to-day life. They argue that, once empowered, people view themselves as socially and politically competent, and seek meaningful, egalitarian relationships in other facets of life. But they have rarely looked in detail at specific examples of the empowerment process. Consequently, a number of important questions remain unanswered.

What social contexts facilitate popular activism? Under what circumstances is activism most likely to occur? How are those who participate affected by their participation? How does it change their views of themselves, their home lives, their relationships to work or to the community? How do people come to understand their place in the world and their relationship to the system of power relationships in which their community is embedded? More importantly, how do they come to believe that those relationships can be different, and that their own actions can alter them?

This essay reflects our preliminary attempts to address these questions and to generate hypotheses which might facilitate their investigation. The case study we have chosen to explore in detail centers on the public struggles which twentieth-century women in Barcelona initiated in reaction to threats to the quality of life in the city.[6]

Why "the city," and women's struggles within it, as focal points for our investigation? Cities provide a vantage point from which to view many important social processes. Modern city space, encompassing both the built and social environments, is a creation of both capitalist relations of production and the patriarchal organization of households, the most important manifestation of which is the separation of residence and workplace.[7] A reading of the urban landscape thus helps make explicit key relationships between reproduction, production, and the sexual division of labor. Each of these relationships generates tensions which can then become the locus of struggle around such issues as housing and quality of life.[8] As Castells points out, it is the collective character of the way in which these contradictions are produced and managed by urban governments that creates the conditions for the discovery of common interests among urban residents, and may, through struggle, demystify the social relations of both capitalism and patriarchy.[9]

> [U]rban space ... Its close association with social movements ... expresses the fact that people always need a material base on which to organize their autonomy against the surveillance of the political apparatuses controlling the spheres of production and institutional power. Only in the secrecy of their homes, in the complicity of neighborhoods, in the communication of taverns, in the joy of street gatherings, may they find values, ideas, projects and, finally, demands that do not conform to the dominant social interests. The control over space is a major battle between people and the state.[10]

Women, in particular, have had a complex relationship to cities. On the one hand, urban areas have drawn those seeking to escape the confinement of patriarchal rural settings in favor of a culture and public space that challenge socially-imposed gender roles and nurture women's creative autonomy.[11] On the other hand, the city has imposed its own constraints on women's freedom; for it, too, has been largely a masculine creation.[12]

Symbolically, the urban environment of massive scale has become associated with governance, the enforcement of laws, and the transaction of business—all functions which, within recent Western cultures, at least, are thought to be less suited to women than to men. The nature and location of housing and jobs also create oppressive barriers for women—especially women of color and single parents. These problems have been augmented, and women's role in sustaining urban life made more difficult, as the feminization of poverty has reduced the quality of urban life. Yet cities have also enabled some women to gain new insights, and support for their shared struggles.[13] Historically, the experience of working-class women in the city has led them to mediate between the "public" and "private" spheres within capitalist cities, and has often involved them in a range of activities and social issues that challenge the assumption of a dichotomy between workplace and community (see Chapters 1 and 2, above). Women's involvement in strike activity has often served to broaden the struggle into a community-wide action.[14] Cities have also provided a context for women to re-design urban space and social life.[15]

Our focus on the participation of women in urban struggle is based on our recognition of the potential contribution of that participation to the development of a critical consciousness. Struggles which directly involve issues of control over space, or which draw attention to the spatial manifestations of gender, class, and race inequality (housing, school desegregation, community safety) occur with great frequency in cities, and often involve much participation by women. Thus, despite the challenges it poses to daily living, the urban context can provide the social space to challenge gender, class, and race oppression.[16] As Susan Squier has summarized, "In its many guises—as symbol, theme, setting, even character—the city speaks fluently of woman's public and private life ... of her ... confinement in patriarchal models for experience, and of her struggle to win freedom from such circumstances."[17]

The Social Landscape of Protest

The extensive movement of Barcelona women within and between various neighborhoods during their protest actions in 1918 provides a focus for examining more closely the relationships between urban space and the radicalization process.[18] These women left the "safety of their neighborhoods and the familiarity of daily routines," says Kaplan, to visit places in the city where they had seldom been before and to confront male authority."[19] What role did this physical movement through the city play in the protest actions themselves, and, more importantly, in the changing consciousness of the women involved?

In the case of the women of Barcelona, the impetus for protest came initially from the immediate need for food and shelter: women organized within their neighborhoods to protest the high price and limited availability of fuel and food.[20] Although they could not, in themselves, generate a more sophisticated political understanding, these concerns were pressing enough to involve women in new and courageous forms of direct action against the state and capital. The long queues outside foodshops and coal suppliers provided the social space to discuss the worsening situation and to plan assaults on coal trucks and marketplaces. These took place in five major districts of the city, involving bands of five hundred to one thousand women at a time. Demands to lower prices were made both face-to-face with suppliers and indirectly through posters. On occasion, the coal or meat itself was appropriated from a supplier and auctioned off by the women at lower prices.[21]

The precise nature and focus of these struggles altered the consciousness of the participants, as reflected in escalating demands on the part of the protesters.[22] What distinguished these consumer riots from other mass demonstrations was the total and exclusive involvement of women, and their *offensive*, rather than *defensive*, posture. Participants refused to continue coping with a decline in the quality of life. They began looking for the social power and physical means to alter the structures and institutions directly responsible.

To understand more fully the centrality of women in these struggles, we must examine their place in the political economy of Barcelona at that time. In Barcelona, women occupied a social space which blurred the boundaries between "production" and "consumption." Although capitalist industrialization had brought about some physical and social separation of workplace and residence (production and consumption), most urban residents moved back and forth between these spheres. In one sense, the separation was sharpest for men, who left their homes and communities each day for work. They defined themselves primarily as workers, and their social life revolved around activities and relationships formed at the workplace. Even so, they were surely aware of the connection between conditions of work and the quality of community life. For women, on the other hand, the primary definition was as caretaker of the home, and their social lives centered around neighborhood events (marketing and laundry, for example). These activities, nevertheless, brought them into daily contact with the producers and distributors of consumer goods. In short, to fulfill their roles as caretaker of home and community, they had to move beyond their immediate domestic environment and become sensitive to changes in the cost and availability of housing and consumer goods, thus criss-crossing arenas of production, distribution, and consumption.[23]

Women—and particularly working-class married women—spent most of their days with other women. Changes in the cost of living felt by one would be felt by all, and modes of adaptation could be readily shared and/or observed. Such a situation proved ideal for spontaneous organizing that builds on shared consciousness.[24] In such a context, it quickly became clear that the increasingly difficult economic situation was a social (or public), rather than an individual (or private) problem.[25] In fact, the communication among women was so "natural" that many who participated in the actions could barely describe how they happened.

Peer pressure was readily applied, and it usually worked: it was difficult to withstand being "called out" by one's neighbors! Women in factories—usually unmarried working-class girls whose situation was believed to be temporary and whose general position was, thus, hardly viewed as distinct from that of the others—readily joined in the strikes. Far from being separated from the public arena, these women understood their roles as women precisely to act *in it*.[26]

The Physical Landscape of Protest

Early twentieth-century Barcelona mirrored other capitalist cities in terms of its divisions into distinct class-based neighborhoods, and industrial and commercial districts. However, it also maintained some ties with the pre-industrial past. Poor and working-class neighborhoods were located largely in the outer rings of the city or by the wharves. Thus, most workers had to commute to their jobs on the wharves or in factories closer to the city center.

During many weeks of struggle, Barcelona women ventured out from their neighborhoods to cover an enormous expanse of urban territory. Protest actions and attempts to capture direct control over social life took them from local merchants, fuel distributors, markets, and churches to the harbor, government offices, cabarets, red-light districts, factories, slaughterhouses, trolley lines, and department stores. These foci of protest were not, however, randomly chosen. Each mobilization originated with a concern about an important issue, and each culminated in a specific demand. There was not a precise linear progression of issues, demands, and spatial focus. Nevertheless, as demonstrations moved through prominent public spaces, women raised larger social issues and made more radical demands. We can also identify a backward and forward movement between issues of immediate and long-term concern.

Protests and direct action against high prices and the shortage of necessities spread outward along major transportation lines into parts of the city considered off-limits to women (such as provincial government offices), factory and commercial districts, and even wealthy residential sectors. On the way to these rallies, routed through streets housing textile factories, housewives called upon factory women to join them.[27] As the protests spread into non-residential areas, women raised more controversial issues related to lay-offs and unemployment, low wages and status for women in the workforce, high rents, war and peace, prostitution, and lack of education.[28]

Interestingly, these actions were, evidently, viewed with ambivalence by the anarcho-syndicalist labor confederation, the CNT. Although that organization had declared a one-day general strike in November 1916 to protest the rising cost of living, connections between workplace issues and those relating to women's subordinate status in either workplace or community were rarely made by the mainstream movement. In fact, in January 1918, both the CNT and the UGT (the socialist labor union federation) were weak and relatively disorganized in the wake of the protracted, and, ultimately, unsuccessful general strike in Barcelona in August 1917 and the repression which followed it. Thus, it was (largely unorganized) women who initiated and maintained the subsistence strikes of January 1918.[29]

A few men in the CNT recognized and applauded these women: *Solidaridad Obrera*, the newspaper of the CNT, reported, for example: "Yesterday you placed the standard of revolutionary conduct at such a height that you left the majority of the men who believe themselves to be able revolutionaries looking very small."[30]

Others were clearly threatened by the women's independent action: "the hour for justice has sounded with the heroic greatness of the women. Either we take advantage of it or we should give our testicles to the dogs to eat."[31] Those who appreciated its significance, however, were clearly in the minority. Thus, for example, when the Catalan Regional Federation of the CNT held a congress at the end of June 1918, not a single female delegate was present. Virtually none of the female-dominated industries or workplaces were unionized; and those which were unionized (e.g., La Constancia) were represented by men.[32]

Still, one of the major speakers at that congress addressed the role of women in the January 1918 strikes. Enric Rueda, representing the lampmakers of Barcelona, declared:

> Women ... have clearly demonstrated their capacity to participate in social struggles, the only struggles which derive, at their core, from a desire for harmony, the only wars which are pursued with the goal of peace, justice, and equity.
>
> After August, when we were persecuted, surrounded by the brutality of the bourgeois regime; when they could no longer meet their children's needs because of our absence and, more importantly, because of the avarice and egoism of the voracious bourgeoisie, our *compañeras* knew to take to the streets to demand what, for the most part, no one wanted to give them: their rightful bread.
>
> The Catalan woman is prepared, by her social orientation and by her energy, to be an important element in the struggle for emancipation. No longer does she go to the confessional; no longer does she fear our going out into the streets in open protest. Today, she incites us to defend freedom, she inspires us to continue with our struggles. Women: correcting social injustice, we, who are a self-conscious and responsible force, we say to you that you are equal to men, that you have the same rights, that you have the same needs, as men. We must devote ourselves to organizing women in syndicates of resistance.[33]

Although the organization did pass resolutions advocating the unionization of women, they focused almost entirely on incorporating women into already-existing unions, thus ignoring the vast majority who were located in non-unionized textile shops (especially out-workers), or, even more importantly, in domestic service.[34]

But for the women themselves, it seems clear that the spatial focus of protest reflected a growing political consciousness; and, in particular, an awareness of the connections between workplace and community issues. Violent marches on lavishly-lit music halls and "palaces of leisure" in the harbor district served to emphasize the need for fuel conservation and women's right to control the use of electricity.[35] Women also made forays into government offices to demand a halt to out-of-province shipments of food and fuel. As the focus moved from consumption to production, strikes were launched in all the major textile industries (which were centers of women's employment) and in many male-dominated workshops.[36] Marches on major department stores, drawing women employees outside, shifted the focus back from production to consumption and on to distribution. Gradually, simultaneous demands arose from the women for reduced rents and lower food and transportation costs; rehiring of railroad workers; increase in job alternatives and education for women; an end to war and a return to peacetime concerns; an end to hierarchy in both the unions and the family; and an end to the Church's participation in economic exploitation through its sponsorship of piecework shops which competed with the women employed in the large textile factories.[37]

The Politicization of Protest

Given the origins of the protest activities in a narrow set of consumer/survival issues, the expansion of protest to encompass these issues of labor market segmentation, patriarchy, anti-militarism, discrimination and religious hypocrisy marks a truly significant growth of consciousness and political sophistication. This personal and collective growth occurred in part as a cause, but more as a result, of the march of the women out from their secure neighborhoods into urban territories where they interacted with representatives of the state, capital, and the male establishment.

While the protests may have been motivated by the women's vague sense of a need for solidarity in the struggle for survival, the movement between residential, production, and distribution centers reinforced their awareness of the strong connections between forms of economic and social domination. Similarly, the backward and forward march of women between centers of political decision-making, neighborhood and family space, and the workplace served to highlight the hierarchical nature of political, social, and economic authority structures. As Kaplan points out, each woman-led struggle highlighted daily life as a problem for the entire community. "Women's work" thus became a public responsibility, and women themselves became more aware of the "essential though invisible services which they perform."[38]

Female networks formed in neighborhoods with a deeply-rooted radical tradition influenced women from other parts of the city, infusing them with consciousness and self-confidence. As one observer commented:

> The women of San Martín [a working-class district] were very revolutionary. And when the strikes came, they came. They were the first who got people to go out. People would say, "Here come the women from San Martín, here come the women from San Martín."[39]

By the time the protest activities were at their peak, women had succeeded in closing down most factories which employed women and seriously disrupting urban life. They managed to touch not only all the nodal points of women's lives in the city, but also the male bastions of political and social power. And they had visibly occupied, and at least temporarily controlled, the largest public plazas.

In our view, the political sophistication evident in these actions distinguishes them from what E.J. Hobsbawm, for example, described as the narrow and limited understanding which such protests reflect of the broader social origins of local problems. In fact, our analysis of these events, and our review of other scholarship on popular protests, suggest that struggles which begin as protests focused on consumption issues may well generate a deeper political understanding.[40]

In fact, the shifting social and spatial terrains of protest in Barcelona may have had a more significant effect on the consciousness of the protesters, and may have gone further in exposing them to the roots of their own exploitation, than any single struggle organized either at the workplace or in the community. The Barcelona "Women's War" thus suggests that radicalization is very much a dual process involving the reappropriation and limited, or symbolic, transformation of both physical and social space. A focus on the latter component suggests that development of a critical social consciousness capable of placing individual problems within a larger social, economic, and political framework is an active process. Far from involving leaps of faith and understanding achieved by listening to explanations of domination and inequality provided by a radical leadership, the route to radicalization for the women of Barcelona came from direct involvement in struggle and in the design of alternative social institutions.

All women were encouraged to participate in the protest actions and were recruited by extensive informal networks originating in working-class neighborhoods and female-dominated workplaces. This combined with the deliberate actions against authority to provide a context for a growing political consciousness. The primary factors responsible for this orientation were the non-hierarchical posture of female leadership and the interchange of experiences and ideas among women and between women and figures of authority. Both factors had the effect of (1) reducing the women's distance from facts concerning their life circumstances and the root causes of injustice; (2) providing knowledge of past struggles and of the contributions of working-class people (women in particular) to their communities and workplaces; and (3) increasing women's ability to envision social and economic alternatives and their confidence to act on them.

These levels of consciousness and activity were not lost in subsequent years. Although the women's demonstrations in Barcelona did not topple the government, patterns of organization established then provided crucial models for the anarchist movement in the years to follow. Through the development of storefront schools and cultural centers, workplace organizing, and other local activities, anarchists were able to create and enlarge "free spaces" in the cities and in the countryside. Over time, these activities prepared people to take their places in the social revolution that accompanied the Spanish Civil War. By 1936, anarchist organizations and practices were so well established in Barcelona that the social revolution transformed both the city and its inhabitants:

> The atmosphere then [during the War], the feelings, were very special. It was beautiful. A feeling of—how shall I say it?—of power, not in the sense of domination, but in the sense of things being under our control, if under anyone's. Of possibility. We had everything. We had Barcelona; it was ours. You'd walk out on the streets, and they were ours—here, CNT; there, Comité this or that. It was totally different. Full of possibility. A feeling that we could, together, really do something. That we could make things different.[41]

In preparing the way for this larger struggle (the Civil War of 1936–39), the Barcelona Women's War of 1918 thus had some lasting effects on the city. The collective memory retained by its working-class neighborhoods kept alive both social criticism and debate about what city life, in its cultural and spatial forms, ought to be like.

Interpreting Urban Struggles

Cities have often attracted women seeking to escape domestic rural confinement. But cities have, in turn, imposed their own constraints on women's freedom, some of which are based in differences of class and race, and some of which cut across class and race divisions. Both in the 1918 demonstrations and in the context of the social revolutionary activities of the Spanish Civil War period, women's actions took them across the boundaries social theorists have constructed between workplace and residence, "public" and "private." Such patterns of activism are echoed in many contemporary urban struggles.

Early analyses of these struggles, however, did not focus on the relationship between the participants in the protest and the form and content of their activities. Instead, the literature on urban struggle [at least through most of the 1980s] moved in two different directions. One focused on the relationship between capitalism and the patterning of urban space, and on the ways in which that relationship structures urban social struggles.[42] A second focused on the participants in struggles, and on the targets of their protest, especially the condition and cost of housing.[43]

Marxist and feminist urbanologists devoted considerable attention to the patterning of urban space and social struggle. Both focused on the social division of labor under capitalism—the increasing separation between "public" and "private" arenas, or "workplace" and "home."[44] Most generally, the separation of workplace from home, and the largely unstated assumption that society is composed of heterosexually-constructed nuclear families, has defined "work" as that which takes place in the public arena of (paid) economic exchange. The male is perceived as the primary wage-earner for the family, the one who acts in the "public" arena; whereas the female is perceived to act only within the home. "Politics" is then defined as that which relates to "public" matters, and in which women are perceived to have little or no place.

But while non-feminist Marxists have tended to treat the community/ workplace split as a consequence of capitalist industrial development, and have largely ignored its implications for women, increasing numbers of feminist critics have insisted that the patterning of urban space is a product both of capitalist industrial development and of patriarchal heterosexual social norms.[45] They make clear that the consequences of spatial segregation fall differently on women and men. They insist that residences, too, are workplaces, and recognize the connection between urban spatial structure and women's exploitation both at home and at work.[46]

Although this interpretation offers a richer understanding of both "residence" and "community," it still reflects a distinction between "workplace" and "community." Women are portrayed as disadvantaged in traditional workplaces, and as both exploited in, and identified with, residential workplaces. The resolution these critics offer is to open up paid work to women on an equal basis with men, and to recognize the dependence of the entire set of relationships on the exploited domestic labor of women.

In the "real world" of political action and social struggle, however, such a distinction breaks down. The orientation of women toward "domestic" concerns has not resulted in their absence from politics. On the contrary, it has generated a longstanding tradition of women's activism, particularly around quality-of-life issues. As Levy and Applewhite note, for example, in their study of "women of the popular classes" in the French Revolution, "the popular classes had no political power, except in their ability to threaten public order, but they understood how political power operated to affect their livelihoods."[47]

Feminist historians of popular protest movements have also noted the prominent role of women in urban movements. Lawson, Barton, and Joselit suggest that women's "numerical predominance" in tenant organizing in New York City is attributable, in part, to "woman's role as homemaker and budget supervisor."[48] Temma Kaplan argued that women's prominence in these activities is a consequence of a specific "female consciousness" that derives from women's particular place in the social-sexual division of labor. That sensitivity to quality-of-life issues—even before the era of the welfare state— led women to demonstrate, riot, and demand that the state fulfill its "proper" role in providing adequate services.[49]

In our own time, the social relations of what is left of the welfare state often serve to highlight the relationship between domestic needs and public policy.[50] We argue, then, that the daily realities of poor and working-class women's lives in cities explode the presumed dichotomy between workplace and community, public and private spheres. British feminist Cynthia Cockburn argues persuasively that the responsibility to maintain the household and its members means that women (even those who are not engaged in waged labor) must be active in the urban arena considerably beyond the limits of the so-called domestic sphere.[51]

Thus, because of their place in the sexual division of labor, urban poor and working-class women experience, day-to-day, very specific relationships not only with the males to whom they are related, but also with shopkeepers and landlords, employers, and agencies of the state. These women's roles let them experience the interpenetration of public and private arenas. Thus, to treat a "sphere of reproduction" as distinct from a "sphere of production"—even for analytical purposes—is to miss both the complexity of women's lives and the implications of that complexity for the development of women's social and political consciousness.[52]

Consequently, it does not make sense to speak of struggles at work as separate from struggles in the community, or to describe struggles over community-based issues as somehow "political," rather than "economic."[53] A recognition of the relationship between workplace and household issues also alters the nature of workplace struggles. For example, some workers have extended negotiations and strikes to take account of the effect of work rules and policies on home life and on the conditions of work.[54] Newspapers have reported efforts by communities to buy out or take over factories employing local workers when multinationals threaten to close them down.

Quality-of-life protests—even if undertaken in defense of what might be seen as narrowly-domestic concerns—can change consciousness by challenging women's own understanding of their place in the family and the community, and of the broader political and economic context of local problems. Lois Gibbs and others at Love Canal may have initially protested the dumping of toxic wastes out of an understanding of their role as protectors of home and community, but their experiences changed them fundamentally. Those experiences led them to challenge the bases of their marriages and into political action on a wider scale: moving from a demand that business become socially responsible to a questioning of the right of businesses to maintain secrecy.[55]

During the 1960s and 1970s, a flurry of community activity around civil rights, housing, and local autonomy issues beckoned would-be social-change activists to incorporate the "neighborhood" along with the "workplace" in the search for a revolutionary undertow in society. The answers to the questions raised then still elude us: What factors transform local struggles into larger movements for change? How does participation change people? What factors determine whether, over the long-term, local community activism will produce "radical" social change?

In the years since, there has been a curious coming together of those who once lent unquestioning support to every variety of community activism and those of the Marxian left who did their best to ignore it. Many Marxists acknowledge the importance of community action, while many defenders of community organizing recognize its often shaky potential for radical change.[56] Both groups agree that certain participatory struggles have the potential for popular and collective transformation. The central question continues to be how to create a climate and culture in support of radical social change.

We can begin to construct a rudimentary picture of the radicalization process from the work of historians and social theorists. Through this work, we are made aware, for example, of the importance of creating autonomous institutions through which people can formulate a counter-hegemonic understanding of their condition, or what Nancy Fraser has referred to as "subaltern counterpublics."[57] As organizing and protest activities attract larger numbers of people, they can contribute to the development of what Lawrence Goodwyn termed a "culturally unsanctioned level of analysis."[58] Finally, people can create the institutional means to share new ideas in "an autonomous political way." The progression of struggle, in Goodwyn's analysis, thus emanates from involvement in cooperative activity (and the resistance it meets), as well as from the creation of a new collective movement culture.[59]

Harry Boyte, Sara Evans, Frances Fox Piven, Richard Cloward, and Manuel Castells agree that decentralist movements often grow from collective organizing experiences which mold discontent into grievances against specific targets. They also point out that progression usually entails a change in the focus of a struggle from (simple) opposition to the active resistance to power, and the search for creative alternatives in the organization of the workplace or community.[60]

Studies of the Barcelona movements confirm these descriptive generalizations. Initial dissatisfaction with the current circumstances of life and a desire for community led people in struggle to an understanding of the interrelationships between economic and social life, and to an ability to place daily troubles in a larger context. Opposition then gave way to an alternative vision and efforts to challenge authority by trying to realize this vision. As self-confidence and critical understanding grew, there was an increased desire to act. Increased scope of the struggle also meant that many levels of society came under assault simultaneously.

What these descriptive generalizations lack is the specificity necessary to uncover the factors behind this progression—the role of women, daily life, and the urban environment in the generation of a radical social movement. How do individuals subjected to various forms of domination mediate and resist its effects? What is the role of Henry Giroux's "oppositional culture" in the home, the neighborhood, the school, and the workplace? What factors enable those in socially subordinate positions to seize distinct "moments of cultural and creative expression" and inform them with a different counter-hegemonic logic? How do these varied cultural experiences coalesce during the course of struggle to oppose and resist power and authority?

Answers to such questions require a shift in emphasis away from an exclusive examination of the structural determinants of inequality to a view of people as actors rather than passive victims. It also requires that we avoid romanticizing the power of the dominated. What we seek, instead, is a truer sense of the conflict that results when culture, race, gender, and class interact in relationships between home, community, and workplace.

At this juncture, however, it may be possible to establish some criteria for identifying potentially progressive local struggles. One could ask, for example, whether the struggle is informed by a dominating or liberating logic. Is it an effort to achieve greater control over one's life, or a mere reaction to powerlessness?[61] Do those involved in struggle develop a more holistic understanding of social domination? Are they beginning to appropriate their own histories and to reinterpret local and national events in light of this understanding? Is cultural and creative expression incorporated into struggle?

The following hypotheses reflect our preliminary efforts to identify those elements or forces that seem to facilitate personal radicalization and the collective development of a social movement.

I Radicalizing Forms of Participation

The development of a critical consciousness is an active process which involves participation in social struggle and in the design of change. Collective confrontation with structures of authority and/or the creation of some new social-political reality in the interstices of existing power relations often generates changed consciousness and energizes continued action (resistance). Based on our analysis of the cases we have examined, we hypothesize that the kind of struggle most likely to produce changed consciousness has certain characteristics:

- It reduces participants' distance from the facts of their lives, enabling them to recognize the significance of the larger social context in which their oppression takes place.
- It allows people to learn more about their history, especially if it brings together members of different generations and/or cultures.
- It leads to increased confidence: recognizing that one is not alone and can act with others is an empowering process.
- It demands changes which cannot be met by mere adjustment and adaptation (parallel to André Gorz's classic distinction between "reformist" and "structural" reforms)[62] and, therefore, generates a momentum for continued involvement.

II Multi-Focal Protests

Any successful movement for change will have to confront the encroachment of capitalism and political centralization into all facets of economic and social life. Struggles with radical potential must wage battle on multiple levels and in many different economic and social arenas simultaneously. Separate protest activities which address a multitude of issues (such as high food and housing costs, low wages and uncertain job tenure, schools and child care, the safety of living environments, and race and gender discrimination) hold enormous consciousness-raising potential. As we have seen, the interrelationship between family, community, economy, and national politics becomes more visible as the range of protest activities widens and the information and opposition each generates increases.

III The Reappropriation of Space

The transformation of popular forms of opposition into meaningful movements for social change is facilitated when those involved in protest make a concerted effort to reappropriate and transform their physical and social space. Environments themselves neither dominate nor liberate. They do, however, play a crucial role in maintaining socially-constructed categories of gender, race, and class, while at the same time providing a context within which these categories may be resisted and altered. Landscapes of subterfuge, relatively free of the influence of political, economic, and cultural domination, can provide the "social space" necessary for the incubation of counter-hegemonic interpretations of daily problems.[63] Active participation in community institutions and in struggles to create alternative public spheres may provide the opportunity to define oneself anew. Moving the physical site of protest activity from the local area to the workplace, and to centers of political power, raising issues of local and global concern, may also increase the depth of popular understanding of social and political domination. Efforts to reclaim access to particular spaces (abandoned houses, expensive means of transport, etc.), or to alter the environment to better meet a community's needs, may, in turn, generate repressive acts that highlight the connections among hierarchical authority structures.

IV Women, Workplace, and Community

Finally, the prominence of women in many of these struggles is not coincidental. Working-class women's roles as "family caretakers" link them to both workplace and neighborhood, and provide a context for them to experience their physical and social environment in a way different from that in which most men do—even those men of similar class and ethnic-cultural background. Paradoxically, the specific gender expectations for women may facilitate the development of a radical consciousness, since their roles force them (at least at moments) to see the connections between workplace and neighborhood concerns and the state (or political authorities), as manifest at Love Canal and Three Mile Island, in tenant organizing, or the women's peace and disarmament movements. The feminization of poverty and current changes in family structures and living situations—particularly rising numbers of female-headed and alternatively-structured households—may well intensify these tendencies.

Underlying each of these hypotheses is the recognition that neighborhoods, like workplaces, are neither necessarily all-encompassing "footholds of domination"[64] nor the loci of revolution. Although they are marked by contradictions, they may contain the possibility for emancipatory struggle. A focus on opposition and resistance within environments of community and work, and on the differing experiences of men and women with regard to locality, ideology, and the state, deserves further exploration.

This case study of women's struggles in urban Spain provides a basis for potentially rich new areas of inquiry. It also raises many additional questions.

- In what ways did more contemporary movements—e.g., Love Canal and Three Mile Island, or women's peace camps at Seneca Falls/Romulus, NY, or Greenham Common, in England—provide contexts for organizing comparable to those of the city squares and markets of early twentieth-century Barcelona? What were the most significant differences?

- An approach focusing on empowerment suggests that activities most fruitful for generating radical consciousness are those which have at least some chance of success.[65] Are there cracks and crevices, relatively free social spaces, in our society today? How can a vast area, or a large group of people, be organized? And how can local organizations, or groups with a specific focus, sustain their integrity and join with others in coalitions? In the case of tenant movements in New York City, males (and particularly the Socialist Party) took over direction of the larger movement. As activities moved beyond the neighborhood level, women and issues of immediate concern to them tended to be relegated to a secondary position.[66] What factors accounted for this? Are similar patterns evident today? [To what extent does the internet make such concerns almost superfluous?] What can we learn, for example, from the experience of the National Congress of Neighborhood Women, which has attempted to maintain and encourage autonomous organizing on the part of women? (see below, Chapter 10).

- How are levels of critical understanding acquired in one particular arena of struggle (the family or community, for example) carried forth into another arena (such as the workplace)?

Feminism challenges us to examine how a disaggregated population, divided by differences of race, class, and gender, is affected by environments not of its own creation. It challenges us also to examine how these populations create environments supportive of new social forms and "a symbolism and imagery that captures ... repressed hopes."[67] The built and social environments we currently occupy will continue to provide a backdrop for this resistance. It remains for us to explore further these varied and potentially-subversive terrains.

Acknowledgments

We wish to thank Ardis Cameron, Philip Green, Joan Landes, and Robert Rakoff for helpful comments on earlier drafts of this chapter.

II

CHALLENGING DICHOTOMIES

Dependency, Privacy, Identity, Power

4

DEPENDENCY OR MUTUALITY[†]

A Feminist Perspective on Dilemmas of Welfare Policy

Concern about the "feminization of poverty" and the perpetuation of a "culture of dependency" characterizes much of the debate about welfare policy, both among mainstream policy-makers and policy analysts, and among feminist critics and commentators. Many critics of US welfare policy—whether from a left- or right-wing perspective—seem to have accepted the claim that "welfare perpetuates dependency," and that "dependency" is inconsistent with citizenship in a democratic society. Feminist historians and state theorists have focused on the historical development of the welfare state and, specifically, on the creation of a two-track or two-tier system that was (and remains) both gender- and race-biased.[1] Others have suggested that theorists and policy analysts ought, more basically, to begin to explore constructions of "difference" that lead to such policies and to our "fears of dependency," themselves.[2]

Where do these fears come from? What implications do they have for the ways we examine and evaluate policy alternatives? In this chapter, I explore some of the political, analytical, and ideological legacies on which contemporary feminist analyses of female poverty and "dependency" seem to draw, their relationship to theories of citizenship, their implications for our understandings of policy alternatives in the area of welfare, and the limitations of these perspectives. I argue, first, that to evaluate welfare programs solely, or primarily, in terms of their alleged contribution to "dependency" is limited and misleading; and, further, that the stigmatizing of particular relationships as "dependent" that underlies many contemporary critiques makes invisible other kinds of interrelationships that are crucial to the social whole. I do not offer here a fully articulated alternative view. But I will end with a plea for developing new ways of looking at these issues that might enable us to avoid the difficulties posed by the use of the term "dependency."[3]

Liberal and Marxist Legacies of Western Feminisms

Western feminist theorizing, particularly that dominant in US circles, has drawn primarily on liberal and Marxist-socialist traditions. Although

59

psychoanalytically-based theories have also found resonance in feminist circles, I focus here on liberal and socialist traditions since I believe these have been of most influence on policy analysts, and have had the greatest impact on popular activism and thinking.

The Liberal Tradition

The western liberal political tradition—beginning with Hobbes and Locke, and continuing in our own time with the work of John Rawls, for example—is deeply embedded not just in US law and custom, but in many of our ways of thinking about the world. I examine here the ways that tradition has constructed our understandings of dependence (and independence), their meanings, and their implications for the political community. As both Carole Pateman and Barbara Nelson have argued, the liberal tradition embodies a number of contradictory perspectives on dependence, independence, and women's roles in a polity.[4] On one hand, liberalism articulated a revolutionary position vis-à-vis traditional patriarchal communities, placing a high value on individuality and individualism, and insisting that people earn their places in a social and political community on the basis of their individual accomplishments rather than on the basis of feudal or caste relationships. More than any other set of claims, I think, this perspective marked the radical character of Hobbesian and Lockean liberalism.

On the other hand, the liberal tradition limited the province of that individuality in important ways. First, it linked respect for self-worth to self-support and/or to the bearing of arms. That is to say, any person able to support himself and/or to bear arms in defense of the state was considered worthy of citizenship. As Michael Walzer noted—although seemingly without awareness of the gender implications of his analysis—a citizen is, in Hobbes' words, one who can "protect his protection."[5] Independence, as the ability to support oneself and (later, with the introduction of the "family wage system") one's family, came to be defined as a basis for citizenship. But, as may already be clear, notions of citizenship derived from that perspective had gender and class built into them. Carole Pateman has argued, further, that gender has been inscribed in an analogous way even into the "participatory democratic" stream of political thought which developed as a radical alternative to those theories. Participatory democrats, like the traditional liberals they criticized, assumed a citizen body composed primarily of self-supporting—though politically and economically *engaged*—males.[6]

But the liberal position which connected citizenship with self-support resulted in an ambiguous citizenship status for all who were not self-supporting males. Even in the so-called democratic polities of England and the US, property qualifications for voting effectively excluded poor men from full citizenship rights until well into the nineteenth century.[7] For blacks in the United States, the disabilities were doubled—or, to put it more accurately, perhaps, the "grounds" which could be used to exclude them from citizenship were multiplied. Slaves, of course, were not self-supporting by definition. Beyond this, racist notions of moral and intellectual inferiority further served to deny full incorporation of black males into the polity, even long after the passage of the so-called Civil Rights Amendments in the post-Civil War period.

The situation was similarly problematic for women, both white and black. In this case, the public–private split, deriving from the Aristotelian tradition that women (along with, in Aristotle's view, slaves, children, farmers, and laborers) were "necessary conditions," but not "integral parts" of the political community, ensured that women would not be considered eligible for citizenship as defenders of the state (after all, they were the ones the male citizens had to rush out to defend!) nor as self-supporting laborers, since their "work" was defined as domestic and, therefore, not-work. The movement for (white) women's suffrage was, in essence, a demand that women be recognized as full citizens of the polity, regardless of their dependent economic status and their exemption from military service.

Nelson and Pateman argue effectively that liberal political theory and practice accepted the ideology of separate spheres at its core. It was, therefore, only white, propertied men who were fully and unambiguously citizens. Women were included in the citizen body only quite late in the game; and only with the presumption that they were, and would continue to be, economically dependent on men. In effect, as Linda Gordon has also noted, even after women won the suffrage, they were excluded from full political participation, since political life continued to be considered outside the proper sphere of women's attention and understanding.[8] More importantly, from the point of view of our concerns here, women were also excluded from the full presumption or expectation of economic autonomy and independence that was otherwise taken to be the ground for political independence.[9] Similarly, in participatory democratic theory, to the extent that women (or men) are accorded political equality, it tends to be based on their active participation in the (paid) economic arena. But, as Pateman has argued, this approach assures women citizenship only to the extent that they are "like men." Once again, citizenship is linked to (economic) independence.[10]

These views of the relationship between (economic) independence and citizenship, and of women's relation to both, had important implications for the construction of the US welfare state. The budding welfare state incorporated this heritage of unequal treatment of people in terms of class, gender and race. Welfare programs created both before and during the New Deal (with participation of middle-class women reformers and women's organizations) assumed that women would enter into, and participate in, the wage labor market on terms very different from those of men: as temporary, or secondary, workers, certainly not as the main supporters of their families. Social insurance schemes were premised on the assumption that men would earn a "family wage" to support their families and that most women would be attached, in some way, to a male (either father or husband). Programs oriented toward women (e.g. Mothers' Aid or, later, Aid to Families with Dependent Children) attempted to deal with what were labeled "anomalies," i.e. women not attached to men and, therefore, excluded, in some sense, from the mainstream. Women were, thus, covered by programs not as (potential) workers, but as mothers. As Myra Ferree has put it, the US welfare state was built on the assumption that "women's state is essentially domestic and dependent."[11] In a sense, the economic dependency of women, first on men and then on the state, was built into the structure of welfare state programs from the very beginning, along with (and mutually reinforcing) assumptions about the separation of spheres and the sexual division of labor.

The Marxist-Socialist Tradition

While it offered a strong challenge to the individualism of liberal theory and practice, socialist tradition has fallen prey to similar problems with respect to the question of dependency. In important ways, for Marx as for liberals, self-realization was tied to work—not, of course, alienated wage labor, but true work under socialism. Capitalism prevented people from experiencing themselves fully as human (productive, communal) beings. In his early works Marx discussed this claim under the rubric of "alienation," but similar concerns appear in his later works as well. He wrote in *Capital*, for example:

> [M]eans for the development of production transform themselves into means of domination over, and exploitation of, the producer; they mutilate the laborer into a fragment of a man, degrade him to the level of an appendage of a machine, destroy every remnant of charm in his work and turn it into a hated toil ... they distort the conditions under which he works, subject him during the labor-process to a despotism the more hateful for its meanness; they transform his life-time into working time and drag his wife and child beneath the wheels of the Juggernaut of capital.[12]

The primary issue for Marx was not *individual* dependence or independence, but class-based exploitation.[13] At the level of the individual, capitalism exploited people, denied them awareness of the ways all members of society are *interdependent*, and set workers in competition with one another so that they experienced other workers not as comrades but as enemies. Importantly, however, exploitation would be overcome not through individual achievement but through *collective action* leading to the overthrow of capitalism. In the process, both men and women would finally be able to respect themselves and each other, and come to experience themselves as fully equal members of a community.

Marx criticized the so-called public/private split in liberal capitalist democracies, insisting that economic and political life cannot be easily separated and that formal political equality in the context of a capitalist economic system only perpetuates and masks the inequality and exploitation of workers.[14] Marxist-socialist analysis viewed poverty not primarily as a condition of *dependence* but, rather, of *exploitation*. The solution to it was political, even more than economic: the incorporation of working people into the paid labor force (and, in particular, industrial waged labor) would create the conditions under which workers could come to consciousness of themselves as a class, with a joint interest in overcoming private property and the social division of labor. Economic action would be, at the same time, political, and have the consequence of overthrowing both capitalism and the supposedly autonomous political system.

The question of how the specific subordination of women is to be understood in Marxist terms has been the subject of considerable debate. Marx and Engels both recognized and acknowledged the particular subordination of women under capitalism, but their analyses of it, and prescriptions for overcoming it, were not always consistent. In general, they seemed to treat subordination as a function of women's relation to the division of labor, specifically, their exclusion from the paid labor force. Most explicitly in *The Origins of the Family, Private Property, and the State*, Engels argued that women's subordination under capitalism was a function of private property and the division of labor, and that the full entry of women into the wage-labor force, on equal terms with men, would be the key to their emancipation.[15] Nevertheless, in at least some of his writings, Marx asserted a "natural" division of labor between men and women, which need not imply subordination, and which would not necessarily end with the establishment of socialism. Thus, as Alison Jaggar has noted, in *The German Ideology* Marx and Engels refer to the "division of labor in the sexual act" as "natural." Further, in *Capital*, Marx claims that "within a family ... there springs up naturally a division of labor, caused by differences of sex and age, a division that is consequently based on a purely physiological foundation."[16] Presumably, even under socialism, the sexual division of labor would continue; however, it would no longer result in women's subordination.

But, as socialist-feminist critics have noted, although Marx insisted throughout his work that human nature—and particularly social inequality—is *socially-constructed*, he seemed to ignore that insight in the case of gender difference. Nowhere did either he or Engels explain in what sense the sexual division of labor was "natural," nor *why* women should necessarily continue to be responsible for domestic duties once capitalism had been abolished. Both Marx and Engels noted—but then ignored the significance of the fact—that the sexual division of labor (and the domination of women by men) *predated* capitalism. Thus, neither their theoretical analyses nor their prescriptions for change attended either to the realities of women's subordination in the domestic arena or, more significantly, to the interrelationship between the domestic and public arenas. Once again, while Marx and Engels were critical of the public/private split in general, they seem to have ignored its significance for women and for male–female relationships.[17] Their analyses assumed that women's emancipation would be accomplished through the abolition of capitalism and the establishment of socialism. However, attention to their own analytical framework, as well as to more recent historical studies, leads to the conclusion that male dominance is neither so simply explained nor so simply overcome, and that without specific attention to gender relations, women's subordination to (or dependency on) men will continue under socialism.[18]

Contemporary Feminist Perspectives

Contemporary feminists are heirs to both the strengths and the weaknesses of these theoretical traditions. Liberal feminist theorists and critics, when they address issues of women's poverty, have tended to argue that the solution to "female dependency" is to get women out of the home and into the job market, so that they can be economically self-supporting, the equals of men.[19] Fundamentally, these critics accept the liberal premise that individual worth is measured by one's ability to earn—provided, of course, that discriminatory barriers in the job market are eliminated. Such a perspective has little to say to the situation of women who are *in* the paid labor force, and not earning enough to survive, especially when there are many men in the same position—a situation increasingly common, given that major job growth in recent years has been in the low-paid service sector. In addition, since this premise measures worth by earning capacity, it cannot value the work of those who are not, and for one reason or another (their own disability; responsibility for the care of dependent children, elderly, or disabled; or inadequate skills or education, for example) cannot be part of the paid labor force. It is difficult for liberal feminists to affirm the value of unpaid nurturing activity without seeming to reinforce a "separate spheres" doctrine which also keeps women dependent.[20]

Socialist feminist critics, on the other hand, have focused primarily on the nature and consequences of the sexual division of labor, the construction of women as consumers within a capitalist society, the nature of domestic labor, and women's roles as producers and reproducers of labor power.[21] These debates and discussions have, in turn, provided the context for proposals for wages for housework and "caregiver wages," as ways of recognizing and validating women's (unpaid) work in the domestic sphere.[22]

The common theme of all these socialist-feminist studies is that "dependent" women have important roles as supports for men, children, the elderly, and other groups and, therefore, do much work that is essential to the maintenance of social and economic life. There are two aspects to this argument. First, women are *perceived* as dependent—and they may *be* so economically—because much of the domestic work women do is not paid.[23] Second, any adequate political-economic analysis must not only look beyond the public/

economic context to the domestic arena; it must, as well, explore the inter-dependence *between* these domains, and the way gender structures *both of them*.[24] The economic dependence of women on male wages is socially constructed and can be eliminated only through a total social reorganization that must address not only the economy but also gender—that is, familial and kinship structures and the social division of labor by sex.[25] Thus, even though it may start from a position quite critical of liberal individualism, this analysis, too, has as one focus the goal of economic self-sufficiency for women.

Barbara Taylor recounted the transformation and bifurcation of nineteenth-century British utopian socialism into a class-conscious socialism that is relatively gender-blind and a gender-conscious feminism that is relatively class-blind.[26] Similarly, in the US context, we find analyses that would have women make "independence," rather than collective empowerment, their goal; analyses, incidentally, that now make it very difficult to counter the claims that "feminism has failed women," in that it told women they could "have it all." Multiple articles in *The New York Times Magazine* and elsewhere that have focused on women dropping out of professional careers are premised on the assumption that "feminism" was about individual-level success, rather than about collective empowerment that was aimed at profound restructuring of the organization of work. And those perspectives that did focus on collective empowerment (e.g. socialist or black-nationalist groups) tended to marginalize women or to treat gender issues as of only secondary importance. Yet, both within the feminist community and outside it, analyses offer very different visions of what "independence" means and of what must be done to achieve it.

The implications of these perspectives for welfare programs and for activist organizing are multi-faceted. Both feminists and anti-feminists tend to define women's "dependence" as the problem. For many feminists—both liberal and socialist—the issue is that women's dependency on men has been replaced by women's dependency on the state: but dependency of either sort is viewed as problematic. For many anti-feminists, on the other hand, it is not women's dependency on *men* that is the problem, but only women's dependence on the state—and, in particular, on welfare and employment-support programs. Ironically, both camps seem to agree that the solution is to eliminate the dependence: to make women independent (whether of men or of the state), presumably by eliminating the welfare system or by providing education and/or job-training. In yet another twist, William Julius Wilson argued that the problem of (black) female dependency on the state is a consequence of (black) male unemployment; he advocated employment programs to enable black men, in particular, to support black women and children.[27]

Beyond "Dependency"

As many critics have noted, those policies which have been developed to address women's poverty are confused and contradictory—and, importantly, unsuccessful.[28] However, critics are far from agreed on what approaches or programs should replace them.

It is now a commonplace that the welfare state has ambiguous consequences for its clients. On the one hand, beginning with Piven and Cloward's *Regulating the Poor* (1976), some critics have viewed welfare programs as mechanisms for the exercise of state control. On this view, welfare "dependence"—fostered by the state—has the consequence of moderating resistance to the social inequality created by industrial capitalism. Even education and job training programs, which were originally designed to get people "off welfare" and into a condition of "independence" are, themselves, state-sponsored. Some might well argue, then, that participation in such programs is a manifestation of precisely the "dependence" they are presumably designed to overcome.

Following from this perspective, critics Irene Diamond and I termed "state skeptics" focused specifically on the impacts of state-sponsored welfare programs on women's family and sexual lives. Jean Elshtain, Kathy Ferguson, Irene Diamond, Barbara Nelson, and Gwendolyn Mink, for example, "emphasize the bureaucratic and disciplinary techniques through which the contemporary welfare state organizes family life and sexuality."[29] Isaac Balbus pointed to the transformation of "citizens of a limited state" into "clients of an unlimited state," a concern that, if anything, has only been getting stronger in recent years.[30] These perspectives might well lead us to be wary of *any* state-sponsored welfare programs, on the ground that they increase dependency or, more generally, decrease women's ability to control their own lives.

On the other hand, as many of these same critics have argued, welfare state programs have also afforded important resources for empowerment.[31] Many such programs have been of tremendous value to women—whether by providing employment within the welfare-state bureaucracy (and, thus, directly "lifting them out of dependence") or by providing needed, though inadequate, benefits to those who are clients. Thus, for example, although her focus is less on *group* organizing and more on the ways in which individual, subordinated, immigrant women were able to use social service agencies—even while also being abused by them—Linda Gordon's work on family violence and social control makes an important argument about the complex nature of the relationship between so-called agencies of social control and their clients.[32]

Further—and perhaps most importantly—women and poor people have been able to use many of the programs and institutions created by the welfare state precisely to organize *against* the state, demanding better services and benefits. In the process, "clients" can come to experience, for themselves, precisely the stronger self-image and the collective sense of empowerment which many anti-poverty organizers take to be their goal. Thus, state programs often serve as the contexts for major organizing against the state, not only on behalf of greater welfare benefits, but also for more equality. On this view, organizing becomes a form of consciousness-raising and empowerment, as well as a means of self-protection and self-assertion. The welfare state comes to be seen not just as a mechanism of control over the poor, but as a product of the demands made, and resistance offered, by poor and working-class people to changes in the class relations of advanced capitalism in the United States.[33]

I do not believe that anyone has yet successfully resolved the dilemmas entailed in looking to the state to foster "independence." Can programs and institutions created by the state be used to create the conditions for over-coming dependence? (We certainly assume they can in the case of educational institutions!) Can there be a "progressive welfare policy," or are all efforts at reform of state welfare programs merely routes to more "tractable forms of domination"?[34] So far, we have seen that all of these analyses begin from the (often-unstated) assumption that dependency is undesirable; where they differ is in their evaluation of what contributes to its perpetuation or elimination. I wish to argue here, however, that the basic problem in addressing these dilemmas is not simply one of strategy, but of the assumption on which the strategies are based, namely, that all forms of human economic dependency—whether on other individuals or on the state—are problematic, and should be eliminated whenever possible.

If we return to the review of the legacies of feminist theorizing offered at the beginning, it becomes clear that what is at issue in the case of welfare and women's poverty is not a question of dependence versus independence. In fact, virtually no one in this society is totally independent in any meaningful sense. Liberal theory to the contrary notwithstanding (and even liberal theorists acknowledge that the state of absolute independence which they termed the "state of nature" was long since past, if not entirely hypothetical), societies are composed not of independent individuals, but of networks of relationships, characterized by *inter*dependence.

In fact, talk of women's dependence *highlights* economic dependence while *making invisible* other kinds of dependency—emotional, for example.[35] In pre-industrial and early industrial periods, family relations were characterized by mutual dependency: all members of the family contributed to its upkeep, and the work of each was recognized and valued. However, with the creation of a capitalist industrial workforce, and privatized households based in sepa-rate spheres, women came to be viewed as economically dependent on men. More particularly, the inauguration of the "family wage system"—at least at the ideological level—both assumed and served to legitimate women's eco-nomic dependence on men. The system had obvious negative consequences both for those men (and their associated families) whose wages were not sufficient to sustain a family and, especially, for those women not tied to wage-earning men.

Contemporary discourse about "welfare dependency" tends to criticize *some* groups of women for their failure to be economically self-sufficient. But it is important to note that *who* is devalued (and on what basis) varies greatly with class and race, and also with the social position of the evaluator. Black single mothers and single heads of households, for example, are often criticized for being dependent on the *state*, rather than on men; poor single women of whatever racial/cultural background are frequently criticized on similar grounds. Middle-class women, on the other hand, may find themselves criticized by feminists for their "dependence" (if they are not in the paid labor force), or by conservatives for their "independence" (if they are)!

Nevertheless, throughout this period—whether of early, middle, late or advanced capitalism—women have done the largely unpaid work (which has rarely been recognized *as* work) on which others depend in fundamental ways, whether those "others" be husbands, children, elders, communities, or employers (theirs or their husbands'). The concepts of "caregiver wages," wages for housework, and the like were developed precisely to validate that work, and to make it visible—although they, in turn, may run the risk of reinforcing the so-called traditional sexual division of labor.

In fact, I believe we must move beyond these dichotomies to revalue many types of dependence, whether on other people or on communities, that are at the root of social life, and that ought to be viewed as potential sources of empowerment, rather than as symptoms of powerlessness.[36] As Marx argued, and as resistance movements in the US and around the world have demonstrated repeatedly, collective action is based in mutual dependence (or interdependence), not in individual struggles for "independence." It is people's connections to one another, often—though not always—rooted in shared experiences of oppression, that have provided downtrodden people with the power and the vision to engage in collective resistance against what might well appear to be insuperable odds. Dependence—or, better, *mutuality*—is not to be avoided but, rather, is a fact of life to be acknowledged and even celebrated.

On this view, what is problematic is not dependency, per se, but *unequal* dependence resulting in relationships of domination and subordination, in which one person, or group, holds the power to define the nature and/or life-chances of another.[37] Obviously, there are some situations where dependence—and even unequal dependence—cannot be avoided; they must be recognized as inherent in the life of human communities: for example, the dependence of children on their elders, of elderly on the young, of the sick or disabled on the healthy. Other forms of dependency—for example, those rooted in race or gender oppression—are socially-constructed and potentially changeable. The aim of social movements and social policy, rather than being defined in terms of *independence*—which represents the adoption of an inappropriate (and inaccurate) idealized liberal vision—ought to be to enable people to achieve relationships of meaningful *interdependence* and mutuality. In such a context, value would be attributed not according to earnings, and not even necessarily on the basis of the paid work one did, but on the basis of one's place as a member of an interdependent community.[38]

The recognition that people are rooted in communities, that our lives find meaning in relation to the others with whom we live them out, and that the struggle to overcome subordination is a collective, rather than an individual, one—served as the basis for the individual and collective empowerment many women experienced through consciousness-raising in the early days of the "second wave" women's movement. It was also a primary source of the collective and individual empowerment experienced by those who participated in the civil rights, welfare rights, anti-Vietnam War, and anti-nuclear movements in this country within recent years. It is that power that has animated and sustained resistance movements throughout history. It is, finally, the only power that can provide a full meaning to "citizenship" in a democratic political community which recognizes its constituents as more than isolated, atomistic, individuals.

Feminist rethinking of welfare policy, then, must begin to take more fully into account the knowledge we have gained over the past many years of organizing. Welfare state programs are ambiguous and problematic: they can reinforce domination, and they can also empower. If we focus on either side of the equation and ignore the other, we lose touch with the totality. If we focus only on overcoming dependence, and ignore the important work of nurturing that undergirds any community, we slip into a false vision of a society characterized by "independence" and "autonomy," ignoring to our peril the heretofore largely invisible work that has supported those supposedly autonomous persons. Our goal, then, ought to be to move toward a vision and description of *mutuality*, one which values both autonomy and interdependence, and which recognizes—and celebrates—the variety of ways people can and do contribute to the maintenance and transformation of the community as a whole.

5

PRIVACY, PUBLICITY, AND POWER[†]

A Feminist Rethinking of the Public–Private Distinction

(with Mary Lyndon Shanley)

The distinction between public and private has been a central feature of liberal political discourse since its inception. Both classic and contemporary texts of political philosophy have debated understandings of public and private as part of a discussion about the place of politics, economics, and domestic life in human society. Many contemporary feminist theorists have criticized the public/private distinction for categorizing women's activities and household life as "private," and in doing so simultaneously excluding women from such public activities as voting or holding public office, and shielding what happens in the home, including violence against women and children, from public scrutiny.[1] At the same time, feminists have also worked hard to develop the notion that women have various rights to privacy, from the right to retain custody of their children, to the right to choose a life partner, to the right to reproductive freedom.

Privacy is not something natural or pre- or extra-political, but a politically constructed and contested good. Calling some activity or sphere of action private can, depending on the circumstances, either reinforce the allocation of power, goods and benefits along lines of race, gender, class, and sexual orientation, or constitute a claim to political power and autonomy. Disputes over what is private and what is public therefore cannot be resolved simply by greater refinement and precision in the definition of these terms; part of the definitional resolution will involve a political settlement.

In this chapter we examine various disputes over what American law and society should regard as public and what as private, as a way of sharpening our perception and increasing our appreciation of the political judgments inherent in any particular use of these terms. The permeable and mutable nature of the boundary between public and private makes their meanings constantly subject to negotiation and change. When the issue of where to draw the line between public and private arises in legal and public policy

70

debates, the deployment and configuration of political, economic and social power is invariably at stake.

The History of the Public/Private Distinction in Western Political Theory

"Public" and "private" have always been defined, and have taken on political meaning, in relationship to one another. Aristotle, for example, in defining the public (or political) arena as the realm where free and equal citizens engage in striving together toward the common good, distinguished it from the private domain, which, he argued, was characterized by relationships of inequality, dependence, and concern for meeting the necessities of life. Political philosophy, as he understood it, dealt with the public world of citizenship and equality; relations among unequals (e.g. between freemen and slaves, men and women, parents and children) were necessary conditions of politics, but not properly the concern of political analysis.

Early liberal theorists retained a distinction between public and private domains, but shifted their focus of attention in significant ways. In addition to addressing public and political roles and responsibilities, they attempted to define a zone of privacy as a way of delimiting the power of the state. Taking individual freedom as their point of departure, liberals focused on protecting individuals against the arbitrary exercise of power, a threat they perceived as emanating primarily from the state. Thus, both Hobbes and Locke argued that the only grounds for depriving a person of his freedom—the only way one becomes obliged to obey the orders of another—is his own consent (presumably for his own protection). From this perspective, the "public" came to be understood both as the socially-constructed realm of power and domination *and* (following Aristotle) as the site for the exercise of political freedom; whereas the "private" was taken to be an unconstructed realm of "natural" freedom, free from relations of power and domination properly understood.[2] Along with this division went the assertion that politics had to do with relations *between relative equals* in the artificially-constructed public realm; and that, insofar as relations of inequality appeared in the private realm, they were "natural" in origin, and therefore irrelevant to politics.

These definitions led later theorists to explore two sets of issues: (1) what constituted "public" and "private," and (2) where the line between them ought to be drawn. First, the primary concern of theorists with respect to the "private" domain seems to have been to set limits on state power. A claim to privacy was a claim to a realm where others had no right to intervene. At the same time, the assertion of a distinction between public and private reflected the assumption that relationships within the so-called private realm, relationships of voluntary (economic) exchange, of intimacy, and of domesticity, were not about power. Second, the "private" was taken to include everything that was not "political"—i.e. economic relationships, friendships and voluntary associations, and domestic and familial relationships.

By the late nineteenth century, the development of industrial capitalism, and, in particular, of Marx's critiques of relationships under capitalism, had led even many non-Marxists to expand the notion of the "public" to include economic activity. Theorists began to recognize both that relations of power and domination were structured into the so-called free market, and also that concentrations of economic power deeply affected political relationships. Marxists criticized liberals for limiting their analysis of power to the realm of "politics," and insisted that the public, the realm where the analysis of power is appropriate, had to be extended to include economic—and especially market—relationships. While this perspective offered a powerful critique of the dominant liberal view, it still left largely intact the liberal assumption that the remaining private (and therefore "natural") sphere was not an important locus of constructed power relationships and was, therefore, largely irrelevant to "politics."[3]

Hannah Arendt worked with this construction of the boundaries of public and private, but returned to a more Aristotelian emphasis on the public. Arguing that there are, in fact, three realms of activity characterizing the human condition—labor, work, and action—she stressed the importance of "action" (analogous to Aristotle's notion of the public/political) as the expression of human freedom and dignity, the realization of each individual's unique personality. "Labor," by contrast, corresponds to the cyclical biological processes of birth, growth and decay. It is defined primarily by necessity, and takes place largely in the family, the private or household domain. The activity of such labor—though necessary for the perpetuation of life and the species—is repetitive, uncreative, and private, and hardly expressive of the full range of human possibility. "Work" is characterized by self-conscious "fabrication" and construction, and may involve collective activity that realizes important creative aspects of human personality. Nevertheless, it is limited; it remains focused on those tasks necessary to maintain human life, tasks so bounded by necessity that they do not provide opportunities for the expression of individual freedom. For Arendt, then, the distinction between "public" and "private" takes on much more the connotation it had for Aristotle: the "private" domain may be necessary and important for human *existence*, but human *freedom* is fully realized only in the public arena, where (as Mary Dietz put it) "the revelation of individuality amidst collectivity takes place."[4] In this formulation, Arendt provides an important link between earlier liberals and more radical participatory democrats insofar as what she defines as "public," or the realm of "action," is also the realm of democratic politics. At the same time, her claim that the realm of necessity (and significantly of economic inequality) has no place in politics links her to a more conservative tradition.

What remains common to virtually all these formulations (despite their differences as to what is included within the "public" domain) is an understanding of the private as *domestic*, and a fundamental distinction between that realm and everything else. Where economics fits in this schema remains, to some extent, in dispute; but a wide variety of theorists agree that the domestic, intimate, familial, and sexual relationships belong to the private. Further, these thinkers limit analyses of power, and especially of political power, to the public domain.

Two democratic theorists did examine relationships among household members and how these might influence public life, with quite different results. Jean-Jacques Rousseau argued that the domestic education of boys and girls would influence their understanding and performance of their roles as citizens. Although the discussion of the socialization of citizens in *The Social Contract* is apparently gender-neutral, and focuses on institutions and practices that allow for the realization of the General Will, Rousseau's more specific treatment of (moral) education in *Emile* is sharply differentiated by sex. In that text, the education of boys focuses on the development of their autonomy and independence while that of girls emphasizes their *dependence* and the importance of molding their behavior to conform to social expectations. For Rousseau, such differentiation and gender inequality (in the context of an overall insistence on human equality) were justified on the ground that family stability depended on gender-differentiated roles and behavior, and family stability was essential to social stability. Hence difference or hierarchy between family members was, in Rousseau's eyes, not inevitable or natural (although it rested upon inherent differences between the sexes) but it was socially necessary.[5]

John Stuart Mill, by contrast, argued that because the moral training for citizenship began in the home, and because women should be active in political life, the education of boys and girls should be identical (or at least very similar). Mill also fervently believed that relationships of male domination and female subordination in the household would foster habits of willfulness in men that would be antithetical to the respect for reciprocity essential to democratic political life. Mill's belief that sexual equality in the family was a prerequisite for a fully democratic political life was, however, an exception among Western democratic theorists. For most, the household and the polity appeared to be of different orders and were to be evaluated by quite different criteria.[6]

Feminist Challenges to the Public/Private Distinction

Feminist theory offers a rich and multi-faceted challenge to the traditional understanding that public and private domains are conceptually distinct and that activities are easily assigned exclusively to one or the other. Feminists have explored the ways the distinction obscures the exercise of power within the so-called private realm; masks the maleness of the public realm; and ignores the ways the public/private distinction itself is a social construction that reflects the exercise of power and the allocation of resources in *both* realms. The main focus of our discussion here concerns the way the social construction of private and public involves profoundly political struggles that affect not only our understanding of these terms, but the status of those who have different resources and authority both as private beings and as citizens.

The publication of essays like Jean Bethke Elshtain's "Moral Woman and Immoral Man" and Teresa Brennan's and Carole Pateman's "'Mere Auxiliaries to the Commonwealth'" focused attention on the ways the construction of the public/private distinction in Western liberal thought masked the maleness of actors in the public realm.[7] Elshtain pointed out that, since Aristotle, a public realm defined as the domain of power and domination had been counterposed to a private realm ruled by moral principle. She noted that Machiavelli and Weber, as well as Aristotle, associated the private sphere with women who, because of their identification with it and morality, were effectively deemed unfit for political life. This split between morality and politics, women and men, necessarily relegated women to the sidelines, and severely restricted both the content and conduct of politics by removing women's voices and concerns from political debates, and denying the relevance of "morality" to political life.[8]

Brennan and Pateman, for their part, showed that the supposedly gender-neutral citizen of a liberal polity was, in the writings of both Hobbes and Locke, clearly a male head-of-household. That and later work of Pateman made clear that structures of political participation, understandings of the meaning of "consent," and notions of what constituted the autonomy necessary for citizenship were all predicated on unstated assumptions about the availability of individual citizens to participate in political activity. These unstated assumptions included, most significantly, that the daily activities of the nurturance and sustenance of the male "citizen" and his family would be taken care of by someone else, either his wife or other women of his household. But the question of any political role for those women, or of the nature of their relationship to the man, was completely ignored. Familial or household relationships were relegated to the status of "nonpolitical" or private issues. Thus, while the categories of "public" and "private" were central to classical liberal theory, the theory itself was quite unconscious about the gendered nature of its categories. The much-vaunted public sphere of democracy and participation was, effectively, the exclusive domain of men.[9]

Other theorists explored the implications of this split between public and private for a more feminist vision of the social and political order. Michelle Rosaldo, a cultural anthropologist who attributed universal "sexual asymmetry" to the gendered differentiation of public and domestic spheres of activity in virtually every known society, found the roots of that differentiation in women's association with child-birth and childrearing. Everywhere, she argued, the biological fact of women's childbearing is elaborated into a complicated social system in which "men, in their institutionalized relations of kinship, politics, and so on, define the public order," and women "are their opposite."[10] As a result, "characteristic aspects of male and female roles in social, cultural, and economic systems can all be related to a universal, structural opposition between domestic and public domains of activity." Key to overcoming the subordination of women, Rosaldo argued, is the abolition of this dichotomous distinction—an abolition to be achieved not only by women engaging in the public world, but by men "taking on the responsibilities of the home."[11] Public and private would, then, continue to exist as somewhat separate domains characterized by different types of activity, but the boundaries between them would no longer be coincident with gender divisions.[12]

More recent critics—including Rosaldo, herself[13]—have questioned whether the distinction between public and private can ever be separated from its gendered origins, and point, as well, to the dynamics of power and domination at the core of *both* dichotomies. They argue that revealing the dichotomous gender construction of the public and private was very important but the spheres are neither distinct nor discrete; injustices in one affect relationships in the other as well. Catharine MacKinnon has argued, for example, that all male–female relationships, whether intimate or not, exist in the context of social structures that reflect and encourage male sexual domination of women. Even if not all relationships directly manifest such domination, power imbalances infuse multiple dimensions of the social world:

> Men's physiology defines most sports, their health needs largely define insurance coverage, their socially designed biographies define work-place expectations and successful career patterns, their perspectives and concerns define quality in scholarship, their experiences and obsessions define merit, their military service defines citizenship, their presence defines family, their inability to get along with others—their wars and rulership—defines history, their image defines god, and their genitals define sex … For each of men's differences from women, what amounts to an affirmative action plan is in effect, otherwise known as the male-dominant structure and values of American society.[14]

Most specifically, MacKinnon asserts that legal rules and the legal system, while ostensibly gender-neutral, inscribe and perpetuate the power of men over women in both the so-called public *and* the private domains.

More generally, feminist critics have demonstrated, it is impossible to distinguish once and for all what is public and what is private. Both concepts are socially constructed, and each is implicated in the other. What each encompasses changes with time and place. "Privacy" implies a realm of freedom and intimacy, sheltered from the incursions of other individuals or of the state, and guided by love and reciprocity rather than justice or power; this boundary, however, is anything but firm or impermeable. As Susan Moller Okin has argued, "the domestic sphere is itself created by political decisions, and the very notion that the state can choose to intervene in family life makes no sense."[15] The categories public and private are mutually interdependent and cannot be evaluated apart from one another; therefore, feminist analysis must address the ways power is exercised within each realm as well as in the distinction between them.[16]

It is impossible, then, to distinguish clearly and permanently "public" from "private": not only is the meaning of each understood in part by contrast to the other, but each category contains aspects of the other.[17] To offer just one example: the family, the quintessential domain of privacy, exists by virtue of laws that define who and what constitute a family.[18] Legal definitions of "family" are contested not only by those who demand that the state recognize the "privacy" due to their non-traditional families (e.g. protests against midnight searches by state welfare departments in the homes of welfare recipients; or claims for domestic partner benefits or for the right to marry for gay and lesbian couples); but also by those who demand that the state *deny* familial privacy to those who abuse women and children within families.[19]

At this point we might well ask whether the feminist critique of the public–private distinction has so revealed the gender-based and permeable nature of the concepts of public and private that we should throw them out altogether. We think not. These analyses of the indeterminacy of public and private suggest that the meaning and application of these concepts are the locus of severe political struggle. US feminists and radicals of various stripes have repeatedly battled to redraw the boundaries of public and private, and to reveal the political uses to which the public/private distinction has been put. Rather than attempting to develop yet another set of criteria by which these determinations might be made more effectively, we suggest that such an attempt can never finally succeed. An examination of several moments of contention over privacy reveals that what is at stake is not (or is not solely) the correctness of a definition, but, rather, a struggle over the configuration and distribution of power and resources.

Power, Political Struggle, and the Public/Private Distinction

Women's resistance has often expressed itself in struggles over the boundaries of private and public. In the United States, such efforts have included the anti-slavery movement, the anti-lynching campaigns of the late-nineteenth and early-twentieth centuries, recent efforts to stop sexual harassment and domestic violence, welfare mothers' rights movements, and the gay and lesbian rights movement, to name just a few. In each of these cases, a challenge to the accepted legal or social understanding of what was public and what was private also called into question conventional views of gender, race, class, and/or sexual orientation. Sometimes the struggle to define public and private involved asserting a right to privacy for people who had been denied it and the freedom it entails; at other times it meant piercing a curtain of privacy that kept oppressive relations from public view and judgment. Always the struggle over the construction of public and private has gone beyond disputed definitions to address the exercise of power.

Slavery: privacy and the denial of privacy

Black women under slavery led the effort to analyze the construction of the role of the public/private dichotomy in maintaining a system of racial and sexual domination. Thus, Harriet Jacobs' *Incidents in the Life of a Slave Girl* made clear how defining the plantation as the slave-master's private domain made possible his virtually limitless power over black women and men. In claiming slaves as their personal property, slave owners denied slaves any privacy. The fact that the legal system provided no realm of privacy—including marriage and family—for human chattel was one of Jacobs' most strongly-felt indictments of slavery. As Jacobs explained, "If slavery had been abolished I, also, could have married the man of my choice; I could have had a home shielded by the laws; ... but all my prospects had been blighted by slavery."[20]

Jacobs' appeal to northern women abolitionists focused not so much on the denial of civil rights to enslaved blacks, but on the denial of a private realm, which Jacobs seemed to treat as a necessary foundation of citizenship. To be chattel, Jacobs argued, means to have no private life. Not only is the individual at the constant beck and call of the master, but, more fundamentally, enslaved people are denied the privacy necessary for establishing and maintaining family life, setting conditions for their own lives, or expressing any independent will. The argument, here, about public and private is two-fold: (1) the denial of privacy to the enslaved is a violation of human rights; (2) the denial of privacy to the enslaved, as well as masking white male power by treating its abuses as "private," is a deeply political issue, one that allocates power and resources in ways that go far beyond the specific issue at hand. It affects not only the possibility of slave marriage, but any recognition that those enslaved may claim human rights.

Challenges to lynching as challenges to privacy

At the turn of the century, in her analysis of lynching, Ida B. Wells carried this argument forward in exploring the centrality of social understandings of the "private" realm of sexuality and sexual relations to the maintenance of white power in both the public and private arenas. Wells attacked the myth that lynchings were mob reactions to the rape of white women by black men. She documented the fact that the majority of those lynched in the South between 1896 and 1900 were not even accused of rape, but were killed in response to economic competition, self-assertion or "insubordination."[21]

Wells argued that the (false) link between rape and lynching revealed how myths about black sexuality provided an essential underpinning for white domination over blacks in both sexual (i.e. private) and political (i.e. public) domains. The stereotype of black male sexual appetite made consensual sexual relations between white women and black men appear impossible; any such relationship would be considered rape: hence, it would be a matter of public concern and a justification for lynching. Because the black community well knew that the vast majority of lynchings were not responses to rape, but rather to other forms of challenge to white hegemony (e.g. economic competition, "insubordination," etc.), and because occasions for lynching were almost totally unpredictable, lynching served as an instrument of terror that stifled black self-assertion and initiative in all areas of life. Conversely, the legacy of white men's ready access to slave women and the stereotype of black women's promiscuity made it virtually impossible for a black woman to claim that any relations between herself and a white man were *not* consensual. Hence, such relations were always regarded as "private," and rape prosecutions were virtually unknown. The intersection of these stereotypes of race and gender thus affected people in both their intimate and their civic relations. Wells' analysis exposed the ways the distinction between public and private constituted an exercise of power, both by constraining the terms of debate and by undermining the possibilities of resistance.[22]

Taken together, Jacobs' and Wells' analyses illuminate two dimensions of public and private: Jacobs emphasized the importance of privacy, seen as autonomy and the ability to set the terms of one's life course, as a necessary condition of citizenship, while Wells demonstrated how some claims to privacy mask the exercise of power. Both these dimensions are evident in some contemporary social and political movements that manifest how the distinction continues to be contested.

Welfare rights and the claim to privacy

Those who have been recipients of public assistance—both in the US and in many other western countries—have often had to struggle for the recognition of any zone of privacy free from public interference. Even before the days of "friendly visitors" (forerunners of contemporary social workers), those who dispensed public charity often treated poverty as a manifestation of social incompetence that justified intervention by those more favorably situated.[23] Barbara Nelson has demonstrated, for example, that, from its origins in Mothers' Aid, Aid to Families with Dependent Children carried with it elements of intervention and social control that were far more exacting than those of Workmen's Compensation, Social Security, or unemployment insurance.[24] Programs were designed with the sense that poor people either had no need for, or no right to, the kind of privacy generally granted to "citizens" as a matter of course. By the mid-1960s, spurred on by the consciousness-raising of the Civil Rights movement, black women welfare recipients strenuously objected to the unannounced late-night searches for a "man in the house" (presumably designed to protect the state against fraudulent claims for support) perpetrated by welfare offices against their overwhelmingly female (and often black) clientele. In those cases, both class and race seemed to conspire to devalue the privacy of welfare recipients; and the demand to be free from such searches associated a right to privacy with basic citizenship rights.[25]

Although those searches were discontinued, the assumption that the internal relationships of families receiving welfare benefits are "fair play" for public scrutiny remains, and continues to be a focus of resistance on the part of recipients. Thus, Daniel Patrick Moynihan's characterization of black female-headed families as manifesting a "tangle of pathologies" attempted to justify public policy intervention in the family, and became the subject of numerous attacks and counter-claims.[26] In the contemporary period, attempts to use criminal law and/or welfare policy to regulate fertility (via the implantation of progesterone patches to prevent pregnancy) or to control marriage and childbirth (via proposals to penalize women for bearing children and/or to reward them if they marry) indicate that the line between public and private may be drawn very differently when those affected by the proposed policy are poor and/or non-white. The situation of female recipients of AFDC, or now TANF, seems to deny them a zone of privacy in a way reminiscent of Jacobs' complaint about slavery. In the contemporary cases, however, class and/or economic dependency, rather than race or slave status, seems to have become a justification for regulating sexual and reproductive life.

Domestic violence and the call for intervention

While many aspects of the welfare rights movement highlighted ways the denial of privacy to poor families constituted an inappropriate exercise of power, activists in the battered women's movement have argued that the state has traditionally been all-too-ready to declare the home off-limits to public investigation and intervention in the face of accusations of spousal or child abuse. Police are often reluctant to make an arrest when answering a call about a "domestic disturbance": they might try to quiet things down and urge the husband/abusive partner to "cool off" and curb his temper. Prosecuting cases of domestic violence is often a low priority in District Attorneys' offices. Courts are sometimes reluctant to issue orders of protection, on the grounds that doing so might mean splitting up a family. Probation offices are often slow to serve orders of protection.[27]

Activists in the battered women's movement point out, however, that state reluctance to intervene in the family "has often served to reinforce the power of its economically or physically more powerful members." Abuses of power directed against women and children within the family may become difficult if not impossible to discern because of reluctance to scrutinize family relationships too closely. Noting that "between 1.8 and 5.7 million women in the United States are beaten each year in their homes," Susan Okin argues that "the privacy of the home can be a dangerous place, especially for women and children."[28] If law and society label intervention to halt violence and prosecute abusive action as "interference" in family matters, family privacy becomes a cloak for what, in another context, the law would recognize as criminal assault.

We noted above that the state and other public welfare groups have often been more willing to intervene in poor families than in middle-class or wealthy ones. The pattern seems to hold true for cases of spousal and child abuse, as well as in welfare rights cases. Yet, as Linda Gordon has noted in her study of the history of domestic violence, poor and working-class women have often called upon "outside" institutions for protection for themselves or their children, despite the danger that those agencies might be as likely to remove a child from a home characterized by poverty as to prosecute an abusive father or husband.[29] Apparently, no matter the extent of their subordination both in the home and in the political arena, women who claim a right to be free from abuse and intimidation in their homes are recognizing an important connection between citizenship rights and the public/private distinction. The harm done by domestic violence affects its victims not only as private individuals, but as public persons or citizens as well, and failure to prosecute such offenses not only denies justice to that individual, but also intimidates all victims of domestic violence.

Gay and lesbian rights, publicity and privacy

As did women in the welfare rights movement, advocates for gay and lesbian rights have struggled for a right to the privacy of their domestic arrangements. At the same time, like advocates for battered women and children, they highlight the ways existing laws obscure the privileging of heterosexual relations in the same way that familial privacy obscures male power. The gay and lesbian rights legal reform agenda has been multifaceted, including civil rights legislation to prevent housing and job discrimination; legal recognition of same-sex domestic partnerships or marriage; elimination of prejudice against divorced parents who are gay or lesbian in child-custody determinations; elimination of prohibitions against gays and lesbians being foster or adoptive parents; and repeal of the ban on military service for gays and lesbians. Not all activists support all these goals with equal fervor, of course, and a focus on gaining the right to legal same-sex marriage has taken center stage in recent years. But a variety of organizations, including the National Gay and Lesbian Task Force, Lambda Legal Defense Fund, and the National Center for Lesbian Rights have all pushed for equal civil status for lesbians and gay men.

Many of the arguments for lesbian and gay rights invoke the argument that consensual sexual activity between adults is a private matter that should be shielded from state scrutiny. Criminal statutes against same-sex activity, which took the form of anti-sodomy statutes, were eventually found to deny gays and lesbians rights of privacy that the Supreme Court articulated in a number of decisions during the 1960s and 1970s that we discuss below; and the prohibition against same-sex marriage would seem to contradict the Court's ruling in *Loving v. Virginia* 388 US 1 (1967) that the choice of a marriage partner is "one of the 'basic civil rights of man.'"[30] The struggle to obtain legal recognition of a right to privacy in consensual sexual conduct was, therefore, central to the agenda of the gay and lesbian rights movement.

The development of the legal right of privacy began in 1965, and seemed to hold out the promise that same-sex couples would, before too long, be able to invoke that doctrine to shield their relationships (and themselves) from charges of criminal activity. The Court's first articulation of a constitutionally-protected "right to privacy" was found in *Griswold v. Connecticut* 381 U.S. 479 (1965). *Griswold* struck down a Connecticut statute that prohibited both the use of contraceptive devices and the act of counseling others to use such devices. The majority opinion, written by Justice Douglas, argued that marital sexual relations belong to "a zone of privacy created by several fundamental constitutional guarantees." Seven years later, in *Eisenstadt v. Baird* 405 U.S. 438 (1972), the Court held that this right of privacy pertained to individuals as such, not only to married couples: "If the right to privacy means anything, it is the right of the *individual,* married or single, to be free from unwarranted governmental intrusion into matters so fundamentally affecting a person as the decision whether to bear or beget a child." These decisions invoked privacy to protect the freedom of nonprocreative sexual expression for consenting adults.[31]

The Court also displayed concern to protect consensual intimate relationships in *Loving v. Virginia* 388 U.S. 1 (1967), which struck down a Virginia statute prohibiting marriage between white persons and persons of different races. The Court declared that marriage is a basic civil right and "one of the vital personal rights essential to the orderly pursuit of happiness by free men." The choice of a marriage partner was a liberty protected by the Due Process Clause that the state could not abridge. The Court held that anti-miscegenation laws violated the Equal Protection Clause as well as the Due Process Clause. Such laws affected not only the possibility of marital intimacy, but the civil equality of blacks and whites as well; anti-miscegenation laws were inevitably "an endorsement of White Supremacy."

While, in 1986, the Supreme Court denied the relevance of these precedents, holding that the right of privacy did not prohibit states from outlawing acts of sodomy between consenting adults (*Bowers v. Hardwick* 106 S.Ct. 2841 [1986]), the Court reversed itself a decade and a half later in *Lawrence v. Texas* 539 U.S. 558 (2003). The *Lawrence* Court argued that anti-sodomy laws "seek to control a personal relationship that, whether or not entitled to formal recognition in the law, is within the liberty of persons to choose without being punished as criminals. The liberty protected by the Constitution allows homosexual persons the right to choose to enter upon relationships in the confines of their homes and their own private lives and still retain their dignity as free persons." The Court clearly depended on arguments about what should be public and what private in its claim that "liberty gives substantial protection to adult persons in deciding how to conduct their private lives in matters pertaining to sex."

Recent state-level cases about same-sex marriage have articulated not just a right to the privacy of sexual/living arrangements, but a corollary right to *public* recognition of those relationships through the institution of marriage. Thus, speaking for the Court in *Goodridge v. Department of Public Health* (MA SJC-08860), Chief Justice Margaret Marshall clearly incorporated the right to marriage within the guaranteed rights of citizenship:

> barred access to the protections, benefits, and obligations of civil marriage, a person who enters into an intimate, exclusive union with another of the same sex is arbitrarily deprived of membership in one of our community's most rewarding and cherished institutions. That exclusion is incompatible with the constitutional principles of respect for individual autonomy and equality under the law.

Similarly, the Supreme Court of California declared that

> core substantive rights include, most fundamentally, the opportunity of an individual to establish—with the person with whom the individual has chosen to share his or her life—an *officially recognized and protected family* possessing mutual rights and responsibilities and entitled to the same respect and dignity accorded a union traditionally designated as a marriage.

The ability to form such relationships, the Court continued, is a "vitally important attribute of the fundamental interest in liberty" that is guaranteed by the Constitution of California.[32]

Courts in Massachusetts and in California (though not in New Jersey or New York) recognized the importance of Harriet Jacobs' insight, echoed in *Loving v. Virginia* and in *Lawrence*, that the right freely to construct relationships of intimacy is not only an essential human right, but also an important foundation of citizenship. These rulings stand in sharp contrast to military regulations that exclude (open) gays and lesbians from the US military. Struggles in the early 1990s over the ban on military service by gays and lesbians claimed that all people should be able to assume the rights and responsibilities of citizenship, regardless of sexual orientation. These regulations, in constructing gay and lesbian relationships (as distinct from heterosexual relationships) as matters of public, rather than private, concern, simultaneously deny a right to privacy and justify public interventions that reinforce heterosexual privilege.

Hearings on the confirmation of Clarence Thomas and the confusions of public and private

These and other social movements over the course of the last century have highlighted the ways the public/private distinction both masks and reinforces exercises of power in society on the bases of race, gender, class, and sexuality. At times, claims to privacy assert the civic personhood of those denied privacy; at other times, those same claims protect the powerful from challenges to their domination.

Many of these complicated dynamics of power were strikingly revealed in the Senate hearings on the nomination of Clarence Thomas to the Supreme Court. Anita Hill's charges that Thomas had sexually harassed her when she worked for him at the EEOC constituted a claim that his "private" behavior was relevant to the public debate on his suitability for the Supreme Court.

The dynamics of the Thomas hearings were very complex, with Thomas himself being the object of racial stereotyping and hatred, and his supporters invoking damaging stereotypes of black women.[33] By accusing the Committee of engaging in a "high-tech lynching," Thomas raised the specter of racism and the legacy of white supremacy in an effort to shield his behavior from public scrutiny. In casting himself as the victim of a racially-motivated, trumped up charge of sexual misconduct meant to scuttle his rise to power, Thomas saved his nomination but distorted the analogy between his own situation and that of victims of lynching. His use of the analogy obscured the fact that his accuser was not a white woman or her white male "defender," but a black woman; and not a person more powerful than he, but his employee.

By its nature, sexual harassment, "the imposition of unwelcome sexual demands or the creation of sexually offensive environments," is usually not witnessed by others even when it takes place in the workplace. Harassment often involves "anxiety, depression, and loss of status and self-esteem" for the individual, while for women as a group, it serves "to perpetuate views of females as sexual objects, to intimidate them from entering nontraditional occupations, and to impair their educational and employment performance, all of which reinforce patterns of gender inequality."[34] According legal recognition to the concept of sexual harassment meant that behavior that had previously been treated as "private," and dismissed as "'dalliance,' 'flirtation,' 'game,'" or "petty slights suffered by the hypersensitive," was now seen to have public consequences.[35] Like domestic abuse, sexual harassment constitutes an exercise of power that limits a woman's "private" (in this case workplace) participation and, relatedly, her ability to exercise her rights of citizenship.

In the context of the confirmation hearings, Thomas successfully portrayed Hill and the Senate Committee, rather than himself, as guilty of violations of privacy. He denied that the behavior Hill complained of had ever taken place, and contended that all questions about, or allusions to, his sexual behavior constituted inappropriate intrusions into his private life. Thomas was largely successful in his efforts to privatize those issues through arguments that manipulated both race and class identity.[36] Thus, his accusation that the charges against him appeared racially motivated effectively silenced the all-white Senate Committee. No one thought to point out that the analogy was deeply flawed: lynch mobs had used trumped-up charges of rape of white women to kill black men and terrorize the black community; no lynching recorded by Ida B. Wells or uncovered by subsequent research was perpetrated by an accusation from a black woman.[37] Thomas appropriated black racial identity for himself, and made Hill's racial identity invisible, rendering her symbolically white.

A similar strategy confused issues of class identity. Thomas consistently painted himself as a hard-working black man, who had scraped his way up from the poverty of his share-cropping grandfather. These images both called upon and challenged dominant stereotypes of the "lazy black man." At the same time, he contrasted his own climb to the top with that of his "welfare mother sister," who didn't know what to do when the check was delayed. As a number of commentators pointed out, however, Thomas' self-presentation denied the ways his climb to the top—portrayed by him as his personal, "private" triumph over adversity—was facilitated by the policy achievements of the civil rights movement and affirmative action programs.[38] Further, and more significantly, he painted an inaccurate picture of his sister which played heavily on conventional racial stereotypes of "black welfare mothers."[39] Left out of the story was the fact that his sister had only recently joined the welfare rolls, and had been forced to do so when she undertook to care for their aging aunt, a "private" responsibility that had fallen to her rather than to Thomas, apparently, because of gender.[40] Further, the hearings consistently erased Anita Hill's own class background (which was as poor as Thomas') and identified her with her white, middle-class supporters. That identification made it difficult for the Senators (or the television-viewing public) to recognize the exercise of economic power or domination that constitutes an important (although usually hidden) component of sexual harassment.

Conclusions

Both "public" and "private" are contested and highly political terms. Not only is the line of demarcation between public and private socially, juridically, and politically constructed, but determinations of what is private and public are significantly influenced by sex, race, class, and sexual orientation. Many of those who have addressed issues of privacy have (rightly) pointed out how relegating women to the private domain kept them out of the public world of paid labor and political participation. Others, including Harriet Jacobs, have recognized that the ability not to be consigned by *others* to the private sphere, but to claim it for oneself, is an important right of citizenship and a significant measure of political power.

Nevertheless, although this overview suggests the importance both of helping women to assume public roles and responsibilities and of providing protection for individual autonomy, it also makes clear that to think of either "public" or "private" as a fixed category is misguided. There is no typology or set of procedures that will allow us to draw a line between public and private that will be appropriate for all times and circumstances.

The multiple uses of the word "privacy" around matters of human reproduction and family life show how deeply implicated questions of power and resources are in this term. Many women claim the right to use birth control or obtain an abortion as a right to privacy. Such an assertion insists that individual women, not individual men or the state, make these fundamental decisions about their procreative activity. At the same time, supporters of women's decisional autonomy also acknowledge that other aspects of childbearing and childrearing should not be thought of as private or as affecting only women. The state should recognize its obligation to provide children with adequate nutrition, medical care, and education, and individual men should take responsibility for their sexual activity and the rearing of their offspring. Both the demands for reproductive rights and for recognition of the profoundly social dimension of care for children involve contestations over what is private and what is public about family life. If the resolution of those struggles seems to come from greater refinement in our understanding of those terms, it is because that refinement will incorporate political decisions about the configuration of decision-making authority and the allocation of goods and services both within the household and in the larger society.

Both the history of the public/private distinction in Western political philosophy and the variety of policy debates examined here indicate that when the line between public and private becomes a matter for public debate, we should take it as a signal to scrutinize the configurations of power that have a stake in the issue under discussion. What constellation of power is manifest in the existing practices? Whose power is being challenged by the claim of a right to privacy? Whose interest would be served if the demand for public "intervention" were met? Although we cannot definitively draw a definitional line between public and private for all circumstances and all times, we must be alert to the issues of power and influence at stake in any particular attempt to do so.

6

GENDER, RESISTANCE, AND CITIZENSHIP

Women's Struggles with/in the State

(with Mary Lyndon Shanley)

This chapter looks at two distinct historical moments when women's unexpected political activity radically challenged prevailing understandings of what constituted "public" and "private" business and, in the process, made evident the ways state power depended on particular constructions of gender: the early phase of the anti-lynching movement in the United States (1890–1920) and the protests of the Mothers of the Plaza de Mayo in Argentina in the 1970s and 1980s. Although these may seem like disparate movements, both were directed against state-condoned or state-sponsored terror used as an instrument of social and political control. Both movements were initiated by women who had no formal means of access to institutions of political decision-making.[1] In their protests against state terrorism, women not only protested illegitimate state actions or inaction, but also effectively *politicized gender* and used it to challenge both state power and the setting of the agenda of politics for all citizens.

These two movements, we argue, provide striking illustration of the deep interrelationship between what is thought of as public, or political, power and the so-called private world of sexuality and reproductive life. They illuminate the argument made by some feminists that the construction of gender has political consequences—that social understandings of proper roles and behaviors for men and women both affect power relationships within the home and provide differential access to influence and power in the public realm. In challenging the power of the state *as women*, both anti-lynching activists and the Madres were able to use gender to articulate new understandings of citizenship, involving not simply the extension to women of formal political rights (such as the vote) previously enjoyed only by men, but also a deep transformation in how a society understands the domains of "public" and "private," and the relationship of these to concepts of masculinity and femininity.[2]

Indeed, the evidence these movements provide of the profound interdependence of "public" and "private" power, and of notions of gender, is striking precisely because those conjunctions were not the initial focus of either group. Yet neither could achieve its political goals without confronting, and to some degree changing, social constructions of gender. In doing so, they altered understandings of what was legitimately the subject matter of political debate and decision-making, and of who could appropriately take part in such discussions.

I. Anti-Lynching Campaigns, 1890–1920

Lynching—mob murder, often following the torture of the victim—first appeared in the US during the colonial period, and then became common practice in western frontier towns of the United States. Particularly in the second and third decades of the twentieth century, it was practiced against Italians and other "foreigners" in urban labor struggles.[3] But blacks in the post-Reconstruction South were the most frequent targets of lynch mobs. According to a study by the NAACP, 4951 persons were lynched in the US between 1882 and 1929, of whom 3500 (71 percent) were black.[4] A study conducted by the Tuskeegee Institute found that blacks constituted 73 percent of the victims of lynchings committed between 1882 and 1968; and 84 percent of all lynchings took place in the states of Alabama, Arkansas, Florida, Georgia, Kentucky, Louisiana, Mississippi, Missouri, North Carolina, Oklahoma, South Carolina, Tennessee, Texas, Virginia, and West Virginia.[5] Frederick Douglass spoke out against lynching, and was active in establishing the Afro-American League in the late nineteenth century; the National Association for the Advancement of Colored People (NAACP), founded in 1909, made anti-lynching one of its top priorities; and the Council on Interracial Cooperation (CIC) and the American Society of Women for the Prevention of Lynching (ASWPL) conducted a concerted drive for a Federal anti-lynching statute (known as the Dyer Bill) in the 1930s. As lynching subsided during the late 1930s and into the 1940s, legislative efforts to protect voting and other civil rights replaced anti-lynching statutes as priority concerns for groups concerned with black rights in the United States.

Mob-initiated punishment was a violation of the protections of due process and fair trial guaranteed by the US Constitution, and many of those who opposed lynching did so on the grounds of its extra-legal nature. Jane Addams, for example, condemned lynching as an affront to civilized politics:

> certain well-established principles underlie all self-government and ...
> to persistently disregard these principles is to endanger self-government itself. When this disregard constantly occurs any section of a self-governing country has a right to enter its protest against any other section, just as the civilized nations interfere with any one nation whose public acts throw back the whole of civilized progress.[6]

It was black women in the United States around the turn of the century, however, who identified and gave voice to the fact that the evil of lynching lay not only in its violent and extra-legal character, but in the interpretive discourse which framed the understanding of lynching advanced by both its defenders and its opponents. Lynching, they pointed out, was almost universally described as the retaliatory act of an incensed mob seeking vengeance for the rape of a white woman by a black man. Even Jane Addams, for example, in her article *condemning* lynching, perpetuated the view that lynching was a response to rape:

> We would send this message to our fellow citizens of the South who are once more trying to suppress vice by violence: That the bestial in man, that which leads him to pillage and rape, can never be controlled by public cruelty and dramatic punishment, which too often cover fury and revenge. That violence is the most ineffectual method of dealing with crime; the most preposterous attempt to inculcate lessons of self-control.[7]

Black women, led by Ida B. Wells, a Memphis school-teacher, newspaper publisher, and publicist, argued forcefully, however, that lynching was not about rape at all, but about *power*. In her view, lynching was a form of terrorism designed to preserve the social, economic, and political power of southern white males, who were threatened by the small gains some blacks had made during Reconstruction.[8] Wells, Mary Church Terrell, and other black women who organized the early anti-lynching campaign developed an analysis of lynching in the South that highlighted the use of sexuality and gender ideology in reinforcing race- and class-based power. They addressed the issue of the boundaries between so-called "public" and "private" domains, and insisted that issues of sexuality and sexual propriety were not simply private matters, but affected the allocation of power and rights throughout society. They opposed lynching not only because it was "uncivilized," but also because it systematically disempowered black and white women and black men. Lynching was not so much about punishing black men, as about structuring politics and power in such a way as to exclude black men and all women.

Wells' first focus was on the myth of the black rapist. Significantly, her own crusade against lynching was sparked by the March 1892 lynching at "the Curve," of three black men (Thomas Moss, Calvin McDowell, and Henry Stewart) who had recently opened a grocery store in a "thickly populated colored suburb" of Memphis that had previously been served only by a white grocery.[9] One after another, her articles and speeches pointed out that the overwhelming majority of those lynched in the South—like Moss, McDowell, and Stewart—were not even *accused* of rape. Her study of lynchings perpetrated between 1896 and 1900 (based on data compiled by the *Chicago Tribune*) indicated that, in 1896, "less than 39% of the negroes lynched were charged with this crime; in 1897, less than 18%; in 1898, less than 16%; and in 1900, less than 15%."[10]

Mary Church Terrell, who was to become president of the National Association of Colored Women's Clubs, responded to the Memphis lynchings by arguing, in "Lynching from a Negro's Point of View," that rape was not the cause of lynching; rather, "it is simply the pretext" for organized violence against the Negro. Further, rape is not committed by black men against white women out of a "desire to assert racial equality" (another common myth). Nor was it true that black people did not understand the immorality of rape: if blacks sympathized with lynching victims, she asserted, it was because they believed them innocent. What, then, was the cause of lynching? Race hatred and lawlessness: "Hostility toward the negro in the South is bitter and pronounced, and ... lynching is but a manifestation of this spirit of vengeance and intolerance in its ugliest and most brutal form."[11]

Wells, Terrell, and other black women developed a broad analysis of the ways in which the mythology of the black rapist (and of the vulnerability of white women) reinforced prevailing relations of both gender- and race-based power. Most obviously, both the falsity of the charge of rape, and the sexual and racial components of those false accusations, contributed to the ways lynching served to maintain white male power.[12] The fact that lynchings occurred for a wide variety of supposed offenses (including "inflammatory language," "mistaken identity," "making threats"), meant that blacks never knew what would provoke a lynching.[13] Prudent blacks would therefore avoid any actions which could be interpreted as insubordinate or worse. The charge of rape, however false, also made all but the most formal contact between black men and white women dangerous to both. Wells argued, in fact, that false charges of rape directed against black men were designed to cover up the reality of *consensual* relations between black men and white women. Following the lynching at "the Curve," she wrote in an editorial:

> Nobody in this section of the country believes the old threadbare lie that Negro men rape white women. If Southern white men are not careful they will overreach themselves, and public sentiment will have a reaction. A conclusion will then be reached which will be very damaging to the moral reputation of their women.[14]

Wells' observation hit such a raw nerve that it led to the destruction of the offices of her newspaper, *Free Speech*, and a warning, which she heeded, not to return to Memphis for fear of her life.

The accusation of rape against black men also deflected attention from white male rape of black women. As Wells wrote:

> White men who had created a race of mulattoes by raping and consorting with Negro women were still doing so wherever they could,

these same white men lynched, burned, and tortured Negro men for doing the same thing with white women; even when the white women were willing victims.[15]

Such interracial rape was sometimes excused by the myth of the "loose" black woman, the female counterpart to the myth of the black rapist. Fannie Barrier Williams, a black woman activist who spoke at the World Columbian Exposition in Chicago in 1893, addressed claims about black women's supposed immorality. As Paula Giddings reports:

> [T]he onus of sexual immorality did not rest on black women but on the white men who continued to harass them. While many women in the audience were fantasizing about black rapists, she implied, black women were actually suffering at the hands of White ones. If White women were so concerned about morality, then they ought to take measures to help protect black women.[16]

In short, lynching, and the myth of the black rapist associated with it, reinforced existing gender hierarchies, keeping white women and black women, as well as black men, "in their place." As Bettina Aptheker has argued:

> In defending the racial integrity of black manhood, Wells simultaneously affirmed the virtue of black womanhood and the independence of white womanhood. For the dialectics of the lynch mentality required the dehumanization of black men (as rapists), black women (as prostitutes), and white women (as property whose honor was to be avenged by the men who possessed her). Just as rape was used to justify the lynching of black men, so the mythology of the black woman's sexual promiscuity and aggression were the main ideological vehicles used to "explain" the appetite of white men for black women.[17]

In these ways, sexual and racial tensions were put at the service of maintaining both gender and racial hierarchies, reinforcing the political and economic dominance of white men over blacks in the South, making a mockery of any notions of equal citizenship supposedly guaranteed by the so-called Civil Rights Amendments of the 1870s. Further, as we will see, constructions of race and gender became both inseparable from, and constitutive of, the boundaries of public and private, delimiting what was legitimately an issue available for public/political debate.

The claim that lynching was designed to preserve and protect white dominance in the economic, as well as social and political, realm finds further support in the ways international pressure eventually helped bring an end to lynching. As the Mothers of the Plaza de Mayo would do some one hundred years later, Wells took her case to the international community, conducting speaking tours in England, and writing for the British, as well as US, press.[18] This appeal to the conscience of "outsiders," both nationally and internationally, through media and speaking campaigns, represented an important aspect of the effort to develop new methods of political power and influence. In the end, many observers credited that campaign with having a significant impact on lynch practices in the South: by the 1920s and 1930s—as Wells and others had hoped—white southerners themselves began to oppose lynching on the grounds that it was giving the South a "bad name," and might have negative consequences for the international cotton trade. Robert Ingalls has argued that "the critical factor in explaining both the persistence of lynching and its eventual disappearance was the attitude of the local elite." In the pre-1920 period in Tampa, Florida, for example, he found that local elites participated in and/or condoned lynchings, as a way of preserving "white supremacy and the cigar industry." Lynching stopped in the 1930s "when it threatened to undermine that order."[19]

The power of black women's analysis of lynching derived from their understanding of the relationship between public power and their society's constructions of both racial and sexual inequality. Their analyses of lynching highlighted the fact that what was truly at stake were the *boundaries* of "politics," the borderlines between "public" and "private," and the ways constructions of gender were used to delineate—and to reinforce—those boundaries.

Wells' analysis of the gender and race dynamics of lynching and "rape" insisted that that which had been made a matter of *public/political* attention and defined as rape—i.e. white women's consensual relationships with black men—must be allowed to remain *private*. Conversely, that which had been *privatized* and kept off the political agenda—i.e. white men's rape of black women—must be *publicized* and opposed. It was precisely the denial that lynchings and white–black sexual relations in the South had a public or *political* dimension that Wells' campaign was designed to challenge. Although lynchings were, in effect, public events, southern law enforcement officers repeatedly claimed that they could not identify the perpetrators. Threatened with lynching herself if she returned to Memphis, Wells turned to the media to make others "witness" to the events in the South, to engage those others in the struggle, to politicize the outrages and, eventually, to force lynchings onto the agenda of politics for broader discussion and action.

Black women's awareness of the linkages between myths about sexual behavior and social and political control also made them strong advocates of guarantees for black voting rights and women's suffrage. The post-Reconstruction South had attempted, using Jim Crow laws, to deny rights granted by the 14th Amendment and the Civil Rights Acts of 1866–68. In effect, southern white males attempted to repeal federal protections for citizenship rights and to insure that relations between whites and blacks remained outside of federal control. Wells saw clearly the connections between political disenfranchisement, lynching, and the racial and economic subordination of black men:

> The right of the Afro-American to vote and hold office remains in the Federal Constitution, but is destroyed in the constitution of the Southern states. Having destroyed the citizenship of the man, they are now trying to destroy the manhood of the citizen.[20]

Their analysis of the interlocking and mutually-reinforcing politics of racial and sexual subordination also led black women to call for the extension of suffrage to women. The sexual and racial economies that allowed white men access to both white and black women, but which demanded the lives of black men who crossed racial lines in their emotional or sexual lives, and ostracized white women who did the same, both reflected and sustained a white male monopoly of political power. Depriving black men of the vote robbed them of the means to defend either themselves or the women in their families. Depriving black women of the vote removed a tool for "race advancement" and also made such women vulnerable to male authority (both white and black). The disenfranchisement of white women perpetuated their dependence on their white male so-called protectors in both political and economic matters.

Ultimately, then, Wells, Terrell, and other women who championed the anti-lynching cause not only developed new ways to engage in public life (which they had, perforce, to do since, as women, they had no formal access to decision-making institutions), but new criteria for what constituted politics, insisting that it required publicizing (and attending to) both the rape of black women and the lynching of black men and women. In the process, they challenged both prevailing gender relations and understandings of the rights and privileges of citizenship: it was impossible to insert these new issues into the public arena without "overstepping" the bounds of what "women" were supposed to do and talk about. Their analyses demonstrated, further, that the public power of white males was integrally linked to constructions of sexuality that were both race- and gender-specific.

II. The Madres de Plaza de Mayo

Although the context for the activities of the Madres de Plaza de Mayo in Argentina was very different from that of the black women's anti-lynching movement, the demonstrations of the Madres de Plaza de Mayo against the "disappearances" of their children under the military juntas of 1977–1982 were similar to the anti-lynching campaigns in a number of respects. Like the earlier movement, the Madres' actions were simultaneously a protest against human rights abuses, a rejection (albeit ambiguous) of prevailing cultural definitions of appropriate gender roles, and a challenge to the existing boundaries between "public" and "private." While their condemnation of human rights abuses was explicit, the Madres' challenge to prevailing gender norms was by-and-large tacit, communicated by their actions and the symbols they employed in their demonstrations. Yet the Madres' demands for the return of their children confronted traditional understandings of women's proper conduct and concerns, and of the domains in which they were expected to act. The Madres also contributed to an ongoing redefinition of what constituted "fitting" topics for political discourse and debates. Although they claimed to be non-partisan, they engaged in a profoundly "political" discourse about the most fundamental structures and values of both state and family in late-twentieth-century Argentina.

In March, 1976, a military coup deposed President María Estela (Isabel) Perón, who had been elected successor to her husband, General Juan Perón as President of Argentina. The three-man Junta vowed to end what they labeled as economic and political chaos.

During the period of restructuring that followed, known as "el Proceso," the government pursued stringent economic measures aimed at decreasing the rate of inflation, and launched a massive campaign against guerrillas and those it considered to be politically dangerous. The campaign consisted both of military engagements with guerrillas and the abduction of suspected subversives. Those abducted were held, and often tortured, in a nationwide system of 340 clandestine detention centers. While some dissidents were formally arrested and held, even if neither charged with a crime nor brought to trial, others simply disappeared. An official report published after the restoration of democracy documented the disappearance of 8,960 people, including some 130 infants, who were never accounted for.[21]

As a few of the *detenidos* were released and recounted their experiences of jail and torture, those actively looking for information about friends or family members realized that government agents were complicit in the detentions, torture, and withholding of information. Yet to challenge the clandestine abductions was to risk disappearance for oneself or another family member. Thus many people who knew of the disappearances were effectively silenced, much as lynchings had silenced and terrified far more blacks in the United States than they had victimized directly.

On 30 April 1977, fourteen women appeared in the Plaza de Mayo in Buenos Aires and paraded silently around the monument to the independence movement of 1810. They repeated their walk around the monument every Thursday at 3:30 p.m.[22] The government quickly labeled them "las locas (crazy women) de Plaza de Mayo." Nonetheless, the ranks of the Madres gradually swelled. The Madres abjured partisanship, claiming to "have no politics," by which they seemed to mean that they never asked one another their party affiliations, and made no explicit pronouncements about economic policy, social issues, or political institutions. The Madres demanded nothing more (and nothing less) than that the government release their children or tell them where they were. Once the third military junta fell in the wake of the Falklands/Malvinas War in 1982, and some democratic processes were restored, the Madres added to their demands that those responsible for the disappearances be tried by a civilian court.

Initially, the Madres' emphasis on their maternal role protected them from governmental retaliation. For the first two years, the Junta refrained from moving against the Madres (and the Grandmothers of the Plaza de Mayo, who formed a similar protest group) with overt brutality, undoubtedly because of the outrage clubbing or arresting such women in the Plaza would have provoked. In December, 1978, however, a thousand women were expelled from the Plaza by the police; the Madres suffered continual harassment throughout 1979, and had to abandon their demonstrations during much of 1980.[23] Some Madres themselves disappeared, among them Azucena Villaflor, one of the first members of the Madres, who was abducted as she was leaving a meeting of Madres held in a church.

The actions of the Madres de Plaza de Mayo were simultaneously radical and couched in traditional language. Evocations of maternal responsibility and mothers' anguish had strong resonances in a Catholic country where the veneration of the Virgin Mary augmented the respect paid to mothers.[24] The white kerchiefs the mothers wore were an example of the complicated imagery of their protest. Kerchiefs are traditionally worn by Catholic women in church, a sign of women's respect, obedience, and acceptance of authority. These white kerchiefs were also visual reminders of diapers, a symbol of their missing children. The Mothers embroidered these kerchiefs with the names and the dates of the disappearances of their children, using a traditional womanly skill on what could be read simultaneously as a piece both of women's and of children's clothing to voice an uncompromising political challenge. They carried pictures of their children, frequently family snapshots, at their breast, transforming private moments and memories into public, political statements.[25]

The names and pictures of disappeared children also served as a constant reminder of the torture to which the young people had probably been subjected. Imprisonment in clandestine detention centers was often accompanied by excruciating torture, much of it of a sexual nature.[26] The Madres insisted that sexual behavior that occurred in the context of torture was not unspeakable or "private" abuse, but political, an exercise of *public* power for which there must be *public* accountability. Implicitly, the Madres claimed knowledge of all that men and the state had traditionally characterized as unfit for women's eyes, ears and tongues, just as nineteenth-century black American women refused to accept the state's denial of the rape of black women by white men and of love affairs between white women and black men. The content of what they spoke about, as well as their "breaking silence" by public demonstrations, challenged the boundaries of public and private as well as prevailing structures of gender. The Madres, like the women of the anti-lynching movement, insisted that their anguish was not simply personal and private, but a matter of *public* business. Their anguish gave the lie to the Junta's claim that it was "protecting" women from the violence of social disintegration.

As had the women of the anti-lynching movement, the Madres found important sources of support—including financial, moral, and political resources—in the broader international context. While the Argentine Junta attempted to silence the women—and any reports of their activities—within Argentina, women's organizations in the US, the Netherlands, and elsewhere *publicized* the issues within their own countries, and, over time, forced their governments to raise issues of human rights with the Junta.[27]

Many feminists sympathetic to the Madres' cause worried that the Madres unintentionally subverted both the goal of women's emancipation and the development of a broad political agenda for Argentina. By waging their protest so explicitly and exclusively as mothers, by demanding simply that the regime produce their children alive or account for their whereabouts, these critics argued, the Madres were doing nothing to challenge—indeed were reinforcing—women's exclusive responsibility for children and their exclusion from activities outside the home.[28] Some Argentine feminists told Jean Elshtain in 1982, for example, that the Madres, by grounding their protest so explicitly in their duties as mothers, "wound up deepening and legitimating the mourning mother as the ideal-typical female identity."[29] Marysa Navarro concluded that the Madres

> were compelled to act not on moral or political grounds or out of concern for gross human rights violations, but because they were mothers. Their refusal to acquiesce in the loss of their children was ... a coherent expression of their socialization, of their acceptance of the dominant sexual division of labor and of their own subordination within it.[30]

María del Carmen Feijóo saw the Madres' confrontational tactics as effective against the military dictatorship but worried that "a defense of human rights based on women's reproductive roles reinforces the conventional sexual division of labor," and limits the issues and the grounds on which women can engage in political activity. "'We are life' can become a trap for women as the forces of change are stymied by the weakness of women's discourse and as the most traditional aspects of that discourse are appropriated by a political class dominated by men." She concluded that unless the political mobilization of women is more than "a matter of 'human rights' or of 'helping others,'" and unless men take up those issues of education, health, and welfare which have been perceived as "'typically feminine,'" women will remain "vicarious vehicles for the needs of others," not political actors in their own right.[31]

Along with others, however, we believe that the fact that the Madres effected their protest using traditional language about motherhood existed in tension with, but did not negate, the transformative potential of their protest. The Madres' use of maternalist language in their search for their children had what Laura Rossi, Jennifer Schirmer, and Jo Fisher have each characterized as the unintended and paradoxical consequence of politicizing the family and breaking down artificial barriers between the "public" and "private" spheres of women's activities. The Madres turned the notion of maternal responsibility on its head, insisting that their duty to care for their children took them out of their homes and into the streets as political protestors.[32] All mothers, they insisted, had reason and the right to address issues of due process, habeas corpus, and military and political accountability. As women had to move out of the "private" sphere and into the "public/political" sphere "as mothers, in order to survive," their "private" anguish, expressed collectively, led them to "challenge the state and cross its artificial boundary from private mourning to public politics."[33]

In the post-Junta, period the Madres continued to challenge the regime. They rejected Alfonsín's "compromise" that only the generals be tried and punished, and some continue to insist that everyone engaged in the torture of their children be tried in civilian courts. The Madres have refused to engage in partisan politics, and have disparaged those who do, on the grounds that such engagement, in the absence of juridical judgment of those responsible for the disappearances, constitutes a betrayal of the disappeared. A number of observers have criticized this position. Mark Osiel has argued that, by taking such an "uncompromising" position, the Mothers demonstrate their unwillingness to engage in "politics," properly understood (i.e., compromise), and contribute to a potential destabilization of the regime. In his view, they ought to let go of the memory of the disappeared, and get on with their lives and with "normal politics." María del Carmen Feijóo argues that the Madres must transform themselves from a movement of opposition to a more traditional "political" grouping. The task confronting the Madres, she says, is "how to go from the rules of the game of opposition to the rules of the game of constructing civilian peace?"[34]

While the accusation that the Madres are "stuck" in some "pre-political," oppositional mode that is inappropriate to the new democratic order is understandable, there is also truth to the Madres' insistence that unless individuals are held accountable for human rights violations, not only through *private* documentation but through a collective, public (juridical) proceeding, one of the most essential foundations of democracy is weakened. The Madres are saying, in effect, "we have seen the consequences of amnesia/silence vis-à-vis the disappeared in the past. We fought against the privatizing of grief with the juntas; why should we accept it from a democracy?" They force us to ask, who bears the consequences of the limiting of the political agenda? Is democratic "stability" to be purchased at the same price as authoritarian "stability"—through the silencing of women? That is, the Madres seem to us to be acting not out of naiveté, but out of a conscious effort to create a new understanding of what constitutes the agenda of politics and the dimensions of appropriate political behavior.[35]

Preliminary Conclusions

We are struck by some significant similarities between these two case studies, particularly in what they seem to suggest about women's activism in the absence of formal routes of access to politics and about the relationship between gender roles, the boundaries of "public" and "private," definitions of "the political," and state power.

Redefining the Scope of Politics

Feminist scholars writing about women's activism in a variety of contexts have suggested that "collective action … grew out of the quotidian."[36] The actions of women in the anti-lynching movement and in the Madres de Plaza de Mayo both conform to, and challenge, this model. The form of activism each group adopted was necessarily "non-political" (as politics was conventionally defined in each context), because of their exclusion from formal political institutions. And, as we have seen, it grew out of their day-to-day efforts to deal with the realities of terrorism and oppression in their lives and in the lives of their loved ones and friends. The terrorism they confronted, however, was hardly "quotidian" in the usual sense of the term; and the modes of participation they created effectively *challenged* political authorities, forced new issues onto the political agenda, and attempted to create new political space for all citizens.

Our study seems to provide additional evidence for Tilly and Gurin's efforts to frame this phenomenon as one of "fluid boundaries between proto-politics and politics."[37] Feminist historians of US politics in the late nineteenth and early twentieth centuries have noted that, since women lacked the vote during this period, their lives were characterized by "voluntarism and "domesticity." Nevertheless, these did not exclude women from political life. To the contrary, voluntary organizations—usually thought of as outside the arena of "politics"—became the bases for women's political activism. Some have argued, in fact, that these voluntary organizations or "interest groups," originally created by women in response to their political marginality, effectively changed the face of mainstream politics in the United States.[38]

In the cases we have considered here, neither the black women active in the anti-lynching movement nor the Madres de Plaza de Mayo defined themselves as explicitly *political*. Nevertheless, their activities clearly had a *public* dimension, designed to challenge existing structures of power. When the Madres called themselves "non-political," they seemed to mean "non-partisan." It was the regularity and publicity of the Mothers' marches around the central plaza—rather than any formal political organization—that was their most powerful resource. Although both Ida B. Wells and Mary Church Terrell made occasional appeals *to* political parties, on the issue of women's suffrage as well as of lynching, neither put much faith in parties. Over time, they came increasingly to rely on the pressure that could be brought to bear on governors, sheriffs, or other political officials through direct action and/or lobbying. In each case, although the form of activism seemed—to them—to derive from the "dailiness" of their particular struggles, other groups eventually joined them in those practices and even adopted those practices as their own.[39]

In redefining the relationship between politics and non-partisanship, the activities of the anti-lynching women and the Madres also challenged traditional understandings of what is "public" and what is "private." In the context of a society that was deeply structured by gender (and, at least in the US case, by race), concerns that were held to be private—located outside of politics in the realm of sexuality, family, and intimate personal relations—were shown to be both deeply political and essential constituents of the agenda of politics. What was at stake, then, was not simply an assertion of some "woman's interest," but a redrawing of the boundaries of public and private, of what was considered appropriate subject matter for public political discourse. In the case of the anti-lynching movement, black women's analysis asserted that sexuality and intimate relations were not simply "women's concerns," and not issues that could or should properly be relegated to the private, or domestic, arena. Rather, they were *fundamental* to the structuring of public life and of social, economic, and political power. In the case of the Madres, while the Juntas were still in power, the Madres rejected the regime's characterization of their grief as "private," and insisted that they would not forget their lost children. Their activities forced the question of the disappearances onto the public, political agenda and, at the same time, opened up possibilities of political opposition for others. Their challenge to the regime on the question of the boundaries of public and private broadened the terrain of politics for everyone. Their continued opposition during the post-Junta period suggests their commitment not only to a public judgment of those responsible for the torture and disappearances, but also to creating a more broadly participatory citizen body that challenges traditional interpretations of political behavior.[40]

Exploring the Relationship Between Gender and State Power

Because, in most societies and certainly in the two under study, gender roles are deeply enmeshed with defining the borders of public and private, women's engagement in issues in the public or political domain necessarily challenges both definitions of appropriate gender roles and definitions of state power.

The cases we have explored provide evidence for these claims along a number of different dimensions.

In both the US and in Argentina, regimes assumed the silence of women. In neither case were women expected to speak publicly, least of all about such "inappropriate" topics as sexual assault, rape, or sexual torture. When women did become active and speak, therefore, their activities made evident the dependence of state power and authority on gender expectations and, in particular, on women's silence.

In each instance, women asserted their right to both political and sexual knowledge—kinds of knowledge of which they were presumed to be ignorant. In the process, their activities pointed out that politics was significantly *about* sexuality. The connections are, perhaps, easiest to see in the case of Wells' analysis of lynching and "rape." While she began with an effort to debunk the myth of the black rapist, she soon came to insist on the links between the myth of the black male rapist and the myth of black female promiscuity *as part of* her analysis of lynching. In calling on the state to intervene to protect the civil rights of black men, she was, at the same time, speaking new truths about black women and white women, truths which posed fundamental challenges to the dominant ideology of white male supremacy. Significantly, Wells' struggle was not just with the *white* power structure: her autobiography provides numerous examples of opposition from men in the black community who questioned the "appropriateness" of a black woman's engaging in public debate and activism around such issues.[41]

The political opposition they mounted to state-sponsored or state-condoned terrorism led both groups of women to open up issues of gender politics. Talking about a supposedly gender-neutral human rights issue *required* them to talk about sexual violence, sexual repression, and torture. Breaking silence also exposed the myth that women, although "outsiders" to politics, were protected by those men who were full members of the polity. According to dominant constructions of gender in both societies, women's exclusion from full citizenship was "justified" on the grounds that women could rely on the state—or on their husbands or fathers—to defend and protect their "interests."[42] But the activities of both the anti-lynching women and of the Madres proclaimed that they had *not* been protected, that "their men" were not able to protect them, that the state was complicit in the terror, and, further, that their own silence was protecting the perpetrators of violence.

In the case of the anti-lynching movement, Wells pointed out the state's toleration of racist institutions and practices that allowed lynching to take place and lynch mobs to go unpunished. These practices rendered black women doubly vulnerable: both to the loss of their men and to rape by whites. What began, for Wells and Terrell, as an effort to enlist the state to protect black men became an exposition of the race *and* gender dimensions of political power. In the case of the Madres, what began as a direct appeal to the executive (General Videla) to find their disappeared children became an exposition of the complicity of the state in the disappearances and torture and, ultimately, of the oppressive nature of traditional gender structures in families and organizations as well. Breaking silence shattered the gender assumptions which had excluded women from politics and rendered them and others vulnerable to state violence. At the same time, it made evident the reliance of state power on those very gendered assumptions, and the silences they presumed and enforced.

This dynamic, in which a challenge to state power exposes the gender structure undergirding that power, can be found in other instances of women's political mobilization as well. In South Africa, for example, black women's opposition to the extension of the Pass Laws to women in the 1950s exposed the extent to which the structures of apartheid depended on maintaining the *ideology* of traditional families while undermining *actual* black families both in cities and in the "homelands." Women's protests against passes revealed both apartheid's reliance on "traditional" families and gender roles and its denial of any meaningful support to black families. In short, the apartheid system was structured by gender, as well as by race.[43] In the contemporary United States, the battered women's movement challenged the construction of the home as a "private" space that must be shielded from state scrutiny and intervention. The power of the state in this case is exercised in its *refusal* to intervene to stop battering, on the ground that what goes on in the home is "private." Activists in the battered women's movement demonstrate how the widespread cultural acceptance of the privatization of the home masks the workings of both male dominance and state power.[44]

These cases suggest that definitions of politics and constructions of state power are predicated upon particular understandings of gender. Both the anti-lynching campaign and the struggles of the Madres confronted the assumption that women and their concerns (including children) are properly part of the "private" realm, and that, if they are in need of protection, they will receive it from men, who are properly part of the "public" realm. Yet both cases provide examples of women coming to the realization that gender is not just a private matter, and that cultural understandings of gender are a critical component of the construction and exercise of state power. In their unconventional challenges to definitions of both appropriate gender roles and politics, these women revealed links among politics, gender and citizenship that scholars and activists alike must continue to explore.

7

RETHINKING ANARCHISM/
RETHINKING POWER

A Contemporary Feminist Perspective

The collapse of socialism in the Soviet Union and Eastern Europe, combined with the growing popularity of post-modernist criticism in the academy, has left both activists and theorists largely bereft of models for social and political transformation. The old formulas no longer compel. Neither class, nor race, nor gender seems, on its own, sufficient to offer a fool-proof basis for transforming pervasive relationships of oppression and inequality. At the same time, however, the post-modernist suspicion of "totalizing" discourses has not provided an alternative way of thinking about the categories of political struggle that enables us to deal simultaneously with the complexities of identity while developing a strategy for action.[1]

A focus on eradicating domination links many formulations of feminism with anarchist perspectives. Classic communalist anarchism (in the collectivist tradition of Proudhon, Bakunin, Kropotkin, Malatesta, Goldman and, more recently, Murray Bookchin) offered a critique of contemporary society that focused on relations of domination and subordination, a vision of an ideal (egalitarian, non-hierarchical) society, and a strategy for achieving it, based on direct action and what Colin Ward has termed "spontaneous organization."[2]

To an extent, one could argue that anarchism participated in the same Enlightenment-inspired search for "primary causes" and "universalizing theories" that characterized the socialism, radical feminism, and other theories so profoundly criticized by post-modernist theorists. Communalist anarchists, after all, tended to focus on hierarchy, as such, as *the* manifestation of oppression, and to direct their strategic attention to the state. Yet, at the same time, anarchist theories and practices challenge the claim that there exists one "primal cause" or most basic form of domination and subordination. A focus on hierarchy can lead to exploration of the *multiplicity* of relations of domination and subordination, and of the connections among them.

Still, to the extent that much anarchist theorizing envisioned a mutualist society *without* relations of power and domination, its discourse grates against contemporary sensibilities.[3] In an intellectual and political climate in which we are constantly made aware of the pervasiveness of power and of domination, it

101

may be difficult to take seriously those who call for an end to all such relationships. This chapter offers a brief overview of communalist anarchism, and then explores its analyses of power and domination, and of strategies for change, through the lens of feminist criticism and activism. It then turns to what an anarchism revised in the light of these critiques might have to offer to contemporary political analysis and strategy.

Communalist Anarchism: A Brief Overview

The main tenets of the communalist anarchist tradition can be summarized fairly simply. First, communalist anarchists are committed to freedom and community: they insist that freedom is a social product, and that people become free to develop themselves fully only when they are members of an appropriately organized, supportive, community. Personal freedom and social life are not mutually antagonistic, but interdependent and mutually supportive.

Second, an anarchist society would be one without hierarchical relationships, and without institutionalized patterns of authority. Anarchists claim that people can organize and associate themselves on the basis of need, that individuals or small groups can take the necessary initiative, and that centralized political coordination is both harmful and unnecessary. Anarchists criticize both the so-called neutrality of the state, and the actual practice of politics: neither is free of relations of domination. That is not to say that there never can be or will be leaders, or those who take initiative. It is to say, however, that the right or authority to direct or command a situation should not inhere in roles or offices to which some people have privileged access, or from which others are systematically excluded.[4]

Third, the anarchist vision is of a society characterized by diversity: one that not only tolerates, but positively supports, differences among groups of people, and also among people within such groups. It is a society in which, as Colin Ward has described it, harmony is achieved through complexity.[5] And, along with a commitment to non-dominating relationships among people is a commitment to non-dominating relationships with the environment.[6]

In addition, the anarchist vision is of an egalitarian society. Not only should there be no one who (by virtue of sex, race, class, etc.) has the authority to order others around, but neither social nor economic inequality is necessary to sustain social organization. In place of economic inequality, anarchists propose mutualism and reciprocity. People can organize themselves on the basis of mutual interdependence, and need neither centralized work authority, nor inegalitarian work incentives and salaries, to keep social and economic life on an even keel.

Finally, anarchism implies a theory of social change, a revolutionary strategy, which can best be termed the theory and practice of direct action. That strategy means, first, that the process that creates the new society must be consistent with the aims and relationships in the society which is the goal.

Thus, there can be no leadership or hierarchy in the process of social change. And, second, the way to create a new society is to *create* a new reality. The new society is to be built up from and, in fact, the revolutionary process *consists of*, social organizations which change existing reality (specifically relations of domination and subordination). It is only *by participating* in communal, mutualist, institutions that people learn how to participate in them, i.e. how to live in a communalist, anarchist society. And it is only by acting in ways consistent with mutualism and reciprocity that those institutions and practices can be created.[7]

Power and Domination

Classical anarchist theorists argued that the exercise of power (particularly the unrestrained power that accompanies holding specific positions in political, economic, religious, or social life) brutalizes both the wielder of power and the one over whom it is exercised. With respect to the first, one who holds power tends to develop an ever-increasing desire to maintain it. The powerful come, ultimately, either to think of themselves as indispensable or to act as if they did. Bakunin argued, for example, that "nothing is as dangerous for personal morality as the habit of commanding ... Two feelings inherent in the exercise of power never fail to produce ... demoralization: contempt for the masses, and, for the one in power, an exaggerated sense of his own worth."[8] Kropotkin made the point equally strongly: "any group of people entrusted with deciding a certain set of activities ... of an organizational quality always strives to broaden the range of these activities and its own power in these activities."[9] Formal hierarchical authority structures may well create the conditions they are supposedly designed to combat: rather than preventing disorder, anarchists have argued, governments are among its primary causes. Hierarchies make some people dependent on others, blame the dependent for their dependency, and then use that dependency as a justification for the further exercise of authority.[10]

Conversely, to be always in a position of being acted upon, and never to be allowed to act, is to be doomed to a state of dependence and resignation. Those who are constantly ordered about and not allowed to think for themselves, anarchists insist, soon come to doubt their own ability to think or act for themselves. Bakunin argued that political authority debases the individual by not allowing one to make one's own free choices (thus negating freedom). And Kropotkin faulted political authority for preventing that spontaneous cooperation among people which he saw as the foundation of moral action.[11] Thus, government becomes its own justification: the more we are governed, the less we feel we can do without it. Mutual aid is replaced by a one-way dependence on external authority.

Many anarchist theorists and activists have devoted attention to the way participation in relationships of domination and subordination undermines the sense of self, of self-confidence, and of possibility, on the part of those in subordinate positions. In 1903, for example, the Spanish anarchist, José Prat argued that "Women's 'backwardness' is a consequence of the way she has been, and still is, treated. 'Nature' has nothing to do with this ... If woman is backward, it is because in all times man has kept her inferior."[12] While the subordination of women has social roots, it also has psychological effects. Emma Goldman went so far as to argue that "true emancipation [for women] begins neither at the polls nor in courts. It begins in woman's soul."[13] In short, relationships of domination and subordination have complex and multiform consequences for those who participate in them.

Classical anarchists recognized that there are different kinds of power and that it is important to distinguish the sort of *institutionalized* power I have been discussing from other sorts of authority. Even these anarchists, who rejected the argument that formal authority is necessary for social order,[14] acknowledged that, in many situations, someone will know more than others about a particular task and how to do it, so others will defer to him or her on that basis. Or, as Bakunin and Kropotkin argued, some may have greater knowledge or understanding of natural or scientific laws, and be able to exercise what they term "natural authority" on the basis of such knowledge; similarly, some people may have overwhelming personalities that seem to "compel" obedience. But anarchists distinguish sharply between these sorts of authority—which people may *decide freely* whether to follow or not—and formal, institutionalized authority, which there are sanctions for disobeying.[15]

Classical anarchist theory, then, seems to imply a discernible distinction between *formally recognized* power or authority, on the one hand, and a kind of "free followership," based on acknowledgment of superior knowledge or understanding, on the other. The former is considered incompatible with freedom (or the vision of an ideal anarchist society); the latter is not only not incompatible, but possibly even necessary for its smooth functioning.

A number of contemporary anarcha-feminists have argued that one of the most significant (for feminists) aspects of anarchism is precisely its critique of power relationships. Thus, in the words of Carol Ehrlich:

> Social anarchists and radical feminists share the belief that power relationships (that is relationships in which one has the ability to compel another's obedience or control another's actions) are inherently coercive, competitive, and inegalitarian, and that institutionalized forms of inequality are rooted in power relationships ... Anarchist feminism works to end all forms of inequality, beginning (but not ending) with patriarchy.[16]

It is *power* that is "key to class and sex inequality alike, and to all the other forms of inequality as well."[17] The goal for (anarchist) feminists is the elimination of those organizational forms that institutionalize unequal access to resources; i.e., that support and manifest relationships of power and domination.

Marsha Hewitt argues, similarly, that "the core of both anarchist and feminist theory is an ongoing preoccupation with power ... feminism and anarchism complement each other because they are both concerned with, and struggle against, domination in its every form," and attend to the impact of power on both the political and the internal-personal levels.[18] Most dramatically, perhaps, L. Susan Brown argues that "anarchism goes beyond feminism in its ceaseless attempts to annihilate power itself."[19]

But what does this mean? In the context of many contemporary feminist efforts to "empower" women (or to define feminism as the empowerment of women), or to reconceive power as capacity, is it appropriate even to *aim* at "annihilating" power?[20] And in an era defined significantly by the legacy of Michel Foucault, and by the feminist insistence that "the personal is political" (and, therefore, not free from relationships of power), can we even imagine that it would be possible to end all relationships of domination and subordination?

It is precisely the effort to make a sharp distinction between "formal" and "informal" power which is difficult for many contemporary feminists (postmodernist and otherwise) to accept. As Marx, Foucault and many others have made clear, power is much more complex than such a formulation would imply. "Informal power," for example, is almost invariably concentrated in the hands of individuals who are otherwise socially-privileged. Further, there is virtually no arena of our lives free from the exercise of power of some sort; and, at the same time, virtually no context in which there is not also resistance. What, then, does it mean to advocate the "annihilation" of power, or to suppose that such a goal is even desirable? Is it possible to imagine new understandings of power (such as power as capacity, or "empowerment") that would not be imbued with relations of domination?

Kathleen Jones has suggested that one key to the problem is the definition of power as *sovereignty* that demands, or depends upon, an enforced unity.[21] Jones argues that it was the construction of sovereignty (by Hobbes) as the overcoming of difference that has been fundamental to "establishing authority as a 'command-obedience relationship.'"[22] In its place, she draws on Hannah Arendt to call for an understanding of authority as an "augmentation of our common life": "contrary to the restricted understanding of authority as contingent on conflicting individual and, primarily, male wills, authority is here seen as the construction of a meaningful world ... the vitalizing of community itself." Authority, then, becomes a way of describing shared meanings, "cohering and sustaining connectedness."[23]

The attempt to think about power *other* than as a mechanism for enforcing unity is one component of a more complex understanding of power. But contemporary debates have also highlighted other necessary dimensions of such a reconceptualization—specifically, the multiple faces of power and resistance. Here, feminist questions focus on how to analyze relationships of domination (and resistance) so as to recognize the multiple domains and dimensions of power while not succumbing to analytical incoherence and/or political resignation.

Perhaps the most serious (and strategically compelling) charges leveled against the various interpretations of "feminism" that developed over the course of the Second Wave is that each focuses on one particular relationship of domination and subordination as critical, effectively ignoring or marginalizing the others. Increasing numbers of feminist activists and theorists, however, have found these approaches inadequate. Either they could not account for differences of class or race or sexual orientation among women, or they treated one or another of these characteristics as "secondary." But women who exist in a world characterized by multiple "fault-lines," who find themselves members (or non-members!) of a variety of collectivities, with multiple loyalties, have found such approaches overly-simplified and oblivious to the complexity with which they live.[24]

The problem is clear. In the words of Ernesto Laclau and Chantal Mouffe, the problem facing contemporary radical activists is the loss of "privileged points of rupture": contemporary US and Western European societies are characterized by a "diffusion of social conflictuality to more and more numerous relations."[25] Neither Marxism's claim to explain all relations of domination and subordination on the basis of class, nor radical feminism's claim to explain it all on the basis of sex, is adequate. On the one hand, there are too many other lines of cleavage which seem to generate challenges to existing structures of power and, on the other, there are too many ways in which the supposed grounds of resistance are undermined and constrained.

> There is no *unique* privileged position from which a uniform continuity of effects will follow ... There is therefore no subject ... which is absolutely radical and irrecuperable by the dominant order, and which constitutes an absolutely guaranteed point of departure for a total transformation.[26]

If there is no one privileged "point of rupture," no necessary assumption of homogeneity of experience or consciousness, no particular form of domination and subjection that can or will guarantee the final degree of resistance, whence comes the will or force to change, to overcome the relations of domination and subordination that limit us?

Like a number of contemporary activist/theorists, Laclau and Mouffe insist that the recognition that there is no "fundamental contradiction" signals not an end to politics, but its beginning. If any and all perspectives are necessarily partial, then effective political action requires what they term "articulation"— the successful linking of one's struggles with those of others—in short, "coalition-building."[27] We can see this perspective foreshadowed in the communalist anarchist insistence that the focus of analysis (and of resistance) need not be on any *single* relationship of domination and subordination (i.e. one based on class, on race, on gender, on age, or on religious affiliation, for example), but rather on *relations of domination and subordination as such*[28]—a perspective about power that fits well with contemporary understandings of its multiple faces and dimensions. And we see it named, again, in Gail Stenstad's call for what she terms "atheoretical," "anarchic thinking" that is characterized by "openness to ambiguity and multiple interpretations, attentiveness to the strange-within-the-familiar ... " that "empowers a multiplicity of voices and of possibilities for thought and action."[29]

Another context in which feminist explorations of the ambiguities of power has been developed quite extensively in recent years is in theories of the state. Anarchists, of course, are best known for their anti-state perspective, the insistence that there can be *no* legitimate political authority, and that the so-called neutrality of the state is always a mask for relations of domination and subordination.[30] Contemporary feminists have been quite divided about the role of the state and its particular implications for women; and many of these critical writings can be helpful in exploring anarchist approaches.

For example, feminist scholarship has made clear that welfare states have ambiguous consequences for their clients. On the one hand, beginning with Piven and Cloward's *Regulating the Poor*, some critics have viewed welfare programs as mechanisms for the exercise of state control. They have focused specifically on the impacts of state policies generally, and of state-sponsored welfare programs in particular, on family and sexual lives. Some emphasize the ways contemporary welfare state policies organize family life and sexuality, in Balbus' view, transforming "citizens of a limited state" into "clients of an unlimited state."[31] Others have explored the ways legal structures legitimize certain definitions of "family" and acceptable sexuality, and marginalize others.[32] And still others have focused more specifically on the ways state welfare programs have created and/or reinforced hierarchical relationships of gender and race, specifically through the creation of a two-channel welfare system.[33]

On the other hand, state programs can also provide sources of empowerment.[34] Many such programs have been of tremendous value to women— whether in providing employment within the welfare-state bureaucracy, or in providing needed, albeit often inadequate, benefits to those who are clients. Further, women and poor people have been able to use programs and institutions created by the welfare state precisely to organize *against* the state, demanding better services and benefits. In the process, "clients" can come to experience, for themselves, precisely the stronger self-image and the collective sense of empowerment which many anarchists have taken as a goal. Thus, critics argue, state programs could serve as the contexts for major organizing against the state, not only on behalf of greater welfare benefits, but also for more equality. The welfare state comes to be seen not just as a mechanism of control over the poor, but as a product of the demands made, and resistance offered, by poor and working-class people to changes in the class relations of advanced capitalism.[35]

In short, the state is a much more complex set of institutions and practices than early anarchist theory acknowledged. While contemporary feminists are hardly agreed about what to make of this complexity, or how best to relate to "the state," most seem convinced that issues of power must be addressed in all their complexity. The state can neither be ignored, nor simply opposed in the sense that anarchism (at least as traditionally understood) would have advocated. In that respect, contemporary feminist perspectives pose important challenges to those anarchist views. Unlike traditional anarchists who wanted to eliminate the state, many feminists advocate a state that is accountable to its citizens, and genuinely responsive to, and representative of the interests of, *all* its citizens.

Strategies for Change

The key question for all theories of domination and resistance (of which socialism is one, feminism another, and anarchism yet another) is to develop an analysis not only of the workings of domination, but also of the possibilities of resistance and transformation. For both socialism and feminism, that process has generally been referred to as the problem of consciousness-change. How do people come to recognize (collective) grievances and their capacity to take action to overcome them? How can such consciousness and action be coordinated and sustained into a more broadly-based movement? It has become clear that a simple "oppression/resistance" or "oppression/consciousness" model is inadequate. On the one hand, as theorists as different as Michel Foucault and Piven and Cloward have noted, power is never exercised without there being resistance to it. Yet, it is also the case that resistance is never automatic, and a consciousness of grievances does not necessarily follow from even the most horrific abuses of power.[36]

Anarchist analyses of resistance and the strategic prescriptions deriving from it center on direct action and the consistency of means and ends. Recognizing the existence of conflicting realities in the world is central to the anarchist strategy for social change. Just as there is no power without resistance, there is no hierarchy without a variety of understandings of those relationships.[37] For anarchists, the perspectives of those subject to domination and oppression provide the bases for social change. To overcome domination is, in fact, to create a new reality, and to do so by asserting, and acting upon, a different conception of what constitutes knowledge, one's own nature, and the relationships in which one finds oneself. In addition, through such action, people effectively *change themselves*. By acting differently, they convince both themselves and others that they are not "naturally subordinate," that the dependency or submissiveness that has characterized them, for example, is not definitive of their being.[38]

This relationship between "personal" change and "political" change helps to explain why anarchists argue so strongly for the consistency of means and ends. One cannot establish an egalitarian society through hierarchical organizations which recreate in different form long-standing patterns of subordination. To live as members of an egalitarian, communalist, society, people must re-socialize themselves as new persons. They must come to see themselves, and to act, on the basis of a new (alternate) reality. And this they can do only by acting—with others, and on a non-dominating basis.

In the anarchist view, previously-dependent people come to recognize their grievances and their capacity to take action to combat them by a combination of education (including "propaganda by the deed," exemplary action that recruits adherents by the power of the positive example it sets) and engaging in action, both of which reflect new understandings and manifestations of "power," and which become self-sustaining activities.

But how can these actions and consciousness be sustained and coordinated into a broad movement? Anarchists' answer to this question differs significantly from that of Marxists—and fits well with much feminist practice. For anarchists argue that change cannot be achieved through centralized organizations that manifest the traditional, hierarchical understanding of power, but must develop out of the widest possible sort of participation. This must be so because any particular action or organization is necessarily *partial*, even as it is also potentially a building-block of a new society. People must act "locally," i.e., where they feel called to act; and no centralized organization can direct that.

This is what both anarchists and many feminists have meant by strategies of "empowerment," what Spanish anarchist women termed *capacitación* [39] When people join together to exert control over their workplace, their community, the conditions of their day-to-day lives, they experience the changes they make as their own. Instead of reinforcing the sense of powerlessness that often accompanies modest improvements granted from the top of an hierarchical structure, a strategy of direct action enables people to *create their own power*. This is not power in the sense of domination; but power/authority in Kathleen Jones' sense of "augmentation" or connection, power that both enables and constitutes the work of what Laclau and Mouffe refer to as "articulating" differences. Acting in this way increases people's self-confidence, and fortifies them to continue to act.[40] It is not surprising, in this context, that so many women felt *strengthened* by the consciousness-raising sessions that were characteristic of early stages of the "second wave" of the women's movement— sessions that enabled people to share a different reality, and then to act upon it. That acting together strengthened women further, and gave them the power to continue to act, even against obstacles. The women of Mujeres Libres (a Spanish anarchist women's organization, active in Spain during the time of the Spanish Civil War, and committed to "emancipating women from their triple enslavement to capital, to illiteracy, and as women") reported similar experiences of overcoming their own embarrassment and timidity about speaking in public, for example. Those who act together with others in non-traditional ways are often perceived as threatening (and ridiculed or dismissed as "hysterical" or "disorderly") precisely because they are challenging some long and dearly-held beliefs about how the world does and should operate.[41]

Laclau and Mouffe challenge us to redefine understandings of domination and subordination in more complex ways. In their view, the problem of "consciousness" must be renamed: "Our central problem is to identify the discursive conditions for the emergence of a collective action, directed towards struggling against inequalities and challenging relations of subordination ... our task is to identify the conditions in which a relation of subordination becomes a relation of oppression ..."[42] They take "relation of subordination," to mean "that in which an agent is subjected to the decisions of another"—the relationship of employee to employer, for example, or of women to men in "certain forms of family organization." By "relations of oppression," they refer to "those relations of subordination which have transformed themselves into sites of antagonism." The problem then becomes to explain that process of transformation.[43]

For both Laclau and Mouffe and for Piven and Cloward—although in different ways—that process is fundamentally *political*. If there is nothing automatic about resistance—and, in particular, about resistance expressed in collective forms—then it must be created or constructed. But what are the conditions for doing so? Both sets of authors look to the larger context in which the relationships are located. Laclau and Mouffe, Yeatman and Temma Kaplan, for example, focus on "discursive conditions," in particular, the "profound subversive power of democratic discourse" that enables those experiencing relationships of subordination to understand them as subordinating, and therefore unjust according to commonly-accepted democratic principles, and then to resist.[44] For Piven and Cloward, as well, the larger political context matters, but these authors tend to focus on the state of relationships/consensus/alignments among those who are *exercising* power, rather than on the discursive context, noting that the possibilities for successful resistance and realignment of power relationships is greatest when disruptive protest can splinter existing alignments and allegiances.[45] While anarchist writers have tended to focus on the ways action, in itself, can help to develop alternative perspectives, contemporary writer/activists such as Piven and Cloward, Boyte and Evans, and others have argued that openings for successful resistance are often quite fleeting: it is only in the (often temporary) interstices of power that alternative views and practices can really begin to develop and flourish.[46]

Here is where feminist *practice* has much to offer to anarchist theory. Consciousness-raising groups brought together women who—consistent with the dominant cultural consensus—had perceived dissatisfaction with their lives as their "personal problems," and enabled them to recognize both the "commonness" of those issues and their socially-constructed aspects. The recognition that "the personal is political" became the watchword of the women's movement, and allowed people to develop and then to share changing perceptions of self and world. But consciousness raising, and the making of connections between "personal problems" and social/political practices, was not limited to the privacy of living rooms. To give just two examples: Self-help health clinics enabled people to recognize that they *could* understand at least some of what was going on inside their bodies, and that they could *participate* in making decisions about how to care for themselves. Food co-ops arose from a growing recognition of the ways food production and distribution were designed to further the interests of distributors, rather than of either producers or consumers; and, at the same time, they effectively empowered the women (and others) who created and participated in them by enabling them to work with others and to take greater responsibility for the context of their daily lives. Here, we can see important connections with much contemporary feminist post-modernist theorizing about "local" actions, the importance of what Laclau and Mouffe term "articulation," and what others discuss as the work of "politics" in a context of partial and unstable identities.[47]

Barbara Epstein's study of the non-violent, direct action movement makes a number of similar claims. She emphasizes the importance to movement activists of *personal* transformation as well as the achievement of more broadly "political" goals. In her view,

> [I]n late twentieth-century United States, protest politics must be utopian, in the sense that it must hold out a vision of a nonviolent and egalitarian society, and that it must build the new society within the shell of the old by creating a space within which these values can be realized as far as possible.[48]

She sees most contemporary movement groups as anarchist in inspiration and practice. Yet she argues that it is another side of that anarchist legacy which poses the greatest problem for the movement:

> [T]here is an assumption running through the direct action movement that constructing an egalitarian, nonviolent society requires abolishing power relations and doing away with conflict ... [But the] movement's suspicion of power and conflict makes it difficult to make strategy and to build the kinds of organizations that can weather changes in issues or tactics.[49]

While she favors eliminating centralized state power, she thinks it fanciful "to believe that power itself should be or can be abolished."

My own sense is that the wariness of "power" expressed in Epstein's analysis, and manifest both in the movements she studied and in so much of feminist and anarchist theorizing, reflects the complexities of power I have been exploring in this chapter. On this point, Jones' call for us to rethink power/authority in more "woman-friendly" ways that do not assume that unity must be enforced through the repression of differences becomes particularly relevant. Critics of both anarchism and feminism, for example, have warned of the dangers of their communalist/collectivist side. All-too-often, these critics argue, the consensus-oriented decision-making strategies associated with both movements have either faltered because of differences, or else reinforced the power of the majority in the name of the collective. Of course, these problems are not limited to consensus-based organizations: they are surely manifest, as well, in liberal democratic systems such as that of the US.

Much of the discussion of the coercive nature of "community" has focused on these more "collectivist approaches."[50] Nira Yuval-Davis and Floya Anthias, Iris Young, Audre Lorde, Patricia Hill Collins, Elizabeth Spelman, Gloria Anzaldúa, Susan Okin, and a host of others have all pointed to the dangers of basing feminist utopian visions on some unitary/homogeneous notion of "community" which is almost necessarily exclusive of differences among women.[51] The question then becomes, how to develop a conception of community/politics that is multivocal, and based on diversity, rather than on univocal concepts of power that are rooted in enforcing homogeneity or conformity.

Conclusion

And so we return, in the end, to the questions of difference, conflict and strategy we raised earlier. How can we realize the goal of collective action that unites people across differences, but does so without creating new, centralized, hierarchical structures, and without either denying differences or reifying them into permanent identities?

Contemporary feminist perspectives offer crucial rethinkings of locally-based, direct action strategies. For, it is *through politics*—that is to say, efforts to coordinate perspectives and activities with others—that we come to develop our own identities (however temporary and unstable) and capacities, and to learn about others'. Laclau and Mouffe are correct in saying that "articulation" is all. While we may not be able to eliminate power, we can move toward challenging the dominating, hierarchical, structures of power in and through which we interact. Much progressive protest politics, in fact, consists of actions that express such challenges. Further, people do (and seemingly will) question and resist those forms of dominating power by which they are oppressed and to which they have access, once the possibility of such resistance becomes a reality (a process that happens through what has been described as changing discourse—e.g. the spread of democratic ideas; as "propaganda by the deed"; or as finding the "cracks" in existing patterns or institutions of control).[52]

Those who resist dominating power (and, in the process, create a different kind of power)—whether in their daily lives, or in more formal protest organizations—do not necessarily have fully-developed long-term strategies formulated in their minds. While the absence of such strategizing has often tended to make us doubt the legitimacy or effectiveness of the resistance, feminist/anarchist perspectives challenge us to recognize that such skepticism is unwarranted. In fact, I would argue, "local action"—action taken not on the basis of some universalized narrative about "revolution," but on the basis of challenging *particular* oppressive relationships—partial and limited though it might seem, is the only politics consistent with a commitment *not* to deny the differences among us.[53] Such a politics—e.g. of women's health collectives, food co-ops, of bus boycotts, lunch-counter protests, ACT-UP demonstrations—recognizes the particular circumstances in which people live their lives, and in which they experience relations of domination, at the same time that it provides a context to challenge those relationships and to participate with others in creating a "new self."

There is yet another side to this "local" politics. In a paper on "Coyote Politics," Shane Phelan described both lesbians and feminists as "shape-shifters," who not only *do* shift perspectives, behaviors, attitudes, etc. in response to changing circumstances, but ought to celebrate and take pride in that multiplicity, as it is the only way to deal with a world of great complexity.[54] Similarly, María Lugones has used the language of *mestizaje*, and metaphors of "curdling," to address the complexities of identity and resistance, specifically the "impure resistance to interlocked, intermeshed oppressions." She urges us to think in terms of "multiplicity" (which communicates a sense of the "messiness" of identity), rather than of "fragmentation," which, in the guise of attending to differences, implies the possibility of a "clean separation" between parts of a self, a separation that can be accomplished—if at all—only through domination.[55] And Gloria Anzaldúa writes of the spiritual, sexual, and psychological borderlands where cultures, classes, and races touch, "where the space between two individuals shrinks with intimacy," and calls upon her readers to live with the contradictions, in those borderlands, to live "without borders" to "be a crossroads."[56] It is not coincidental that such calls for action that is open to difference, and for a politics that does not freeze people into particular identities, comes from those who have been "marginalized," or "particularized" by the traditional universalizing discourses. Yet it is from these margins that we find arising both theory and practice/resistance.

For too long—blinded by efforts to understand this resistance in terms of conventional theories of protest and organization—feminists and progressives have denied the significance of seemingly disparate and fragmented activities. If a rethinking of anarchist perspectives does nothing more, it should at least make us aware of the importance of such forms of resistance, and offer a framework within which to understand it. Partial, fragmented, identities may not seem to offer as sound and solid a basis for organizing and resistance as did traditional claims to class, race, or sex-based unities. But they *do* form the basis of actual resistance struggles. The task now is to explore the ways those struggles challenge domination while attempting to create new, more mutualist, expressions of power.

III

IS CITIZENSHIP THE GOAL?

8

EXCLUSION OR INCLUSION?

The Ambiguities of Citizenship

Feminist theorists and activists have recently been embracing two discourses they had earlier criticized: "citizenship" and "the public sphere." The popularity of these frameworks stems partly from the apparent inability of the traditional left (whether in the US or in much of Western Europe) to respond to the collapse of the Soviet Union and the fall of communism in Eastern Europe; and partly from efforts—in response to feminist and post-modernist criticism in the academy—to find non-essentializing ways of talking about processes of resistance and social change. As Engin Isin and Patricia Wood put it, "the political question (or perhaps anxiety) of our times is whether cultural politics can form an effective resistance to injustice, inequality, domination and oppression engendered by advanced capitalism and institutionalized by neoliberalism."[1] The language of citizenship *seems* to be free of the complications of both identity politics and socialist universalism,[2] while, particularly in the US context, drawing on powerful images of successful movements for inclusion (e.g. abolitionism, the Civil Rights Movement, and the Women's Suffrage Movement).[3] Related to this attention to citizenship is a growing interest in the theoretical and practical possibilities offered by Habermas' notion of the public space of "discursive" or "deliberative" democracy, to provide critical purchase on the practices of democratic politics.[4]

The resulting explorations have been fruitful. And yet, as many have pointed out, both frameworks are fraught with problems. Habermas' conceptualization of the public sphere as a space for deliberation and democratic citizenship effectively masks many of the inequalities and hierarchies that he is explicitly attempting to avoid.[5] Beyond that, citizenship, itself—at least as it exists in most western welfare-state societies—has been constructed through a variety of exclusions, based on gender, class, race, etc.[6] This chapter explores the contradictions and possibilities offered by a focus on citizenship or "democratic public space" as a goal and strategy of political struggle.

117

The Oppositional Potential of "Citizenship" and the "Public Sphere"

Sylvia Walby has captured much of the appeal of citizenship as an oppositional category, while also taking into account the ambiguities of its usages:

> Today, citizenship means universalistic democratic rights of social and political participation. In popular political discourse it entails the full integration of all adults regardless of "race," ethnicity, sex, or creed. In this way it is a modernist, universalistic concept. However, it is also a national project, a location which places limitations on its universalism. Nevertheless, the new meaning of the term citizen, with its attempt at a democratic and universalistic project, rather than the limited notion utilised in ancient Greek city-states from which women and slaves and aliens were excluded, is useful for social science. Access to citizenship is a highly gendered and ethnically structured process. Yet the concept is potentially suited to the conceptualisation, investigation and theorisation of the varying degrees of social integration and participation in contemporary society.[7]

Citizenship has many dimensions. It refers to those who are considered to have "standing" to make claims against the state—e.g. for the protection of life, liberty and property—commonly referred to as *civil* rights; to those who have the right (or duty) to participate in decision-making and/or in the exercise of political power—e.g. voting for candidates, serving in public office, deliberating on matters of local or national policy—commonly referred to as *political* rights; and to those who are entitled to make claims for access to the necessities that make possible the exercise of these civil and political rights—what Marshall characterized as the "whole range from the right to a modicum of economic welfare and security to the right to share to the full in the social heritage and to live the life of a civilised being according to the standards prevailing in the society"[8]—usually referred to as *social* rights. Nevertheless, treating the provision of these latter goods as a matter of "right," or as a critical component of citizenship, has been much more commonly acknowledged in European contexts than in the US.[9] In this chapter, I focus primarily on citizenship as "standing," or status, but I will also be discussing a second meaning, as active participation in public life; that is, citizenship as *practice*.[10] In the US, workers, African Americans, women, and now gays and lesbians have couched demands for equal rights and political inclusion in the language of citizenship. T.H. Marshall, himself, noted that, while citizenship can function to justify social inequality, the language and practices of citizenship can also tend to impel people toward greater *equality*.[11] Or, as Ruth Lister has commented, "as an inspiration and a yardstick, it ... offers a political tool."[12] In important ways, then, the language of citizenship is a language of inclusion.

If citizenship has offered, historically, a powerful language for inclusionary political movements, many contemporary theorists argue that Habermas' notion of the "public sphere" can provide an even more effective, perhaps less problematic, language to address issues of inclusion and engagement in contemporary democracies. Seyla Benhabib, for example, notes that Habermas' discursive model highlights the *openness* of democratic modernity: (a) "the consensual generation of general norms of action through practical discourses"; in which (b) "the development of individual identities becomes increasingly dependent on the reflexive and critical attitudes of individuals in weaving together a coherent life story"; and (c) "the appropriation of cultural tradition becomes more dependent upon the creative hermeneutic of contemporary interpreters."[13] In short, the "public sphere" is a site for enacting broad, and activist, understandings of politics or citizenship. And this broadening—seemingly without slipping into the essentializing categories of that much-maligned "identity politics"—is surely a significant dimension of its appeal for contemporary inheritors of 1960s "participatory democratic" political perspectives.[14] As Anne Phillips has summarized:

> Rejecting both the false harmony that stamps out difference and the equally false essentialism that defines people through some single, authentic, identity, many look to a democracy that maximizes citizen participation and requires us to engage and contest with one another.[15]

Both "citizenship" and "the public sphere," then, have been used to rally people in the name of broadening political participation, and to oppose policies that limit either social benefits or democratic controls over political life. Activists in post-Soviet Eastern Europe drew heavily both on discourses of activist citizenship and of civil society to explain and/or legitimate their resistance to Soviet power and their struggles to institutionalize democratic regimes and practices. And in both the US and Western European contexts, the language of citizenship has been used to justify the creation of programs of social provision, and continues to be used to oppose contemporary cuts in such programs.

Finally, of course, these two frameworks are connected in more basic ways. Struggles over who has "standing" as a citizen are often equally struggles about what states *owe* their citizens and, more significantly, over what fora are available for discussion of these matters and who can participate in them. Debates over access to the "public sphere," or a public space of discussion and debate, are equally struggles over what is to be discussed, and who will decide. Thus, both "rights of citizenship" and "access to the public sphere" can serve as points of condensation for a variety of contemporary resistance struggles, particularly in self-proclaimed democratic polities.

Nevertheless, as feminist and other critics have been arguing for some years, the discourse and practices of citizenship—particularly in the US—are deeply gendered and racialized; and Habermas' notion of the "public sphere" participates in some of the same problematic dualisms (especially that between public and private) that characterize traditional liberalism. I now turn, then, to an examination of some of those criticisms, as a step toward exploring whether, and in what ways, those concepts might be refigured as part of a developing politics of social-political change.

The Problematics of "Citizenship" and "the Public Sphere"

Although marginalized groups have used claims for equal citizenship to mobilize and struggle for inclusion in the polity, the practices of citizenship, particularly in the US, have been, and remain, deeply ambiguous and exclusionary. These practices have been structured around, and participated in, a number of tensions and dichotomies, which can also be expressed in the form of oppositions or exclusions: (a) workers/citizens; (b) workers/women; (c) women/citizens. These dichotomies, in turn, are related to two others that have been critical to both feminist scholarship and to understandings of the politics of race and class in the US: public/private and dependence/independence.

Public/private

As discussed above (Chapters 2 and 5), the so-called public/private split goes back at least to Aristotle, who described a public/political arena as the realm in which free and equal citizens engage in ruling and being ruled in turn, while striving for the common good. But this domain—as Aristotle was well aware—depended on the existence of a private/domestic arena, characterized by relationships of inequality and *de*pendence, and focused on meeting life's necessities (a formulation taken up later by Hannah Arendt, among others). This private realm was profoundly gendered, classed, and racialized, peopled by women, slaves, laborers, "barbarians," and others who failed to meet Aristotle's criteria for the "rationality" necessary for citizenship.

Although it differed in many respects, the liberal tradition also limited full citizenship to those who were defined as "independent," and who were understood to have the means to participate "unencumbered" in the public realm. That was to mean, at least until the early nineteenth century in the US (later in Europe) not those who were slaves, or waged workers (who were considered "dependent" on others for their wages), or persons who were perceived as not "working" (e.g. women). It further assumed that citizenship is acted out in the *public* domain, and that private or domestic activities are not the activities of "citizens." This conceptualization constituted one part of a legacy of at-best marginal citizenship status for those defined as located in the private/domestic arena—in the US, slaves, women, and non-workers. At the same time, it offered some women an alternative basis of incorporation into the polity as "republican mothers," integrated on the basis of their domestic activities, and, specifically, their contribution to the care and education of future generations of citizens.[16] Nevertheless, as Nancy Fraser has argued (following Habermas), this simplistic public/private binary not only obscures the interrelation of these "spheres," but also ignores other important dimensions of contemporary life. In fact, there are really two different separations under "classical capitalism": that between the (official) economy and the "private" nuclear family, and that between the state (particularly in its bureaucratic/administrative dimensions) and the public sphere as an arena for public contestation and debate. Each arena, or domain, interacts with the others in complex ways; and each is deeply gendered. Thus, although some version of a conceptualization of public and private can be helpful for understanding the dynamics of power in contemporary societies, these terms must be used carefully, in ways that do not continue to mask the relations of which they are constituted.[17]

Dependence / independence

In the liberal tradition, citizenship was clearly linked to independence, defined in two ways: self-support and bearing of arms. Full citizenship—as I discussed above (Chapter 4)—was deemed to be incompatible with dependency.[18]

Such a formulation, of course, resulted in an ambiguous status for all non-self-supporting males—including poor free white men, slaves, free blacks in the post-Emancipation/pre-Civil Rights era, and women. Even white women were not eligible for full citizenship as defenders of the state—since they were the ones the males were supposedly defending! Nor were they considered to be self-supporting, since women's (domestic) work was not counted as "work," and—through much of the nineteenth century, and well into the twentieth—they were sharply limited in opportunities for paid employment. Even when they *did* work for wages, employers justified paying women below-subsistence wages on the grounds that they were (or ought to be) dependent on men for their support.[19] In short, dependence was understood to be—at least for white women—women's "natural" or "appropriate" condition.

For black women and other women of color, expectations were sharply different. During the era of slavery, of course, dependency was considered to be black women's (and men's) "natural" condition. But even in the post-slavery period, neither free Black women, Latinas, nor many immigrants were allowed to participate fully in the ideal of female domestic dependence. Most were expected to work for wages (usually in domestic employment), although at wages which did not allow for self-sufficiency; they were faced "with a double-bind situation, one that required their participation in the labor force to sustain family life but damned them as women, wives, and mothers because they did not confine their labor to the home."[20]

Nevertheless, when citizenship came for (white) women, it was based on their assumed *dependency*, and justified on that ground, and on women's *difference* from men. But both the more "prudentialist" arguments for women's suffrage, and those for state-supported welfare benefits for women and children, reinforced the sense that only women could be dependent adults and still merit the status of citizen.[21] It is, nevertheless, true that female social reform activists deliberately *used* those understandings of women's "proper" place—with many of which they disagreed—to argue for social rights that women (and later men) would not otherwise have had. Still, both "independence" and "dependence" were also gendered.

Feminists, of course, have criticized both these dichotomies: they have pointed out that so-called public and private domains are mutually-constituted, as well as gendered; and they have explored the mystifications inherent in any concept of "independence."[22] But no one is, in reality, completely independent: the seeming independence of some actually rests on the dependence of others (and vice versa). In addition, the valorization of independence that characterizes liberal political thought has, as its obverse, devaluing the care-taking work that is performed mostly by women and people of color.[23] Further, Carole Pateman's *The Sexual Contract* argued powerfully that the mythical social contract, which grounds US political self-understanding, obscures the *sexual* contract which assures that both citizenship and paid work are defined in gendered terms: "sexual difference gives rise to a patriarchal division of labor not only in the conjugal home, but in the workplaces of civil society."[24] Indeed, the "employment contract presupposed the marriage contract."[25] Or, as Nancy Fraser has noted, "there is ... a very deep sense in which masculine identity in [male-dominated classical capitalist societies] is bound up with the breadwinner role."[26] The "independent" role is a male one; it is defined (and supported, at least in part) by contrast with the situation of the women and children dependent on him. Not coincidentally, the contemporary public discourse of "dependency" (especially in relationship to welfare "reform") constructs it as a condition of *personal status or character*, ignoring or denying its socio-economic dimensions and attempting to privatize relations of dependency in the family.[27]

Workers and citizens

These and other exclusionary aspects of citizenship shaped and deformed the struggles of workers for inclusion in the US polity. Thus, even though workingmen drew on the language of equality and inclusion—claims that "all men were created equal"—to challenge their *exclusion* from full citizenship, those challenges, themselves, proved ambiguous. First, they relied on the exclusion of others (e.g. blacks and women). In addition, within the context of the paid economy, workers clearly were *not* equal to their bosses. They had, therefore, to tread a fine line: explicit acknowledgment of the (economic) inequality they were struggling against could undermine their own claims to inclusion (as equals) in US public life.

A successful incorporation of workers into the polity, then, meant reconciling the equality and independence supposedly required for citizenship in a democratic polity with the hierarchy of a capitalist wage-labor system. Marshall phrased the dilemma well, noting that the growth of citizenship constitutes a movement toward equality, yet

> its growth coincides with the rise of capitalism, which is a system, not of equality, but of inequality ... How is it that these two opposing principles could grow and flourish side by side in the same soil? What made it possible for them to be reconciled with one another and to become, for a time at least, allies instead of antagonists?[28]

Marshall's argument was that social citizenship, itself, provided the basis for the reconciliation, by offering benefits geared to what he termed "class abatement," aimed "at making the system less vulnerable to attack by alleviating its less defensible consequences."[29] But this argument, of course, is more appropriate to the British context than to the US, where citizenship for workers pre-dated any significant state welfare provision.

Alternatively, Carole Pateman argues that the root of the successful (though, in her view illegitimate) reconciliation is to be found in the concept and practice of *contract* which, in the guise of creating an egalitarian relationship of free exchange, in fact creates a relationship of domination and subordination: for "what is required [by the employment contract] is that the worker labors as demanded. The employment contract must, therefore, create a relationship of command and obedience between employer and worker."[30] It is this very mystification that legitimates the obedience—by, in effect, personalizing or privatizing the *social* relations of capitalism (or, in Habermasian terms, removing them from the public sphere and relegating them to the private—the paid economy). Nevertheless, this fiction is useful: it creates, for the worker, the illusion that he [*sic*] *is* still independent. And, it is deeply connected with our understandings of citizenship. For the employment contract both masks the dependency of the (male) worker *and* seemingly differentiates it from the (supposedly differently-constructed) dependency of women in marriage.

In a somewhat different vein, Judith Shklar's discussion of the reconciliation of "worker" and "citizen" in the US context focuses on the construction of the worker as "free" and "independent" in opposition to the slave, on the one hand, and the "idle aristocrat," on the other. In the US, "earning offers citizens their standing ... Not to work is not to earn, and without one's earnings one is 'nobody.' ... When they cease to earn ... whatever the character of their work, Americans lose their standing in their communities."[31]

Thus, the specter of dependence—whether expressed in the language of slavery or in the language of domesticity—loomed large in the consciousness of newly-industrializing US workers in the nineteenth century. Eric Foner argues that the analogy between northern "wage slavery" and southern chattel slavery formed an important part of workingmen's rhetoric in the mid-nine-teenth century. "For those reared in the tradition of the independent artisan, working for wages seemed a form of slavery, for it entailed a loss of personal autonomy and of a sense of control over one's own destiny."[32] Amy Bridges argued, similarly, that labor organization in the 1850s "was accompanied by a protest against the degradation from independence to 'wage slavery.' ... Strikes would ... enable labor [quoting a union broadside] to 'take that posi-tion which God intended men should fill—truly independent of his fellow, and above the position of mere 'wage-slaves.'"[33] While workingmen eventually had to give up that individualist understanding of independence and shift to a new understanding that made wage-work compatible both with independence and with citizenship, the shift was not an easy one, and did not happen without a struggle.[34]

Elizabeth Bussiere argues compellingly that, in the early nineteenth century, workingmen in the United States developed a significant counter-tradition to the emerging liberal individualist paradigm. An "artisan republicanism," while emphasizing the value of *work*, emphasized the *social* context of the creation of wealth, and the consequent responsibilities owed by the community to its members. Her argument focuses on the ways this tradition might have pro-vided grounding for claims to a constitutional right to subsistence.[35] What interests me here, however, is that, for all its radicalism, this tradition, too, contributed to what came to be the prevailing view that connected work (and the "independence" it supported) with the rights of citizenship.

Eventually, the peculiarities of the US political context resulted in a parti-cular accommodation on the part of American workingmen: while they did not abandon class-consciousness, their activities were split between workplace-focused unions and politically-focused parties. The split was far from total: in many cases, the critique of industrialism was political as well as economic; and workers argued for "rights" as *obligations* on the part of government and/or their social "betters" to meet subsistence needs well into the mid-nineteenth century. But, in the end, as Shefter notes,[36] there developed a distinction between the claims workers asserted against their employers and those they asserted against the state. In effect, a public/private distinction, that relegated economic struggles to the "private" context of labor relations, left intact a sense of independence, which could then be acted out in the political arena.

Workers, Citizenship and the "Public Sphere"

In accepting "independence" as a criterion of citizenship, US workingmen effectively defined themselves through a series of oppositional exclusions—as *different from* slaves, immigrants, and women. Judith Shklar's *American Citizenship* explores how the standing of "citizen" was defined in opposition to that of slave. Similarly, a focus on independence also placed workers in an ambivalent relationship to immigrants, who were seen as threatening to labor at least in part because of their presumed "dependence."[37]

Further, the construction of workers as "independent" was also profoundly gendered. Most workers apparently ignored the situation of their "dependent" wives, sisters, or daughters (or else, more probably, saw it as confirming their own independence). Nor were labor unions particularly concerned about the much-lower wages of women workers—wages that prevented them from becoming independent in any meaningful sense—except in trying to exclude women from the labor market, and from unions, as rate-busters. Although some women workers and their allies were arguing for equal pay for equal work as early as 1860, they were not especially successful in rallying the support either of the mainstream labor movement or of the women's rights movement.[38] Both the Knights of Labor and members of the National Labor Union did take up the cause of unionization of women, and made the argument for equal (or at least "reasonable") pay; but both apparently did so in ways that treated women's dependency as normative. As Susan Kennedy summarized, "a victory for the Knights, in the form of decent wages for men, would eliminate the need for women to perform wage labor."[39]

In short, although workers used the language of inclusion to argue for their incorporation as citizens, that same language constrained even their own sense of its broader possibilities. This ambiguity in the discourse of citizenship might offer an additional perspective on what Martin Shefter and Ira Katznelson, among others, have chronicled as the split between "economics" and "politics" (in Fraser's conceptualization, between the [official] economy and the state) in the consciousness of US workers.[40] To review: workers' organizations recognized their relative powerlessness in the *economic* arena, where they struggled against the unfair labor practices, low wages, long hours, etc. that constructed them as dependent. And they made demands in the so-called *political* arena (public sphere) vis-à-vis the state for policies guaranteeing the right to organize, etc. But they did not make *political* demands *as workers* to address their relationship to industrial capitalism, perhaps because the recognition of such a relationship would have compromised the foundation of their own presumed independence that served, in turn, as the foundation of their claims to citizenship; or, perhaps, because—as Bussiere argues—they had already lost the struggle for broader recognition of individual/communal *interdependence* with the earlier failure of "artisan republicanism." In any event, the result was a split between their rights as *workers* and their rights as *citizens*, which meant that they could not make demands as *(male) worker-citizens* for protection, support, or relief from the excesses of capitalism. This construction of the "public sphere," then, not only excluded women, slaves, immigrants, and others from participation; it also defined attention to conditions of "dependence" as irrelevant to (or inappropriate for) public debate or discussion. Thus, the incorporation of workers as citizens entailed the acceptance of significant exclusionary understandings—of who could be a worker, of what constituted work, and of what could legitimately be brought into the arena for public discussion—exclusions that were both challenged and re-enacted in women's struggles for incorporation into the polity.

Women, Work, and Citizenship

If the role of "independent worker" was gendered masculine, so was that of "citizen." And a number of feminists have pointed out that the capacities for consent and speech which, for Habermas—as well as many liberal theorists— define the minimal necessities for citizen participation in political debate and opinion formation (i.e. in the public sphere) are "capacities that are in myriad ways denied to women and deemed at odds with femininity."[41] Discourses of both independence/dependence and of public/private served to exclude women from official arenas of political participation.

As we saw in the case of workers, so too with much early women's activism, whether focused on gaining the suffrage or on expanding prevailing conceptions of the bounds of "public business": this activism, too, was constrained and deformed by the terms of debate it both adopted and challenged. The paradoxical aspects of this process can be seen very clearly in studies of the role of women and women's organizations in the construction of welfare provision in the US.

The process of establishing social supports was very different in the US than in Western Europe (where it was impelled by a combination of labor union agitation and capitalist pressure on governments to provide social insurance as a way of co-opting labor militancy). As Suzanne Lebsock described the US experience in the late nineteenth and early twentieth centuries, in the absence of attention from the state, women reformers took it upon themselves to salvage "the human wreckage of industrial capitalism."[42] White middle-class women founded and staffed settlement houses and women's clubs; they conducted research on the working and living conditions of new immigrants; they assisted unionization efforts and supported union organizations in their struggles with employers; and they pressured local and state governments to institute legislation to protect women workers, to limit child labor, to provide free public education, to stop the exploitation (or what they perceived as neglect) of children, and a variety of other activities.[43] Black women undertook similar efforts, at both local and national levels, to meet the day-to-day needs of poor blacks—otherwise ignored by most white reformers—for health care, shelter, and schooling; to counter racist stereotypes; to oppose lynching; and, more generally, to develop programs of education and "race uplift."[44]

US women reformers of the early twentieth century created structures and practices to meet real needs; and—at the urging of many of these same women and their allies—many of the programs they created were eventually taken over by governmental bodies. Further, by deliberately drawing on existing stereotypes of women as "domestic caretakers," women reformers succeeded in getting the *issue* of social provision onto the agenda of mainstream politics at both the state and national levels. Wendy Sarvasy has argued, in fact, that these practices effectively constituted the basis for a new understanding of citizenship—not as political participation (from which they were formally excluded), but as feminist social service.[45] Paula Baker and William Chafe have argued, along somewhat different lines, that these forms of activism changed the shape of citizenship—and definitions of politics—not only for women but for men as well.[46] Thus, by the end of the Progressive Era, and largely through struggles led by women, that which had been considered the stuff of charity work—concern over industrial conditions, education, nutrition, maternal and child health—and accordingly relegated to a "private" sphere, was more generally agreed to be a new and necessary domain of state action. As Paula Baker put it, "social policy became public policy."[47]

Nevertheless, while these reformers (as well as suffragists) did open the activities of citizenship to women for the first time, and succeeded in transforming the boundaries of the "public sphere," they did not escape the discursive framework of US politics, which continued to define women as dependent. In the end, both suffragists and maternalist reformers (however "reluctant" their maternalism), claimed rights to citizenship, protection, and/or governmental provision on the basis of women's presumed *dependence*, even though many of the women who worked to establish social welfare programs were themselves, economically "self-supporting." And the programs they established (particularly the maternal-child welfare programs in the Shepard–Towner Act, eventually incorporated into the Social Security Act of 1935 and its later amendments) both assumed and reinforced that dependence—and did so in ways that further hardened differences along race and class lines.[48] Finally, because even what we might term a "right to dependency" was understood in gendered and racialized terms, Black, Latino, and Asian women were effectively excluded from more "generous" welfare provisions until the mid-twentieth century; and programs to address the problems of dependent *men* became virtually impossible to conceive, let alone to enact.

Thus, whether we refer to status or to practice, citizenship in the US is deeply gendered and racialized. Historically, women (and children) could make claims to rights vis-à-vis the state (or have such rights claimed on their behalf) that men could not, rights that they were "owed" *because* of their presumed *natural* condition of dependence (typified, in the case of women, by motherhood, or the possibility of being a mother). Compensatory programs—mothers' pensions, widows' pensions, protection for women workers, Aid to Dependent Children, even OASDI benefits—assumed (and reinforced) a condition of dependency as *constitutive* of women's status. And when (white) women won "full citizenship rights" in 1920, they did so, at least in part, on the basis of their *difference* from men—a difference defined in significant ways through their presumed dependence—and, in part, on the strength of their potential role in assimilating and "taming" the threat to white supremacy and dominant values posed by massive immigration. Citizenship for (white) women, then—as it had been for white men—was constructed through a series of exclusions and oppositions, although these were *different* from those earlier exclusions, and may have served as "opening wedges" to the extension of rights (e.g. in the form of workplace protections) to men as well.

Since men's citizenship was premised on *in*dependence, there were limits to what they could or would demand in the way of "social rights." Rights to organize, yes; rights to vote; rights to act on their presumed independence. But not (with the exception of Jacksonian artisan-republican workingmen)—at least until the cataclysm of the Great Depression—rights to social supports of any significant degree, since that would have been inconsistent with the independence deemed constitutive of (male) citizenship. Thus, notions of "manly independence" contributed to a further marginalization of men who were not part of the organized labor force (especially new immigrants and black Americans) as threats to male independence, even as these same exclusivist practices contributed to ensuring their dependence.

Ambiguities, Citizenship, and the Public Sphere

In the present—despite formally "universal" citizenship, now inclusive of women, the poor, and members of minority communities—citizenship and the public sphere in the US remain structured by exclusions and inequalities. Both the definition of what is appropriately a matter for public discussion and debate, on the one hand, and understandings of independence that underlie dominant conceptions of citizenship, on the other, have been constructed and maintained through gendered and racialized exclusions. And yet, the language of citizenship and of a "democratic public sphere" has frequently served to rally people for emancipatory, oppositional ends. What are we to make—strategically—of these ambiguities?

As Nancy Fraser has noted with respect to "needs discourse," "for the time being," these discourses are "with us, for better or worse."[49] Further, each of these frameworks provides openings that have been drawn upon, and could continue to be tapped, as resources to expand and democratize public debate. Ernesto Laclau and Chantal Mouffe, for example, direct us to "the profound subversive power of democratic discourse" that enables those experiencing relationships of subordination to understand them *as subordinating* and therefore unjust according to commonly accepted democratic principles, and then to resist.[50] Or, as Marshall wrote over fifty years ago: "societies in which citizenship is a developing institution create an image of an ideal citizenship against which achievement can be measured and towards which aspiration can be directed."[51] Can we, then, draw upon these discourses in oppositional ways, in calls to restructure political life in accordance with the values to which they point?

Seyla Benhabib, while noting that the notion of a public sphere presupposes a distinction between the public and the private that feminists have identified as a site of domination and subordination, nevertheless argues that we need a *"critical model of public space and public discourse"* that can distinguish between "publicity" in the all-too-common form of a "bureaucratic administration of needs," on the one hand, and "collective democratic empowerment over them" on the other.[52]

Similarly, Mary Ryan argues that, although "from the first the American public sphere was constructed in the shadow of both gender restrictions and an emerging private sector of social life," nevertheless, politics in the US has been democratized, precisely by groups challenging their marginalization. To recognize this paradox, she insists, is to shift our perceptions away from the notion of *a* public sphere, and to adopt a more plural and decentered vision of *multiple* arenas for participation. At the same time, we must remember that the "public" has maintained its resilience through progressive incorporations, and that crucial political actions may be perceived (or dismissed) as unruly, outrageous or disorderly.[53]

And Nancy Fraser, as well, while noting that Habermas' claims about the public sphere as a space for citizenship mask the inequalities and hierarchies he's trying to avoid, and that, even in the absence of formal exclusions, "deliberation can serve as a mask for domination," nevertheless claims that his model offers important resources. The focus on a seemingly-free floating "discursive arena" can easily mask relations of domination. Nevertheless, discussions of politics that focus on the "public sphere" can alert us to the need for "subaltern counterpublics," "parallel discursive arenas where members of subordinated social groups invent and circulate counterdiscourses to formulate oppositional interpretations of their identities, interests, and needs."[54] Jane Mansbridge has made similar arguments with respect to "enclaves of protected discourse,"[55] as has Shane Phelan with respect to community: " ... we can only come to community by negotiating about what we will have in common, what we will share, and how we will share it."[56]

Of course, these formulations raise further questions: what is necessary to sustain "subaltern counterpublics"? How do we establish—and maintain—"enclaves of protected discourse"? What are the criteria for assuring that discussions in which we "negotiate about what we will have in common, what we will share, and how we will share it" do not, themselves, perpetuate the relationships of exclusion, of power and domination, that feminists and others have worked so hard to uncover and contest?

These remain the critical questions for a contemporary politics of inclusion and resistance. It is one thing to set out the criteria for what would constitute a truly democratic public space; it is quite another to create the conditions for realizing it. These processes—both of imagining a democratic public space and of engaging people in popular actions to broaden understandings both of citizenship and of the domain of political life—are, of course, the "stuff" of politics. I have argued above (Chapter 7) that "it is *through politics*—that is to say, efforts to coordinate perspectives and activities with others—that we come to develop our own identities (however temporary and unstable) and capacities, and to learn about others." And, further, that such local activism "partial and limited though it might seem, is the only politics consistent with a commitment *not* to deny the differences among us."[57] In short, the way to address questions of difference and domination without reinscribing the domination is to keep those issues constantly at the fore.

Similar arguments can be made in the cases of citizenship and a "public sphere." These discourses, while on the one hand, constituted by exclusions, have, on the other, provided a space for the contesting of those same exclusions. Indeed, as I am concluding this chapter (November 2008), Barack Obama has just won the presidential election, after a campaign which successfully mobilized large numbers of people *across* traditional boundaries of race, gender and class. The possibilities of a more inclusive citizenship have come dramatically to the fore. At the same time, however—as we see in the treatment of immigrants, and in debates over immigration policy—the terms of citizenship remain deeply problematic. If we are to continue to draw on these concepts, we must keep the exclusions which have structured them at the forefront of consciousness, debate, and resistance. Struggles over a more inclusive notion of citizenship (whether in terms of membership or participation)—or over a broader conception of what is to be the focus of public debate—must keep at their center precisely the ambiguities of exclusion and inclusion that have both structured those practices and impelled resistances to them.

Acknowledgments

This chapter grew out of a presentation at the conference, "Women, Citizenship, and Difference," held at the University of Greenwich, July 16–18, 1996. I am especially grateful to Nira Yuval-Davis and to Verena Stolcke for helpful comments on early versions of these ideas. A version of it was presented at the 1998 Annual Meeting of the American Political Science Association, Boston, MA.

9

BROADENING THE STUDY OF WOMEN'S PARTICIPATION

Why should we be concerned with broadening the study of women's participation in US politics?[1] One might well argue that such efforts are unnecessary: rates of participation by women in conventional politics are rising, and fast approaching those of men; women are making gains in the electoral-political arena, especially at the local level, but increasingly at the state and (though more slowly) federal levels. And, further, what have traditionally been defined as "women's issues"—ranging from access to abortion or birth control, parental or family leave, child-care, health care, welfare, or education—are making it onto the mainstream national political agenda. Isn't it sufficient to assume that these trends will continue, and to go about measuring and/or studying women's participation within traditional channels?—e.g. by examining recruitment of candidates, fund-raising, the role of the media, the relationship to parties, issues of leadership, race and class differences, organizational strategies, and the like?

Yet, without diminishing the significance of these gains (and the importance of research that will allow us to explore their limits and what can be done to overcome them)—and even in the aftermath of the 2008 election season that foregrounded women's electoral political roles as never before—it remains the case that a focus on the electoral arena, and on traditional forms of participation, offers us only a partial view of politics and participation in this country, and, in particular, the participation of women. For, large numbers of women have been, and remain, active *outside* of traditional political arenas—or in other than traditional ways. Such activities have a significant impact on the formal electoral/political arena, and would be worth studying if only for those effects. But, as I have argued above (Chapters 1, 2, and 6), these activities also constitute important forms of politics in themselves and deserve study, as such. Non-electoral forms of what is sometimes termed "collective behavior" (e.g. demonstrations, protests, the creation of alternative institutions, etc.) can, at the very least, exert pressure on mainstream organizations and may make them more amenable to change from traditionally-structured groups.[2] At times the alternative organizations and/or modes of behavior they create can serve as models for, or challenges to, existing institutions and practices.[3] Or, we might look to the ways the Obama campaign effectively melded movement

131

and electoral strategies to create a powerfully effective hybrid. More broadly, non-electoral activities may express ways of engagement with, or involvement in, the public business that effectively broaden our understandings of that business, i.e. of "politics," itself.

In short, and most immediately, broadening our study of women's participation is critical to an accurate understanding of the full range and extent of women's activism in what is generally termed public life. It challenges us to break through dichotomized ways of thinking about political participation versus social mobilization or collective behavior, for example, to recognize that politics, properly understood, necessarily includes both and that, in fact, the distinction, itself, is more misleading than helpful. More significantly, and in the longer range, attention to a broader concept of *women's* participation has much to contribute to a rethinking of the meanings and practices of citizenship and participation for *everyone* as we attempt to meet the challenges of the twenty-first century.

Democracy and Women's Participation: The Challenge of Theory and History

Public, Private, and the Definition of the Political

Much early feminist work, in both history and the social sciences, focused on the supposed separation between public and private domains, pointing out that the division obscured the exercise of power within the private realm, masked the maleness of the public realm, and ignored the relationship between the relegation of women to the private domain and their subordination in the public.[4] Later work challenged that dichotomization further, pointing out the gendered nature of both public and private domains, and the interdependence of each on the other.[5] And some critics have added to this discussion of the public/private dichotomy a related critique of the construction of the categories of "dependence" and "independence" as similarly gendered and raced.[6]

These dichotomies affect definitions of politics and participation in critical ways. Carole Pateman, for example, has argued that the concept of a social contract, which anchors US political self-understanding, is grounded in a dichotomous (and gendered) understanding of public and private.[7] The myth of a *social* contract, which purports to unite free and equal individuals, obscures the *sexual* contract on which it depends, and which assures that both citizenship and the paid work which has come to be identified with "independence" are defined in totally male terms—and, further, depend on the support of women in the "private" realm. Our common understandings of both citizens and of workers assume that each will have someone at home to take care of his [*sic*] needs, and make it possible for him to work or to engage in public/political life.[8] Politics is "public business" that takes place in the "public" (i.e., male) domain. In short, our most basic understandings of citizenship and public participation, and the institutions through which they are realized and expressed, are gendered at their core. Women and workers *cannot but remain* second-class citizens (a kind of support-staff of public life) as long as these institutions continue to define and structure our politics. On these grounds alone, then, we could make a claim for the necessity of "broadening the study of women's participation"!

Further, Pateman argues, the metaphors of consent and contract which ground our political institutions are flawed in other ways, as well. At best, citizens have the option of voting or not voting, but we have little role in defining or structuring what will be voted on, or whether we consent to a regime as such. While she draws on metaphors of male–female relationships, Pateman's critique of contract—and of contractual understandings of political life—goes considerably beyond questions of gender:

> Consent must always be given *to* something; in the relationship between the sexes, it is always women who are held to consent to men ... An egalitarian sexual relationship cannot rest on this basis; it cannot be grounded in "consent" ... Perhaps the most telling aspect of the problem of women and consent is that we lack a language through which to help constitute a form of personal life in which two equals freely agree to create a lasting association together.[9]

If that is true for marriage, however, the force of her argument is that it is similarly true for social and political relationships: no more do we have a language through which to help constitute a form of social life in which *any* equals (however differently constituted) freely agree to create lasting relationships. The limits of consent and equality in marriage, then, point also to the limits of consent and equality in liberal democratic politics. We need new models and new metaphors to constitute a more broadly inclusive and democratic politics. Attention to women's participation in a wide range of activities may give us some clues as to how to move beyond the limits of existing models and practices of democracy.

Activism without Access: Women and the Welfare State

Related to this questioning of the construction of politics and democracy in the liberal state (and the US in particular) is a series of questions about "the state" and its relation to women. In its broadest formulation, the question takes the form "is the state an arena for the domination of women or for their empowerment?" The literature on this topic is vast; and much of it focuses on the construction and operation of welfare state policies and programs.[10] Early work by Frances Fox Piven, Piven and Cloward, and Zillah Eisenstein, for example, argued that welfare programs arose from women's struggles, and have provided important contexts for women's empowerment.[11] These perspectives were challenged by Isaac Balbus, Irene Diamond, Jean Elshtain, Kathy Ferguson and others, who focused on the welfare system as a site for the bureaucratic and disciplinary regulation of sexuality and family life.[12]

Recent work by a wide range of authors has continued to explore this complex and multi-faceted relationship, noting the role of welfare policies and institutions in controlling women at the same time that it emphasizes women's roles in the *construction* of those same welfare state policies. The issues here are many, and I have explored them in greater depth in Chapter 4 above. These studies begin from a recognition that neither power nor participation can most effectively be studied in dichotomous ways: modern social and political life is complex and ambiguous. Practices are neither *simply* emancipatory nor simply oppressive.[13] Nevertheless, and at the same time, these scholars point to women's roles in opening up new avenues for women's participation—and, importantly, for dramatically changing societal understandings of the domain of politics, itself—even at a time when women, themselves, were denied formal access to mainstream politics. As William Chafe put it:

> women's history [of the Progressive Era] has caused scholars to reconsider the definition of politics itself, broadening that area of inquiry to include informal networks of influence that helped shape public policy and highlighting the intersection of the personal and the political.[14]

Thus, Mimi Abramovitz, Linda Gordon, Seth Koven and Sonya Michel, Gwendolyn Mink, Barbara Nelson, Jill Quadagno, Wendy Sarvasy, Kathryn Kish Sklar, and Theda Skocpol, among others, have explored the roles of women in creating what came to be major welfare state programs, especially AFDC, Social Security, unemployment benefits, and Workman's Compensation.[15] None of these studies sees these women's accomplishments as unproblematic: the institutions they created were fundamentally structured by race and class, even as they attempted to address the problems of relatively powerless women and children. Nevertheless, each study also provides important evidence of the ways women's activities outside the formal political realm (at times when women did not have official access to that realm) were critical to the development of these institutions.

In fact, attention to women's activism does much more than provide information about the construction of the US welfare state: it offers clues to a fuller understanding of the changing nature and practices of politics and citizenship. Thus, Suzanne Lebsock, focusing on the broad range of women's voluntary associations in the nineteenth century, argues that "long before they were voters, they were political actors." Through their activism, the WCTU, club women (white and black), settlement house workers, labor union activists, "direct action radicals" such as Emma Goldman, Margaret Sanger and Elizabeth Gurley Flynn, and suffragists "helped change the political landscape in the forty years surrounding the turn of the century."[16] Paula Baker has suggested that the combined effect of an ideology (and practice) of separate spheres—of defining "politics" as male and "domesticity" as female—while excluding women from formal electoral/political participation, effectively created a separate arena of women's politics characterized by voluntarism and an attention to social needs. As white women were eventually included in the formal political arena, they brought with them this penchant for voluntary association (rather than party-type organization), and an attention to "social issues", both of which profoundly influenced the practice of politics in the United States.[17] Black women—effectively excluded from formal political participation in many areas until the mid-1960s—nevertheless continued to perform important "public" work in their communities, to raise issues, and to create institutions to meet communal needs.[18] Women's activism broadened the shape and domain of politics, and eventually redefined what counted as "political" for everyone. Sarvasy draws on this history (with all its race and class biases) to argue that women's activism in the early part of the twentieth century provides practices of "social citizenship" that offer important models for contemporary revisionings.[19] In short, we cannot properly understand "politics," let alone political change, unless we broaden our understanding of the varieties of (women's) participation to include activities which, at any given moment, might well be considered "beyond the pale."

"Insiders" and "Outsiders"

As I suggested above, attention to activities considered "outrageous" and "inappropriate" has been another important focus of feminist research and revisionism in the study of American politics. On the one hand, branding certain types of activities "disorderly" or "unseemly" has been a way both of excluding women (and others) from formal political life, and of denying the *political* significance of activities they have undertaken.[20] Thus, it is important to examine the boundaries of what is considered appropriate political behavior, for these presumed boundaries both define its limits and offer an opportunity to explore differences in those limits by race, class, or gender.

In addition, other feminists have directed our attention to the relationship between "radicals" and "traditionalists," or between those who work "inside" and those who work "outside" formal political institutions. While, as Mary Katzenstein reminds us, women are never wholly *in*side, nor wholly *out*side institutions, nevertheless, there are differences in strategies and tactics between those who operate in "protest" modes and those who try to work within institutions (what she has termed "unobtrusive mobilization"). Her work—and that of Cathy Cohen, Janet Flammang, Jo Freeman, Joyce Gelb, Gelb and Marian Palley, Viven Hart and Sheila Tobias—reminds us of the complicated relationships among women "inside" and those "outside," and their interdependence. Once again, they insist, we cannot fully comprehend the success and failure, or even the strategies and tactics, of those inside institutions if we fail to take account of their relationships with (or, at the very least, awareness of) those acting more autonomously, or in more contestatory modes, outside them.[21] Or, to put it more generally, we cannot assume that there is a dichotomous distinction between "insider" politics and that of "outsiders": as in so many other arenas, feminist explorations point to the ways that dichotomous assumptions can blind us to the much more complex character of political life.

Questions/Topics for Further Research

This brief overview has demonstrated the importance of broadening the study of women's participation. Feminist historians and sociologists have pioneered the exploration of "women's culture and politics," and, increasingly, have attempted to draw out the implications of women's activities in this broader context for politics and social change in the more narrowly-constructed arena. But feminist political scientists have been somewhat slower to take up this challenge, especially with respect to studies of contemporary US activism. Much feminist political science research still focuses primarily on questions of who gets involved in elections, parties, running for office, lobbying politicians, or working in the bureaucracy. While there are studies of contemporary grassroots movements, few have seriously addressed their implications for politics and citizenship more generally.[22]

One of the main reasons for this narrowness of focus has to do with methodological biases within the discipline of political science itself, and especially within the field of US politics. Since the 1950s, the study of US politics has been dominated by the "behavioral" approach—a focus on quantitative studies, based on survey research, of supposedly "objective" phenomena, such as voting patterns, rates of turnout, party identification, and comparative measures of "interest" in politics.[23] Since these methodologies defined (and continue to define) the discipline for years—affecting patterns of research funding, and evaluation of research for purposes of tenure and promotion—a great deal of feminist research on women and politics has conformed to this norm. Of course, feminist behavioral research in political science differs from traditional mainstream work in its insistence on the significance of examining *women's* particular patterns of participation and the ways they are similar to, or different from, those of men.[24] Nevertheless, as Janet Flammang has noted, studies undertaken with quantitative methodologies necessarily focus on actions and behaviors, and have tended to be much less concerned with the *meanings* people (and especially women) attach to those behaviors.[25]

In order to address the sorts of questions that historians and theorists have raised for us—questions that, I am arguing, are necessary for a fuller understanding of women's participation in politics—scholars will need to challenge the dominance of these narrowly-quantitative methodologies, and to supplement them with more qualitative methods, including participant observation, interviews, and case studies. Ferree and Miller would take the methodological challenges even further: "analysis of participation in terms of cognitive structure and organizational strategies of recruitment, rather than in terms of the specific motives *or* incentives individuals have for joining movements, reintroduces the old problem of participation in a new and potentially productive manner."[26] Of course, given the hegemony of behavioral methods within the discipline as a whole, these new approaches will not necessarily meet with easy acceptance. Nevertheless, as recent works amply demonstrate, they have much to offer, not only to the study of women and politics, specifically, but also to the broader study of political science.[27]

I suggest four general areas in which new research might be undertaken, and then look more specifically at the issues to be addressed under each rubric: (1) What are the patterns of women's mobilization into politics?: who gets involved and why? (2) What are the patterns of consciousness-change?: what happens to those who participate in "non-traditional" political activism? what is the relationship between grassroots activism and "politicization" more generally? (3) How do we evaluate the effectiveness of various strategies and/ or approaches to activism, e.g. "outsiders" vs. "insiders," efforts to create alternative institutions, protest vs. policy-making? and (4) What are the places where we are "stuck" either theoretically or politically, and can the study of non-traditional forms of participation contribute to addressing these dilemmas?

Mobilization: Who Gets Involved in Activism and Why?

Over the past decade or so, historians and feminist theorists have offered a variety of models to explain patterns of participation (or non-participation) by women. Temma Kaplan claimed that many women are activated by what she termed "female consciousness" (the understanding of what it is to be a woman that is specific to a particular culture and historical moment), a perspective that, although derived from the prevailing sexual division of labor may, nevertheless, generate compelling concepts of rights and obligations that can provide a context for radical collective action. And she suggested that, under certain circumstances, relatively conservative "female consciousness" can be transformed into a more contestatory "feminist consciousness."[28] Others have argued that it is women's concern for the safety and continuity of their families and communities that seems to engage them in political activity. Sara Ruddick and Jean Elshtain, for example, suggest that it is not so much a female consciousness as "maternal thinking" that characterizes the world-view of many women activists, and provides a framework for understanding their mobilization and goals.[29]

Mary Dietz, by contrast, has suggested that both female consciousness and maternal thinking are too limited in focus, and that women are activated by (and ought to be mobilized around) notions of citizenship and inclusivity. Darlene Clark Hine, Cheryl Gilkes, Nancy Hewitt, Deborah Gray White, and others, argue that, in the case of many black women activists, a key mobilizing factor is some notion of "race uplift." And, as we have seen, Wendy Sarvasy suggests that what motivated many women activists in the early years of the twentieth century was a notion of "social citizenship," which might be seen as another version of what Jane Addams referred to as "municipal housekeeping."[30]

Studies of women activists could explore whether any of these perspectives are helpful in understanding either patterns of mobilization or the construction of agendas for activism. Further, are there differences in patterns of engagement, or in grounds of mobilization, by race? class? age? region? Do participants' understandings of the grounds of their participation change over time? As a consequence of activism? In what ways? Do some of these perspectives/ideologies appeal to particular groups more than to others? If so, to which, and why?

There is room, here, for both historical and contemporary studies. Existing historical studies of communities and organizations can be re-examined for what light they shed on patterns of mobilization and for what they say about the relationship between the larger cultural/political context and women's participation. Do openings in more formal electoral or bureaucratic arenas seem to mean more or less nontraditional participation by women? Are there variations by class, race, ethnicity? What is the relationship between changing definitions of politics and women's participation in both formal and informal arenas? New studies of women's organizations might focus on some of these questions with an eye to their implications for participants' understandings of politics, participation, and citizenship. Do those who engage in so-called nontraditional forms of participation see it as second-best to electoral participation? Or do they see themselves as engaging in "politics by other means"? Do they understand themselves to be engaging in a critique of "normal politics"? To be struggling to change definitions of "the political"?

Beyond these questions, there is the issue of the contexts in which women *come* to politics: do their paths follow those predicted/described by pluralist models (i.e. of coming to an awareness of an interest, and then finding others who share it, and joining with them to insert their interest into the general political fray)? Or, does (women's) activism reflect a different understanding of the relationship between individuals, communities, and politics?[31] I have suggested above (Chapters 1, 2, 5, 8) that much women's activism belies both the distinction between public and private, and the extreme individualism, which ground dominant theories of political behavior. And I have argued that attention to it could lead us to question the relevance of those individualist models to men, as well as to women, leading, perhaps, to broader understandings of citizenship. Research on women who are engaged in such activities could help to shatter false dichotomies, and determine whether the apparent challenges to these ways of thinking and to individualist under-standings of mobilization into politics hold more broadly, and what their applications might be for how we understand both the domain of politics and the possibilities of citizenship.

Patterns of Consciousness-Change

What happens to participants once they engage in political activism (however defined)? Temma Kaplan wrote of the possibility of a shift from "female consciousness" to "feminist consciousness" as activism contributes to a con-sciousness of broader political issues.[32] Other studies of activists have suggested that a sense of empowerment comes from engaging with others in collective action. As one of Cynthia Cockburn's informants expressed it, "when you start getting involved, you find you're not a cabbage any more. You've got a mind and can do things."[33] How common are such transformations?: of a sense of self?; in relation to other family members?; to the larger community?; to other organizations?; to the political system more generally? What are the contexts in which such changes occur? What factors in the social/political context affect the likelihood of that transformation, and how do they vary by class, ethnicity, race, age, and sexual orientation? Do the patterns or processes differ as between formal and informal types of participation?

And what about that broader consciousness, or sense of empowerment, the recognition that one is "not a cabbage any more"? Does it transfer from one issue to another? Can we talk of people or groups empowered by their experiences in ways that change their orientation to politics and participation more generally? Or, to put it another way, is activism "addictive"? Many studies of politics and participation have suggested that *unsuccessful* activism has serious negative consequences—i.e., that those with experiences of protest without success are more likely than ever to be resigned to their fate.[34] Can these factors be overcome? Is *any* success better than none? Or does the sig-nificance of the issues addressed matter?[35] What is the relationship (if any) between "cooptation" and consciousness change? Does a changed conscious-ness lead to less likelihood of cooptation (as some studies might suggest)? What do we mean by "cooptation" in this sense? Do we understand it to mean (as many critics do) entry into the more formal or traditional political arena? If so, should we rethink its connotations?

More generally, it would also be important to know about cross-over or carry-over between grassroots/oppositional activism and more mainstream participation. Participation in civil rights movement organizations is one sort of case: there are well-known examples of male activists moving from civil rights movement organizations into electoral politics (e.g. Julian Bond, Jesse Jackson); and also of white women, for example, moving from activism in the civil rights movement into more explicitly feminist activities.[36] The con-sequences of women's participation in the National Welfare Rights Organization, however, are much less well-known. Although that organization had been established mainly by black male activists, the majority of its activists were women recipients of AFDC. Many of them, apparently, were politicized by their experiences and experienced themselves as more effective politically as a result of their participation. It would be important to explore further both what happened to their consciousness about the nature and meaning of politics, and what effect their participation had on their later activism in other contexts.[37]

How many women become active in their neighborhood or community in collective actions of one sort or another (e.g. school-related issues, environmental concerns, abortion rights, health care, etc.) and move from that into more conventional politics? (Mary Ford, the former mayor of Northampton, Massachusetts, for example, traces her political origins to the protest politics of the 1970s. Sally Martino Fisher and Marie Leanza, both of whom were active in local community struggles with the National Congress of Neighborhood Women in Brooklyn in the 1970s, are now involved in local NY City politics.) What factors make such cross-overs likely? or unlikely? Are there different patterns for people who get involved in different issues? Do patterns differ by age, race, class, sexual orientation? Are there differences between women and men? In short, do participants see these various forms of participation along a continuum (challenging, in yet another context, dichotomous ways of thinking about participation), or do they perceive a step-wise difference between grassroots and mainstream politics? In this regard, it will be interesting to be attuned to the effects of Barack Obama's recent electoral victory: what will happen to the millions of volunteers who were involved in the hybrid of electoral and community-based organizing that characterized his campaign?

Finally, what is the relationship between grassroots activism (or collective action) and politicization more generally? How, if at all, does participation in activities outside of the mainstream political arena affect (women's) overall interest in politics? Does it affect patterns of voting? of lobbying? of following local or national issues? Again, is there a continuum of politics that effectively includes informal, as well as formal, participation? Are there differences in awareness, in behavior, in attitudes between those who are engaged in mainstream institutions and practices and those who engage in more non-traditional forms? What institutional/structural factors affect mobilization into different types of activism? or the consciousness-change that does (or does not) take place as a result of it? Is the distinction that political scientists (and many politicians) tend to make between activism in organizations *versus* electoral participation a valid or helpful one?

Alternative Strategies: Strengths and Limits

One set of questions concerning strategies has to do with the relationship between the "insiders"—those working as elected policy-makers and bureaucrats (policy implementers)—and "outsiders"—protesters, demonstrators, those who attempt to establish alternative institutions, and the like. Rather than pose the question of the relative value of insider vs. outsider perspectives—thereby reinforcing a dichotomous understanding of these phenomena—I think more fruitful research would look at the relationship between the two modes or contexts of activism. Gelb, Gelb and Palley, Katzenstein, and Hart, for example, all point to the mutual interdependence of outsider and insider activists—the outsider activists need people in positions of authority and/or responsibility within institutions who can put into effect the policies they desire; whereas the insiders need external pressure groups both to serve as support networks for them and to keep pressure on the institutions. More research needs to be done as to what these relationships are, how the different groups perceive their roles, and what they count as successes. Also, how do those relationships vary with the different dimensions of policy-making: e.g. getting issues onto the agenda, legislating or otherwise formulating policy, and policy implementation? What are the relationships among women (and women's groups) at each stage? How do they vary? Do they change with different policy domains?[38]

What about different *forms* of activism? At the turn of the last century, women were active both in lobbying those with political power to address social issues such as women's labor, child labor, the needs of poor mothers, etc., at the same time that they (or others) were developing programs and institutions to meet some of the needs *not* being addressed by social policy. In our own day, there are those who create shelters for battered women, set up abortion or birth control clinics, develop assistance for those "squatting" in abandoned housing, or build housing for homeless women and their families; there are those who protest and lobby and devote their energies to getting these issues onto the public/political agenda; others who lobby policy-makers to ensure that those issues *on* the agenda will actually be translated into meaningful programs; and still others who are in positions to develop and implement these policy changes. What do relationships look like in each context? Are different types of activism more or less effective in different contexts? How does each group of actors view the others? their relationships? the political process as a whole?

How do these different types of participation affect contemporary understandings of the boundaries of politics? What kinds of activities tend to be labeled "disorderly" or "inappropriate"? Does the application of those labels vary with the class, race, age, or sexual orientation of the participants? Does participation initially labelled disorderly become accepted as orderly or appropriate? If so, by what process? What is the relationship between disorderly participants and political insiders? When, and how, have non-traditional forms of participation broadened the boundaries of politics—either by widening the definition of what constitutes legitimate political action/participation, or by forcing the inclusion of new issues onto the political agenda?[39]

Activism and Contemporary Theoretical Dilemmas

Finally, can broadening the study of women's participation contribute anything to the resolution of (or at least to addressing) some of the critical issues confronting contemporary feminist activists, politicians, and theorists? Here, I would mention two arenas in particular, though there are surely many more.

(a) Tensions surrounding "identity politics" and coalition-building. Both at the level of theorizing, and at the level of political practice, many groups—feminist and otherwise—have been caught up in attempting to address questions of equality and difference among women. These questions, of course, followed from those with which feminists initially engaged: questions of equality/difference between women and men. Early efforts focused on what differences "made a difference." That is to say, feminists recognized that men and women were socialized differently in most societies, and that they differed along biological/genetic lines. Early feminist work addressed questions such as how relevant biological differences were to gender-based patterns of dominance and subordination? On what grounds could one argue for equality between men and women, while yet acknowledging the ways that differences between them might well require different treatment?[40] More recently, analogous questions have arisen with respect to differences (of class, sexuality, race/ethnicity, age, etc.) *among* women. Growing numbers of feminists—especially those who are not white, middle-class, able-bodied, or Christians—are arguing that too much feminist theorizing and activism presupposes some notion of a "universal woman," analogous to that of "universal man," independent of any cultural/ethnic/class context—a notion that, in fact, denies the complex ways in which gender, race, class, sexuality, and ethnicity are socially-structured and mutually interdependent. At the same time, much post-modernist, post-structuralist feminist theorizing challenges the usefulness of fixed identity categories of any sort. The question these critiques pose for feminist theorizing—and for studies of women's participation—is a critical one: How can we move toward some sort of broad-based solidarity among women without (on the one hand) denying the differences of class, race, ethnicity, sexuality, etc. that exist among us or (on the other hand) reifying them and turning them into immutable and unbridgeable differences?[41]

We can find important clues to an answer by looking at the real political activities in which people (especially women) have engaged. With a few exceptions, we have not looked as carefully as we might at those moments where people from a variety of "identity categories" have engaged in real-life political struggle and resistance. We ought to be looking at grassroots participation around issues such as housing cost and availability, school desegregation, toxic wastes, etc. as resources for theory. Much, I think, can be learned from those who are acting and attempting to effect change—people who work with others who share various identity characteristics and at the same time form coalitions, on the basis of those characteristics, with others "unlike" themselves—even while experiencing the contingent and contested nature of their identities.[42]

Attention to such activities can also help us think about the relationship between identity(ies), activism, and coalition-building. What is the relationship between political participation (whether in the broad or narrow sense) and identity? Does grassroots participation engage and/or affect participants with respect to issues of identity differently than does electoral participation?[43] Is there a relationship between participation in politics (however defined) and willingness to engage in coalition-building? If so, in what direction? Is there a difference in the impacts of traditional vs. non-traditional participation on these sorts of changes?

(b) Creating alternatives to contemporary policy. Politically, we are at a major turning point in national policy debates about health care and wealth and income inequality; mortgage foreclosures and poverty are clearly much on the public consciousness. While there are real limits to the boundaries of those debates, and to the creativity and imagination apparently available to policy-makers (and even policy analysts and critics), nevertheless, the 2008 financial crisis may have opened up new possibilities for broad-based con-versation—and action. As resources, there are groups and organizations of women that have been addressing these issues "on the ground" for years—contemporary equivalents of the club women of the late nineteenth and early twentieth centuries, of the settlement house workers, of those who were attempting to establish what Wendy Sarvasy refers to as "social citizenship."[44] As historians look back on that period, they now recognize that activities that were *not* seen as "political" then were, in fact, essential components of the larger political landscape, and had important implications for what eventually met more narrow definitions of politics.[45]

While the larger context of political participation has certainly changed since then, there are, nevertheless, contemporary equivalents of those actors: those who are building housing for homeless women and their children, those who are members of organizations like "Up to Poverty" (a Massachusetts welfare rights organization that insisted that welfare benefit levels ought to be raised at least to support people at poverty levels) or Arise (a low-income and poor people's rights organization in Springfield, Massachusetts, that focuses on community organizing on welfare rights, health care reform, criminal justice, grassroots strategies to end violence against women, housing and homelessness issues, etc.). Cynthia Enloe has commented ironically, in another context, that "the more a government is preoccupied with what it calls national security, the less likely its women are to have the physical safety necessary for sharing their theorizing about the nation and their security within it."[46] But this holds true not only in the case of national security issues; the same could be said of us. Have we looked to the women who are organizing around these issues for any directions in policy-making? I suspect that the answer is not nearly as much as we might. After all, they are neither politicians nor policy-makers;

and most of their activity is taking place outside what we tend to recognize as "the political arena." But that does not mean that there is not much we might learn from it; studies of women's activism in these areas might well help expand our limited imaginations with respect to policy, just as women's activism at the turn of the century dramatically affected understandings of what issues were appropriate to politics and what could be done to address them.

In a variety of ways, then, a broadened study of women's participation becomes an essential component of any research agenda on (women in) American politics in the twenty-first century. Broadening the range of our attention will certainly make possible a more textured understanding of what happens (and why) within the traditional domain of politics. But there is more. Historically, women's participation has created new spaces for politics, and dramatically expanded our understandings of what politics is about. There is no reason to expect any less from contemporary activism (by both women and men). Indeed, the extensive "community organizing" component of Barack Obama's 2008 presidential election campaign—and the breadth of the coalitions formed in that campaign—provide some grounds for the belief that the new president and his advisors are aware of that potential, and prepared to draw on it. In the end, such attention has the potential not only to assist in addressing some critical problems, but to expand and deepen our perspective on the nature and possibilities of both politics and citizenship.

10

WOMEN'S COMMUNITY ACTIVISM AND THE REJECTION OF "POLITICS"

Some Dilemmas of Popular Democratic Movements

Recent studies of gender and citizenship have raised two sets of questions—one practical, one theoretical—that I explore in this chapter. The practical concerns the claim, common among grassroots activists both in the US and elsewhere, that their activities are "not political." In some ways, of course, we might find this perfectly understandable: after a brief respite in the 1950s and 1960s from a rather long-standing bad "rep," politics in the US has again become identified with (often even treated as a synonym for) corruption and sleaze, a set of activities in which supposedly decent people should not want to be engaged. This is a perspective that was certainly common in the US toward the end of the nineteenth century, and has long been familiar in much of Latin America, Africa, and in Eastern Europe. Nevertheless, while this tendency to distance oneself from politics may be all too understandable, it is particularly problematic and disturbing at a time when so much of our national (and international) politics seems aimed at a depoliticization of the populace: increasingly, for example, whether with respect to welfare policy, corporate oversight, or national security, we are told that matters are best left to experts. So, one of my concerns here has to do with the implications of this "rejection of the political" for democratic politics.

The second, theoretical, starting point is the recent growth of feminist writing about citizenship—much of it in response to Jürgen Habermas' call for the reclaiming of a "public sphere." Habermas' notions have proved particularly fertile, and generated a burgeoning literature, including extensive feminist discussions about what Nancy Fraser has referred to as "subaltern counterpublics." While Habermas' (and his critical followers') calls for a reinvigorated, gender- and class-neutral, public sphere are certainly compelling, I often find myself wondering just how such ideals might be put into practice. How do we assure that some newly-formulated public sphere will not simply recreate relationships of exclusion, power, and domination in new guise? Further, what would it take to *sustain* subaltern counterpublics?

145

These two sets of questions came together for me in thinking about an essay by Brazilian feminist scholar Evelina Dagnino who, in her introduction to an anthology on new social movements in Latin America, noted that most of those movements focused on broadening (or creating) a more democratic political arena, and treated "the politico-cultural understanding of differences" as a necessary prerequisite to the creation of democracy—that is, to the building of a political community that can incorporate those (social, cultural, economic) differences in a more egalitarian fashion.[1] Feminist theoretical conversations in the US, of course, have focused on "difference" for some years now; but it has all-too-rarely been the case that our theoretical conversations have had much to do with practical political activism. I have long believed, however, that the practical knowledge activists have gained through working in their communities might be fruitfully brought into more direct engagement with feminist/democratic theorists and theories.

This chapter represents an effort at such a confrontation of practice with theory. I want to set out some questions about the meanings of democracy, politics, and participation in our current context, and then hold them up against the activities of the National Congress of Neighborhood Women (NCNW), an organization founded in Brooklyn, NY, in 1974.[2] I want, that is, to begin the process of exploring what the NCNW might be able to teach us about some of the perquisites of democratic civic engagement.

Citizenship as a Site of Exclusion or of Inclusion? Habermas and his Feminist Critics

Increasing numbers of critics in recent years have pointed to the fact that exclusions and divisions are central to the logic of liberal democratic theory and practice. Scholars ranging from Carole Pateman to Judith Shklar, and from Gwendolyn Mink to Charles Mills have noted that citizenship, as it exists in many western democracies, has been constructed through a variety of exclusions, based on gender, race, class, sexuality, migration status, and so on.[3] A great deal of feminist scholarship, of course, has focused on addressing one important context of exclusion: the so-called public–private split. Critics have pointed out that, while the public realm is presented as one where free and equal citizens engage together in striving for some common good, that arena depends on a private/domestic realm that is characterized by relationships of *in*equality and dependence, and is focused on meeting life's necessities. Furthermore, that so-called private realm tends to be defined in profoundly gendered, classed, and racialized ways. In the US during the nineteenth century and well into the twentieth, such a formulation resulted in an ambiguous citizenship status for all those who were not self-supporting males: including poor free white men, slaves, free blacks in the post-Emancipation/pre-Civil Rights era, and women.[4] And, further, the split meant that the domain of politics (in the sense of public business) was limited to activities that took place only in that public arena. Consequently, inequalities, injustices, and various forms of domination that characterized the household and (for many years) workplaces were deemed private matters, beyond the appropriate domain of politics—or legal regulation. Equally significantly, activities undertaken to *challenge* those categories (or to broaden the domain of politics) could be ignored, or dismissed as irrelevant.

A central focus of feminist scholarly work in political theory has been to call into question this dichotomy and to highlight its relationship to notions of independence and dependence. Feminists have pointed out the gendered nature of both public and private domains, and the interdependence of each on the other. In addition, they have noted the mystifications inherent in any concept of "independence," which had been taken to be the prime characteristic of actors in that "public" domain.[5] The focus on supposedly-independent actors in a public/political arena, however, obscures the fact that no one is truly independent; what appears as the independence of some is premised on the dependence of others (and vice versa). Further, as Carole Pateman has argued, the mythical social contract which grounds US political self-understanding obscures its *sexual* dimensions: the "independent" role is a male one, defined, at least in part, by contrast to the situation of the women and children dependent on him.[6] These perspectives on what defines the domain of the political have far-ranging consequences. They can affect what problems are thought to merit public/political attention, what actions are considered relevant—even legitimate—political behavior, and who will participate with what effects in the larger arena of politics. Conversely, they can result in a tendency to ignore, devalue, or define as outside the appropriate domain of politics those activities which challenge the boundaries of public and private. Finally, to the degree that such frameworks successfully exclude people or issues from the agenda of politics, they can act powerfully to limit effective participation in the formal political realm.

In response to some of the problematic ways citizenship has been defined and regulated, many scholars have turned to the work of Jürgen Habermas—in particular to his notion of a discursive "public sphere"—in the hope that it could offer a framework for constructing a more egalitarian, democratic, inclusive, public space. Building on the claim that citizenship offers a powerful language for inclusionary political movements,[7] these scholars argue that the public sphere can be reclaimed from its exclusivist uses, and reconstructed as a site for enacting broad understandings of politics and citizenship, which incorporate a full range of our diverse population.[8] Although the promises of democracy have not been fulfilled even in many supposedly democratic societies, the vision is still a compelling one. As Anne Phillips suggests,

> [R]ejecting both the false harmony that stamps out difference and the equally false essentialism that defines people through some single, authentic, identity, many look to a democracy that maximizes

citizen participation and requires us to engage and contest with one another.[9]

Rethinking Democracy and the Public Sphere from a Feminist Perspective

Neither this scholarly literature nor contemporary public policy debates about the decline of civil society, however, provide us with very good models for *how* to reconceptualize citizenship along these lines. Indeed, there often seems to be very little relationship between public policy debates about how to increase public interest in, and/or engagement with, political institutions and the scholarly literature that highlights the ambiguities and complexities of both the theory and the practice of citizenship in the US.[10]

Nevertheless, some such work is being done, particularly by feminist theorists. Seyla Benhabib, for example, argues that we need a "critical model of public space and public discourse" that can enable us to imagine (and people to strive for) "collective democratic empowerment over" needs, as opposed to a more distant "bureaucratic administration of" them.[11] Julie White offers a "democratic practice of care" as a way to begin constructing an inclusive arena of public deliberation—particularly over needs. Thus, she proposes *politicizing* what (namely, needs) is often treated as *outside* politics, at the same time that she argues for meaningful incorporation of diverse groups into deliberations about policies.[12] Mary Ryan notes that "the American public sphere was constructed in the shadow of both gender restrictions and an emerging private sector of social life" while recognizing, nevertheless, that US politics has been democratized—precisely by groups fighting their way in from the margins. This paradox points to the need to modify the idea of *a* public sphere, and to move toward a more plural and decentered vision of *multiple* arenas for participation—even while being aware that those who *do* challenge dominant paradigms of appropriate behavior will likely be dismissed as "disorderly."[13]

Nancy Fraser has argued that, even in highly stratified societies—where talk of a "discursive arena" can easily mask relations of domination and subordination—discussions of politics that focus on the public sphere can be valuable in pointing to the need for "subaltern counterpublics," "discursive arenas where members of subordinated social groups invent and circulate counterdiscourses to formulate oppositional interpretations of their identities, interests, and needs."[14] Iris Young argued that civil society "enables the emergence of public spheres in which *differentiated social sectors* express their experience and formulate their opinions ... the public sphere enables citizens to expose injustice in state and economic power and make the exercise of power more accountable" (emphasis mine).[15] Significantly, such visions tend to emphasize the importance of bringing people together in a *reconstructed* public sphere that will incorporate existing differences. Even though those differences may mark lines of differential power and privilege, a public arena for contestation might still allow people to engage more-or-less equally both in determining its agenda and participating in its deliberations. Indeed, as Julie White notes, it may be that *only* in a context where differences are acknowledged and named rather than ignored is there a possibility of meaningful democratic political engagement.[16] Or, as Shane Phelan has put it, "[W]e can only come to community by negotiating about what we will have in common, what we will share, and how we will share it."[17]

Of course, these formulations raise further questions: What is necessary to sustain "subaltern counterpublics"?[18] What would it mean to welcome new groups into the public arena in significant ways? What are the criteria for assuring that discussions in which we "negotiate about what we will have in common, what we will share, and how we will share it" do not, themselves, perpetuate the relationships of exclusion, of power and domination, that feminists and other social critics have worked so hard to uncover and contest? What would it mean to have a truly *diverse* participating citizenry? How would we learn to engage *with* our differences, rather than trying to deny them or insist that they do—or ought—not make any difference? These remain the critical questions for a contemporary politics of inclusion and resistance. Discourses of citizenship, and of a public sphere, while, on the one hand, constituted by exclusions, have, on the other, provided a space to *contest* those same exclusions. Both "citizenship" and "democracy" are powerfully evocative terms. Nevertheless, they remain deeply problematic. Can we reclaim and revive them without reinscribing the exclusions on which they have been based? Or, to phrase it somewhat melodramatically, how do we achieve broad-based participation by a truly diverse citizen body—and survive it?

The Rejection of "Politics" and the Politics of Depoliticization

The insistence on the part of many grassroots activists that their activities are "not political" is, as I suggested earlier, hardly unique to the current (post-Watergate, post-9/11, post-financial crisis) US context. A variety of studies of such activists—focusing on groups as diverse as anti-toxic waste protestors in rural North Carolina, ethnic-cultural identity movements in Latin America, anti-poverty activists in New York and Philadelphia, and even some anti-apartheid activists in South Africa—have pointed out that participants were hesitant to identify themselves as "political." As Nancy Naples noted in her work on community-based "activist mothers" during the War on Poverty, many of them made a separation between what they described as their "community work" and what they identified as "politics."[19] The women saw community work as simply an expression of their roles as wives and mothers, "a logical extension of their desire to improve the lives of their families and neighbors," what Temma Kaplan had earlier termed "female consciousness."[20]

In Kaplan's work on women in a variety of grassroots movements, as well as in numerous case studies of US-based local community activism, and in studies of new social movements in Latin America, we find similar rejections of "politics."[21] Furthermore, we see patterns of mobilization and consciousness that seem to link this "refusal of politics" to a distinction similar to that Nancy Fraser describes as a "politics of needs" as opposed to a "politics of rights."[22] In his study of women's participation in urban movements in Mexico City, for example, Miguel Díaz-Barriga noted that many of the activists denied that they were engaging in politics, which they seemed to identify with "the violent and corrupt public sphere of male politics." Rather, their activism seemed to depend on their understanding of it as separate from more traditional forms of political activity, and as rooted in *"necesidad."* He argued that they believed themselves to be creating a "borderland region between the domestic and public spheres."[23]

This splitting between an activism based on needs and what participants understand to be "politics" represents a theme common to many of these movements. Yet Naples, Kaplan, Molyneux, Díaz-Barriga, and others have all argued that, although many activists may initially be drawn out of their households by relatively conventional understandings of their roles as women, these activities often bring them into confrontation with political authorities, or with men and women of other communities, awakening them to a consciousness of inequality, motivating them to further struggles, and, ultimately, politicizing them.[24] Nevertheless, if the protestors, themselves, reject a construction of their actions as "political," then to what extent *are* they being politicized? How likely are they to translate (or transfer) the knowledge they have gained in their struggles around necessities in their communities to any broader political context? How likely are they to change their understandings of themselves in relation to the larger community? How effective is such activism in creating the building blocks of more inclusive democratic practices? More to the point: under what circumstances do people shift from an *essentialized* understanding of needs as *outside* the realm of politics to a *politicized* view of them as the "stuff" of politics?[25]

It is in such a context that we can see the potentially critical role of the language of democracy. What is needed, here, is a reshaping not just of the ways the *academy* defines politics and activism,[26] but, also, of what constitutes the *public's* understanding of these terms. So, for example, Iris Young defines "civil society" as a kind of activity identified with the "associational life world," rather than with *either* the state *or* the economy.[27] She goes on to describe three levels of associative activity within civil society: private association, civic association, and political association. Political associations are those that "self-consciously focus ... on claims about what the social collective ought to do ... Political activity is any activity whose aim is to *politicize* social or economic life ... to raise questions about how society should be organized."[28] Contrary to much commonly-held belief, to be "political" is not necessarily to engage in the formal electoral/political system, i.e., to engage with the state; but it *is* to struggle, together with others, to influence what will be on the *agenda* of the community. The question remains, however: how to enable/encourage those who see themselves as engaging with others "simply to meet their needs" to recognize that such engagement *is* a form of politics? Does the language of needs contribute to, or inhibit, that recognition? Do people see themselves as citizens or as clients? And how do changes in the realm of public policy affect those understandings?[29]

But the problem with a language of "meeting needs," rather than of "engaging in politics," goes even deeper; for, basing claims on needs can sometimes be more *dis*empowering than empowering. In the US context, for example, Patricia Williams has questioned the value of a needs-based strategy for achieving greater equity for African Americans. If we look historically, she argues, blacks have *not* been well served by a language of needs; on the contrary, their needs have been consistently denied. For African Americans in the US, the critical issue is not to assert needs, but "to find a political mechanism that can confront the *denial* of need."[30] Although a language of rights does not guarantee anything—slaves, for example, were not protected by a rights discourse because they were not granted the basic status of "rights-bearing individuals"—at least it provides an *opening*. Williams' argument is parallel to the claim that the discourse of citizenship can open a space for inclusionary movements, even if it has often been applied in exclusionary ways. What if Williams' claim holds more broadly, however, and those who say they are not engaging in politics, but, instead, are organizing to meet their community's needs, are, in effect, *undermining* their long-term prospects for effecting meaningful change? (Another prime example of the way a language of needs can be *de*-politicizing is, of course, in the discourse of welfare, where those with "needs" for public assistance are increasingly defined in *terms of those needs*, and treated as less than full citizens.)[31]

Finally, many of these same studies also highlight the ambiguous role of the state in providing a context for community-based activism. Naples' study of women anti-poverty activists during the War on Poverty notes that activism was both facilitated and inhibited by state policy.[32] The state often plays a contradictory role as both a "catalyst for, and site of, women's politicization." It "not only supports the reproduction of gender, racial-ethnic, and class inequality, but also provides avenues through which these patterns can be challenged."[33] LaDoris Payne, now Director of WomanSpirit—an NCNW-affiliated organization in St. Louis—got her start as an organizer through the War on Poverty, when she was hired as a Community Outreach worker.[34] In Brooklyn, the NCNW used money from CETA (the Comprehensive Employment and Training Act) to employ low-income women from the neighborhood, and to pay them (among other things) for community organizing. Those funds—together with its neighborhood college program— helped to support and politicize significant numbers of neighborhood women.

Conversely, however, when Federal funds ran dry, many of the organization's programs had to be discontinued or dramatically scaled-back. Ultimately, as Iris Young also argued, effective social change will require not only an active (politicized) civil society, but also engagement in more traditional domains of politics, such as elections, lobbying, and so on.[35] Further, the former may well lead (or contribute) to the latter.

Incorporating Difference: NCNW

A focus on the programs of the National Congress of Neighborhood Women (NCNW) allows us to explore the ways these questions of politics, needs, empowerment, and public space have played out in practice. The NCNW was established in 1974–75, with the aim of "meeting the needs and strengthening the abilities and power base of poor and working class women."[36] Its goal was "to provide a voice for working class and poor women working on issues to improve their communities, families, and their own status,"[37] by (1) working with them to recognize and develop the strengths they already had; and (2) teaching skills to enable them to take more active roles in the revitalization of their neighborhoods and communities. The organization saw itself explicitly as "encouraging political involvement" in broad terms:

> We favor self-determination and self-help for ourselves and our communities, but we believe that government has a responsibility to assist people to help themselves. While we are non-partisan and non-ideological, we encourage political involvement and the use of political activity to accomplish our goals.[38]

This phrasing articulates a rather sophisticated understanding of "political involvement," one not limited to conventional forms of political participation. But it is not always clear that this politicized perspective on community activism was fully shared by all those involved. Equally significantly, I want to explore the relationship between these overtly political goals of the NCNW and its policies and programs on diversity.

Naming Women's Leadership

Why an organization specifically for working-class women? Because, as NCNW literature and spokespersons made clear, the first step toward effective activism is awareness—coming to recognize *oneself* and one's friends/colleagues as capable participants.[39] Further, as Jan Peterson, the founder of the organization noted, both mainstream (largely middle-class-oriented) women's organizations and the overwhelmingly male leadership of the local community were ignoring the needs and concerns of working-class, community-based women. When she moved to Brooklyn in the early 1970s to direct a CETA anti-poverty program in Williamsburg-Greenpoint, Peterson discovered that the traditional leaders of the community were not listening to her, or to other women:

> She could see that the "overseers" and many local leaders were in agreement on one thing: a woman's place was in the home. Even so, many ordinary "housewives" were actually working very hard to sustain and enhance the life of the community through PTAs, block associations, tenants' groups in the projects, political clubs, and churches.[40]

Eventually, Peterson was able to use the framework of CETA to hire some of these women to work on community improvement—in the course of which, they began to recognize their own and one another's skills.

Jan Peterson's background in both the Civil Rights Movement and the women's movement seems to have been quite important to her understandings of "politics" and of activism, and in the consequent formulation of many of NCNW's approaches. In both of those movements, politics was understood to mean connecting the personal and the political through programs of education and consciousness-raising, with the aim of enabling those who had been subordinated to develop, in the words of Martin Luther King, Jr., a sense of being "somebody." Further, her experiences in the Civil Rights movement made Peterson particularly sensitive to issues of incorporating women of diverse ethnic and racial groups within the organization. As she put it: "The civil rights movement saved my life." Additionally, having the CETA money "allowed us to try experiments like that ... We had CETA; we could sit in rooms and argue it out with one another ... It was an incredible luxury; but it also made possible some tremendously important learning."[41]

Both my own interviews with members of the NCNW and others recorded at various points in the history of the organization indicate that many women active in it had an ambiguous relationship to the feminist movement. On the one hand, Jan Peterson, in particular, was a committed feminist, and had ties to feminist organizations in Manhattan, where she had lived before moving to Brooklyn. On the other hand, many of the local women participants in the group—in Williamsburg, initially, mostly Italian-American working-class women; later, and elsewhere, including many African American and Latina working-class and poor women—reported considerable alienation from mainstream feminism. One major source of their suspicions had to do with the place of family and community in their lives. Jan Peterson noted that

> the original feminist analysis was that in order to gain power over our own lives, we had to leave our families and neighborhoods. That's how I got from a small town in the Midwest to New York. The National Congress of Neighborhood Women grew out of the attempt

to support women who have a commitment to family and neighborhood ... There are two different women's movements. Our women's
movement deals with poor and working class women who see their
families and neighborhoods as fundamentally part of who they are.[42]

One local woman who was active in NCNW had actually attended a meeting
of the National Organization of Women (NOW) in Manhattan, but "couldn't
relate to the women there: ... We were family people and we lived for our
families ... We were largely Italian and that means a strong sense of family. In
our eyes, they were telling us to leave our families and homes."[43]

Nevertheless, even though the women saw themselves as rooted firmly in
their families and community, the place where they faced the most blatant
sexism was within community organizations. As one participant wrote,
describing their experiences:

> They live in a world where 'Father knows best,' and if mother knows
> best, she keeps it to herself. The men in the community weren't
> threatened by the women's activities until they began to enter the
> male "sphere." Women worked hard fighting for community issues as
> "auxiliary divisions" of male-based organizations. However, once
> federal funds became available or bows were to be taken, it was
> suddenly the men who did it all.[44]

She went on to cite another's depiction of her first foray into the official public
arena:

> The first time I spoke in public, I was so scared I almost dropped
> dead. The only reason that I could do it was that I was so hopping
> mad at the men in the meeting. They either refused to recognize the
> women who'd had a lot of experience on the issue, or kept shutting
> them up. I sat there for over two hours, just seething and burning.
> Then I spoke over the men's voices: They were all screaming for
> me to sit down. I kept screaming too. That was my first speech.
> Hysterical.[45]

NCNW's programs and training materials addressed both these issues—
"feminism" and the empowerment of women *as* women on the one hand; and
the need to recognize and highlight women's contributions to the community,
on the other. As early as its founding in 1974, NCNW's principles included
the following:

> *Empowerment*: We are committed to building women's consciousness of
> their power and potential, of their right to self-realization, of their
> right and capacity to define and solve their own problems, and to

doing this by stressing recognition of their strengths and by offering education and skill-building in a manner that does not alienate them from themselves and their roots.

Families: We recognize that families come in ever-changing forms; but whatever the form, we affirm the importance of families to the healthy development of both adults and children. And, we are committed to strengthening family life and to helping families function well for all their members.[46]

The framing of issues is also significant here: as early as 1974, and continuing until today, what we find is less a language of women's rights, than of a community's needs; as Jan Peterson described it, "We are *not* rights-based; we're about development. About implementation on the ground, and improving the situation of *communities*, and of women *in* them."[47] Or, in the words of LaDoris Payne, discussing her work in St. Louis:

> The part of St. Louis that I live in is an underdeveloped community within a developed one ... we have no theater, no hospital, no public library. It is a community under threat: gentrifying, and slated for industrial development. Unemployment and health care are our big issues ... I got involved about 30 years ago through War on Poverty Programs as a community outreach worker ... it was as much self-help as anything. I'm not a social worker by training or inclination; I'm a freedom fighter![48]

Virtually none of the many women with whom I spoke used a language of rights; they described their concerns and activities in terms of meeting needs and, most directly, improving the community: establishing a senior center, a day-care center, struggling for traffic lights, and so forth.

Initially, many community women were wary of the organization. Ann Giordano acknowledged that, when she first met women who identified as feminists, she wasn't particularly interested in what they had to say: "We didn't want to philosophize and ideologize about how women are discriminated against." But when Jan Peterson sent around a survey asking what the women might want, "people got interested because it was *doing*, not sitting around and talking ... And they were taking these classes to better their families and the community."[49] Similarly, Habiba Soudan, who has been active in organizing in the African American community in Camden, NJ, for many years, and became involved in NCNW in the late-1980s, noted that NCNW enabled women not just to *find* their voices, but to *use* them—for the betterment of themselves, to be sure, but also, for their communities and families.[50]

The language of "needs" is significant here, in two respects. First, the early organizers approached community women not in terms of what their *(political) demands* were, but what their self-defined *needs* were. This made the process less threatening. But, second, that approach allowed/enabled the women to *participate in the definition and interpretation of their needs*, a process that Julie White, for example, names as critical to what she terms a non-paternalist "democratic politics of care."[51] On a related note, a number of the women pointed out that, when they first got involved with the Congress, they did so out of their concerns as mothers. In the words of one: "I was always a fighter. In my own little way, ... I always fought for the issues—if I knew it would affect my kids, I would fight for that, no matter what."[52] NCNW's programs helped her both to recognize herself *as* a leader, and to see that her activities had political significance beyond the needs of her family.

The organization developed materials that would translate these concepts into simple language—making clear to women who had long been involved in their communities that they *were* leaders, and could—and should—take themselves seriously as such. Thus, a training manual prepared for the James Weldon Johnson Tenant Association in East Harlem, NY (which developed in collaboration with the NCNW) offered a brief quiz, "Am I a leader?" in which it asked readers whether they had been involved with tenant association meetings, PTAs, church suppers, talking with neighbors about community issues, and then went on to insist, "These are all LEADERSHIP ACTIVITIES ... And *you* do some of them! ... YOU ARE A LEADER!!"[53]

In addition to working with the women to help them recognize their own leadership capacities and to develop new ones, the organization reached out to other groups in the community to encourage them to overcome their sexism and incorporate women more fully—insisting that such practices would benefit everyone. So, for example, in February 1981, Jan Peterson sent out a two-page memo to "Neighborhood Leaders" with suggestions about "how to include women effectively in your efforts to revitalize neighborhoods." Its opening paragraph read

> Women have long supplied the raw labor power in grassroots organizations, yet their needs and issues have not been addressed. Volunteer women may organize the church supper to raise money, but they are excluded from the decision-making body that plans how the money is spent. Often grassroots organizing begins with the women, only to have leadership become male as the group mushrooms into coalition with broader recognition or obtains sizeable funding such as the neighborhood community corporations around the country ... Finally, since men and women have been conditioned to different priorities, issues at the local level such as women's health care services and daytime street safety, are not as readily attended to. In fact, most grassroots women's programs like those dealing with wife abuse, rape, etc. are not even perceived as part of the organized neighborhood effort.

> We believe that all of these problems occur because people are not
> aware of how to incorporate women effectively in the effort to revi-
> talize neighborhoods.

This introduction was followed by a list of questions that the organizations
could ask themselves about their programs, such as "Are women involved in
initiation?," "Do women participate in the direction of the project?," "What
are the benefits of this project to women? Directly? Indirectly? Do the participants perceive them as benefits in key areas in their lives … Does the project
contribute to increasing women's access to knowledge, resources, the power
structure?" Finally, "Does this project increase women's options, raise their
status?"[54]

The first step, then, is awareness of—consciousness-raising about—the *need*
for empowerment, for women to take significant roles in their communities.
NCNW took—and continues to take—the issue of empowerment very seriously. At the core of its activities were programs of education and leadership
training.

Leadership Training as Recognizing the Strength in Diversity

> We needed to *talk* about our different experiences so that people could
> understand each other. We *were* different; we couldn't pretend that different
> things didn't bother us.[55]

An early NCNW report on its activities made clear that the development of
an awareness of women's leadership potential was a primary focus of its programs. I want to focus, here, on what seems to me a particularly unusual
aspect of those programs: the NCNW's insistence—in the context of an
otherwise relatively fractured women's movement—that critical to the development of that potential was an ability to work with, and to value, diversity.
In particular, its leadership training program aimed

> [to] help women to see why they need the support of other women
> leaders, how to build and maintain a support system, how to network
> and share skills with other women, and how to build alliances across
> lines that have often divided people and prevented poor and working
> class communities from obtaining power.[56]

As Jan Peterson noted, when asked about the goals of the NCNW:

> [T]he role of NCNW is to strip women of all those kinds of things—
> the indifferences, and divisions of color, culture, religion and all the

other kinds of things that prevent women ... from working together—and *make them deal with them* so that we can work towards the
real goal ... [which] is providing a country that we all feel good
about as women. Where there are decent jobs for all people, decent
salaries for all our people; decent housing for all people.[57]

Before turning to a more in-depth exploration of those programs, however, I
want to acknowledge the complicated place of leadership, and especially of
leadership development, in a participatory-democratic organization. On the
one hand, such programs might seem like contradictions in terms: if one insists
that women are equally capable, along with men, of taking leadership in their
communities; if one insists, in fact, that women *are already* leaders in their
communities, whence a need for leadership training? What is the relationship
between leadership *training* and leadership *support*? Is not any concept of
leadership training self-contradictory?

The short answer to this last question is: yes and no. Many democrats have
acknowledged that democratic skills need to be nurtured and developed.
People are capable of participation; but they will participate more effectively if
they are "prepared" to do so.[58] What is critical is the level of respect accorded
to the perspectives of community people, themselves. Julie White's framing of
a distinction between "paternalism" and a "democratic politics of care" is
helpful here. White calls for a "participatory politics of need interpretation"
that stands in opposition to paternalism, understood "not as the problem of
intervention in the lives of (self-regarding) others, but as speaking for others in
the process of defining their needs." An alternative process would privilege
"the voice of those presently 'in need' in the course of defining 'need' and
determining arrangements of resources to meet those needs."[59] NCNW's leadership training programs should be considered within such a context: they
were developed in response to a survey of neighborhood women in which
those women expressed a desire to improve their organizational leadership
skills.

To return, then, to the place of diversity work within these leadership programs: Virtually every member spoke of the importance of that work as a
central feature of NCNW's activities. Ann Giordano credits the work with a
broad impact on the community of Greenpoint/Williamsburg:

I've always taken pride that we, as diverse as we are, have not had
the kind of problems that Crown Heights has had, that Bensonhurst
has had ... Because the National Congress did so much diversity
work and had so many people out there that even if you don't agree
with it all, you can't sell it out ... You can't buy into racism totally,
even if you are a racist, because there's a part of you that knew a
nice Black person or a nice Hispanic person. So you can't sell that
person out.[60]

Training programs that specifically addressed issues of diversity were a key part of NCNW's goals from the beginning. For example, its 1974 statement of principles included:

> *Support Groups and Networks*: Because of multiple and conflicting demands made upon women which often lead to feelings of inadequacy, isolation, illegitimacy and self-denial, we believe in the importance of women's support groups and supportive networks ... support groups should promote the honest sharing of feelings, information and aspirations in an atmosphere of caring and confidentiality where difference is both recognized and respected.
>
> *Diversity*: We are committed to fostering understanding and respect for personal and group diversity, especially class, race and cultural differences, and to the use of consciously adopted methods to accomplish this. We are convinced that these and other differences must be made visible and celebrated for true tolerance and community to exist.[61]

Early in its existence, NCNW surveyed women in the community who *had* taken some leadership, and asked them what they felt they needed to move to a "next step." Their responses indicated that "they felt they had to develop certain skills to build self-confidence." In addition to developing basic skills necessary for leadership, they needed work on issues of diversity: "Women in these communities haven't had the experience of working together because things are basically structured around the family unit. A lot of these women had never worked with different ethnic or racial groups. In order to make the community survive, they have to have the experience of understanding their common needs."[62] The overall goal of the organization, then, was "not only to empower [low-income and working-class] women, but [to] build coalitions among different ethnic groups ... that are concerned with the same kind of issues."[63] Critical to the achievement of that goal was making face-to-face contact with women, encouraging them, and urging them to be in touch with women in other communities, similarly situated.

The centerpiece of NCNW's programs to develop women's leadership was the Leadership Support Group, designed to enable "women to get together with their peers to share experiences, feelings, ideas, strategies, skills and other resources in a supportive environment."[64] The basic idea was to provide a confidential and non-judgmental context for women leaders to think through, together with others, the issues they are confronting in their neighborhoods and communities. Groups consist of 10 to 15 women, who commit to meet once a week for a minimum of three months, in two-to-four-hours sessions. Suggested plans for sessions include a general discussion topic (e.g. availability of child-care in the community, growing up, relationships with people in other groups ...), and then time for an "individual problem discussion," in which one of the members has an opportunity to present a problem she is dealing with, and to get feedback from the group.

It is in the guidelines for general discussions that we see the explicit addressing of issues of diversity. Many of the suggested topics deal with personal issues, and are designed to give participants a chance to get to know one another, as well as to explore dimensions of their own lives that they might not have thought about in this way. Participants are to think about the question at hand (e.g. "growing up as girls") in terms of a variety of factors that might have affected their experience, including gender, race, class, ethnicity, age, sexual orientation, and others. After addressing personal issues, groups are encouraged to move on to look at institutions (family, financial, churches, educational, media, various movements), thinking about how they (and members of their group) have been affected by them, or might (have) organize(d) to effect change in them. Making attention to issues of difference among the women an explicit focus of every session represented an effort to break down the barriers that often divide women from one another, and that may prevent their building the sorts of alliances and coalitions which would be necessary for any change to occur. The "personal was political," but not in some narrow sense. More accurately, perhaps, "the personal/political is diverse."[65] Participants who reflected back on their experiences noted, repeatedly, that this process of learning about themselves and one another was one of the most valuable aspects of their participation in the organization. Finally, it's important to note that the organization seems regularly to have undertaken these sorts of workshops with its own staff, enabling them to address issues of difference among themselves—including between professional and clerical staff.[66]

Finally, the groups were meant to address women's fears related to taking power, and the tensions that can arise from competition.

> The final issue regarding support is to learn that providing support to another's leadership growth doesn't take away from ours ... Enjoying watching another woman grow and seeing that every woman taking a step means that more of us can do it is essential ... We must get over past hurts and internalized ideas that say that women can't stick together or must claw each other. In our support groups we will learn how to deal with how we have personally hurt each other; learn how women have been historically pitted against each other, and develop ways to change all this and develop relationships built on mutual trust.[67]

By 1982, NCNW was able to report, in a description of its Leadership Development Project, that

> over the past 18 months, with government and foundation support, NW has involved over 400 women leaders in its first National

Leadership Development Project. With the assistance and commitment of a diverse group of ten neighborhood women leaders from around the country, NW has developed a leadership support training model that draws on the experience of poor and working class women's work in their communities. The training helps women to see why they need the support of other women leaders, how to build and maintain a support system, how to network and share skills with other women, and how to build alliances across lines that have often divided people and prevented poor and working class communities from obtaining power.[68]

One of the most important lessons learned from this process was overcoming the resignation that characterized the lives of so many in the community:

A lot of what I do in my work today is ... understanding yes, you're in poverty, but you don't have to stay there ... it's helped me tremendously to ... try and pass on to other women that you never have to accept where you are in life ... The feeling of powerlessness and the acceptance is so strong in people, and how do you break it? It's like a constant struggle ... to show people that you don't have to do it.[69]

Empowered by their participation in these groups, women from NCNW established a college program in the community, organized to "save" a firehouse, worked with others to preserve bus routes in the community (and institute new ones), called local politicians to account, helped rehabilitate an abandoned hospital into housing for low-income families, and engaged in numerous other activities which eventually drew together women from both Italian American and African American neighborhoods in the area.

Beginnings of Conclusions

For the women of the NCNW, the need for civic participation—for women to take a role in improving their communities and in developing plans for the future—was a given. But they recognized that, in a context of inequality and massive structural oppression, such activities would not necessarily come easily or "naturally." Women needed concrete and ongoing support if they were to break free of dominant communal stereotypes (like: women belong in the kitchen), and claim recognition for the roles they were, in fact, already filling in their communities. Activism by isolated, individual women, or activism that was limited to one specific issue was not their goal. Rather, if women were to become more fully engaged citizens on an on-going basis, and see themselves as such, those taking part in activities needed to name what they were doing *as* political engagement, and to recognize themselves as leaders. Only that combination of acknowledgment—of themselves, from others, and from the larger community—would enable them to continue to engage, and to move into larger, and potentially more conflictual, arenas.

But the organization went beyond empowerment at the level of the individual, or even the neighborhood or community. Recognizing that a significant part of the experience of women, in particular, in working-class communities in the US is to be alienated from ongoing structures and institutions of power and influence, to be subject to economic and social forces over which those communities have little control, they insisted that working-class women learn how to build bridges to others who might seem unlike them, to overcome precisely those divisions based on race and ethnicity that have traditionally kept such communities apart from one another, and vying for limited resources. Thus, almost from the beginning, *diversity* work was seen as critical *both* to leadership development *and* to encouraging/facilitating broader participation, that is, to enabling these women to be, and to recognize themselves as, more fully engaged citizens. It is almost as though the confrontation with diverse women's stories is, itself, politicizing.

What does this experience have to contribute to addressing the rejection of "politics" and the construction of alternative public spaces? What can we learn from NCNW's activities that might help us respond to some of the theoretical puzzles with which scholars of gender and citizenship have been engaged?

First, with respect to constructions of "politics." NCNW began with programs rooted in family and community, rather than with abstract critiques, or even with explicit calls for political engagement. But its programs focused on making connections between the women's concerns as wives and mothers, the skills they had developed in those capacities, and the contributions they had already made and would continue to make, to the broader community. They started, that is, with needs; but helped the women to see connections between those needs and their rights as citizens, *and* to perceive commonalities between their needs and those of others. This two-pronged focus on needs became an important part of a process of politicization: overcoming both their suspicion of "politics" *and* their suspicions and wariness of others. Participants came to believe that only *through collective action*—and, at least on occasion, making demands of formal political institutions—did those needs stand a chance of being met.

But what would make collective action possible? Skills training (including the development of analytical tools) and diversity work. NCNW's skills-focused programs (especially the college program[70]) helped the women to locate themselves and their community within a broader political-economic context. Many came to see that action to address the needs of their families required them to think *structurally* about their situation, and to engage with similarly-situated women in other neighborhoods. They developed an *analysis* of their situation, that is, that brought them to a broader understanding of politics, and to an awareness of the political character of their concerns, and may well have helped them to overcome their earlier rejection of "politics." As LaDoris Payne summarized the way she encourages women in her groups to move from personal experience through analysis and onto activism, the questions to ask are: "What? So What? Now What?"[71]

Analysis alone, however, would not have been sufficient to build and sustain what Fraser referred to as a "subaltern counterpublic." NCNW coupled programming that educated its members politically (or politicized them) with programming that helped them address issues of diversity and difference—notably the Leadership Training program. I think we can understand this dimension of its activities as a partial, but critical, component of an answer to the question: What is necessary to sustain a "subaltern counterpublic"? From NCNW's vantage point, a counterpublic must be inclusive; it must have at its core a commitment to dialogue and support across differences of race, ethnicity, religious background, and sexuality. NCNW insisted that the achievement of such inclusion was not automatic or easy: in a society divided by differences of race and ethnicity, in particular, it would have to be deliberately created, at the grassroots, and in small-group settings, to build the trust, and the knowledge of one another, that, alone, would make possible the perception of a shared fate critical to sustained joint action.[72] And what facilitated the building of that trust was, precisely, the ways they developed of *connecting* diverse personal stories in a consciousness-raising context: making manifest, that is, not only that the "personal is political," but that "the personal that is political is diverse."[73]

That the NCNW has been extraordinarily successful in many of its efforts has been documented elsewhere.[74] What this exploration of the Leadership Training Program suggests is that at least one key to the successful politicization of working-class women in their communities—enabling them to see that their actions *are* "political"—is the combination of an explicit focus on difference and diversity and a recognition that effective activism—like any other skill—can be taught, and learned. In such a context, those committed to improving their lives and those of their families by working in their communities need not deny that they are engaged in politics; rather, they can come to take pride in discovering that they, too, are political beings. Perhaps, too, given what we have seen in the Obama campaign's melding of grassroots organizing with electoral politics, these kinds of activities may eventually serve as guidelines for more activist, engaged, practices of citizenship for everyone.

Acknowledgments

I am grateful to Rachel Roth and Joan Tronto for helpful comments and suggestions in response to an earlier draft, comments that I particularly appreciated since I was unable to attend the conference for which this chapter was originally written. I also want to thank Amrita Basu, Mary Katzenstein, Eileen McDonagh, Wendy Mink and Molly Shanley for careful readings and a wonderful conversation; and Jane Mansbridge and the participants in the feminist theory workshop at the March 2004 meetings of the Western Political Science Association, for helping me think through both this chapter and the larger project of which it forms a part.

11

FAMILIES, CARE AND CITIZENSHIP

Notes toward a Feminist Approach

One of my first published pieces explored the limits of contemporary feminist language about solidarity among women, specifically, the use of terms like "family" and "sisterhood" to express strong bonds, despite extensive feminist critiques of the subordination of women reflected in (and effected through) the actual workings of real families.[1] Families are highly political institutions; constructions of family are *ideological*, as well as biological. To use the language of family to express strong bonds of affiliation, I argued, is both to privilege that one form of relationship and to obscure the power and value of other forms, specifically those we refer to in the language of "friendship," i.e. more self-consciously chosen bonds.

I still agree with much of what I wrote there, in discussing six functions we look to families to fulfill—(1) nurturance/caring/support; (2) acceptance/ support for self-development; (3) solidarity/social cement; (4) protection from abandonment and isolation; (5) socialization/reproduction; and (6) sexuality and intimacy. In each case, I pointed out that families do not necessarily do what we look to them to do; and, moreover, that much of the important work in each of these areas—on which families and society depend—is, in fact, done, or supported by, networks of friends and other chosen associates. In such a context, I argued, using the language of kinship to describe powerful bonds masks the power of non kin bonds, further reinforces the ideological primacy of traditionally-constructed families, and obscures the social inequalities that are often perpetuated through families. Finally, while heterosexually-constructed nuclear families are the only officially-sanctioned contexts for sexuality and intimacy, it was evident—and continues to be so now—that they are far from the only contexts in which people *do* experience such intimacy. Although some critics of the "sexploitative" character of US individualist, market-based, relationships argue that families are the only alternative to an individualistic, utilitarian, universe, made up of self-interested monads, it is also clear that "it is possible to agree with the Moral Majority that we suffer from a sort of moral vacuum without accepting either [its] definition of morality or [its] prescriptions for the family."[2] The article called for decentering families as primary social building blocks, and

165

recognizing in our theories the power of the friendships that had animated our movement.

As I look back at this analysis in the light of my own recent experience, and in light of the questions that now concern me in my efforts to think about what feminist citizenship might entail, I am struck by two things: (1) the continuing relative inattention to friendships in feminist theorizing;[3] and (2) my own earlier lack of attention to issues of "dependency" and "care" (other than for young children). These issues were brought home to me quite dramatically as a result of my mother's having lived for almost three years after a severely-impairing stroke, and through watching (and participating in) the struggles of many of my peers to care for ill or aging parents or partners.

How do we think about friends and families now, particularly in the light of increasingly ideological uses of words like "family," "dependency," "independence," to justify massive cutbacks in social provision? As evidenced by the PRWOA of 1996, and the increasing cultural concern over marriage and families (e.g., Defense of Marriage bills at both the federal and state levels, struggles over gay marriage in multiple states, and welfare "reform" strategies designed to force poor women into marriage, to name just a few examples), "family" is carrying ever more cultural weight. What are the implications of these changes? How do we address the inequalities that are structured into familial relationships without falling prey to a liberal-individualist voluntarism, and while insisting that the work of care, traditionally performed in those families, must continue to be done, but not at the cost of women's full and equal participation in the society and polity?

More specifically, how should we think about care work, in particular?[4] About the fact that, whether it is done by family members, or by paid workers who are not family members, the work of assuring that life can go on tends to be underpaid, under-valued, and overwhelmingly performed by women, especially members of minority communities? And, to the extent that more care work *is* being undertaken for pay (because the entry of women into the paid labor force means that they may not be available to do carework for no pay in their own homes), that work is becoming increasingly racialized.

Some years ago, Susan Okin suggested that these social changes were already challenging traditional family structures, and that society would *have* to accommodate to them:

> Women have done and continue to do much of the crucial work of society without compensation or recognition, but their tolerance for this state of affairs has been approaching its limit for some time now. No longer able to assume and ignore the work that women do, society will have to face up to "rethinking the family."[5]

Would that this were so! It may well be the case that those women who are able to find reasonably-paid work outside their homes have lost their tolerance for these assumptions; but that does not mean that "society" *will* face up to rethinking the family in any significant way. Instead, what seems to be happening is that some proportion of the work that had traditionally been done by women within their *own* families, for no pay, is now being done by (largely immigrant) women for *other people's families*, at extremely low pay. The expectation that care work is the *private* responsibility of individual families has simply been shifted over into new social forms that continue to exploit the poor and the immigrant, especially women and men of color.[6]

Questions about care, about women's work, about pay for care work, and the like have been on the agenda of feminists for decades. More books and articles are constantly appearing. How are we to arrange for the work of care in our society? If it is not to be paid, who will do it? At what costs? If it is to be paid, who will pay for it, and at what levels? How are caregivers to be prevented from falling into poverty, themselves? More generally, these studies raise further questions: Why is the work of caring for dependents (whether children, the elderly, the frail or ill) so ill-paid and so disrespected, even as the need and demand for it are rising steadily? My focus here is on questions of care as they relate to constructions of families and the constitution of citizens. What is the relationship between autonomy and support for individuation as (among the) goals of a democratic society and a recognition of a need for care of dependents within that society? What would it mean to think about care as a *positive value*, an important aspect of citizenship, and a necessary component of justice, rather than as a "necessary condition" for the "true work" of politics?[7] More specifically, how do we assure that the work of care will be done without reinforcing a secondary status for those who perform that work?

"Deviant" Families

Recent ideological uses of family have highlighted "deviance" as the source of many of our problems, and have tended to focus on two "deviant" types: single "welfare mothers" (understood to be young women of color) and the families they head, and queers. Although the two groups are rarely discussed at the same time, we might learn something important about families by doing so. For, as a number of feminist critics have pointed out, a focus on "the deviant" masks and obscures the ways "traditional" families are failing their members. Cheshire Calhoun claims, for example, that "historically, gays and lesbians have become family outlaws not because *their* relationships and families were distinctively queer, but because *heterosexuals'* relationships and families queered the gender, sexual, and family composition norms." A focus on specific outsiders, that is, externalizes threats to a presumed "normative family," and enables members of those normative families to "adjust to new, liberalized norms of acceptable gender roles and sexual behavior within families, as well as new, liberalized norms of acceptable family composition."[8] Or, as Linda Nicholson argues:

> The distinction between "traditional" and "alternative" families
> encourages those who experience such clashes [between the way they
> live and the way they are "supposed to live"] to think of them as the
> relatively isolated effects of living a slightly "deviant" life. We need to
> fully acknowledge that in relation to many contemporary definitions
> of "traditionality," most of us are "deviants." Having done that, we can
> begin mobilizing the political power necessary to make our present
> institutions conform more adequately to our needs.[9]

There are clear parallels between the cases of queers and of welfare mothers:
both are derided for being "outside" (or for "wanting in" to privileges associated with) the heterosexually-constructed nuclear family. In each case
(though differently), the *promise* of "the family" is elusive. Of course, these are
hardly the only groups for whom so-called traditional families do not work.
The focus on them as deviants, however, deflects attention from all those
others who are ill-served by the families in which they live, who cannot make
ends meet despite the presence of a male wage-earner, whose relationships are
characterized by abuse or neglect, etc. In short, it diverts attention away from
the failure of "families" to do the work they are expected to do, particularly as
broader social supports are eliminated.

Contemporary families are under enormous pressure. On one hand, the
increasing expectations that accompany societal affluence have resulted,
effectively, in a "speed-up" for virtually everyone. Most families require two
wage-earners to achieve a so-called middle-class standard of living; but jobs
are increasingly precarious, and many workers have had to trade security and
benefits for a job of any kind. The increased number of women in the labor
force has not been accompanied by a parallel increase in social services to
support that work, so that the brunt of the "juggling" of family and job (and of
cutbacks in social services) is borne by women. Furthermore, the increased
mobility that is an essential component of this "new economy" contributes to
the weakening of precisely those institutions that traditionally offered support
in times of dislocation (e.g. neighborhood or community organizations, religiously-based communities, and other local institutions).[10] On the other hand,
when the economy contracts, even precarious jobs with no benefits start to
disappear. While this reality may leave more two-adult families with at least
one potential caregiver at home, it threatens *everyone's* ability either to give or
receive care, and the loss of wages may well mean increased hardship for all.
Furthermore, the ideology of the family has, in effect, served to justify the
continued *privatization* of those costs—and, especially, of the work of caregiving—on the backs of women.[11] It is a minority of families who live in the
idealized nuclear family of the 1950s, with a stay-at-home mom, two children
and a dog, and a father who earns enough to support them all. But our social
policies have barely changed in response. Instead, in boom times, we ostracize
and demean those who do not fit the norm, thus absolving "society" from any

responsibility to address basic questions of care. And, even in times of economic crisis, questions of how the work of *care* will be accomplished—as opposed to how we, as a society, will find jobs for people, or make up for lost income—rarely make it onto the *political* agenda.[12]

Families and Care Work: Feminist Responses

> Feminist research on the "labor of caring" shows that in all industrialized Western countries, welfare—tending to children, the elderly, the sick and disabled—is largely provided in private households by women without pay, rather than by states, markets and voluntary nonprofit organizations; all Western welfare states depend upon this care to a great extent.[13]

The tasks of caring for those who need assistance with the activities of daily living has been treated by most mainstream political theorists, and by most US public policy as a familial, that is private, matter. Care is expected to be provided in the home as a kind of altruistic duty expected of women or, if women are not available to do this in home, by low-paid staff, either in the homes of others or in an institutional setting, arrangements for which are the responsibility of (the family of) the person in need of care. If we combine this formulation with the ideological separation of "public" and "private" in liberal discourse, we can begin to understand how most theorists and policy-makers have assumed that the provision of care is not a matter of *public* policy. Furthermore, if that is the case, then considerations of *justice* need not apply.[14] Hilary Land and Hilary Rose have dubbed this an assumption, or, more accurately, a requirement of "compulsory altruism for women."[15] The assumption that women will "cover" the needs for care within families, of course, removes attention to the work of care from the public agenda, and results in a gross *understatement and underreporting* of the social service work necessary to sustain a society. As Orloff notes, "provision of welfare 'counts' only when it occurs through the state or the market, while women's unpaid work in the home is ignored."[16]

Much feminist analysis has focused on these and other ways in which women's care work is either taken for granted (as in the case of women who have other means of support while they are engaged in such care), or vastly devalued (when it is done by women who have no other means of support). Over the past century, feminists have developed a number of different responses to the devaluation of care work, and of the women who engage in it. Early maternalists, for example, recognized the importance of caring for dependents (at least dependent children!) to the sustenance of families and society, and advocated mothers' pensions or children's allowances that would allow women to continue to perform it. Nevertheless, as Ann Orloff and others have noted, those benefits were never sufficient to allow women to support themselves and their children without a husband; rather, they were meant to provide a kind of temporary "back-up" for the failures of the family wage system: "Nowhere did a maternalist strategy achieve parity between benefits for stay-at-home mothers and wage-earners' benefits or a standard of living for single mothers comparable to their married counterparts."[17]

Early twentieth-century social feminists, on the other hand, attempted to revalue that work of care, and to have it recognized as an important component of citizenship. Wendy Sarvasy has argued, for example, that, by drawing on existing stereotypes of women as "domestic caretakers," women reformers succeeded in getting the issue of social provision (i.e. what we now term "care work," broadly construed) onto the agenda of mainstream politics at both the state and national levels. More significantly, their practices constituted the basis for a new understanding of citizenship based on their understanding of women's difference: citizenship enacted not through electoral participation, but through social service.[18]

Ann Shola Orloff has argued that the dominant strategy of women's movements since World War II has been to pursue a goal of equal rights, which meant, in most cases, a focus on women's labor force participation.[19] Marxist socialists, of course, had insisted that women's subordination in the home would be overcome only by women's full and equal participation in the labor market. Second-wave socialist feminists pointed to the significance of *reproductive*, in addition to *productive* labor, and argued that both needed to be recognized and validated if women's emancipation was to be achieved. On this view, women's subordination was a product of their confinement to the household, in a situation of dependency on men. The solution: more equal access for women to the paid labor force, which would require, in turn, a series of social supports that would make that participation possible, most notably quality child-care at an affordable price.[20] Many of those who advocated greater access for women to the labor market, however, were well aware that paid work, alone, would not be sufficient. Feminists pointed to the "politics of housework" and the need to engage men, as well as women, in the work of care for home and children, if equality were ever to be achieved.[21]

On one level, these critics recognized that taking care of home and family members needed to be recognized and validated *as work*, and as necessary for the continued existence of families and communities. The force of most of these early writings was to argue for some *socialization* of that work; at the very least, to engage male members of the household in it—assuming, of course, that there *were* male members of the household! More broadly, some aimed at the goal of recognizing a *social/communal responsibility* to enable women to work.[22] But there was little attention to what Eva Feder Kittay has come to term "care work" as a special category of work, or to what would happen if it could *not* be provided from within (even more equitably constituted) family networks.[23]

Equally problematic, I think, are the ways arguments about child care, in particular, developed over time, and were incorporated into the dominant social discourse. While some early arguments for the provision of child-care focused on the *value to children* of broadened social networks, educational enrichment, and the like, the discourse soon shifted to justifying social provision of child-care on the basis of a combination of efficiency and remediation: child-care came to be defended as a "second-best" alternative (to care by stay-at-home mothers) that would make possible women's labor force participation and/or provide extra support for children who could benefit from additional pedagogical opportunities (e.g. the Head Start model).[24] We are now seeing some of the (perhaps unintended) consequences of that approach: the assumption that most women *should* work for pay outside the home, and that those who do not (unless they have husbands to support them!) are, in one way or another, derelict in their responsibilities and parasites on the larger society.[25] Strategies adopted to provide for the *possibility* of meaningful work for women who had been excluded from it have been turned into arguments to *punish* those women who do not have work that can support themselves and their children, or who stay at home to care for children, sick family members, or other dependents.[26] Middle-class women's struggle for a right to equal access to work, in short, may have had the effect of making poor women—for whom work rarely represents emancipation—particularly vulnerable to attack.

Beyond the concern for equal access to, and equity within, the waged labor market, however, is the way the work of care in our society is still understood primarily as a private/familial responsibility. Where does this leave all those who do *not* have family members to care for them, either because they live alone, because those with whom they live are not interested in, or capable, of providing that care, or because their "families of choice" are not recognized *as families* as a result of state laws or constitutions limiting marriage to "one man and one woman"? At the same time, how do we take account—whether in our theories or in our public policies—for the phenomenon of *non*-kin-based care networks, such as those who have functioned as "fictive kin" within African American communities for generations, or those who provide care, especially within gay and lesbian communities in the US, in response to the AIDS crisis? We now have the Family and Medical Leave Act on the books; but—even leaving aside its limited reach and supports—"family" is defined quite narrowly, with the result that many of those who have undertaken to care for others (friends or unmarried lovers, for example) are not eligible for its coverage.

Contemporary Debates, Feminist Responses

As many critics have noted, the Personal Responsibility and Work Opportunity Act of 1996 built on many earlier trends to further demonize and stigmatize poor women with children who depended on meager state benefits for their survival. Responses to it developed along a number of lines.

1　Some feminists focused on efforts to stem the attack on poor women, and to advocate for continued, and more adequate, benefits and the elimination of punitive family caps and time-limits. The Women's Committee of 100, for example, argued that "the war against poor women is a war against all women," and attempted to rally mainstream feminist organizations to join with poor women and welfare rights groups to oppose welfare "reform."[27]

2　Another strategy (followed by some of the same activists and writers) focused on the *politics* of welfare cuts, and the ways they functioned to reframe patriarchal control. Frances Fox Piven argued, for example, that welfare cuts have *economic* aims: to enlarge the pool of people desperate for low-waged work, thus increasing insecurity and driving down wages for all.[28] Marilyn Friedman argued that the issue is not just economic: welfare cuts do reinforce patriarchy, although in new ways: "Many low-income women now occupy a *class* position in relation to middle and upper income families which parallels the position which the traditional wife occupied in relation to her husband." That is, they carry out nurturant reproductive labor for families, have no bargaining advantages as a group, are engaged in care for bodily needs, and are hemmed in by lack of respect and few opportunities for advancement. state control reappears as control by higher-income families: "Class-based market patriarchy is a systemic phenomenon in which certain socio-economic classes, via their familial unit, acquire a portion of that control over (low-income) female domestic labor which has historically been usurped by male 'heads of households' and, more recently, by the state." Or, to put it another way, "even the patriarchal family is, in many cases, no longer a nuclear self-contained domestic unit. It is surviving through the deprivatization of some of its domesticity. The patriarchal family has 'gone public.'"[29] In short, changes in family structures, and the challenges of providing care, highlight the fluid boundaries between "public" and "private." Care work is not a *private* matter, nor should it be exempted from considerations of justice that presumably apply only to a *public* domain.

In addition, the combination of cutbacks in benefits for the poor and increases in benefits for the (relatively) wealthy seems designed to enforce and reinforce a particular version of the patriarchal nuclear family. While the lack of sufficient federal funding for child-care means that publicly-supported child-care is inadequate and of poor quality, tax policies are supporting child-care deductions (and IRAs for stay-at-home moms) for the middle and upper classes at ever higher levels.[30] Or, as Orloff notes,

> [S]ome women are tied to the welfare state *as mothers*, while others are tied to the state *as wives* ... This distinction can be significant politically because it reinforces differences

between two-parent families and single-parent families, as has occurred in the United States.[31]

Further, the public policy focus on *child*-care again deflects attention from questions of *care work more generally*, of which child-care is simply one manifestation. When we treat child-care as if it were the *only* type of care on the agenda, and in a way that assumes that the primarily responsibility is on the individual family—and, in particular, on mothers—we seriously underestimate the extent of the "care crisis" in US society and, perhaps more significantly, narrow the potential base of allies for a political struggle to address it.[32]

3   In addition to these political strategies, feminists have also questioned the meaning of "dependence" and "independence" in liberal theory and in contemporary Western societies, insisting that no one is, in fact, truly independent, and that our theories and policies must recognize *inter*-dependence and support those who do the essential work of social support.[33] As I argued above (Chapter 4), a focus on economic independence as a criterion for full citizenship fails to recognize that even those who are thought to *be* economically independent are, in fact, dependent on the work of many others (wives, mothers, etc.) to do the care work that enables them to "go to work." As Susan Okin pointed out, "assumptions about the care that takes place within families allow [William Galston] not to see that even the minority of citizens he considers independent are not really so, for in important everyday ways they do not, of course, take care of themselves."[34] More significantly, perhaps, Eva Feder Kittay's work highlights the ways that holding autonomy and independence as goals places those who *do the work of caring, as well as those who are explicitly "cared for"* in subordinate positions. All too often, those who are caregivers are, themselves, in need of care—both emotional and financial—because carework is so undervalued in our society. Thus, "the well-being of dependents *and* caretakers *and* the relation itself between caretaker and dependent must be seen as requirements of public understandings of social cooperation."[35] In short, those who are caring for others are not, themselves, fully autonomous—they are limited by the needs and demands of those dependent on them.

Kittay, Kornbluh, Mink, Folbre, Young and others have all argued for the necessity of *adequate pay for caregivers*, and the recognition of caregiving work as an essential *public* good. In part, their arguments focus on ending the stigmatization and demonization of those receiving public benefits under AFDC, now TANF. In part, however, they raise much broader questions of what constitutes the "public interest," and how carework—and not just care for children, or care for family members—is to be incorporated into an understanding of citizenship.[36] Developing this latter line of argument is, it seems to me, one of the most critical "next steps" for feminist theorizing and politics related to both families *and* friends.

Toward a Rethinking of Carework, Justice, and Families

I have been wary of making notions of care central to theorizing about women and politics, for fear that to do so would be to reinforce the societal expectation of women as caretakers, and to undermine feminist claims about the importance of socializing this work. I am becoming convinced, however, that it is important *politically*, as well as theoretically, to start thinking more practically about the place of care in feminist conceptions of justice and citizenship. As the dominant discourse becomes ever more individualistic, and as communitarian perspectives (which tend to be quite conservative with respect to families and gender roles) have become the dominant counter-discourse, it is ever more important for feminists to articulate arguments for women's agency—and full citizenship—that do not reinforce either liberal individualism or conservative familialism. As Joan Tronto has argued,

> virtually every political debate in the US comes down, sooner or later, to a desert claim that grows out of the "work ethic": that people are entitled to what they have because they "earned" it. The care ethic posits a very different set of standards for desert: people are entitled to what they need because they need it; people are entitled to care because they are part of ongoing relations of care.[37]

Martha Minow and Molly Shanley make a related claim in developing a notion of "relational rights": "the individual must be seen simultaneously as a distinct individual and as a person fundamentally involved in relationships of dependence, care, and responsibility." Further,

> A conception of relational rights and responsibilities ... would not regard "rights" as belonging to individuals and arising from the imperative of self-preservation, but rather would view rights as claims grounded in and arising from human relationships of varying degrees of intimacy. Relational rights and responsibilities should draw attention to the claims that arise out of relationships of human interdependence.[38]

Or, as Tronto argues, attending *politically* to the place of care in human communities helps us to challenge and reframe traditional understandings of equality, as well as of autonomy: "we recognize that citizens are not self-sufficient. All people depend upon others ... Recognition of our mutual states of dependence and conditions of vulnerability provides a different basis for equality."[39]

Uma Narayan offers an important caveat: claims about care and dependence have, of course, been used as a justification for colonialism and domination (for example, by John Stuart Mill, in justifying British colonial rule in India): "care discourse can sometimes function ideologically to justify or conceal relationships of power and domination."[40] Patricia Williams expressed a similar concern about the dangers of "needs" discourse for African Americans: asserting needs has never been a firm ground for rights, she argued; rather, the issue for African Americans has been "to find a political mechanism that can confront the *denial* of need."[41] We must be wary, then, of how—and in what contexts—we make arguments about care. Nevertheless, as both Narayan and Tronto point out, the effort to pay attention to care *and* justice at the same time can open up *both* concepts to important revisions. As Narayan argues,

> [A] more serious commitment to, and enforcement of, the claims of justice might, at least in some cases, be a precondition for the possibility of adequately caring for and about some people ... Social relationships of domination often operate so as to make many who have power unable to genuinely care about the marginalized and powerless [while] adequate attention to justice may, in some instances, be a precondition for adequately caring policies.[42]

Virginia Held has argued, similarly, that it is important to treat justice and care *in relationship to one another*; for each makes the other possible. It is not self-evident, she writes, that "justice is the primary value of political institutions." Rather,

> [C]are is the wider moral framework into which justice should be fitted. Care seems to me the most basic moral value ... we can say that without care we cannot have life at all ... within a network of caring, we can and should demand justice, but justice should not then push care to the margins.[43]

What is crucial to realize in such conversations, however, is that we *have* models for treating care and justice together. Wendy Sarvasy's work on early twentieth-century social feminists offers one. Sibyl Schwarzenbach notes that—interestingly enough—Aristotle provides another. She argues that, for Aristotle, political friendship (care and concern for one's fellow citizens) "emerges as a necessary condition for genuine justice." Furthermore, "Aristotle repeatedly urges a 'common care' when advising his statesmen in the *Nichomachean Ethics*, and he uses the term 'care' in a political context throughout his *Politics*." And, in response to the feminist concern that a focus on care may contribute to the continued subordination of women as the main societal caregivers, Schwarzenbach offers this thought:

That so many ancient philosophers including Aristotle—white, male, and from the upper classes—acknowledge care's central importance suggests ... that perhaps *all* persons, even those in their prime and in prime social positions (and even those who might have reason to deny it), need give and receive care if their lives are to flourish. If this is the case, the real feminist concern should not be to deny the importance of caring activity but to account for why it has been denied particularly in recent times and to attempt to rectify the vast injustices in the distribution of its benefits and burdens.[44]

Nancy Naples' work on low-income community workers in CAP agencies provides yet another example, and offers a somewhat more contemporary model. Naples argues that, while engaging in community (caretaking) work, women community workers were also developing new understandings of citizenship that effectively blurred boundaries between public and private, individual and community. She suggests, in fact, that they were like the early social-democratic feminists in refusing to "consider citizenship an individual possession. It is something achieved in community and for the benefit of the collectivity." Further,

[C]ommunity workers understood that full participation for low-income people of color in American society required access to certain basic social and economic protections. Like the early feminist social reformers, they also recognized that bureaucratization threatened this access and required participatory strategies to sustain a democratic environment for the provision of social support.[45]

Annelise Orleck's recent study of Black women anti-poverty activists in Las Vegas makes a similar argument.[46]

Placing issues of care—both its receipt and its provision—onto the political agenda could also provide contexts to rethink both the definition of "family" and the place of families in US political life. For, while dominant political rhetoric suggests that care and concern for "families" is a central public policy concern, the reality is that *real* support for families as they are, *or for the care work they do*, rarely finds its way onto the political agenda. Rather, as Iris Young and others have pointed out, many of those who profess to advocate policies supportive of "families" are, in fact, advocating (continued) privatization of care, without needed social supports, and, in consequence, a secondary citizenship status for those who offer that care.[47] As she argued, "a more just society would provide the home help, child care, transportation, workplace accommodation, and flexible work hours that would enable ... people to make meaningful contributions." Further, it would recognize that *no one* is fully independent, and that "dependency work makes a vast and vital social contribution," and should be recognized "by giving those who do it decent material comfort."[48] Finally, it would mean "promot[ing] and enourag[ing] the ends and purposes of families" without "punishing or favoring families based on their composition alone."[49]

What we need, in short, is a further articulation of T.H. Marshall's notion of social citizenship, one that would incorporate *care* and *relational rights* as essential components of citizenship. Such a conception could, I believe, tie together feminist critiques of the privatization of care work, arguments for an expanded (rather than punitive) system of social provision, *and* calls for the validation of the political significance of friendship and of "alternative" familial forms. It would be based on a vision of political community with a number of dimensions. First, it would recognize that communities are *necessarily*, and at root, composed of *interdependent* members; that those relationships of dependence are often *unequal*; and that such inequality should not necessarily stand in the way of fully equal *citizenship* rights. Second, and following from this, it would argue for a system of social provision that is adequate, *generous*, and non-demeaning, one which flows from the obligations and responsibilities of citizenship. Those who enable society to function through caring for *its* dependents (whether in the form of child-care, education, health-care, etc.) are performing crucial work for the *common good*; the need for care ought not be treated as a private problem to be solved by individual families, and those who provide it should be appropriately compensated. Third, such a revisioning of relational obligations and citizenship could further open up our understandings of what constitute legitimate, acceptable, social, sexual, and/or familial relationships.

This last point returns me to my earlier claim about the potential power of "deviance," and offers some interesting possibilities for making common cause between recipients of social benefits (e.g. "welfare mothers") and queers. Karen Struening and Cheshire Calhoun, in different ways, have argued for what we might term a "freedom of intimate association," a position usually associated with the struggles of gays and lesbians for rights to marry and/or to claim full citizenship status. Calhoun, for example, argues that gays and lesbians have been denied the benefits of the "private sphere," in that they have not been able to claim access to that domain through marriage. The case for legal recognition of "gay marriage," then, is really a "bidding for access to the same privilege that heterosexuals now enjoy, namely the privilege of claiming that *in spite of their multiple deviations* from the norms governing the family, their families are nevertheless *real* ones, and they are themselves naturally suited for marriage, family, parenting *however* these may be defined and redefined."[50] Struening argues for a "freedom of intimate association" that "consists not just in redefining the structure and composition of the conventional family, but in redefining the roles of mother, father, husband, wife, lover and friend and the meaning of family, friendship, and other forms of intimate relationship and association," a point taken up and developed, as well, by Traci Levy.[51] In important ways, these arguments parallel those of Gwendolyn Mink and the

Women's Committee of 100 in their claims that the attacks on "welfare mothers" ought to be understood as attacks on *all* women's rights to define how and with whom they will constitute families. There is room here, in short, for significant—and potentially powerful—coalition-building among all those whose families do not fit the heterosexual norm; but also among those providing or in need of care.[52]

What might be the political possibilities if not only feminists, but also gays and lesbians, made common cause with welfare rights advocates to expand the definition of what constitutes "family," and who can constitute a family? Such an approach involves walking a fine line; it runs the risk of re-centering families as *the* institutions for provision of care, even if families take new forms. But families, in some form or another, are likely to be with us for the foreseeable future. In our current political climate, we may need, simultaneously, to point to the limits of what families can be expected to do, and to insist on more meaningful, and generous, forms of social provision, even as we press to expand the boundaries of who and what families are. In the process—by making clear the ways attention to families, and to issues of care provision, force us to question dichotomous understandings of dependence/independence and of so-called public and private domains—such an exploration could offer grounds for richer understandings of the practices of citizenship, itself.

12

DEMOCRACY AND (IN)EQUALITY[†]

Community Activism and Democracy in a
Time of Retrenchment

Mary Louise Pratt remarked that "building democracies and ending inequality are ultimately what is at stake" for the writers in a recent anthology on Latin American social movements.[1] Indeed, these might well be described as the goals of virtually *all* movements for progressive social change. Further, while, in the words of Evelina Dagnino, "a hegemonic building of democracy" has emerged as the major project of Left movements in Latin America, that project, in turn, treats the "politico-cultural understanding of differences" as a necessary prerequisite to the creation of democracy, i.e., of a political community that can incorporate those differences in a more egalitarian fashion.[2]

As I have suggested in earlier chapters, it would seem that such a concern for the "politico-cultural understanding of differences" aptly describes many studies that explore the range and varieties of contemporary (women's) activism, in the US and elsewhere. Activism—even women's activism—of course, is not necessarily always progressive; movements span the gamut from left to right. Nevertheless, attention to the varieties of recent (women's) activism can offer us an unusual opportunity to reflect on the current state of, and possibilities for, meaningful local democratic participation in an increasingly global—and financially precarious—political economy.

Despite some recent "victories" of democracy—however those might be defined in this increasingly complex time—and even in the aftermath of Barack Obama's successful presidential campaign, prospects for progressive social change often seem bleak: Socialist models no longer compel; the identity politics that replaced socialism and which seemed, initially, to offer equally powerful grounds for mobilization, has not succeeded in providing alternative frameworks on a broad basis. Yet the post-modernist critiques that proved so popular in the academy have not necessarily provided clear alternatives in practice. They have not, that is, helped those committed to change to deal with the complexities of identity while, at the same time, developing strategies for action that are responsive to the day-to-day realities of those who have been most marginalized.[3] In response, many feminist and democratic theorists have turned to discourses of citizenship, civil society, and public sphere, in

179

hopes of escaping socialist universalism, identitarian particularism, and post-modernist paralysis.[4] Yet, as I have argued, too many of these conceptualizations of civil society or the public sphere effectively mask the inequalities and hierarchies by which these (and, indeed, citizenship, itself) are constituted.

Explorations of efforts on the part of relatively power*less* people to effect changes in their respective societies and communities can help us to navigate these complexities. In the contemporary Euro-American context, a dominant question for progressives, including feminists, is: How do we defend those state-supported provisions (including guarantees not only of civil rights, but of what T.H. Marshall[5] referred to as "social rights," such as income supports, health care, education, housing, and unemployment) that came into existence during the past century, and that are now under increasing attack from neo-capitalist "globalists," while not pretending that they are anywhere near adequate to meet real needs?[6] And how—if at all—do we extend these and add new rights, such as protections from environmental toxins and against the commercialization of reproduction, to name just a few of the multiple struggles being undertaken in the Western Hemisphere? At the same time, what meaning does "democracy" have for anyone, when those excluded from meaningful decision-making power at both local and national levels now include not just the traditionally marginal—e.g. the poor, immigrants, women, the aged, and members of minority communities and cultures—but even many of the white middle-class, whose concerns are routinely dismissed with the claim that economic factors set the parameters of political possibility? Indeed, precisely at the moment when women and members of minority cultural groups are organizing to assert their needs and rights, it often seems as though any meaningful *politics* has died, and been replaced by a determinist economism that is anything but Marxist in its intents and effects.[7]

Meanwhile, in many areas of Latin America and Africa, and among the countries of the former Soviet Bloc, the fall of non-democratic regimes has not eliminated vast inequalities; indeed, in many cases those inequalities have only increased. In each of these contexts, activists struggle for redistribution of both political and economic goods, while also demanding recognition and (re)valuation of previously-marginalized ethnic-cultural groups. Still other groups are simultaneously mobilizing to maintain those inequalities and/or to reassert the dominance of particular ethnic-cultural identities. How are meaningful changes to be accomplished when economies and economic policies (and the politics and polities sustained by them) seem ever less amenable to local control?

While all the movements discussed in this chapter engage, to some degree, questions of democracy, citizenship, participation, and difference, they do so in different ways, and draw on different theoretical frameworks. Nevertheless, among them, we can find some significant themes, methods, and questions. First, to what extent do new social movements (or, in the language more common in the US context, does "community activism") contribute to an expansion of civil society and the opening of new possibilities for democracy? Typically, those who participate in such movements are those who have been marginalized, or who have understood themselves to be relatively disempowered, in their political-social contexts. Does expanding the base of participation in local movements necessarily broaden people's understandings of what constitutes politics or the public agenda, more generally? Whose needs are being represented, heard, or responded to? Does the appearance of such movements necessarily signal greater democratization? Or, can they be (are they being) manipulated by governments desirous of *relieving* themselves of the responsibility to address social ills?

Second, how do we understand the processes of politicization? Many authors argue that activism rooted in what are perceived as unmet familial, neighborhood, or communal needs often leads to broader political challenges. Such local activism would seem to fall into the category of what Nancy Fraser described as "'oppositional' forms of needs talk, which arise when needs are politicized 'from below,'" and which "contribute to the crystallization of new social identities on the part of subordinated social groups."[8] But a number of studies also raise important caveats: Is a politics of needs necessarily democratizing? What are we to make of the fact that many of those who are mobilized into such movements do *not* see themselves as engaging in "political action," but, rather, as "taking care of their communities"? How might these studies help us to understand the multiple dimensions of politicization and consciousness-change? Interestingly, in the US and Western Europe, which claim to *be* democracies, meaningful participatory citizenship is being constrained *in practice* by the dismantling of the welfare state, even as we tout the value of democracy for others. Many US-based activists rarely use the language of "democracy"; rather, they talk of "community movements," and refer to themselves as "community workers." Conversely, in Latin America, the *rhetoric* of democracy remains a powerful tool for opposition movements, even though the possibilities of meaningful democracy seem limited by what are termed economic "realities." In fact, many of these organizations identify themselves as "social movements" and are *explicit* in stating that their goal is to expand or redefine the meanings of "politics." What, then, can we learn from attending simultaneously to US and non-US movements?

Third, since women are disproportionately represented in many of these movements—though too-often ignored by historians and social scientists who study them—we might well ask, "why women?" What accounts for—and what are the consequences of—the particular presence of women in community-based social movements? Is there a connection between the presence of women and a needs-based politics? Further, how might we understand the complex, and often contradictory, ways these movements either respond to, or draw on, the specific politicization of mothers and motherhood?

Fourth, often, "new social movements" are described as having goals that are *cultural* as much as (or more than) *political*. Yet many contemporary movements seem to be both cultural *and* political, at once. How do our understandings of politics—and of political transformation—change once we begin to take seriously the politics of *cultural change*? Does an explicitly *cultural* politics contribute in particular ways to the processes of democratization? Finally, we find both divisions and connections within activist communities along the lines of gender, race, and class, which can allow us to explore how identities are complexly constituted through their interaction. This examination may lead us to question, once again, the boundaries between "politics" and "personal/private life."

Nancy Naples' *Grassroots Warriors* is a fascinating exploration of the lives and activities of women who were involved in community-based organizations in New York and Philadelphia during the War on Poverty (roughly 1964–74). Her core data are composed of interviews she conducted with approximately sixty of these women and through which she attempted to explore questions such as what motivated them to undertake community work in their neighborhoods; how race, class, and gender intersected in their political biographies and their consciousness; how bureaucratization and professionalization affected their participation; and how the changing political economy and political culture affected their work.[9] From the vantage point of late-2008—when concerns about "welfare reform" seem to have been pre-empted by calls for ever-larger economic stimulus packages—she raises a fascinating question: what was the role of the state in shaping women's "community work" and/or in creating or expanding arenas for citizenship? The idea that the state might actually *create*, rather than effectively *constrict*, opportunities for citizenship is particularly compelling at a time when we find ourselves in the US at the cusp of a potentially "new New Deal"; at a moment where there are considerable pressures to *increase*, rather than decrease, government involvement in the economy.

One of the most valuable aspects of Naples' study is its evocation of a different, and rather more hopeful, political-economic moment, when "maximum feasible participation of the poor" rather than warding off a major depression (or rescuing financial services firms) was the watchword of social policy. Naples explores the impact of that differing policy context on the poor women who were the primary actors at the local level, examining their routes into activism through what she terms "activist mothering," the ways they were changed by their participation, and the ways their participation affected their understandings of themselves as (previously non-) political beings. "Activist mothering," she writes, "highlights the community workers' gendered conceptualization of activism on behalf of their communities ... Central to their constructions of 'community' was a convergence of racial-ethnic identification and class affiliation." In a striking parallel to the programs of the National Congress of Neighborhood Women I discussed above (Chapter 10), she argues that "activist mothering," by those involved in activism during the

War on Poverty "includes self-conscious struggles against racism, sexism, and poverty."[10]

Being a mother, however, does not automatically generate an oppositional consciousness; in fact, Naples' informants point to a number of different paths into activism, including religious involvement (particularly for black women and those involved in the Catholic Worker movement), social work, radical politics, participation in other social movements (e.g. the civil rights movement), and black women's traditions of community care-taking. Interestingly, most of these activists did *not* identify themselves as "politically-engaged" and made a separation between what they understood as their "community work" and what they identified as "politics" (by which they seemed to mean voting, lobbying their elected officials, and so forth). These women saw their community work as simply "a logical extension of their desire to improve the lives of their families and neighbors," what Temma Kaplan originally defined as "female consciousness."[11] Yet, Naples argues,

> [Their] gendered identities as women, daughters, mothers, or workers intersected with racial, ethnic, class, professional, and political identities to create a complex and oftentimes contradictory set of forces that informed their consciousness of inequality as well as motivation to fight for social and economic justice.[12]

Many were profoundly changed by their experiences, coming to see themselves, first, as "community workers" and then as empowered *citizens*, with a right, and an *obligation*, to act on behalf of their communities, and to make claims against the state.

Significantly, Naples attempted to draw lessons from that time for her own. Thus, she notes, "the War on Poverty, with its emphasis on maximum feasible participation, transformed their previously unpaid community work into paid work and, at the same time, empowered them as residents of low-income communities—resulting in a merging of social and political citizenship."[13] Yet, she recognizes the limits of this strategy as well: Increasing pressure for professionalization limited the ongoing participation (and influence) of these community workers even in the heyday of the War on Poverty. Furthermore, the state that had facilitated politicization and empowerment through its policies could, by cutting back on those same programs, limit and virtually eliminate their participation. Naples acknowledges the "contradictions of state-sponsored, community-based employment" as a strategy to end poverty, both economic and political. But, she insists, the contemporary move away from income supports and the "fragmentation of social life into discrete policy arenas fails to capture the mutually constitutive relationships between family income, childcare, health care, housing, education, employment, and so forth."[14] Effective social policies to address poverty must address the interconnections among these problems, and must recognize not just women's "double duty" of paid employment and care for household and family, but a third component, as well: "community work." Only when that work is recognized, validated, *and compensated*, and when women's contributions in that arena are effectively incorporated into our social policies, are we likely to make any real progress toward a more democratic and egalitarian society.[15]

Many studies of the activism of low-income women focus on the relationships among gender, class, race, ethnicity, culture, and sexuality in constructing communities of resistance. As we have seen, all-too-often, gender differences have been treated—both by social movement activists and by those who study them—as of only *secondary* concern or (even more problematically) as threatening to the already-fragile unity of an ethnic- or racially- or class-based movement. That approach, of course, parallels the ways some wished to deny (or at least ignore) the significance of differences of race, ethnicity, or class within the women's movement. Virginia Rinaldo Seitz' study of the Family Auxiliary of District 28 of the United Mineworkers of America, for example, notes that when they began, the women were "a group of people whose experiences, contributions, concerns and dreams were rarely acknowledged and little heard"—even by themselves!—and that their position of marginalization "was constructed for them by subordinate female gender roles, the depressed socioeconomic conditions of the region, and a cultural ideology defining them as Appalachian." Yet, those same conditions provided the context for their empowerment, which Seitz defines as "both a process and an outcome of collective identity and political praxis."[16]

As we saw in the case of the National Congress of Neighborhood Women (above, Chapter 10) and in the case of the women of early twentieth-century Barcelona (above, Chapter 3), women's collaborations *can* create additional community resources, enabling them to develop new bases of power. Along similar lines, Feldman, Stall and Wright, echoing Kaplan and others, note that "the empowering experiences of appropriating spatial resources provide a central, crucial means for low-income women of color to develop resources for collective power." Nevertheless, such collaborations are often quite precarious, "too fragile and sporadic to supplant the role of state and federal programs and non-profit organizations."[17]

Virtually all the essays collected by Naples in *Community Activism and Feminist Politics* emphasize the roles of women as community-builders and care-takers; and the ways that, in the course of their activism, they both draw on, and help to sustain, existing neighborhood, religious, and friendship networks. Further, many explore the complex and ambiguous nature of "activist mothering." In some cases, women were spurred to action *as* mothers, challenging governmental bodies to live up to their role as "protector" (for example, in cases of toxic waste dumping, school struggles, and domestic violence). In other cases, women's engagement in protest activities resulted in (often unintended) challenges to the dynamics of family structures and relationships.

A number of articles examine whether—and how—an oppositional consciousness can be "translated" from one context or environment to another. As Naples notes, the "process of politicization" often requires women's "painful recalculation of their taken-for-granted beliefs about democracy and social justice."[18] Feldman, Stall, and Wright examine the shift from community organizing to economic development strategies among women in the Wentworth Gardens public housing project in Chicago, emphasizing the "skill building" that goes along with women's participation in community work; and Mary Pardo notes that the stories of Mexican-American women in EastSide Los Angeles "convey a sense of movement from household to neighborhood institutions."[19] It is not always clear, however, to what extent the empowerment these women experienced *in* their communities carried over into a broader political arena—or, if it did, how long it lasted.

A number of essays explore the ambiguous role of the state as a site for both empowerment and control. Judith Wittner argues that domestic violence courts provided a context that (in however limited ways) helped women to "restructure relations with men who threatened and beat them."[20] Yet Karen Kendrick criticizes the shelter movement for treating battered women "as clients, rather than as experts of their own experiences and needs."[21] In short, as Naples aptly summarizes, "the state not only supports the reproduction of gender, racial-ethnic, and class inequality, but also provides avenues through which these patterns can be challenged." As a result, "the contradictory role of the state as both a catalyst for, and site of, women's politicization forms another significant theme in research on women [sic] community activism."[22]

Kathleen Blee, and others who have studied right-wing women remind us to be wary of assumptions that women are somehow more peace-loving and nurturing than men. Even studies that acknowledge the existence of right-wing women often tend to treat them merely as pawns of male leaders, ignoring the fact that "women have been involved and even leaders in virtually every major right-wing and antifeminist movement in US history."[23] Blee defines radicals as "those who envision fundamentally new social arrangements or who fervently guard existing social arrangements against forces of change,"[24] thus potentially incorporating activists on both left and right.

Her edited volume contains essays that examine women's roles in US radical movements of the past 50 years, ranging from civil rights to the Ku Klux Klan, from the Boston anti-busing movement to union organizing in Appalachia. Despite the left-right differences, there are some significant unifying threads: (1) how gender shapes political identities and political consciousness; (2) how informal, often emotional, ties, as well as the formal goals that make up the content of movement ideologies, attract individuals to radical movements; and (3) the resulting disjuncture between movement ideologies and individual beliefs.

A number of essays examine the ways women's activism "fits" (or doesn't) into conventional beliefs about women's character and behavior. Belinda

Robnett explores the mobilization of people *into* movements, arguing that most movement histories of the US civil rights movement focus on institutional structures and male leaders, thereby missing the roles of women as charismatic leaders in crisis situations. They also underplay the role of spontaneity and emotion in "micromobilization and group solidarity."[25] Beth Roy, in an article about participants' memories of the struggle to desegregate Central High School in Little Rock, Arkansas, discusses the complicated ways stereotypes about class, race, and gender interact with memory to construct reactions to, and stories about, the activities of that year. On a somewhat different note, she asserts that "women's activism always challenges domestic as well as public power relations, because by the very act of taking a position in the public domain women violate their patriarchal assignment to domesticity."[26] Yet, Julia Wrigley argues that women's activism in the anti-busing movement in Boston was a reflection of a "gender-specific assignment of political tasks," and that the gender segregation that characterized white working-class culture in South Boston effectively reinforced women's power and control in the movement.[27] Although women's activism did put some stress on families, she suggests, it generally fit with community norms and traditional values. Thus, participation in these activities did not really change the participants to any significant degree. In another context, Sally Ward Maggard notes that the women engaged in a hospital workers' strike in Kentucky did not receive the widespread community support they expected, apparently because they were violating local gender norms. In turn, however, that lack of support effectively radicalized them. As one put it:

> They thought we was just a bunch of dumb women out there. Well, we was a bunch of women out there, but I don't think we was quite as dumb as they thought we were. We may not have got the union, but we got them straightened out a little bit ... The experience of this now is worth more than gold![28]

As many of these writers have noted, consciousness changes often in unexpected ways.

Many of these same themes can be found in studies of women's activism in the Middle East, Argentina, Kenya, Nigeria, Italy, and Central Europe, as well as in the US, collected in *The Politics of Motherhood*.[29] These essays explicitly explore the ways motherhood has been politicized—both as a means to control women and as a means by which women have attempted to assert control over their own lives and those of their children and communities. The cultural, social, and political contexts in which these mothers act are, of course, vastly different. But, as Annelise Orleck notes, "Motherhood is always a politicized role ... The institution of Motherhood ... regulates acceptable behavior, restricts expression, and designates appropriate spaces for action." Those mothers who conform to the norms are rewarded; those who don't are punished. "It is against this nexus of power relations that mother-activism must be assessed."[30]

Echoing the findings of many other studies, virtually all of the mothers report becoming involved in activism out of fear or concern for their children, and/or to address basic survival needs of their communities (motivations consistent with Temma Kaplan's concept of "female consciousness"). Yet, it is also clear that many were deliberately *using* their status as mothers to justify activism that not only violated community norms, but may even have placed both them and their children in danger. Women, that is, can take advantage of the politics of motherhood, as well as be manipulated by it. One group well known for such strategizing, of course, is the Mothers of the Plaza de Mayo in Argentina (see above, Chapter 6). Diana Taylor notes, in this regard, that the Mothers were engaged in a "performance of motherhood"; that once they decided to march, "their self-representation was as theatrical as the military's."[31] But they were hardly alone. Simona Sharoni argues that Israeli women peace activists used images of motherhood strategically "to mobilize support for peace without appearing threatening and being relegated to the margins of Israeli-Jewish collectivity."[32] Their strategy seemed a wise one, at least in the short run; those who identified as "feminist peace activists" met with much more—and more violent—opposition. In an interesting parallel, Rema Hammami notes that, within the Palestinian movement, mothers were "socially-acceptable symbols of women's political struggle."[33] Self-identified mother-activists were better able than other women to escape repression— whether on the part of Israeli occupying forces, or local fundamentalist elements.

Temma Kaplan's fascinating essay on the "Aba Women's War" in Nigeria in 1929 explores both the Aba women's use of their sexuality as a defense against military/police repression (they undressed in front of soldiers, in an effort to shame them and prevent them from attacking), and Kaplan's (and her students') discomfort with such practices. The Nigerian women, Kaplan argues, used their maternal sexuality, and traditional values about it, in their attempts to assert political power. The tactic was quite effective against Nigerian soldiers, who shared their cultural background, and were shamed by the display; but it failed totally in relation to the British occupying force, which took the behavior of the women as further example of their "uncivilized nature," and opened fire. Kaplan's analysis does not stop there, however; for she wishes to explore the "troubled silence about the nakedness of mature women" on the part of US feminists. She points out that in Nigeria—where the culture accorded an independent role to women in certain social and political domains—cultural traditions recognized a connection between fertility, childbirth, sexuality and women's power. In that context, the display of women's naked bodies seemed to challenge male authority. US and Western European women, on the other hand, tend to ignore (or reject?) the power of maternal, or mature women's, sexuality. Kaplan offers a provocative challenge to our discomfort, suggesting that it may be "time to read the palms and confront our anxieties about the power inherent in maternal sexuality."[34]

Other essays focus on women who actively engage *as mothers* in hate movements. Claudia Koonz, for example, "investigate[s] the explosive connection between xenophobia, misogyny and maternal concerns as evidenced in the post-Cold War world." Echoing some of the issues raised by Susan Marshall in Blee's volume, Koonz argues that many of the women involved in these movements act out of fear. The question then is: What circumstances transform fear into panic—the sort of panic that leads to participation in racist hate-groups? Members of these groups, she suggests, are not conventional conservatives but "backlash conservatives," striving to restore a lost world. They organize in distinctly modern ways against feminism, where "feminism" becomes a stand-in for the confusion about, and challenges to, traditional values. In Eastern Europe, in particular, where the end of communism had much harsher impacts on women than on men, feminism and women are effectively taking the blame for the resulting social and cultural insecurity. (Many observers have noted a similar phenomenon with regard to the New Right in the United States.) In sum, in situations of crisis and panic, "difference trumps equality"—women/mothers may accept a secondary position vis-à-vis men in return for policies that maintain their superiority over "others."[35] Here, paradoxically, mothers' activism may, indeed, (temporarily) *expand* the base of political participation, but with the goal of *limiting* citizenship and constraining democracy.

Finally, Marianne Hirsch and Sara Ruddick offer important self-critical reflections on the politics of motherhood and motherist politics. Hirsch calls for a "mother-inclusive feminism" and a "feminist motherist politics."[36] Ruddick, whose *Maternal Thinking* (1989) has become a classic text of "difference feminism," seems to be tempering, if not recanting, the enthusiasm of her earlier work. While she has frequently argued against her critics that she never meant to identify nurturant caring as an essential characteristic of women, *The Politics of Motherhood* makes abundantly clear that "there are war mothers as well as peace mothers, racist as well as anti-fascist mothers." Ruddick does not shy away from the challenge this poses to her own position, nor from the complex ways motherhood has been politicized in the contemporary US. In the end, she argues that, while there is nothing necessary or "natural" about a progressive maternalist politics, there is, still, an important place for it: "There is no natural mother love, let alone a maternal love waiting to be politicized for peace, or care, or justice. Maternal politics will have to be invented."[37]

Kaplan's *Crazy for Democracy* is explicit in its concern about the connections between women's activism and expanded possibilities for democratic citizenship. Her case studies of the lives and activities of six grassroots women activists from the US and South Africa can serve as models for redefining politics and citizenship in an era of ever-more-distant, and seemingly unresponsive, government.

The use of the term "grassroots" to describe their activism refers to its "being free from any constraining political affiliations and being responsible to no authority except their own group."[38] Kaplan is explicit here about a phenomenon that we see reflected in many studies of women in social movements: that the women come to their activism through a concern for "what affects ordinary people every day." When they recognize needs, they act as good "democratic citizens," and call on governmental authorities to do something to meet them; if those authorities do not respond, the women take action to try to force them to do so. And in doing so, Kaplan argues—through creating local community groups in the US, or NGOs elsewhere—these activists effectively open up a "third space that is neither public nor private." They help to bring into being what is variously referred to as "civil society" or the "public sphere."[39]

Through case studies, Kaplan is able to explore issues in a relatively sustained way. She notes the connections many of these women came to see between motherhood and citizenship, the ways their activism led them to develop an analysis of "environmental racism," how they drew on pre-existing social networks, and how their activism led them to redefine human rights and articulate a new understanding of politics and citizenship. She insists, in fact, that these activists understand themselves to be acting *as* democratic citizens—not in a traditional electoral sense, but in the sense of politics as "public business." She finds, then, in the examples of their activism, "new and promising directions for democracy."

In a final theoretical chapter, Kaplan aims to explain why so many of the activists in contemporary peace, environmentalist, and community movements are women. She returns to "female consciousness," and to Maxine Molyneux's notion of "practical gender interests,"[40] both of which attempted to explain why and how women who are acting out of traditional gendered understandings of their roles can challenge established political authorities, often in quite radical ways. As have many students of (women and) social movements, Kaplan argues that seemingly "apolitical" women can come into confrontation with authorities when they believe themselves to be acting on behalf of survival needs. Beyond that, women "move back and forth between specific survival needs and general demands for human emancipation and justice."[41] Although she does not say so directly, Kaplan implies that the answer to the question "why women?" is that, precisely because of the gendered division of labor in these societies, women experience themselves, and are expected by others, to be the prime caretakers of families, neighborhoods, and communities—and, therefore, are the ones especially placed to make demands for their protection.[42]

True, much social movement theory ignores or undervalues the roles of women in these communities, or dismisses the activities in which they engage as ephemeral or peripheral. But Kaplan sees women's activities as critical to the revival of democracy precisely because of their refusal to separate "social need" from politics:

> Democracy is certainly not possible in the new millenium if it applies only to politicians elected to office through the work of campaigners who then withdraw and expect their candidates to intuit their will … Without citizens' commitments to put their own bodies on the line and their willingness to demonstrate in front of courthouses and congresses, there can be no democracy.[43]

In short, if women who are among the most marginalized and powerless in their societies can, nevertheless, effectively organize themselves and others to demand attention to their needs, there is, indeed, hope for democracy.

Contributors to *Cultures of Politics, Politics of Cultures*, focused on grassroots movements in Latin America, share Kaplan's explicit concern to examine popular movements within the framework of democratic citizenship. However, they contextualize their theoretical concerns somewhat more broadly. As the editors state, their aim is to "investigat[e] the relationship between neoliberal renditions of citizenship, social adjustment, and the cultural politics of social movements."[44] Virtually all the contributors approach their subjects through Gramsci's insight that politics is not simply about manipulations of economic power, nor is it to be identified with "the state," alone. Rather, political transformation, as Evelina Dagnino notes, involves "the process of building a new hegemony, which implies a new world conception [in which] the role of ideas and culture assumes a positive character."[45] It is in this context that "civil society" takes on such importance; for it is in this realm of civil society that cultures are articulated, identities are created, and politics, itself, comes to be defined and/or transformed. Dagnino argues, in fact, that social movements both extend and deepen democracy, not just "the democratization of the *political* regime but of the society as a whole, including therefore the cultural practices embodied in social relations of exclusion and inequality." How do they do so? Through redefining, in practice, notions of citizenship, human rights, and, ultimately, politics itself. Culture, then, constitutes an important ground of *political* struggle; and, conversely, "the redefinition of the notion of citizenship, as formulated by social movements, expresses not only a *political strategy* but also a *cultural politics*."[46]

These processes are neither simple nor straightforward. Cultural politics is ambiguous; the politics of cultural change are complex. Verónica Schild, Sonia Alvarez, and Elizabeth Jelin, for example, all point to the ways in which seemingly democratizing feminist social movements can serve other purposes. Schild argues that social movements may, themselves, "contribute to the emergence and development of new forms of domination." While women may be central to movements that address the basic needs of their communities, the membership, and especially the leadership, of such organizations is usually more wealthy, better-educated, and more white than are most members of the communities the organizations arise to serve. To the extent that governmental (or transnational) bodies turn to such organizations for policy-making or policy-implementation, "the terms of gendered citizenship and community" may "increasingly be ... established by some women in the name of all."[47] Ultimately, she suggests, the key question comes down to: Who has the right to define the terms of women's struggles? Sonia Alvarez and Elizabeth Jelin raise similar caveats about the roles of feminist NGOs in democratization projects. As Alvarez notes, tensions have already arisen—both within the Latin American context and at the Beijing International Women's conference—between the "*institucionalizadas*," those active within bureaucratic/institutional contexts, and the "*independistas*"; between the "*ongistas*" (members of NGOs) and "*el movimiento*," as to who speaks for women. NGOs, thus, cannot legitimately take on the burden of democratization in their societies, as they are not necessarily accountable to anyone—other than those who fund them! Even the growth of civil society, then, is no guarantee of full equality or of the representation of new interests or needs.[48]

There is another sense, as well, in which it is dangerous to assume that new social movements simply open new political space, and contribute to greater democracy. George Yúdice reminds us that organizations that form to articulate or to meet local needs *can* be expressions of democratic self-empowerment; but they can also be manipulated by neo-liberal regimes intent on "sloughing off" traditional governmental responsibilities. "Does not the effervescence of NGOs cut two ways," he asks—echoing many US progressives' reactions to George H.W. Bush's talk of "a thousand points of light": "helping to buttress a public sector evacuated by the state and at the same time making it possible for the state to steer clear of what was once seen as its responsibility?"[49] Alberto Melucci warns that "the myth that social demands can be straightforwardly translated into decision-making through an allegedly open competition ... fosters an ever more procedural version of democracy which serves to conceal new forms of domination and power."[50] And David Slater notes that "politics," as the "ensemble of practices, discourses, and institutions that seek to establish a certain order," is often about the "taming" of "the political," the tensions and antagonisms inherent in society. Paradoxically, "depoliticization is the most established task of politics."[51] More participation does not necessarily mean more democracy or equality; we must constantly attend to the contexts in which that participation takes place, and the uses to which it is put.

A number of authors address directly the meaning of *cultural* politics. Kay Warren explores how recent moves away from class-based activism in Guatemala and toward the creation of a "unified left" have, paradoxically, increased the *in*tolerance for indigenous groups and their agendas. Critics of the Pan-Mayanists, for example, dismiss them with the claim that they ignore political battles in favor of cultural ones. But, Warren argues (and we can surely hear, both in the critics and in her response to them, echoes of debates within the contemporary US feminist movement), Pan-Mayanists' efforts to articulate a "tactical and situational essentialism" that recognizes their cultural particularity make clear how deeply culture and politics are intertwined. In fact, she argues, "class" is as constructed a concept as is "culture."[52] Similarly, Libia Grueso, Carlos Rosero, and Arturo Escobar argue that the self-constitution and redefinition of *black* communities along the southern Pacific coast region of Colombia as *ethnic-cultural* communities is a *political*, as much as a cultural, activity. Indeed, it points to the "doubleness" of identity as both essential *and* constructed.[53]

Finally, many studies explore processes of politicization and consciousness-change, and particularly the ways social movements can challenge and transform the very definitions of politics. They point to the fact that many of these movements, rooted in meeting the subsistence needs of communities, can lead participants considerably beyond the "everyday" and into broader confrontations with the authorities. Ultimately, they can even become focused explicitly on expanding the boundaries of political life. What is, finally, at stake in these struggles, is democracy, itself: "the right to participate in the very definition of the political system, the right to define that in which they wish to be included."[54] Participatory social movements contribute to the actualization of a new definition of citizenship (in the view of Sergio Gregório Baierle) as "the right to have rights." Such movements, then, effectively redefine both "politics" and the "institutions that formulate 'responses.'"[55] Similarly, David Slater notes that "contemporary political movements have challenged and redrawn the frontiers of the political."[56]

Nevertheless, this "translation" between local/familial/communal "needs" and a radical questioning and redefinition of the political terrain is, as we have seen, complex and ambiguous. As Miguel Díaz-Barriga acknowledges, many of these activists deny that they are engaging in "politics," which they tend to identify with the "violent and corrupt public sphere of male politics." Their participation in grassroots activism seems to depend on their understanding of it as *separate* from (traditional) political activity. In rooting their activism in *"necesidad,"* they believe themselves to be creating a "borderland region between the domestic and public spheres."[57] Díaz-Barriga is not arguing, here, for the existence of a separation between "public" and "private" spheres; rather, he asserts (as have many feminist and other observers of social movements) that it is precisely the blurring of those boundaries that politicizes the participants and grounds the radical redefinition of politics and citizenship to which these movements give rise. But one wonders to what degree such movements *do* challenge definitions of politics, if the participants in them do not necessarily understand their actions in those terms. In fact, that very separation of "struggles around necessities"—or "community work"—from "politics" may leave the larger political system effectively untouched. In any case, there does not appear to be any necessary or easy "transfer" of what participants learn—either about themselves or about relationships of power—in a local context to what they conceive of as the larger political arena (see also Chapter 10).

More caveats are in order. Elizabeth Jelin tempers enthusiasm about the proliferation of NGOs and the growth of social movements, reminding us that polarization and economic inequality have been increasing dramatically throughout Latin America, despite substantial political democratization. Nevertheless, she is still hopeful about the potential contributions of these movements to democratizing projects. In language reminiscent of Kaplan's, she suggests that "the expressive role in the construction of collective identities and social recognition, and the instrumental role that challenges the existing institutional arrangements, are both essential for the vitality of democracy."[58]

Alberto Melucci welcomes the growth of social movements and notes that it is "impossible ... to separate collective action from struggles for citizenship, for civil and democratic guarantees." And, at the same time, "It would be an error to collapse collective action into politics." To do so would be to ignore, or to mask, the neoliberal project of reducing the scope of institutional politics and relegating to civil society organizations the responsibility to attend to community needs. More significantly, "the transformation of social demands into new rules and new rights is an open-ended task of democracy, a never-accomplished process." Democracy cannot eliminate power; at best, it can make its exercise more visible, and, therefore, open to contestation. In his view, then, the main contribution of social movements to democratization is that, in remaining to some degree outside the formal political system, they make conflicts visible, and allow power to be "called into question and negotiated in new forms."[59]

What is, perhaps, most striking here is the commonality of concerns and questions across these many studies. I trust it is not simply a result of my own disciplinary (political science) commitments that I take from them some lessons about the continuing significance of *politics*, in a broad sense. Most of those whose activism is described here have been, and continue to be, marginalized, if not completely excluded, from fully-equal participation *and power* in their respective political systems. Nevertheless, for all of the warnings these studies offer about the ways popular participation can be manipulated and undercut, virtually all argue that it is only *through* such activism that democracy is *being* enacted—or, at least, demanded—in many contexts around the world.

Over forty years ago, E.E. Schattschneider, Peter Bachrach, and Morton Baratz argued that power is wielded most effectively *behind the scenes*, not in efforts to control the *outcomes* of political conflicts, but, rather, through strategies to control the *agenda*, what is considered to be a legitimate focus of political attention and debate in the first place.[60] Building on that analysis, Frances Fox Piven and Richard Cloward argued in their provocative *Poor People's Movements* that the only power that the poor and marginalized really possess in a democracy is the power to disrupt "politics as usual." Piven has carried that analysis further in *Challenging Authority*, arguing that the power the dispossessed have is the power to withdraw their consent. They may be able to use that power occasionally, and in so doing to expand the boundaries of what are considered appropriate political issues; but the power is necessarily ephemeral and limited.[61]

The studies cited here seem both to confirm and to challenge those earlier perspectives. Stories of struggles on the part of those who would seem to have *no* grounds for hope are truly inspiring. Movements for environmental justice such as those inspired by Lois Gibbs and Dollie Burwell, in the US, and Wangari Maathai, in Kenya, not only introduced new items onto the political agendas of their respective communities and states, but actually secured new resources and contributed to the redirection of social policies. Sometimes, projects created by activists have been taken up and served as models for new governmental programs;[62] more frequently, alas, such programs are shut down, or taken over by government agencies to very different political effect. Nevertheless, they do remain as models; and those who experience them may well be changed by the process. How else can people learn about—or even learn to want more—democracy, other than by experiencing its effects? In this respect, I find it hard to ignore the claims of Díaz-Barriga and others that the activities they report "indicate ... new and promising directions for democracy."[63]

Significantly, virtually all of these studies have been written in the shadow of what is variously called "globalization" or "retrenchment." "Globalization" is the term typically used to refer to the impact of broader economic factors on Third-World countries and movements; in Euro-American contexts, discussions more often refer to "retrenchment," or budget crises. What is becoming increasingly clear, however, is that the political-economic processes at work in all of these contexts are similar. While it is true that economic and political conditions in the US, Canada, and Europe may be significantly different from those in Latin America, Africa, Asia, and Eastern Europe, nevertheless, treating "social movements" in Latin America, Africa, Asia, and Eastern Europe as though they were subject to completely different factors than "community activism" in the US, can make it difficult to see the similarities between them, and the mutual learning that can take place. Importantly, it minimizes the larger political-economic forces to which they are all increasingly subject. US feminists and social activists would do well, then, to attend to the stories of movements in other contexts, despite the readily-apparent differences between them.

Finally, what have we learned about women? Multiple studies of women in right-wing movements should certainly shatter the belief that women are somehow naturally open, nurturant, and more "progressive" than are men. Nevertheless, these studies do provide support for the claim that women play a particular role in community-based struggles around basic needs. Since, in the contemporary political-economic environment, it is frequently community-based struggles around basic needs that draw people into activism, we can probably expect that women will continue to figure prominently in such struggles. Whether, and under what conditions, the focus on meeting familial/communal needs will turn into a broader challenge to existing relations of authority—including relations of gender and race—remain open questions. But these are some of the most compelling reasons to continue attending to women's activism in all its many dimensions.

NOTES

INTRODUCTION

1 E.E. Schattschneider, *The Semi-Sovereign People: A Realist's View of Democracy in America* (New York: Holt, Rinehart and Winston, 1960), p. 35.

2 Note, for example, Robert Dahl, *Who Governs? Democracy and Power in an American City* (New Haven, CT: Yale University Press, 1961); Nelson Polsby, *Community Power and Political Theory* (New Haven, CT: Yale University Press, 1963); Robert Lane, *Political Man* (New York: The Free Press, 1972). Schattschneider's *The Semi-Sovereign People: A Realist's View of Democracy in America*; Peter Bachrach and Morton Baratz, "Two Faces of Power," *American Political Science Review* 56, 4 (Dec. 1962), pp. 947–52 and Peter Bachrach, *The Theory of Democratic Elitism: A Critique* (Boston: Little, Brown, 1967), of course, stood out as critical voices; but Matthew Crenson's *The Unpolitics of Air Pollution* (Baltimore, MD: Johns Hopkins University Press, 1971) and P. Bachrach and M. Baratz's *Power and Poverty: Theory and Practice* (New York: Oxford University Press, 1970) had not yet appeared. I am tremendously grateful to Isaac Balbus, whose courses, and whose own study of 1960s urban uprisings, offered us a model for examining contemporary political movements with political-theoretical lenses. See Balbus, *The Dialectics of Legal Repression; Black Rebels Before the American Criminal Courts* (New York: Russell Sage Foundation, 1973).

3 Robert Dahl's *A Preface to Democratic Theory* (New Haven, CT: Yale University Press, 1956) attempted—through the concept of "polyarchy"—to hold American practices up to some theoretical standard; but, at the time, we viewed those efforts as largely apologetic. See also, Dahl, *After the Revolution: Authority in a Good Society* (New Haven, CT: Yale University Press, 1970) and *On Democracy* (New Haven, CT: Yale University Press, 1998). His recent *How Democratic Is the American Constitution?* (New Haven, CT: Yale University Press, 2001) takes a more explicitly critical view. What was fascinating, of course, was that this was largely a disciplinary phenomenon: sociologists studying community power had long been finding entrenched structures of class-based power. See, e.g. Robert S. Lynd and Helen Merrell Lynd, *Middletown: A Study in Contemporary American Culture* (New York: Harcourt Brace, 1929); and Floyd Hunter, *Community Power Structure: A Study of Decision Makers* (Chapel Hill: University of North Carolina Press, 1953).

4 I remember our shock when, after a presentation of what we took to be a devastating critique of the (pluralist) literature on community power and local politics, Ron Zuckerman and I were told that our critique of the pluralist paradigm lacked empirical support.

5 E.g. Isaac Balbus, *The Dialectics of Legal Repression*; Lewis Lipsitz, "The Grievances of the Poor," in P. Green and S. Levinson, eds., *Power and Community* (New York:

Pantheon, 1970); Crenson, *The Un-Politics of Air Pollution*; Bachrach and Baratz, *Power and Community*; and Steven Lukes, *Power: A Radical View* (New York and London: Macmillan, 1974).

6 I have explored some of the dimensions of this "disconnect" in "Personal Identities and Collective Visions: Reflections on Identity, Community, and Difference," in *Contemporary Anarchist Studies: An Introductory Anthology of Anarchy in the Academy*, ed. Randall Amster, Abraham DeLeon, Luis A. Fernandez, Anthony J. Nocella, II, and Deric Shannon (New York: Routledge, 2009), pp. 259–69.

7 For one discussion of the ways in which feminist scholarship challenged conventional academic formulations, see Marilyn Schuster and Susan Van Dyne, "Stages of Curriculum Transformation," in *Women's Place in the Academy: Transforming the Liberal Arts Curriculum* (Totowa, NJ: Rowman and Allanheld, 1985), especially pp. 15–22.

8 *The Body Politic: Foundings, Citizenship and Difference in the American Political Imagination* (New York: Routledge, 2001), p. 176.

9 Frances Fox Piven and Richard Cloward made this case very powerfully in the U.S. context, especially in *Poor People's Movements: How They Succeed, Why They Fail* (New York: Pantheon, 1977); Piven has followed it up most recently with *Challenging Authority: How Ordinary People Change America* (Lanham, MD: Rowman and Littlefield, 2006). My thinking about the place of *women's* resistance, and that of the disempowered more generally, was also given impetus by my studies of anarchist activism and through my participation in a panel at the Berkshire Conference of Women Historians, Wellesley College, 1987, along with Jaccqueline Dowd Hall, Temma Kaplan, and Ardis Cameron, entitled "Disorderly Women." Along similar lines, Holloway Sparks has developed the notion of "dissident citizenship"; see "Dissident Citizenship: Democratic Theory, Political Courage, and Activist Women," *Hypatia* 12, 4 (Fall 1997), pp. 74–110.

10 The classic argument here is, of course, that of T.H. Marshall, "Citizenship and Social Class," in *Citizenship and Social Class and Other Essays* (Cambridge: Cambridge University Press, 1950), especially pp. 6–27. See also Judith Shklar, *American Citizenship: The Quest for Inclusion* (Cambridge, MA: Harvard University Press, 1991); Ernesto Laclau and Chantal Mouffe, *Hegemony and Socialist Strategy: Toward a Radical Democratic Politics* (London: Verso, 1985); Chantal Mouffe, "Democratic Citizenship and the Political Community," in Moutte, ed., *Dimensions of Radical Democracy: Pluralism, Citizenship, Community* (London: Verso, 1992), pp. 225–39 and Nancy Fraser and Axel Honneth, *Redistribution or Recognition? A Political-Philosophical Exchange* (London: Verso, 2003). Zillah Eisenstein made a related argument about the logic of liberal discourse in *The Radical Future of Liberal Feminism* (New York: Longman, 1981).

11 My thinking on these issues is much indebted to the work of Nira Yuval-Davis, especially her recent writing on "Belonging and the Politics of Belonging," *Patterns of Prejudice* 40, 3 (July 2006), pp. 197–214 and Nira Yuval-Davis, Floya Anthias and Eleonore Kofman, "Secure Borders and Safe Haven and the Gendered Politics of Belonging: Beyond Social Cohesion," *Ethnic & Racial Studies* 28, 3 (May 2005), pp. 513–35. Questions of inclusivity and exclusivity, central to the final chapters of this volume, have also been explored by Judith Shklar, *American Citizenship: The Quest for Inclusion* (Cambridge, MA: Harvard University Press, 1991); Ruth Lister, "Inclusive Citizenship: Realizing the Potential," *Citizenship Studies* 11, 1 (February 2007), pp. 49–61; Shane Phelan, *Sexual Strangers: Gays, Lesbians, and Dilemmas of Citizenship* (Philadelphia, PA: Temple University Press, 2001); and Engen Isen, *Being Political: Genealogies of Citizenship* (Minneapolis: University of Minnesota Press, 2002) and Isen, "Engaging, Being, Political," *Political Geography* 24, 3 (March 2007), pp. 373–87,

where he notes that his work is an effort to investigate "citizenship historically as a generalized problem of otherness" (p. 374).

12 Luke Desforges, Rhys Jones and Mike Woods, "New Geographies of Citizenship," *Citizenship Studies* 9, 5 (November 2005), pp. 447, 448. See also Ruth Lister, "Inclusive Citizenship," pp. 55–56; and Archon Fung and Erik Olin Wright, *Deepening Democracy: Institutional Innovations in Empowered Participatory Governance* (London: Verso, 2003); and Archon Fung, *Empowered Participation: Reinventing Urban Democracy* (Princeton, NJ: Princeton University Press, 2004).

13 "Inclusive Citizenship," p. 56, citing Plummer, "The Square of Intimate Citizenship: Some Preliminary Proposals," *Citizenship Studies* 5, 3 (2001), pp. 15, 68.

14 "Obama's Personal LinkedIn," *The New York Times*, Monday, Nov. 10, B1, B6.

1 WOMEN'S COLLABORATIVE ACTIVITIES

1 See, for example, Frances Fox Piven and Richard Cloward, *The New Class War* (New York: Pantheon, 1982); and Sheldon Wolin, "The People's Two Bodies," *democracy* (January 1981), pp. 9–24.

2 See Ira Katznelson, *City Trenches* (New York: Pantheon, 1981); William Kornblum, *Blue Collar Community* (Chicago: University of Chicago Press, 1974); Thomas Bender, "The End of the City?" *democracy* (Winter 1983), pp. 8–20.

3 See, for example, Darlene Gay Levy and Harriet Applewhite, "Women of the Popular Classes in Revolutionary Paris, 1789–95," in *Women, War and Revolution*, eds. Carol R. Berkin and Clara M. Lovett (New York: Holmes and Meier, 1980), pp. 9–35; Temma Kaplan, "Female Consciousness and Collective Action: The Case of Barcelona, 1910–18," *Signs* (Spring 1982), pp. 545–66; Ronald Lawson, Stephen E. Barton and Jenna Weissman Joselit, "From Kitchen to Storefront: Women in the Tenant Movement," in *New Space for Women*, eds. Gerda Wekerle, Rebecca Peterson, and David Morley (Boulder, CO: Westview Press, 1980), pp. 255–71; Cheryl Townsend Gilkes, "'Holding Back the Ocean with a Broom': Black Women and Community Work," in *The Black Woman*, ed. LaFrances Rogers-Rose (Beverly Hills, CA: Sage Publications, 1980), pp. 217–31; Cynthia Cockburn, "When Women Get Involved in Community Action," in *Women in the Community*, ed. Marjorie Mayo (London: Routledge and Kegan Paul, 1977), pp. 61–70; E.M. Ettorre, "Women, Urban Social Movements and the Lesbian Ghetto," *International Journal of Urban and Regional Research* (October 1978), pp. 499–520; and Elisabeth Wilson, "Women in the Community," in *Women in the Community*, ed. Marjorie Mayo (London: Routledge and Kegan Paul, 1977), pp. 1–11.

4 See, for example, Nancy Cott, *The Bonds of Womanhood* (New Haven, CT: Yale University Press, 1977); Susan Saegert, "Masculine Cities and Feminine Suburbs: Polarized Ideas, Contradictory Realities," *Signs* (Spring 1980), pp. S96–111; Cheryl Townsend Gilkes, "'Holding Back the Ocean with a Broom'"; Cynthia Cockburn, *The Local State* (London: Pluto Press, 1977); Ellen Ross, "Survival Networks and Domestic Sharing in an East London Neighborhood, 1870–1914," paper presented at the Berkshire Conference on the History of Women, Vassar College, Poughkeepsie, New York, June 1981, and see also Ross, *Love and Toil: Motherhood in Outcast London, 1870–1918* (New York: Oxford University Press, 1993); Mary P. Ryan, "The Power of Women's Networks," *Feminist Studies* (Spring 1979), pp. 66–86; Laurel Thatcher Ulrich, "A Friendly Neighbor: Social Dimensions of Daily Work in Northern Colonial New England," *Feminist Studies* (Summer 1980), pp. 392–405; and Carol Gilligan, *In a Different Voice* (Cambridge, MA: Harvard University Press, 1982).

5 For urban communities specifically, see Sam Bass Warner, *Streetcar Suburbs* (Cambridge, MA: MIT Press, 1962) and *The Private City* (Philadelphia: University of Pennsylvania Press, 1968). For looks at broader metropolitan areas, see Michael N. Danielson, *The Politics of Exclusion* (New York: Columbia University Press, 1976), and Anthony Downs, *Opening Up the Suburbs* (New Haven, CT: Yale University Press, 1973).

6 Katznelson, *City Trenches*, p. 71.

7 Ibid., p. 45.

8 Ibid., p. 194.

9 Wolin's argument in "The People's Two Bodies," as well as those of Piven and Cloward and Bender discussed below, is clearly indebted to E.E. Schattschneider's *The Semi-Sovereign People* (New York: Holt, Rinehart, 1960), which first drew connections between the restriction of the agenda of politics and its implications for democratic participation and control. See also Walter Dean Burnham, "The Changing Shape of the American Political Universe," *American Political Science Review* 59, 1 (March 1965), pp. 7–28.

10 *The New Class War*, p. 99.

11 "The American Road to Socialism," *democracy* (Summer 1983), pp. 58–69.

12 Ibid., p. 59. Michael Walzer made a similar argument in "Town Meetings and Workers' Control: A Parable for Socialists," *Dissent* (Summer 1978), pp. 325–33; see also Philip Green, *The Pursuit of Inequality* (New York: Pantheon, 1981).

13 Bender, "The End of the City?" *democracy* (Winter, 1983), p. 20.

14 *City Trenches*, p. 64.

15 Ibid., p. 45, also p. 71.

16 Elizabeth Lawrence, "The Working Women's Charter Campaign," in *Women in the Community*, ed. Marjorie Mayo (London and Boston: Routledge and Kegan Paul, 1977), cited in Ettorre, "Women, Urban Social Movements, and the Lesbian Ghetto," p. 510. Compare, for example, Cynthia Cockburn's report of her conversation with a woman activist:

> May Hobbs, a couple of years after the night cleaners' campaign in which she played a leading part, said to me: "People always wanted me to speak about cleaners, nothing but that. That was, a small part of it for me. I'm a woman. It's one big struggle, a woman's struggle, it's not just organizing round our jobs, but it's to do with housing, health, everything that affects you."
> (Cockburn, "When Women Get Involved in Community Action," p. 64)

17 See e.g., *City Trenches* p. 210.

18 See Diana Pearce, "Women, Work and Welfare: The Feminization of Poverty," in *Working Women and Families*, ed. Karen Wolk Feinstein (Beverly Hills, CA: Sage Publications, 1979), pp. 103–24; Jo Freeman, "Women and Urban Policy," *Signs* (Spring 1980, Supplement), p. S6; and Margaret Sims, "Women and Housing: The Impact of Government Housing Policy," in *Families, Politics and Public Policies*, ed. Irene Diamond (New York: Longman, 1983), p. 131.

19 Freeman, "Women and Urban Policy," p. S13.

20 Ann R. Markusen, "City Spatial Structure, Women's Household Work, and National Urban Policy," *Signs* (Spring 1980, Suppl.), p. S23; see also Eva Gamarnikow, "Introduction," The Women and the City Issue, *International Journal of Urban and Regional Research* (October 1978), pp. 395–97.

21 See also Dolores Hayden, *The Grand Domestic Revolution* (Cambridge, MA: MIT Press, 1981) and (although these had not yet been published at the time this article was originally written) *Redesigning the American Dream: The Future of Housing, Work, and*

Family Life (New York: W.W. Norton, 1984), and *Building Suburbia: Green Fields and Urban Growth, 1820–2000* (New York: Pantheon, 2003).

22 Val Burris and Amy Wharton, "Sex Segregation in the U.S. Labor Market," *Review of Radical Political Economics* (Fall 1982), pp. 51–52; Mary Lindenstein Walshok, "Occupational Values and Family Roles: Women in Blue-Collar and Service Occupations," in *Working Women and Families*, ed. Karen Feinstein (Beverly Hills, CA: Sage Publications, 1979), pp. 65–67; Freeman, "Women and Urban Policy," p. S16; and Markusen, "City Spatial Structure," p. S30.

23 Downs, *Opening Up the Suburbs*; Dennis W. Roncek, Ralph Bell, and Harvey M. Choldin, "Female-headed Families: An Ecological Model of Residential Concentration in a Small City," *Journal of Marriage and the Family* (February 1980), pp. 167–68; Sims, "Women and Housing"; and Gamarnikow, "Introduction," pp. 400–1.

24 See Helen Znaniecki Lopata, "The Chicago Woman: A Study of Patterns of Mobility and Transportation," *Signs* (Spring 1980, Suppl.), pp. S161–69; Freeman, "Women and Urban Policy," p. S12; Danielle Chabaud and Dominique Fongeyrollas, "Travail domestique et espace-temps des femmes," *International Journal of Urban and Regional Research* (October 1978), pp. 429–31; and J. Contras and J. Fagnani, "Femmes et transports en milieu urban," *International Journal of Urban and Regional Research* (October 1978), pp. 432–39.

25 Markusen, "City Spatial Structure," p. S37.

26 In addition to Pearce, "Women, Work and Welfare," already cited, see Elliott Currie, Robert Dunn and David Fogarty, "The New Immiseration: Stagflation, Inequality and the Working Class," *Socialist Review* (November–December 1980), pp. 7–31; Ruth Sidel, "The Family: A Dream Deferred," in *What Reagan Is Doing to Us*, ed. Alan Gartner, Colin Greer and Frank Riessman (New York: Harper and Row, 1982), pp. 54–70; and Steven Erie, Martin Rein, and Barbara Wiget, "Reagan Revolution: Thermidor for the Social Welfare Economy," in *Families, Politics and Public Policies*, ed. Irene Diamond (New York: Longman, 1983), pp. 94–119.

27 Duran Bell, "Why Participation Rates of Black and White Wives Differ," *Journal of Human Resources* (Fall 1974), pp. 465–79; Nancy S. Barrett and Richard D. Morgenstern, "Why Do Blacks and Women Have High Unemployment Rates?" *Journal of Human Resources* (Fall 1974), pp. 452–64; Steven Erie and Martin Rein, "Welfare: The New Poor Laws," in *What Reagan Is Doing to Us*, eds. Alan Gartner, Colin Greer and Frank Riessman (New York: Harper and Row, 1982), pp. 74–75; Chester Hartman, "Housing," in *What Reagan Is Doing to Us*, eds. Gartner, Greer and Riessman, pp. 141–61; and Margaret Sims, "Women and Housing," pp. 130–34.

28 U.S. Bureau of the Census, *Money, Income and Poverty Status of Families and Persons in the United States: 1981* (Advance Data from the March 1982 Current Population Survey), Series P-60, no. 134 (Washington, DC: Government Printing Office, 1982), Table 18. The corresponding figures for 2006 were 28.3 percent of all families headed by a woman fell below the poverty level; 36.4 percent of all families headed by a black woman, and 36 percent of all families headed by an Hispanic woman. See www.census.gov/hhes/www/poverty/histpov4.html, accessed July 8, 2008.

29 Simms, "Women and Housing"; Irene Diamond, "Women and Housing: The Limitations of Liberal Reform," in *Women, Power and Policy*, ed. Ellen Boneparth (New York: Pergamon Press, 1982), pp. 109–17; Freeman, "Women and Urban Policy"; Markusen, "City Spatial Structure"; Gamarnikow, "Introduction"; and Hayden, "What Would a Non-Sexist City Be Like?"

30 I am grateful to Irene Diamond for making clear to me the limitations of the apparent determinism of some of their analyses with respect to the relationship between capitalism and patriarchy.

31 In a recent (2008) article, Nancy Hirschmann explores more deeply some of complexities of the relationship between women's work and equality. See "Mill, Political Economy, and Women's Work," *American Political Science Review* 102, 2 (May 2008), pp. 199–213.

32 See Cockburn, *The Local State*, especially Chapters 2 and 6. Socialist-feminist critics have termed this process the "social reproduction of labor." I prefer to avoid that usage, primarily because of its economistic connotations. Clearly, the process of preparing people for full membership in society is a requisite of any ongoing social group.

33 In addition to Cockburn (cited above), see Wilson, "Women in the Community," p. 4; and Lawrence, "The Working Women's Charter Campaign," p. 12. For a discussion of the absorption by women of variations in standard of living (but which does not quite make this argument about the sexual division of labor), see Laura Oren, "The Welfare of Women in Labouring Families in England, 1860–1950," *Feminist Studies* (Winter–Spring 1973), pp. 107–25.

34 "Holding Back the Ocean with a Broom."

35 See Cockburn, "When Women Get Involved in Community Action," pp. 62–66. Myrna Breitbart and I developed aspects of this argument—specifically with respect to the formation of urban women's political consciousness—in "Terrains of Struggle" (Chapter 3 in this volume). Lawrence has noted that women's relationship to home, as well as to work, is fundamentally different from men's. "Thus, home," she notes, "is a radically different experience for male and female workers. For the former it is a compensation for the unpleasantness of work, for the latter it is more work—although both may also perceive the home as an escape from the workplace." Lawrence, "Working Women's Charter," pp. 14–15.

36 *The Local State*, p. 163.

37 "Holding Back the Ocean with a Broom."

38 Marc Raboy, "The Future of Montreal and the MCM," *Our Generation* 4 (1978); see also Cockburn's reports of her interviews with women activists in "When Women Get Involved in Community Action," p. 64.

39 At the time of the original publication of this chapter, Frances Fox Piven and Richard Cloward's, *The New Class War* (1982) offered a particularly acute analysis; see especially pp. 136–42; as did Steven Erie and Martin Rein in "Welfare: The New Poor Laws," especially pp. 82–84. In more recent years, attention to these issues has exploded. See, for example, *Global Woman: Nannies, Maids, and Sex Workers in the New Economy*, eds. Barbara Ehrenreich and Arlie Russell Hochschild (New York: Metropolitan Books, 2002) and Nancy Folbre, *The Invisible Heart: Economics and Family Values* (New York: The New Press, 2001).

40 See Ettorre, "Women, Social Movements, and the Lesbian Ghetto," especially pp. 507–10; Temma Kaplan, "Women and Mass Strikes," paper presented to the Summer Workshop, Project on Women and Social Change, Smith College, June 1981; and Kaplan's more recent *Taking Back the Streets: Women, Youth and Direct Democracy* (Berkeley: University of California Press, 2004); Ida Susser, *Norman Street: Poverty and Politics in an Urban Neighborhood* (New York: Oxford University Press, 1982); and Martha Ackelsberg, "'Separate and Equal'? Mujeres Libres and Anarchist Strategy for Women's Emancipation," *Feminist Studies* XI, 1 (1985), pp. 63–83.

41 *The Local State*, p. 177; see also "When Women Get Involved," p. 62.

42 Much of the analysis to follow was developed with Myrna Breitbart in the process of writing "Terrains of Struggle"; see Chapter 3 in this volume. On women in urban social movements see, in addition to works cited above, Levy and Applewhite, "Women of the Popular Classes in Revolutionary Paris"; Kaplan, "Female Consciousness and Collective Action"; Ronald Lawson and Stephen E. Barton,

"Sex Roles in Social Movements: A Case Study of the Tenant Movement in New York City," *Signs* (Winter 1980), pp. 230–47; Lawson, Barton, and Joselit, "From Kitchen to Storefront"; Annelise Orleck, *Storming Caesar's Palace: How Black Mothers Fought Their Own War on Poverty* (Boston: Beacon Press, 2005); *The Politics of Motherhood: Activist Voices from Left to Right*, eds. Alexis Jetter, Annelise Orleck, and Diana Taylor (Hanover, NH: University Press of New England [for] Dartmouth College, 1997); Nancy Naples, ed., *Community Activism and Feminist Politics: Organizing Across Race, Class, and Gender* (New York: Routledge, 1998) and Naples, *Grassroots Warriors: Activist Mothering, Community Work, and the War on Poverty* (New York: Routledge, 1998).

43 In addition to Kaplan's "Female Consciousness and Collective Action" and *Taking Back the Streets*, see *Crazy for Democracy: Women in Grassroots Movements* (New York: Routledge, 1997).

44 Lawson, Barton and Joselit, "From Kitchen to Storefront," p. 256.

45 Ibid., p. 257. Since this chapter was originally written, much feminist scholarship has focused on precisely these types of activism. I discuss the more recent literature in Chapters 2, 8, 9, 10, and 12, below.

46 My own work on Spanish anarchist women who were active in some of these sorts of struggles confirms the importance of informal networks. Many women were unable, for example, to describe how plans for consumer strikes or bread riots were communicated to the people in the neighborhood: "One simply heard about it," they would report, or "you would be on the street and you would hear that all should be at such and such a place at such and such a time." See *Free Women of Spain*, especially Chapter 2. On the importance of such informal networking—and of women's roles within it—in Spanish urban movements more generally, see also Nick Rider, "The Practice of Direct Action: The Barcelona Rent Strike of 1931," in *For Anarchism: History, Theory, and Practice*, ed. David Goodway (London and New York: Routledge, 1989), pp. 79–105; and Chris Ealham, "The Myth of the Maddened Crowd," in *The Splintering of Spain: Cultural History and the Spanish Civil War, 1936–1939*, eds. Chris Ealham and Michael Richards (Cambridge: Cambridge University Press, 2005), pp. 111–32.

47 "Holding Back the Ocean," p. 221.

48 I discuss the NCNW in more detail in Chapter 10 in this volume. See also Carol Brightman, "The Women of Williamsburg," *Working Papers* (Jan/Feb 1978), pp. 50–57; Ida Susser, *Norman Street*; Tamar Carroll, ed., "How Did Working-Class Feminists Meet the Challenges of Working Across Differences? The National Congress of Neighborhood Women, 1974–2006," available at www.alexanderstreet6.com/wasm; and Carroll, "Unlikely Allies: Forging a Multiracial, Class-based Women's Movement in 1970s Brooklyn," in *Feminist Coalitions: Historical Perspectives on Second-Wave Feminism in the United States*, ed. Stephanie Gilmore; foreword by Sara M. Evans (Urbana: University of Illinois Press, 2008), pp. 196–224.

49 Most notably, in the first instance, Carol Gilligan, *In a Different Voice* (Cambridge, MA: Harvard University Press, 1982); see also Susser, *Norman Street*; Saegert, "Masculine Cities and Feminine Suburbs." For more recent explorations of these issues see Chapters 2, 6, 9, and 10 in this volume.

50 Research in this area has exploded since this chapter was originally published. In addition to sources cited then [Carol Smith-Rosenberg, "The Female World of Love and Friendship," *Signs* (Autumn 1975), pp. 1–29; Nancy Cott, *The Bonds of Womanhood* (New Haven, CT: Yale University Press, 1977); Mary P. Ryan, "The Power of Women's Networks: A Case Study of Female Moral Reform in Antebellum America," *Feminist Studies* (Spring 1979), pp. 66–86; and Martha Ackelsberg, "Sisters or Comrades? The Politics of Friends and Families," in

Families, Politics, and Public Policies, ed. Irene Diamond (New York: Longman, 1983), pp. 339–56], see also Nancy A. Hewitt, *Southern Discomfort: Women's Activism in Tampa, Florida, 1880s–1920s* (Urbana: University of Illinois Press, 2001) and *Women's Activism and Social Change: Rochester, New York, 1822–1872* (Ithaca, NY: Cornell University Press, 1984); Ardis Cameron, *Radicals of the Worst Sort: Laboring Women in Lawrence, Massachusetts, 1860–1912* (Urbana: University of Illinois Press, 1993), Ruth Milkman, *L.A. Story: Immigrant Workers and the Future of the U.S. Labor Movement* (New York: Russell Sage Foundation, 2006); and anthologies such as Ruth Milkman, ed., *Women, Work, and Protest: A Century of US Women's Labor History* (Boston: Routledge & Kegan Paul, 1985), *Visible Women: New Essays on American Activism*, eds. Nancy A. Hewitt and Suzanne Lebsock (Urbana: University of Illinois Press, 1993), *Unequal Sisters: A Multicultural Reader in U.S. Women's History*, eds. Ellen Carol DuBois and Vicki L. Ruiz (New York: Routledge, Chapman and Hall, 1990), and *Women Transforming Politics: An Alternative Reader*, eds. Cathy J. Cohen, Kathleen B. Jones, and Joan C. Tronto (New York: New York University Press, 1997).

51 "When Women Get Involved," pp. 67, 69.

52 See Dimitri Roussopoulos, interview with author (Montreal, Quebec), August 1, 1982 and Marc Raboy, "The Future of Montreal and the MCM," *Our Generation* 4 (1978); on a similar phenomenon among citizen movements in Madrid, see Manuel Castells, *The City and the Grassroots* (Berkeley: University of California Press, 1983).

53 Freeman, "Women and Urban Policy," p. S13.

54 The questions raised here were inspired by—and meant to parallel—those raised by Herbert Gans in his questioning of the conventional wisdom that the West End of Boston was a "slum." See Gans, *The Urban Villagers* (New York: Free Press, 1962); also Carol Stack, *All Our Kin* (New York: Harper and Row, 1975), who challenged the claim that urban black families are chaotic and unstructured; and the related work of Ida Susser, *Norman Street* (New York: Oxford University Press, 1982), with respect to a white working-class community in Brooklyn.

55 Wolin, "What Revolutionary Action Means Today," *democracy* (Fall 1982), p. 27; see also Sara Evans and Harry Boyte, "Schools for Action: Radical Uses for Social Space," *democracy* (Fall 1982), p. 57; Hanna Pitkin and Sara Shumer, "On Participating," *democracy* (Fall 1982), pp. 46, 48; and Michael Walzer, *Obligations* (Cambridge, MA: Harvard University Press, 1970), especially Chapters 10 and 11. In more recent years, a number of other scholars have taken up the question of changes in the nature and practice of democracy in the US. See, for example, Benjamin Barber, *A Passion for Democracy: American Essays* (Princeton, NJ: Princeton University Press, 2000); Matthew Crenson and Benjamin Ginsburg, *Downsizing Democracy: How America Sidelined Its Citizens and Privatized Its Public* (Baltimore, MD: Johns Hopkins University Press, 2002); and Theda Skocpol, *Diminished Democracy: From Membership to Management in American Civic Life* (Norman: University of Oklahoma Press, 2003).

56 The term is Colin Ward's, in a discussion of anarchist practices as they appear in everyday life. See *Anarchy in Action* (New York: Harper and Row, 1973).

57 This problem is, of course, one classic formulation of the liberal dilemma of politics: how to maintain identity and self-interest in the context of a political community; or, conversely, how to form a political *community* out of a conglomerate of self-interested individuals. Nancy Hartsock and Irene Diamond explore the limitations of starting from "interests," an approach which "reduce[s] the human community to an instrumental, arbitrary, and deeply unstable alliance," in "Beyond Interests in Politics: A Comment on Virginia Sapiro's 'When Are Interests Interesting?'" *American Political Science Review* 75, 3 (September 1981), p. 719. I explore some of these

issues in greater depth in *Free Women of Spain*, especially the concluding chapter, and Chapters 10, 12 in this volume.

58 Cockburn, "When Women Get Involved," pp. 69–70.

2 COMMUNITIES, RESISTANCE, AND WOMEN'S ACTIVISM

1 In fact, most theorists seem to assume that the ideal-typical citizen is male. On this point, see T. Brennan and C. Pateman, "'Mere Auxiliaries to the Commonwealth': Women and the Origins of Liberalism," *Political Studies* 27, 2 (1979), pp. 183–200.

2 The most sophisticated contemporary articulation of this perspective is John Rawls, *A Theory of Justice* (Cambridge, MA: Harvard University Press, 1971). Michael Sandel criticizes precisely Rawls's claims of the primacy of "right" over "good" in *Liberalism and the Limits of Justice* (Cambridge: Cambridge University Press, 1982).

3 The clearest explication of this perspective is, of course, Robert Dahl's, *Who Governs? Democracy and Power in an American City* (New Haven, CT: Yale University Press, 1961), pp. 223–25, 276–81; see also Max Weber, "Politics as a Vocation," in *From Max Weber: Essays in Sociology*, eds. H. H. Gerth and C. W. Mills (New York: Oxford University Press, 1958), pp. 77–128, esp. pp. 78–83; and Joseph Schumpeter, *Capitalism, Socialism and Democracy* (New York: Harper, 1950).

4 See, for example, Peter Bachrach and Morton Baratz, "Two Faces of Power," *American Political Science Review*, 56 (1962), pp. 947–52; Isaac Balbus, "The Concept of Interest in Pluralist and Marxian Analysis," *Politics and Society* 1, 2 (1971), pp. 151–77; William Connolly, "On 'Interests' in Politics," *Politics and Society* 2, 4 (1972), pp. 459–77; Lewis Lipsitz, "The Grievances of the Poor," in *Power and Community*, eds. P. Green and S. Levinson (New York: Random House, 1970), pp. 142–72; Michael Parenti, "Power and Pluralism: The View from the Bottom," *Journal of Politics* 32 (1970), pp. 501–30; E. E. Schattschneider, *The Semi-Sovereign People* (New York: Holt, Rinehart, & Winston, 1960); John Gaventa, *Power and Powerlessness: Quiescence and Rebellion in an Appalachian Valley* (Urbana: University of Illinois Press, 1980); and Michael Walzer, "Town Meetings and Workers Control: A Story for Socialists," *Dissent* 25 (Summer 1978), pp. 325–33. More recent explorations of related issues include Matthew Crenson and Benjamin Ginsberg, *Downsizing Democracy: How America Sidelined Its Citizens and Privatized Its Public* (Baltimore, MD: Johns Hopkins University Press, 2002); Theda Skocpol, *Diminished Democracy: From Membership to Management in American Civic Life* (Norman: University of Oklahoma Press, 2003); and Philip Green, *Equality and Democracy* (New York: The New Press, 1998), and *Retrieving Democracy: In Search of Civic Equality* (Totowa, NJ: Rowman & Allanheld, 1985).

5 See, for example, Louise Lamphere and Guillermo J. Grenier, "Women, Unions, and Participative Management: Organizing in the Sunbelt," in *Women and the Politics of Empowerment*, eds. Ann R. Bookman and Sandra R. Morgen (Philadelphia, PA: Temple University Press, 1988), pp. 227–56. On other political changes that have the effect of undermining efficacy see Skocpol, *Diminished Democracy*; Crenson and Ginsberg, *Downsizing Democracy*; Sheldon Wolin, "Inverted Totalitarianism," *The Nation* (May 19, 2003), pp. 13–15; and Sidney Verba, Kay Lehman Schlozman, and Henry E. Brady, *Voice and Equality: Civic Voluntarism in American Politics* (Cambridge, MA: Harvard University Press, 1995). Finally, Lani Guinier's work on electoral districting is, in many respects, an extended essay on structural impediments to political efficacy. See especially Guinier, "Groups, Representation, and Race-Conscious Districting," in Guinier, *The Tyranny of the Majority: Fundamental Fairness in Representative Democracy* (New York: Free Press, 1994), pp. 119–56; "The Tyranny of the Majority," from *The Tyranny of the Majority*, pp. 1–20; Guinier, "Lift

Every Voice," from *Lift Every Voice: Turning a Civil Rights Setback into a New Vision of Social Justice* (New York: Simon & Schuster, 1998), pp. 273–311, and Guinier and Gerald Torres, *The Miner's Canary* (Cambridge, MA: Harvard University Press, 2002).

6 The classic works on agenda-setting are Murray Edelman, "Symbols and Political Quiescence," *American Political Science Review* 54 (September 1960), pp. 695–704; Bachrach and Baratz, "Two Faces of Power," and Bachrach and Baratz, "Decisions and Nondecisions: An Analytical Framework," *American Political Science Review* 57, 3 (Sept. 1963), pp. 632–42; and Schattschneider, *The Semi-Sovereign People*.

7 Edward C. Banfield, *The Unheavenly City Revisited* (Boston: Little, Brown, 1974), esp. 211ff.

8 See, for example, Susan C. Bourque and Jean Grossholtz, "Politics as Unnatural Practice: Political Science Looks at Women's Participation," *Politics and Society* 4, 2 (1974), pp. 225–66; and Jean Elshtain, "Moral Woman and Immoral Man: A Consideration of the Public–Private Split and Its Ramifications," *Politics and Society* 4, 4 (1974), pp. 453–73. More recent writings, that incorporate valuable case studies, include Sandra Morgen, "It's the Whole Power of the City Against Us," in *Women and the Politics of Empowerment*, eds. A. Bookman and S. Morgen; Ida Susser, *Norman Street: Poverty and Politics in an Urban Neighborhood* (New York: Oxford University Press, 1982); Temma Kaplan, "Community and Resistance in Women's Political Cultures," *Dialectical Anthropology* 15, 2/3 (1990), pp. 259–67; Kaplan, *Crazy for Democracy: Women in Grassroots Movements* (New York: Routledge, 1997) and *Taking Back the Streets: Women, Youth and Direct Democracy* (Berkeley: University of California Press, 2004); William Chafe, "Women's History and Political History," pp. 101–18, in *Visible Women: New Essays on American Activism*, eds. Nancy A. Hewitt and Suzanne Lebsock (Urbana: University of Illinois Press, 1993) and Sara Evans, "Women's History and Political Theory," in *Visible Women*, pp. 119–39; and Ardis Cameron, *Radicals of the Worst Sort: Laboring Women in Lawrence, Massachusetts, 1860–1912* (Urbana: University of Illinois Press, 1995). I explore this issue further in Chapter 10 in this volume.

9 See, for example, Sheldon Wolin, "The People's Two Bodies," *democracy* 1, 1 (1981), pp. 9–24; Frances Fox Piven and Richard A. Cloward, *The New Class War* (New York: Pantheon, 1982); Ira Katznelson, *City Trenches* (New York: Pantheon, 1981), and my exploration in Chapter 1 in this volume.

10 See, for example, Bourque and Grossholtz, "Politics as Unnatural Practice"; Elshtain, "Moral Woman"; Nancy Hartsock, *Money, Sex, and Power: An Essay on Domination and Community* (New York: Longman, 1983); Anne Phillips, *Engendering Democracy* (University Park, PA: Pennsylvania State University Press, 1991); and Carole Pateman, "Feminist Critiques of the Public–Private Dichotomy," in C. Pateman, *The Disorder of Women: Democracy, Feminism and Political Theory* (Stanford, CA: Stanford University Press, 1989), pp. 118–40.

11 Among the numerous studies exploring this process of devaluation, see Kristen Amundsen, *A New Look at the Silenced Majority* (Englewood Cliffs, NJ: Prentice-Hall, 1977); William Chafe, *Women and Equality* (New York: Oxford University Press, 1976), especially for his comparison of the Black and feminist movements in this country; and Jacqueline Dowd Hall, "Disorderly Women: Gender and Labor Militancy in the Appalachian South," *The Journal of American History* 73, 2 (Sept. 1986), pp. 354–82.

12 See especially Jo Freeman, "Women and Urban Policy," *Signs* 5, 3 (Suppl. 1980), pp. S4–21; Ann R. Markusen, "City Spatial Structure, Women's Household Work, and National Urban Policy," ibid., pp. S23–44; Gerda Wekerle, "Women in the Urban Environment: Review Essay," ibid., pp. S188–214; Dolores Hayden, *The*

Grand Domestic Revolution: A History of Feminist Designs for American Homes, Neighborhoods, and Cities (Cambridge, MA: MIT Press, 1981), and *Redesigning the American Dream* (New York: Norton, 1983); and Eva Gamarnikow, "Introduction," Women and the City Issue, *International Journal of Urban and Regional Research* 2, 3 (October 1978), pp. 390–402. And see Chapter 1 and Chapter 11 in this volume.

13 Or, as Jean-Jacques Rousseau put it, in describing the sort of transformation that would be necessary for his social contract society to function:

> He who dares to undertake the making of a people's institutions ought to feel himself capable, so to speak, of changing human nature, of transforming each individual, who is by himself a complete and solitary whole, into part of a greater whole from which he in a manner receives his life and being; of altering man's constitution for the purpose of strengthening it; and of substituting a partial and moral existence for the physical and independent existence nature has conferred on us all.
>
> (*The Social Contract*, Book II, Chapter 7)

14 Irene Diamond and Nancy Hartsock, "Beyond Interests in Politics: A Comment on Virginia Sapiro's 'When Are Interests Interesting?' The Problems of Political Representation of Women," *American Political Science Review* 75, 3 (September 1981), pp. 717–21, esp. p. 719. See also Carole Pateman, *The Problem of Political Obligation* (Cambridge: Cambridge University Press, 1980); and Raymond Plant, "Community: Concept, Conception, and Ideology," *Politics and Society* 8, 1 (1978), pp. 79–107.

15 The term "methodological individualism" is explicated in Stephen Lukes, *Individualism: Key Concepts in the Social Sciences* (New York: Harper & Row, 1973), esp. Chapter 17. On the more general point, see Robert Paul Wolff, *The Poverty of Liberalism* (Boston: Beacon Press, 1968), esp. Chapter 5; Michael Taylor, *Community, Anarchy and Liberty* (Cambridge: Cambridge University Press, 1982); Michael Sandel, *Liberalism and the Limits of Justice* (Cambridge: Cambridge University Press, 1982), pp. 59–64, 173–74, and "Conclusion"; Pateman, *The Problem of Political Obligation*; and Castells, *City and the Grassroots*, esp. pp. 292–93 and sources cited there.

16 I explore this process in "Personal Identities and Collective Visions: Reflections on Identity, Community and Difference," in *Contemporary Anarchist Studies*, eds. Randall Amster, Abraham DeLeon, Luis A. Fernandez, Anthony Nocella, and Deric Shannon (New York: Routledge, 2009), pp. 259–69. See also María Lugones and Elizabeth V. Spelman, "Have We Got a Theory for You! Feminist Theory, Cultural Imperialism, and the Demand for the Woman's Voice," *Hypatia*, Special Issue, *Women's Studies International Forum* 6, 6 (1983), pp. 573–81; and Castells, *The City and the Grassroots*, p. 171. Recently, Mary Lyndon Shanley and others have been developing an argument for the existence of "relational rights" within liberalism that would, perhaps, begin to address these issues. See, for example, Martha Minow and Mary Lyndon Shanley, "Relational Rights and Responsibilities: Revisioning the Family in Liberal Political Theory and Law," *Hypatia* 11, 1 (Winter 1996), pp. 4–29; Traci Levy, "The Relational Self and the Right to Give Care," *New Political Science* 28, 4 (December 2006), pp. 547–70; and Jennifer Nedelsky, "Law, Boundaries, and the Bounded Self," *Representations* 30, Special Issue: Law and the Order of Culture (Spring, 1990), pp. 162–89.

17 Wendy Luttrell, "The Edison School Struggle: The Reshaping of Working-Class Education and Women's Consciousness," in A. Bookman and S. Morgen, eds., *Women and the Politics of Empowerment* (Philadelphia, PA: Temple University Press, 1988), p. 145. See also Sandra Morgen's discussion of the contexts of women's developing consciousness in "The Whole Power of the City Against Us," in *Women*

and the Politics of Empowerment, especially toward the end of the article, as well as Cynthia Cockburn, *The Local State* (London: Pluto Press, 1977); Kathleen McCourt, *Working-Class Women and Grass-Roots Politics* (Bloomington: Indiana University Press, 1977); and Ida Susser, *Norman Street: Poverty and Politics in an Urban Neighborhood* (New York: Oxford University Press, 1982); Temma Kaplan, "Community and Resistance in Women's Political Cultures," *Dialectical Anthropology* 15 (1990), especially pp. 259, 263–65, and "Women and Communal Strikes in the Crisis of 1917–22," in *Becoming Visible: Women in European History*, eds. Renate Bridenthal, Claudia Koonz, and Susan Stuard, 2nd ed. (Boston: Houghton Mifflin, 1987), pp. 429–49; Paula Hyman, "Immigrant Women and Consumer Protest: The New York City Kosher Meat Boycott of 1902," *American Jewish History* 70 (Summer 1980), pp. 91–105; and Dana Frank, "Housewives, Socialists, and the Politics of Food," *Feminist Studies* 11, 2 (Summer 1985), pp. 255–85.

18 On "consumer" riots, see Temma Kaplan, "Female Consciousness and Collective Action: The Case of Barcelona, 1910–18," *Signs* 7, 3 (Spring 1982), pp. 545–66; Paula Hyman, "Immigrant Women and Consumer Protest," pp. 91–105; and Ronald Lawson, Stephen E. Barton, and Jenna Weissman Joselit, "From Kitchen to Storefront: Women in the Tenant Movement," in *New Space for Women*, eds. Gerda R. Wekerle, Rebecca Peterson, and David Morley (Boulder, CO: Westview Press, 1980), pp. 255–71. On factory-based strikes, see Ardis Cameron, "Bread and Roses Revisited Women's Culture and Working-Class Activism in the Lawrence Strike of 1912," in *Women, Work and Protest: A Century of U.S. Women's Labor History*, ed. Ruth Milkman (Boston: Routledge & Kegan Paul, 1985); Albert Balcells, "La mujer obrera en la industria catalana durante el primer cuarto del siglo XX" in *Trabajo industrial y organización obrera en la Cataluña contemporánea, 1900–1936* (Barcelona: Editorial Laia, 1974), esp. pp. 45–54. On school struggles, see David Rogers, *110 Livingston Street: Politics and Bureaucracy in the New York City School System* (New York: Random House, 1968); Lillian Rubin, *Busing and Backlash* (Berkeley: University of California Press, 1972); Wendy Luttrell, "The Edison School Struggle: The Reshaping of Working-Class Education and Women's Consciousness," in *Women and the Politics of Empowerment*, eds. Bookman and Morgen; and Andree Nicola McLaughlin and Zala Chandler, "Urban Politics in the Higher Education of Black Women: A Case Study," Chapter 8 of *Women and the Politics of Empowerment*.

19 The complexities of coalition-building and consciousness change are explored in, among others, *Feminist Coalitions: Historical Perspectives on Second-Wave Feminism in the United States*, ed. Stephanie Gilmore (Urbana: University of Illinois Press, 2008) and Kathleen Blee, ed., *No Middle Ground: Women and Radical Protest* (New York: New York University Press, 1998). Lani Guinier and Gerald Torres offer important caveats about the ways electoral/political structures can either promote or inhibit the development of a critical consciousness in *The Miner's Canary*. See also Patricia Hill Collins, *Black Feminist Thought: Knowledge, Consciousness and the Politics of Empowerment* (Boston: Unwin Hyman, 1991) and *Fighting Words: Black Women and the Search for Justice* (Minneapolis: University of Minnesota Press, 1998).

20 Carol Stack, *All Our Kin* (New York: Harper & Row, 1976); Cheryl Townsend Gilkes, "Holding Back the Ocean with a Broom," in *The Black Woman*, ed. LaFrances Rodgers-Rose (Beverly Hills, CA: Sage, 1980), pp. 217–31; "Going Up for the Oppressed: The Career Mobility of Black Women Community Workers," *Journal of Social Issues* 39, 3 (1983), pp. 115–39; and "Building in Many Places: Multiple Commitments and Ideologies in Black Women's Community Work," in *Women and the Politics of Empowerment*, eds. Bookman and Morgen; Paula Giddings, *When and Where I Enter: The Impact of Black Women on Race and Sex in America* (New York: W. Morrow, 1984).

21 Shulamit Reinharz, "Women as Competent Community Builders: The Other Side of the Coin," in *Social and Psychological Problems of Women: Prevention and Crisis Intervention*, eds. Annette U. Rickel, Meg Gerrard, and Ira Iscoe (Washington, DC: Hemisphere, 1984), pp. 19–43. On the roles of women within Latino/a communities, see, for example, Mary S. Pardo, *Mexican American Women Activists: Identity and Resistance in Two Los Angeles Communities* (Philadelphia, PA: Temple University Press, 1998); Carol Hardy-Fanta, *Latina Politics, Latino Politics: Gender, Culture, and Political Participation in Boston* (Philadelphia, PA: Temple University Press, 1993); and Michael Jones-Correa, *Between Two Nations: The Political Predicament of Latinos in New York City* (Ithaca, NY: Cornell University Press, 1998).

22 McCourt, *Working-Class Women*, pp. 220–24, 231–32. This finding is not surprising in the light of studies by Verba and Nie, Baxter and Lansing, and others on the relationship between political efficacy and feelings of racial or ethnic community. See, for example, Sidney Verba and Norman Nie, *Participation in America: Political Democracy and Social Equality* (New York: Harper & Row, 1972), Chapters 8, 20, 12; Verba *et al.*, *Voice and Equality: Civic Voluntarism in American Politics*; Sandra Baxter and Marjorie Lansing, *Women and Politics* (Ann Arbor: University of Michigan Press, 1981). See also Guinier and Torres, *The Miner's Canary*; and Anne Phillips, *Engendering Democracy*.

23 Morgen, "It's the Whole Power of the City Against Us," in *Women and the Politics of Empowerment*, eds. Bookman and Morgen; see also Temma Kaplan, "Female Consciousness and Collective Action," and *Crazy for Democracy*.

24 *Working-Class Women and Grass-roots Politics*, p. 220. See also, e.g. Carolyn Howe, "Gender, Race, and Community Activism," in Naples, ed., *Community Activism*, Chapter 10; and Mary Pardo, "Mexican-American Grassroots Women Activists," *Frontiers* 11 (1990), pp. 1–7.

25 See, for example, Patricia Zavella, "'Abnormal Intimacy': The Varying Work Networks of Chicana Cannery Workers," *Feminist Studies* 11, 3 (Fall 1985), pp. 540–57; Zavella, "The Politics of Race and Gender: Organizing Chicana Cannery Workers in Northern California," pp. 202–24, in *Women and the Politics of Empowerment*, eds. Bookman and Morgen; Ann Bookman, "Unionization in an Electronics Factory: The Interplay of Gender, Ethnicity, and Class," in *Women and the Politics of Empowerment*, pp. 159–79; and Lamphere and Grenier, "Women, Unions, and 'Participative Management': Organizing in the Sunbelt," in *Women and the Politics of Empowerment*, eds. Bookman and Morgen, pp. 227–56.

26 See sources cited in note 20, above.

27 Katznelson, *City Trenches*, passim.

28 Susser, *Norman Street* and "Working-Class Women, Social Protest, and Changing Ideologies," in Bookman and Morgen, *Women and the Politics of Empowerment*, pp. 257–71. See also Sandra Morgen, "'It's the Whole Power of the City Against Us!': The Development of Political Consciousness in a Women's Health Care Coalition," in ibid., pp. 97–115.

29 Cynthia Cockburn, "When Women Get Involved in Community Action," in *Women in the Community*, ed. Marjorie Mayo (London: Routledge & Kegan Paul, 1977), pp. 61–70, esp. 69–70.

30 See, on this point, Richard Sennett, *The Uses of Disorder* (New York: Vintage, 1970); Iris Marion Young, "The Ideal of Community and the Politics of Difference," *Social Theory and Practice* 12 (Spring 1986), pp. 1–26; and "City Life and Difference," Chapter 7 of *Justice and the Politics of Difference* (Princeton, NJ: Princeton University Press, 1990); and Suad Joseph, "Working-Class Women's Networks in a Sectarian State: A Political Paradox," *American Ethnologist* 10 (1983), pp. 1–22; and Chapter 10, in this volume.

31 See Sara Evans and Harry Boyte, "Strategies in Search of America: Cultural Radicalism, Populism, and Democratic Culture," *Socialist Review* 75/76, 14, 3 and 4 (May–August 1984), esp. pp. 75, 87n; Evans and Boyte, *Free Spaces: The Sources of Democratic Change in America* (New York: Harper & Row, 1986); Martha Ackelsberg, "Mujeres Libres: Community and Individuality: Organizing Women in the Spanish Civil War," *Radical America* 18, 4, pp. 7–19; and Craig Calhoun, *The Question of Class Struggle: Social Foundations of Popular Radicalism During the Industrial Revolution* (Chicago: University of Chicago Press, 1982). See also Chapters 3 and 10 in this volume.

32 A study of women jewelry workers by Nina Shapiro-Perl shows how schools, families, and the media socialize people to perceive a distinction between public and private, and thereby profoundly affect the possibilities for workplace-based resistance. See Nina Shapiro-Perl, "The Impact of Gender on Workers' Resistance and Consent" (paper delivered in organized session on Women and Resistance, annual meeting of the American Anthropological Association, Denver, Colorado, November 1984). See also Michael Walzer, "Town Meetings and Workers' Control: A Parable for Socialists," *Dissent* 25 (Summer 1978), pp. 325–33.

33 Louise Lamphere and Guillermo Grenier, "Women's Unions and 'Participative Management'," in *Women and the Politics of Empowerment*, eds. Ann R. Bookman and Sandra R. Morgen (Philadelphia, PA: Temple University Press, 1988), pp. 227–56.

34 Morgen, "It's the Whole Power of the City Against Us," in *Women and the Politics of Empowerment*, eds. Bookman and Morgen; see also her *Into Our Own Hands: The Women's Health Movement in the United States, 1969–1990* (New Brunswick, NJ: Rutgers University Press, 2002).

35 See below, Chapters 3, 6, 8, 10. Also Temma Kaplan, *Crazy for Democracy*; and "Community and Resistance."

36 Carole Pateman makes a similar argument about the "lag" between the day-to-day creativity of feminist and "alternative community" groups in the United States and the recognition of those activities by contemporary political theorists—even theorists of "participatory democracy"—in "Feminism and Participatory Democracy: Some Reflections on Sexual Difference and Citizenship," in *The Disorder of Women* (Stanford, CA: Stanford University Press, 1988). See also Wini Breines, *Community and Organization in the New Left, 1962–1968: The Great Refusal* (New York: Praeger, 1982); Sara Evans, *Personal Politics* (New York: Vintage, 1980); and Barbara Epstein, *Political Protest and Cultural Revolution: Nonviolent Direct Action in the 1970s and 1980s* (Berkeley: University of California Press, 1991).

37 These would include, among others, Harry Boyte and Sara Evans, *Free Spaces*; Benjamin Barber, *Strong Democracy* (Berkeley: University of California Press, 1984) and *A Passion for Democracy: American Essays* (Princeton, NJ: Princeton University Press, 1998); Shane Phelan, *Sexual Strangers: Gays, Lesbians, and Dilemmas of Citizenship* (Philadelphia, PA: Temple University Press, 2001); and Marla Brettschneider, *Democratic Theorizing from the Margins* (Philadelphia, PA: Temple University Press, 2002).

38 I am thinking here, especially, of Sara Ruddick, *Maternal Thinking: Toward a Politics of Peace* (Boston: Beacon Press, 1989); and Jean Elshtain, *Meditations on Modern Political Thought: Masculine/Feminine Themes from Luther to Arendt* (New York: Praeger, 1986) and *Public Man, Private Woman: Women in Social and Political Thought* (Princeton, NJ: Princeton University Press, 1981) and the many writings that have followed from them. Much of the more recent work on "care"—especially that by Joan Tronto and Eva Feder Kittay—has attempted to find a political place for work that has traditionally been done by women without assuming that it is, necessarily, women's work. (See also Chapter 11 in this volume.)

3 TERRAINS OF PROTEST

1 The interview was conducted in 1981 in conjunction with Ackelsberg's research on women's involvement in the anarchist movement in the early twentieth century. "Women with hats" is a reference to women of the middle and upper classes.

2 Interview with Ackelsberg, Paris, France, January 6, 1982.

3 In this respect, the women of Barcelona, and of Catalonia in general, differed from their counterparts elsewhere in Spain, where few women worked outside the home, right up to the time of the Spanish Civil War (1936–39).

4 Lawrence Goodwyn, *The Populist Moment* (Oxford: Oxford University Press, 1978), especially the "Introduction."

5 Michael A. Bakunin, "Federalism, Socialism, and Anti-Theologism" (1867), in Sam Dolgoff, ed., *Bakunin on Anarchism* (Montreal: Black Rose Books, 1980), pp. 102–47; Bakunin, "God and the State" (1873), in Dolgoff, pp. 225–42; Bakunin, "Statism and Anarchy" (1873), in Dolgoff, pp. 323–50; Peter A. Kropotkin, "The Spirit of Revolt," in Roger Baldwin, ed., *Kropotkin's Revolutionary Pamphlets* (New York: Dover, 1970), pp. 34–43; Kropotkin, "Modern Science and Anarchism," in Baldwin, especially pp. 182–90; Michael Walzer, *Obligations* (Cambridge, MA: Harvard University Press, 1970); Frances Fox Piven and Richard A. Cloward, *Poor People's Movements* (New York: Vintage, 1978); Frances Fox Piven, *Challenging Authority: How Ordinary People Change America* (Lanham, MD: Rowman and Littlefield, 2006); Harry Boyte, *The Backyard Revolution* (Philadelphia, PA: Temple University Press, 1980).

6 Temma Kaplan's and Lester Golden's innovative studies of Barcelona in the early twentieth century describe the events considered here and, along with our own research, provide the basis for our analysis. See Temma Kaplan, "Quality of Life and Female Mass Movements in St. Petersburg, Turin, and Barcelona, 1917–18," paper delivered to the Five College Social History Seminar, Smith College, Oct. 29, 1980; Kaplan, "Female Consciousness and Collective Action: The Case of Barcelona, 1910–18," *Signs*, 7, 3 (Spring 1982), pp. 545–67; Lester Golden, "Les Dones com avantguarda: El rebombori del pa del gener 1918," *L'Avenç*, Dec. 1981, pp. 45–52; Golden, unpublished manuscript, 1981.

7 Ann R. Markusen, "City Spatial Structure, Women's Household Work, and National Urban Policy," *Signs*, 5, 3 (Suppl.) (Spring 1980), p. S23; David Harvey, *Social Justice and the City* (Baltimore, MD: Johns Hopkins University Press, 1973); *International Journal of Urban and Regional Research*, Special Issue on the City, 1978; Ira Katznelson, *City Trenches* (New York: Pantheon, 1981).

8 David Harvey, "Labor, Capital, and Class Struggle Around the Built Environment in Advanced Capitalist Societies," *Politics and Society* 6, 3 (1976), pp. 265–95. See also Chapter 1 in this volume.

9 Manuel Castells, *The City and the Grassroots* (Berkeley: University of California Press, 1983), p. 80.

10 Ibid., p. 70.

11 Susan Merrill Squier, *Women Writers and the City: Essays in Feminist Literary Criticism* (Knoxville: University of Tennessee Press, 1984), pp. 4–5.

12 There is extensive literature on this question, beginning, most notably, with the special issues of *Signs* (1980) and the *International Journal of Urban and Regional Research* (1978).

13 See, e.g. Barbara Berg, *The Remembered Gate: Origins of American Feminism: The Woman and the City, 1800–1860* (New York: Oxford University Press, 1978).

14 Temma Kaplan, *Anarchists of Andalusia, 1868–1903* (Princeton, NJ: Princeton University Press, 1977); Ardis Cameron, *Radicals of the Worst Sort: Laboring Women in Lawrence, Massachusetts, 1860–1912* (Champaign: University of Illinois Press, 1995); Meredith Tax, *The Rising of the Women: Feminist Solidarity and Class Conflict, 1880–1917*

(New York: Monthly Review Press, 1980); Barbara Taylor, *Eve and the New Jerusalem: Socialism and Feminism in the Nineteenth Century* (New York: Pantheon, 1983); Ruth Milkman, "Organizing the Sexual Division of Labor: Historical Perspectives on Women's Work and the American Labor Movement," *Socialist Review* X, 1, Jan.–Feb. 1980, pp. 95–150.

15 Dolores Hayden, *The Grand Domestic Revolution: A History of Feminist Designs for American Homes, Neighborhoods, and Cities* (Cambridge, MA: MIT Press, 1981).

16 Cynthia Cockburn, *The Local State* (London: Pluto, 1977); Kaplan, "Female Consciousness"; Harry Boyte and Sara M. Evans, "Strategies in Search of America: Cultural Radicalism, Populism, and Democratic Culture," *Socialist Review*, 75–76, 14, 3–4 (May–Aug. 1984), pp. 73–100; Myrna Breitbart, "Feminist Perspectives in Geographic Theory and Methodology," *Antipode* XVI, 3 (1984); Ronald Lawson and Stephen E. Barton, "Sex Roles in Social Movements: A Case Study of the Tenant Movement in New York City," *Signs* VI, 1 (Winter 1980), pp. 230–47; Ida Susser, *Norman Street: Poverty and Politics in an Urban Neighborhood* (New York: Oxford University Press, 1982).

17 Squier, *Women Writers and the City*, p. 6.

18 While we focus here on the events of January and February 1918, this was not the first time that the women of Barcelona had taken to the streets in protest over quality-of-life issues. For studies of earlier, similar events, see Kaplan, "Female Consciousness and Collective Action"; Joan Connelly Ullman, *The Tragic Week: A Study of Anti-Clericalism in Spain, 1875–1912* (Cambridge, MA: Harvard University Press, 1968), especially Chapter XI; Albert Balcells, "La mujer obrera en la industria catalana durante el primer cuarto del siglo XX," in *Trabajo industrial y organización obrera en la Cataluña contemporánea (1900–1936)* (Barcelona: Editorial Laia, 1974), pp. 45–109. For further exploration of the role of the built environment in anarchist social revolution, see Myrna Breitbart, "The Theory and Practice of Anarchist Decentralism in Spain, 1936–39: The Integration of Community and Environment," PhD dissertation, Dept. of Geography, Clark University, 1978, Chapters 3, 7, 8; Breitbart, "The Integration of Community and Environment: Anarchist Decentralism in Rural Spain, 1936–39," in *The Human Experience of Space and Place*, eds. Anne Buttimer and David Seamon (London: Croom Helm, 1981), pp. 86–119; Nick Rider, "The Practice of Direct Action: The Barcelona Rent Strike of 1931," pp. 79–105 in *For Anarchism: History, Theory and Practice*, ed. David Goodway (New York: Routledge, 1989); and Chris Ealham, "The Myth of the Maddened Crowd," pp. 111–32 in *The Splintering of Spain: Cultural History and the Spanish Civil War, 1936–39*, eds. Chris Ealham and Michael Richards (Cambridge: Cambridge University Press, 2005).

19 Kaplan, "Quality of Life."

20 Kaplan, "Female Consciousness and Collective Action," pp. 555, 560.

21 Ibid., p. 560. Paula Hyman reported similar behavior by Jewish women during kosher meat boycotts on the Lower East Side of New York in the early twentieth century. See Hyman, "Immigrant Women and Consumer Protest: The New York City Kosher Meat Boycott of 1902," *American Jewish History* 70 (Summer 1980), pp. 91–105.

22 Ibid., pp. 562–63; Golden, "Les Dones com avantguarda," pp. 48–50.

23 Kaplan, "Quality of Life" and "Female Consciousness and Collective Action"; for a similar analysis, based on contemporary examples, see Cockburn, *The Local State*, to which we are much indebted. On similar consumption-based actions in the US see Paula Hyman, "Immigrant Women and Consumer Protest"; Darlene Clark Hine, "The Housewives' League of Detroit," in *Visible Women: New Essays on American Activism*, eds. Nancy A. Hewitt and Suzanne Lebsock (Urbana: University of

Illinois Press, 1993), pp. 223–41; and Mary Pardo, "Creating Community: Mexican American Women in Eastside Los Angeles," in Nancy Naples, ed. *Community Activism and Feminist Politics* (New York: Routledge, 1998), pp. 275–300.

24 For a discussion of spontaneous organizing, see Colin Ward, *Anarchy in Action* (New York: Harper and Row, 1974), especially Chapters 2–4.

25 Kaplan, "Quality of Life." For a discussion of an analogous series of protests concerning public transport in Brazil, see José Alvaro Moisés and Verena Stolcke, "Urban Transport and Popular Violence: The Case of Brazil," *Past and Present* 86 (Feb. 1980), pp. 174–91.

26 For an analogous series of events in Lawrence, MA, see Ardis Cameron, "Bread and Roses Revisited: Women's Culture and Working-Class Activism in the Lawrence Strike of 1912," in Ruth Milkman, ed., *Women, Work and Protest: A Century of U.S. Women's Labor History* (Boston: Routledge and Kegan Paul, 1985).

27 Kaplan, "Female Consciousness"; Lola Iturbe, interview with Martha Ackelsberg, Barcelona, Aug. 4, 1981.

28 Golden, unpublished manuscript.

29 Albert Balcells, "La mujer obrera," p. 50.

30 *Solidaridad obrera* 21 January 1918, cited in Golden, unpublished manuscript.

31 Syndicalist from Barcelona, cited in Golden, "Les Dones com avantguarda," p. 50.

32 Balcells, "La mujer obrera," p. 49.

33 CNT-AIT, *Comicios Históricos de la CNT* (Memoria del Congreso celebrado en Barcelona los días 28, 29 y 30 de Junio y 1 de Julio de 1918) (Toulouse: Ediciones CNT Toulouse, 1957), pp. 83–4.

34 See, Balcells, "La mujer obrera," especially pp. 49–50. For more on the relationship between women and unions in this period, see also Martha Ackelsberg, *Free Women of Spain: Anarchism and the Struggle for the Emancipation of Women* (Oakland, CA: AK Press, 2005), especially Chapter 2.

35 Kaplan, "Female Consciousness and Collective Action," p. 561.

36 Golden, "Les Dones com avantguarda," pp. 48–9.

37 Golden, unpublished manuscript.

38 Kaplan, "Quality of Life."

39 Cristina Piera, interview with Martha Ackelsberg, Santa Coloma de Granamet (Barcelona), August 20, 1981.

40 See, for example, Moisés and Stolcke, "Urban Transport"; E.P. Thompson, "The Moral Economy of the English Crowd in the Eighteenth Century," *Past and Present* 50 (Feb. 1971), pp. 76–136; Hyman, "Immigrant Women"; Paolo Freire, *Pedagogy of the Oppressed* (New York: Herder and Herder, 1970).

41 Enriqueta Rovira, interview with Martha Ackelsberg, Castellnaudary, France, Dec. 28, 1981.

42 David Gordon, "Capitalist Development and the History of American Cities," in William Tabb and Larry Sawers, eds., *Marxism and the Metropolis* (New York: Oxford University Press, 1978), pp. 25–63; Manuel Castells, *The Urban Question* (Cambridge, MA: MIT Press, 1978); Castells, *The City and the Grassroots*; Katznelson, *City Trenches*; William Kornblum, *Blue Collar Community* (Chicago: University of Chicago Press, 1974).

43 Lawson and Barton, "Sex Roles and Social Movements"; Ronald Lawson, Stephen E. Barton, and Jenna Weissman Joselit, "From Kitchen to Storefront: Women in the Tenant Movement," in *New Space for Women*, eds. Gerda R. Wekerle, et al. (Boulder, CO: Westview Press, 1980), pp. 255–71; E.M. Ettorre, "Women, Urban Social Movements and the Lesbian Ghetto," *International Journal of Urban and Regional Research* 2, 3 (Oct. 1978); Marjorie Mayo, "The Fallacy of Community Control," in John Crowley, et al., *Community or Class Struggle?* (London: Stage 1, 1977), pp. 65–90.

44 For example, Katznelson, *City Trenches*; Markusen, "City Spatial Structure"; Gordon, "Capitalist Development and the History of American Cities."

45 See, for example, Markusen, "City Spatial Structure," and Eva Gamarnikow, "Introduction," to The Women and the City Issue, *International Journal of Urban and Regional Research* (Oct. 1978), pp. 390–403.

46 For further discussion, see above, Chapter 1.

47 Darlene Gay Levy and Harriet Applewhite, "Women of the Popular Classes in Revolutionary Paris, 1789–95," in *Women, War and Revolution* eds. Carol R. Berkin and Clara M. Lovett (New York: Holmes and Meier, 1980), p. 10.

48 Lawson, Barton and Joselit, "From Kitchen to Storefront."

49 Kaplan, "Female Consciousness and Collective Action."

50 Frances Fox Piven and Richard A. Cloward, *The New Class War* (New York: Pantheon, 1982); Barbara Ehrenreich and Frances Fox Piven, "The Persistence of Poverty: 1. The Feminization of Poverty," *Dissent*, Spring (1984), pp. 162–70. In recent years, of course, the literature on the relationship among poverty, "dependency," welfare policy, and women's status has burgeoned. See, below, Chapter 4; also Linda Gordon, ed., *Women, the State, and Welfare* (Madison: University of Wisconsin Press, 1990); Gwendolyn Mink, ed., *Whose Welfare?* (Ithaca, NY: Cornell University Press, 1999); and Gwendolyn Mink, *Welfare's End* (Ithaca, NY: Cornell University Press, 2002).

51 Cockburn, *The Local State*, especially Chapters 2 and 6.

52 Cynthia Cockburn, "When Women Get Involved in Community Action," in Marjorie Mayo, ed., *Women in the Community* (London: Routledge and Kegan Paul, 1977), pp. 62–3; and Elizabeth Lawrence, "The Working Women's Charter Campaign," in Mayo, ed., pp. 14–15.

53 Cockburn, *The Local State*, p. 163.

54 See Marc Raboy, "The Future of Montreal and the MCM," *Our Generation*, 12, 1 (1978); also Cockburn's reports of her interviews with women activists in "When Women Get Involved in Community Action," p. 64.

55 See Cockburn, "When Women Get Involved in Community Action," pp. 67, 69; Ettorre, "Women, Urban Social Movements and the Lesbian Ghetto," pp. 507–512; Cheryl Gilkes, "'Holding Back the Ocean with a Broom': Black Women and Community Work," in *The Black Woman*, ed. LaFrances Rodgers-Rose (Beverly Hills, CA: Sage, 1980), pp. 219–26; Castells, *The City and the Grassroots*, Boyte and Evans, *Free Spaces*; Virginia Rinaldo Seitz, "Class, Gender and Resistance in Appalachian Coalfields," in Naples, ed. *Community Activism*, pp. 213–36; and Eve Weinbaum, *To Move a Mountain: Fighting the Global Economy in Appalachia* (New York: New Press, 2004).

56 Castells, *The City and the Grassroots*; Boyte and Evans, *Free Spaces*; Kathleen McCourt, *Working-Class Women and Grass-roots Politics* (Bloomington: Indiana University Press, 1977); Kathleen Blee, ed., *No Middle Ground: Women and Radical Protest* (New York: New York University Press, 1998); Blee, *Inside Organized Racism: Women in the Hate Movement* (Berkeley: University of California Press, 2002); Alexis Jetter, Annelise Orleck, and Diana Taylor, eds., *The Politics of Motherhood: Activist Voices from Left to Right* (Hanover, NH: University Press of New England, 1997).

57 Goodwyn, *The Populist Moment*, p. 27; Fraser, "Rethinking the Public Sphere: A Contribution to the Critique of Actually Existing Democracy," in *Habermas and the Public Sphere*, ed. Calhoun (Cambridge, MA: MIT Press, 1992), pp. 119, 124.

58 Goodwyn, *The Populist Moment*, p. xviii; but see also Sara Evans, *Personal Politics* (New York: Vintage, 1980), pp. 219–20.

59 Goodwyn, *The Populist Moment*, pp. 88, 100, 138, 195.

60 In addition to sources cited above, see Henry A. Giroux, "Theories of Reproduction and Resistance in the New Sociology of Education: A Critical Analysis,"

Harvard Educational Review 53, 3 (Aug. 1983), pp. 257–93; Piven, *Challenging Authority*; Breitbart, "The Theory and Practice of Anarchist Decentralism in Spain, 1936–39," pp. 393–99; and Temma Kaplan, *Crazy for Democracy: Women in Grassroots Movements* (New York: Routledge, 1997).

61 We do not mean to suggest that even "mere reactions to powerlessness" may not have empowering effects on participants, but if the activity (and consciousness) do not move beyond that perspective, then (virtually by definition) it will not generate radical social change. I explore these issues further in Chapters 7 and 10 below.

62 A. Gorz, *Strategy for Labor* (Boston: Beacon Press, 1967), pp. 7–8.

63 Breitbart, "Feminist Perspectives in Geographic Theory and Methodology"; on anarchist efforts to claim space in the years preceding the Civil War, see also Pamela Radcliff, "The Culture of Empowerment in Gijón," pp. 133–55, in Ealham, ed., *The Splintering of Spain*. Explorations of the relationships among landscapes, the built environment, and power have burgeoned in the years since this article was originally published. Now-classic studies include Sharon Zukin, *Landscapes of Power: From Detroit to Disney World* (Berkeley: University of California Press, 1991); Mike Davis, *City of Quartz: Excavating the Future in Los Angeles* (New York: Vintage, 1992); Davis, *Ecology of Fear: Los Angeles and the Imagination of Disaster* (New York: Metropolitan Books, 1998); and Dolores Hayden, *The Power of Place: Urban Landscapes as Public History* (Cambridge, MA: MIT Press, 1995).

64 The phrase is Breitbart's; see "Feminist Perspectives in Geographic Theory."

65 See, especially, Douglas Yates, "Political Innovation and Institution Building: The Experience of the Decentralization Experiments," pp. 146–75, in Hawley, et al., *Theoretical Perspectives on Urban Politics* (Englewood Cliffs, NJ: Prentice-Hall, 1976); Piven and Cloward, *Poor People's Movements*; Norman I. Fainstein and Susan S. Fainstein, *Urban Political Movements: The Search for Power by Minority Groups in American Cities* (Englewood Cliffs, NJ: Prentice-Hall, 1974), especially pp. 181–214; Fainstein and Fainstein, "The Future of Community Control," *American Political Science Review* 70, 3 (Sept. 1976), pp. 905–23. Among more recent studies, Frances Fox Piven makes a similar claim in *Challenging Authority*; as does David Meyer in *The Politics of Protest: Social Movements in America* (New York: Oxford University Press, 2007).

66 Lawson and Barton, "Sex Roles and Social Movements"; for an examination of similar patterns of control among early labor union organizations in New York City and Chicago, see Karen Pastorello, ed. "How Did Cross-Class Alliances Shape the 1910 Chicago Garment Workers' Strike?" and Thomas Dublin, Kathryn K. Sklar, and Deirdre Doherty, "How Did the Perceived Threat of Socialism Shape the Relationship between Workers and their Allies in the New York City Shirtwaist Strike, 1909–10?" both available at www.alexanderstreet6.com/wasm.

67 Margaret Cerrullo, "Autonomy and the Limits of Organization: A Socialist-Feminist Response to Harry Boyte," *Socialist Review* 9, 2 (January 1979), p. 95.

4 DEPENDENCY OR MUTUALITY

† Author's note: This chapter was originally published in 1994, and, thus, was written *before* the Clinton Administration's pledge to "end welfare as we know it." I was writing this at about the same time that Nancy Fraser and Linda Gordon were writing their essay "A Genealogy of Dependency," [*Signs* 19, 2 (Winter 1994): 309–36]. The concerns of our two pieces are strikingly similar. I have chosen to reprint this here more-or-less as originally written, because, although the specific language around welfare "reform" may have changed, the issues of dependency and mutuality—and the concomitant need for a politics that recognizes the importance of *relationships*—are still very much with us.

1 Barbara J. Nelson, "Women's Poverty and Women's Citizenship: Some Political Consequences of Economic Marginality," *Signs* 10, 2 (Winter, 1984), pp. 209–31; and Nelson, "The Origins of the Two-Channel Welfare State: Workmen's Compensation and Mothers' Aid," in *Women, the State, and Welfare*, ed. Linda Gordon (Madison: University of Wisconsin Press, 1990), pp. 123–51; Gwendolyn Mink, "The Lady and the Tramp: Gender, Race and the Origins of the American Welfare State," in Gordon, ed., *Women, the State and Welfare*, pp. 92–122; and Mink, *The Wages of Motherhood: Inequality in the Welfare State 1917–1942* (Ithaca, NY: Cornell University Press, 1995).

2 See, for example, Martha Minow, "When Difference Has Its Home: Group Homes for the Mentally Retarded, Equal Protection and Legal Treatment of Difference," *Harvard Civil Rights-Civil Liberties Law Review* 22 (1987), pp. 111–89.

3 Thus, my approach and some of my goals are very similar to those articulated by Nancy Fraser and Linda Gordon in "A Genealogy of Dependency: Tracing a Keyword of the U.S. Welfare State," *Signs* 19, 2 (Winter 1994), pp. 309–36.

4 See Teresa Brennan and Carole Pateman, "'Mere Auxiliaries to the Commonwealth': Women and the Origins of Liberalism," *Political Studies* 27, 2 (1979), pp. 183–200; Pateman, *The Sexual Contract* (Stanford, CA: Stanford University Press, 1988), especially Chapters 3–5; Pateman, "The Patriarchal Welfare State," in *The Disorder of Women* (Stanford, CA: Stanford University Press, 1989); and Nelson, "Women's Poverty and Women's Citizenship."

5 Walzer, "The Obligation to Die for the State," in *Obligations: Essays on Disobedience, War and Citizenship* (Cambridge, MA: Harvard University Press, 1970), p. 82. On the significance of both self-support and self-protection, see also Judith Shklar, *American Citizenship: The Quest for Inclusion* (Cambridge, MA: Harvard University Press, 1991).

6 Pateman, *The Disorder of Women*, pp. 210–25, and "Women, Nature and the Suffrage: Review Essay," *Ethics* 90 (July 1980), pp. 564–75. See also Susan Okin, "Justice and Gender," *Philosophy and Public Affairs* 16 (Winter 1987), pp. 42–72.

7 In England, the Reform Act of 1884 extended suffrage to about ¾ of all adult males, but still excluded many agricultural wage laborers, servants living with their employers, etc. It was not until 1918 that Great Britain adopted universal manhood suffrage, at which time the vote was also given to women over thirty. In the US, universal (white) manhood suffrage dates from the mid nineteenth century, but women's suffrage came much later: although Wyoming granted women the vote as early as 1869, the federal Woman Suffrage Amendment was enacted only in 1920. For a fuller discussion of citizenship in the US, see Martha Ackelsberg, "Citizenship," in *The Reader's Companion to U.S. Women's History*, eds. Wilma Mankiller, Gwendolyn Mink, Marysa Navarro, Barbara Smith, Gloria Steinem (Boston: Houghton Mifflin, 1998), pp. 99–100, and Ackelsberg, "Citizenship," in *Poverty in the United States: An Encyclopedia of History, Politics and Policy*, eds. Gwendolyn Mink and Alice O'Connor (Santa Barbara, CA: ABC-CLIO, 2004), Vol. I, pp. 175–79.

8 Barbara Nelson, "Women's Poverty and Women's Citizenship"; Carole Pateman, "Women, Nature and the Suffrage." See also Linda Gordon, "What Does Welfare Regulate?" *Social Research* 55 (Winter 1988), pp. 609–30; and Jean Elshtain, "Moral Woman and Immoral Man," *Politics and Society* 2, 4 (1974), pp. 453–73.

9 See, for example, John Stuart Mill, *The Subjection of Women* [1869], in *Essays on Sex Equality*, ed. Alice S. Rossi (Chicago: University of Chicago Press, 1970), especially Chapter 3.

10 See Pateman, *The Disorder of Women*, especially Chapter 8; also Shklar, *American Citizenship*.

11 Myra Marx Ferree, "Housework: Rethinking the Costs and Benefits," in *Families, Politics, and Public Policy*, ed. Irene Diamond (New York: Longman, 1983), p. 162. See also Nelson, "The Two-Channel Welfare State"; Gwendolyn Mink, *The Wages of Motherhood* and "The Lady and the Tramp"; Jill Quadagno, *The Color of Welfare: How Racism Undermined the War on Poverty* (New York: Oxford University Press, 1994); and Ira Katznelson, *When Affirmative Action Was White: An Untold History of Racial Inequality in Twentieth Century America* (New York: W.W. Norton, 2005), especially Chapter 2.

12 Karl Marx, *Capital*, ed. Friedrich Engels, trans. S. Moore and E. Aveling (New York: International Publishers, 1947), Vol. I, p. 661.

13 Nancy Fraser and Linda Gordon note that, in the pre-industrial period, the term "dependence" generally connoted *social relations of domination*, and that the term took on its more individualist meanings in more recent years. See "A Genealogy of Dependency," p. 331.

14 Marx most significantly, perhaps, in "On the Jewish Question" and "Critique of the Gotha Program."

15 Engels, "The Origins of the Family, Private Property, and the State," in *Marx and Engels Selected Works* (Moscow: Foreign Languages Publishing House, 1962), Vol. II, especially pp. 217–41.

16 Cited in Alison Jaggar, *Feminist Politics and Human Nature* (Totowa, NJ: Rowman and Allanheld, 1983), p. 68.

17 While there are significant differences among those who define themselves as socialist feminists—especially on the question of the relationship between capitalism and male dominance—virtually all agree in criticizing the traditional Marxist position on "the woman question." See, for example, Michael Albert and Robin Hahnel, *Marxism and Socialist Theory* (Boston: South End Press, 1981); Zillah Eisenstein, ed., *Capitalist Patriarchy and the Case for Socialist Feminism* (New York: Monthly Review Press, 1976); Heidi Hartmann, "Capitalism, Patriarchy, and Job Segregation by Sex," in ibid., pp. 206–47 and "The Unhappy Marriage of Marxism and Feminism," in *Women and Revolution*, ed. Lydia Sargent (Boston: South End Press, 1981), pp. 1–41; Alison Jaggar, *Feminist Politics and Human Nature*, especially pp. 130, 137, 144ff; Joan Landes, "Marxism and the 'Woman Question,'" in Sonia Kruks, Rayna R. Rapp and Marilyn B. Young, eds, *Promissory Notes: Women in the Transition to Socialism* (New York: Monthly Review Press, 1989), pp. 15–28; Batya Weinbaum and Amy Bridges, "The Other Side of the Paycheck," in Eisenstein, *Capitalist Patriarchy and the Case for Socialist Feminism*, pp. 190–205; and Iris Marion Young, "Beyond the Unhappy Marriage: A Critique of Dual Systems Theory," in Sargent, ed., *Women and Revolution*, pp. 43–69. For a more recent discussion of Young's work and its place in this larger conversation, see Mary Hawkesworth, "The Pragmatics of Iris Marion Young's Feminist Historical Materialism," *Politics and Gender* 4, 2 (June 2008), pp. 318–26.

18 See especially Sonia Kruks, Rayna Rapp, and Marilyn Young, eds., *Promissory Notes*.

19 See, for example, Betty Friedan, *The Feminine Mystique* (New York: Norton, 1963); Nancy Barrett, "The Welfare System as State Paternalism," paper presented at Conference on Women and Structural Transformation, Institute for Research on Women, Rutgers University, November 1983; see also Frances Fox Piven, "Welfare and Work," in *Whose Welfare?* ed. Gwendolyn Mink (Ithaca, NY: Cornell University Press, 1999), pp. 83–99; and Gwendolyn Mink, "Aren't Poor Single Mothers Women? Feminists, Welfare Reform, and Welfare Justice," pp. 171–88 in *Whose Welfare?*

20 Among those who have attempted to make the case that "care work" *is* work, and should be remunerated, see Joan Tronto, *Moral Boundaries: A Political Argument for an*

Ethic of Care (New York: Routledge, 1993); Eva Feder Kittay, *Love's Labor: Essays on Women, Equality and Dependency* (New York: Routledge 1999); and Eva Feder Kittay and Ellen Feder, eds., *The Subject of Care: Feminist Perspectives on Dependency* (Lanham, MD: Rowman and Littlefield, 2002). See also below, Chapter 11.

21 See, for example, Heidi Hartman, "Capitalism, Patriarchy, and Job Segregation by Sex," and "The Unhappy Marriage," especially pp. 25–29, 32–33; and Weinbaum and Bridges, "The Other Side of the Paycheck." Both are critical of Eli Zaretsky [*Capitalism, the Family and Personal Life* (London: Pluto Press, 1976)] who, while attempting to incorporate an analysis of patriarchy into a Marxist framework, nevertheless continued to treat class relations as primary.

22 Those who first articulated the theoretical arguments for "wages for housework" were Maríarosa Dalla Costa and Selma James, *The Power of Women and the Subversion of Community* (Bristol, UK: Falling Wall, 1973). See also Deanne Bonner, "Toward the Feminization of Policy: Exit from an Ancient Trap by the Redefinition of Work," in *For Crying Out Loud: Women and Poverty in the United States*, eds. Rochelle Lefkowitz and Ann Withorn (New York: Pilgrim Press, 1986, pp. 285–99; sources cited in note 20, above; and Gwendolyn Mink, "Aren't Poor Single Mothers Women?" in *Whose Welfare?* and *Welfare's End*, especially Chapter 4.

23 Dalla Costa and James argued, in *The Power of Women and the Subversion of Community*, that, since unpaid housework provided a crucial economic support for capitalism, women's demand for wages for their work would constitute an important challenge to capital. For additional developments of that argument, see Bonner, "Toward the Feminization of Policy"; Emily K. Abel, "Adult Daughters and Care for the Aged," *Feminist Studies* 12, 3 (1986), pp. 479–97; Abel, *Who Cares for the Elderly? Public Policy and the Experiences of Adult Daughters* (Philadelphia, PA: Temple University Press, 1991); and *Circles of Care: Work and Identity in Women's Lives*, eds. Emily K. Abel and Margaret K. Nelson (Albany: SUNY Press, 1990).

24 See Hartman, "Capitalism, Patriarchy" and "The Unhappy Marriage"; Jaggar, *Feminist Politics and Human Nature*; Eisenstein, ed., *Capitalist Patriarchy*. Fraser and Gordon make a related argument in "A Genealogy of Dependency."

25 On this point, see especially Gayle Rubin's now-classic essay, "The Traffic in Women," in *Toward an Anthropology of Women*, ed. Rayna R. Reiter (New York: Monthly Review Press, 1975), pp. 157–210 and Iris Marion Young, "Beyond the Unhappy Marriage." Young argues that the work of Hartmann, Weinbaum and Bridges, and other proponents of "dual systems theory" lacks the analytical framework to carry this insight to its logical conclusion—i.e. that the "marginalization of women and thereby our functioning as a secondary labor force is an essential and fundamental characteristic of capitalism" ("Beyond the Unhappy Marriage," p. 58; see also p. 61).

26 Barbara Taylor, *Eve and the New Jerusalem* (New York: Pantheon, 1983); see also Ruth L. Smith and Deborah Valenze, "Mutuality and Marginality: Liberal Moral Theory and Working-Class Women in Nineteenth-Century England," *Signs* 13 (Winter 1988), pp. 277–98.

27 See, for example, William Julius Wilson, *The Truly Disadvantaged* (Chicago: University of Chicago Press, 1987); for a critique of this perspective see, e.g., Linda Gordon, "What Does Welfare Regulate?" *Social Research* 55 (Winter 1988), pp. 626–28, and Fraser and Gordon, "A Genealogy of Dependency."

28 In addition to Gordon ["What Does Welfare Regulate?" *Women, the State, and Welfare*; and *Pitied but Not Entitled: Single Mothers and the History of Welfare, 1890–1935* (New York: Free Press, 1994)] and Nelson, ["Women's Poverty and Women's Citizenship," and "The Two-Channel Welfare State"], see, e.g., Frances Fox Piven, "Women and the State: Ideology, Power, and Welfare," in *For Crying Out Loud*, pp.

326–40; Steven Erie, Martin Rein, and Barbara Wiget, "Women and the Reagan Revolution: Thermidor for the Social Welfare Economy," in *Families, Politics and Public Policy*, ed. Irene Diamond (New York: Longman, 1983), pp. 94–119; Zillah Eisenstein, "The Sexual Politics of the New Right," *Signs* 7 (Spring 1982), pp. 567–88 and "The Patriarchal Relations of the Reagan State," *Signs* 10 (Winter 1984), pp. 329–37; Maxine Baca Zinn, "Family, Race and Poverty in the Eighties," *Signs* 14 (Summer 1989), pp. 856–74; and Gwendolyn Mink, *The Wages of Motherhood, Whose Welfare?* and *Welfare's End* (Ithaca, NY: Cornell University Press, 1998).

29 Martha A. Ackelsberg and Irene Diamond, "Gender and Political Life: New Directions in Political Science," in *Analyzing Gender*, eds. Beth B. Hess and Myra Marx Ferree (Newbury Park, CA: Sage Publications, 1987), p. 513. See Elshtain, "Feminism, Family, and Community," *Dissent* 29 (Fall 1982), pp. 442–49, and "Reclaiming the Socialist-Feminist Citizen," *Socialist Review* 74 (1984), pp. 21–27; Kathy Ferguson, *The Feminist Case Against Bureaucracy* (Philadelphia, PA: Temple University Press, 1984); Irene Diamond, "American Feminism and the Language of Control," in *Feminism and Foucault*, eds. Irene Diamond and Lee Quinby (Boston: Northeastern University Press, 1988), pp. 193–206; and Gwendolyn Mink, *The Wages of Motherhood* and *Welfare's End*.

30 Balbus, *Marxism and Domination* (Princeton, NJ: Princeton University Press, 1982), p. 333. This concern resonates with more recent writing—by Crenson and Ginsberg, Skocpol, Putnam, Wolin, and others—about the decline of civic engagement and the growth of the security state, discussed, above, in the Introduction to this volume.

31 Frances Fox Piven and Richard Cloward, *The New Class War* (New York: Pantheon, 1984); Frances Fox Piven, *Challenging Authority: How Ordinary People Change America* (Lanham, MD: Rowman and Littlefield, 2006), especially Chapter 5; Zillah Eisenstein, "The Sexual Politics of the New Right," "The Patriarchal Relations of the Reagan State," *The Radical Future of Liberal Feminism*, revised edition (Boston: Northeastern University Press, 1993), and *Feminism and Sexual Equality: Crisis in Liberal America* (New York: Monthly Review Press, 1984); Ida Susser, *Norman Street* (New York: Oxford University Press, 1982) and "Working-Class Women, Social Protest, and Changing Ideologies," in *Women and the Politics of Empowerment*, eds. Ann R. Bookman and Sandra Morgen (Philadelphia, PA: Temple University Press, 1988), pp. 257–71; Sandra Morgen, "It's the Whole Power of the City Against Us," in ibid., pp. 97–115; Linda Gordon, ed. *Women, the State and Welfare* and "What Does Welfare Regulate?"

32 Gordon, "Family Violence, Feminism, and Social Control," and also *Pitied But Not Entitled*.

33 See, for example, Piven, *Challenging Authority*; Nancy Naples, *Grassroots Warriors: Activist Mothering, Community Work and the War on Poverty* (New York: Routledge, 1998), Naples, ed., *Community Activism and Feminist Politics: Organizing Across Race, Class and Gender* (New York: Routledge, 1998); Annelise Orleck, *Storming Caesars Palace: How Black Mothers Fought Their Own War on Poverty* (Boston: Beacon Press, 2005); Premilla Nadasen, *Welfare Warriors: The Welfare Rights Movement in the United States* (New York: Routledge, 2005); and Rhonda Williams, *The Politics of Public Housing: Black Women's Struggles Against Urban Inequality* (New York: Oxford University Press, 2004).

34 This latter question was raised specifically by Jennifer Schirmer in comments at the conference "Gender and the Welfare State," Center for European Studies, Harvard University, April 16, 1988; but it has certainly become central to virtually all contemporary considerations of the issue.

35 Fraser and Gordon make a related point in "A Genealogy of Dependency," p. 319.

36 See, for example, Martha Fowlkes, "Katie's Place: Women's Work, Professional Work, and Social Reform," *Research in the Interweave of Social Roles: Jobs and Families* (Westport, CT: JAI Press., 1983), Vol. 3, pp. 143–59, and Fowlkes, *Behind Every Successful Man: Wives of Medicine and Academe* (New York: Columbia University Press, 1980); and Emily Abel, *Hearts of Wisdom: American Women Caring for Kin, 1850–1940* (Cambridge, MA: Harvard University Press, 2000) and Abel, *Who Cares for the Elderly?* My argument here parallels that of Joan Tronto in *Moral Boundaries.*

37 See William Chafe, *Women and Equality* (New York: Oxford University Press, 1978); Michael Walzer, *Spheres of Justice* (New York: Basic Books, 1983); Martha Ackelsberg and Kathryn Pyne Addelson, "Anarchist Alternatives to Competition," in *Competition: A Feminist Taboo?* eds. Helen Longino and Valerie Miner (New York: The Feminist Press, 1987), pp. 221–33; and Martha Ackelsberg, Kathryn Pyne Addelson, and Shawn Pyne, "Anarchism and Feminism," in *Impure Thoughts: Essays on Philosophy, Feminism and Ethics,* ed. Kathryn Pyne Addelson (Philadelphia, PA: Temple University Press, 1991), pp. 159–87. Nancy Fraser and Linda Gordon make a related point about the *social* relations of subordination in "A Genealogy of Dependency," p. 331.

38 Although she argues against "communitarians," Amy Gutmann recognizes the significance of such activities even to liberal societies in "Communitarian Critiques of Liberalism," *Philosophy and Public Affairs* 14 (Summer 1985), especially pp. 320–22. See also Michael Sandel, *Liberalism and the Limits of Justice* (New York: Cambridge University Press, 1982); Martha Minow, *Making All the Difference* (Ithaca, NY: Cornell University Press, 1990); Martha Minow and Mary Lyndon Shanley, "Relational Rights and Responsibilities," *Hypatia* 11, 1 (Winter 1996), pp. 4–29; Traci Levy, "The Relational Self and the Right to Give Care," *New Political Science* 28, 4 (December 2006), pp. 547–70; and Marilyn Friedman, "Feminism and Modern Friendship: Dislocating the Community," *Ethics,* 99 (January 1989), pp. 275–90.

5 PRIVACY, PUBLICITY, AND POWER

† Author's note: This chapter was originally published in 1996, considerably before the decision in *Lawrence v. Texas* (2003) that declared anti-sodomy laws unconstitutional. I have left it in its original form, with the exception of a few paragraphs that focus on gay marriage, rather than on anti-sodomy laws.

1 Carole Pateman, *The Sexual Contract* (Stanford, CA: Stanford University Press, 1988); Pateman, "Feminist Critiques of the Public/Private Dichotomy," in *The Disorder of Women: Democracy, Feminism, and Political Theory* (Stanford, CA: Stanford University Press, 1989), pp. 118–40; Susan Moller Okin, *Justice, Gender and the Family* (New York: Basic Books, 1989); Jean Elshtain, "Moral Woman and Immoral Man: Reflections on the Public Private Split," *Politics and Society* 4 (1974), pp. 453–73, and Elshtain, *Public Man, Private Woman: Women in Social and Political Thought* (Princeton, NJ: Princeton University Press, 1981).

2 See John Locke, *Two Treatises of Government,* ed. Peter Laslett (Cambridge: Cambridge University Press, 1963), pars. 4–9, 54–63, 95–99 on different kinds of freedom; also Jean-Jacques Rousseau, *On the Social Contract, with the Geneva Manuscript and Political Economy,* translated by Judith R. Masters, and edited by Roger D. Masters (New York: St. Martin's Press, 1978), Book I, Chapters 2, 6, 8 on the distinction between "natural" freedom and "political" or "civic" freedom.

3 In some of their writings, Marx and Engels seemed to acknowledge that families, for example, were also affected by relations of domination and subordination; but, for the most part, they saw these relationships as consequences of capitalism and thought such private hierarchies would disappear under socialism or communism.

See, especially, Friedrich Engels, "The Origins of the Family, Private Property, and the State," in *Marx Engels Selected Works* (Moscow: Foreign Languages Publishing House, 1962), Vol. II, pp. 217–41. For some important feminist critiques, see Joan Landes, "Marxism and the 'Woman Question,'" in *Promissory Notes: Women and the Transition to Socialism*, eds. Sonia Kruks, Rayna Rapp and Marilyn Young (New York: Monthly Review Press, 1989), pp. 15–28; Heidi Hartman, "Capitalism, Patriarchy, and Job Segregation by Sex," in *Capitalist Patriarchy and the Case for Socialist Feminism*, ed. Zillah Eisenstein (New York: Monthly Review Press, 1976), pp. 206–47 and Hartman, "The Unhappy Marriage of Marxism and Feminism," in *Women and Revolution*, ed. Lydia Sargent (Boston: South End Press, 1981), pp. 1–41; and Mary O'Brien, *The Politics of Reproduction* (Boston: Routledge and Kegan Paul, 1983). See also my discussion, above, Chapter 4.

4 See Mary Dietz, "Hannah Arendt and Feminist Politics," in *Feminist Interpretations and Political Theory*, eds. Mary Lyndon Shanley and Carole Pateman (University Park, PA: Pennsylvania State University Press, 1991), p. 236; see also Hannah Arendt, *The Human Condition* (New York: Viking, 1968) and *On Revolution* (New York: Viking Compass, 1965); Hannah Pitkin, "Justice: On Relating Private and Public," *Political Theory* 9, 3 (August 1981), pp. 327–52.

5 See Penny Weiss, "Sex, Freedom and Equality in Rousseau's *Emile*," *Polity* 22 (Summer 1990), pp. 603–25 and Weiss, "Rousseau, Antifeminism, and Woman's Nature," *Political Theory* 15 (February 1987), pp. 81–98; Susan Okin, "Rousseau's Natural Woman," *Journal of Politics* 41 (1979), pp. 393–416; and Lydia Lange, "Rousseau and Modern Feminism," in *Feminist Interpretations and Political Theory*, eds. Mary Lyndon Shanley and Carole Pateman (University Park, PA: Pennsylvania State University Press, 1991), pp. 95–111.

6 See Mary Lyndon Shanley, "Marital Slavery and Friendship: John Stuart Mill's *The Subjection of Women*," in *Feminist Interpretations and Political Theory*, eds. Mary Lyndon Shanley and Carole Pateman (University Park, PA: Pennsylvania State University Press, 1991), pp. 164–80; and Christine DiStefano, *Configurations of Masculinity: A Feminist Perspective on Modern Political Theory* (Ithaca, NY: Cornell University Press, 1991).

7 See note 1 above; also Teresa Brennan and Carole Pateman, "'Mere Auxiliaries to the Commonwealth': Women and the Origins of Liberalism," *Political Studies* 27, 2 (1979), pp. 183–200.

8 See also Aileen Kraditor, *The Ideas of the Woman's Suffrage Movement* (New York: Columbia University Press, 1965) and Carl Degler, "Revolution without Ideology: The Changing Place of Women in America," in *The Woman in America*, ed. Robert J. Lifton (Boston: Houghton Mifflin, 1964), pp. 193–210.

9 See also Pateman, "Women and Consent," *Political Theory* 8, 2 (1980), pp. 149–68; *The Sexual Contract*; and "Feminist Critiques of the Public/Private Dichotomy," in *The Disorder of Women* (Stanford, CA: Stanford University Press, 1989), pp. 118–40.

10 Michelle Zimbalist Rosaldo, "Woman, Culture and Society: A Theoretical Overview," in *Woman, Culture and Society*, eds. Michelle Zimbalist Rosaldo and Louise Lamphere (Stanford, CA: Stanford University Press, 1974), p. 34, see also pp. 22–35.

11 Quotations from "Woman, Culture and Society," pp. 35 and 42.

12 Anne Phillips makes a similar argument in her discussion of the public/private distinction in *Engendering Democracy* (University Park, PA: Pennsylvania State University Press, 1991).

13 Michelle Zimbalist Rosaldo, "The Use and Abuse of Anthropology," *Signs* 5, 3 (1980), pp. 389–417.

14 Catharine MacKinnon, *Toward a Feminist Theory of the State* (Cambridge, MA: Harvard University Press, 1989), p. 224.

15 Okin, *Justice, Gender and the Family*, pp. 111, 129.

16 See also Frances Olsen, "The Family and the Market: A Study of Ideology and Legal Reform," *Harvard Law Review* 96, 7 (1983). For a parallel argument about the mutual construction of "dependence" and "independence," see Chapter 4, above.

17 For a useful summary of feminist perspectives on the public–private split, see Pateman, "Feminist Perspectives"; Will Kymlicka, *Contemporary Political Philosophy: An Introduction* (Oxford: Clarendon Press, 1990), esp. pp. 247–62; Anne Phillips, *Engendering Democracy*, Chapter 4; and Patricia Boling, *Privacy and the Politics of Intimate Life* (Ithaca, NY: Cornell University Press, 1996).

18 See *Moore v. City of East Cleveland* 431 US 494 [1977]; *Village of Belle Terre v. Boraas* 416 US 1 [1974]; Olsen, "The Family and the Market"; and Martha Ackelsberg, "Redefining Family: Models for the Jewish Future," in *Twice Blessed*, eds. Christie Balka and Andy Rose (Boston: Beacon Press, 1989), pp. 107–17.

19 On this latter point, see Linda Gordon, *Heroes of Their Own Lives* (New York: Viking, 1988) and "Family Violence, Feminism and Social Control," in *Women, the State and Welfare*, ed. Linda Gordon (Madison: University of Wisconsin Press, 1990), pp. 178–98.

20 Harriet Jacobs, *Incidents in the Life of a Slave Girl* (Cambridge, MA: Harvard University Press, 1987), p. 54. See also Margaret Burnham, "An Impossible Marriage: Slave Law and Family Law," *Law and Inequality* 5 (1987), pp. 187–225.

21 Ida B. Wells, "Lynching and the Excuse for It," *The Independent*, May 16, 1901, reproduced in *Lynching and Rape: An Exchange of Views* by Jane Addams and Ida B. Wells, edited and with an introduction by Bettina Aptheker. Occasional paper no. 25 (New York: American Institute for Marxist Studies, 1977), pp. 32–34.

22 See Wells, "Lynching and the Excuse for It"; also "Lynch Law in All Its Phases," in *Ida B. Wells-Barnett: An Exploratory Study of an American Black Woman, 1893–1930*, ed. Mildred I. Thompson. Vol. 15 of *Black Women in United States History* (Brooklyn, NY: Carlson Publishing, 1990). See also Paula Giddings, *Ida: A Sword Among Lions*, especially Chapters 6–8, 15. We explore Wells' analysis of lynching in a somewhat broader context in Chapter 6, below.

23 For an historical overview, see Karl Polanyi, *The Great Transformation* (Boston: Beacon Press, 1957); also Linda Gordon, *Heroes of Their Own Lives*; Gwendolyn Mink, *The Wages of Motherhood* and *Welfare's End*; Mimi Abramowitz, *Regulating the Lives of Women: Social Welfare Policy from Colonial Times to the Present* (Boston: South End Press, 1988); and Rochelle Lefkowitz and Ann Withorn, *For Crying Out Loud: Women and Poverty in the United States* (New York: Pilgrim Press, 1990).

24 Barbara Nelson, "The Origins of the Two-Channel Welfare State: Workmen's Compensation and Mothers' Aid," in *Women, the State and Welfare*, ed. Linda Gordon (Madison: University of Wisconsin Press, 1990). See also Chapter 4, above.

25 See also Frances Fox Piven and Richard A. Cloward, *Regulating the Poor* (New York: Pantheon, 1971) and *Poor People's Movements: How They Succeed, Why They Fail* (New York: Pantheon, 1979) and Teresa Amott, "Black Women and AFDC: Making Entitlement out of Necessity," in *Women, the State and Welfare*, ed. Linda Gordon.

26 Moynihan's comments, of course, come from *The Negro Family: The Case for National Action* (Washington, DC: Office of Planning, Policy and Research, U.S. Department of Labor, 1965), available at: www.dol.gov/oasam/programs/history/webid-meynihan.htm (accessed September 21 2008). See also Lee Rainwater, *The Moynihan Report and the Politics of Controversy* (Cambridge, MA: MIT Press, 1967). Some of Moynihan's concerns about the structure and internal workings of black welfare families were taken up in new form by William Julius Wilson in *The Truly Disadvantaged* (Chicago: University of Chicago Press, 1988), whose assumptions about welfare recipients were criticized by Martha Fineman, among others, in "Images of

Mothers in Poverty Discourses," *Duke University Law Journal* (1991), pp. 274–95. See also Ange-Marie Hancock, *The Politics of Disgust: The Public Identity of the Welfare Queen* (New York: New York University Press, 2004).

27 See Susan Schechter, *Women and Male Violence: Visions and Struggles of the Battered Women's Movement* (Boston: South End Press, 1982) and Ann Jones, *Next Time, She'll Be Dead: Battering and How to Stop It* (Boston: Beacon Press, 1994).

28 Okin, *Justice, Gender and the Family* (New York: Basic Books, 1989), pp. 128–29. Ann Shola Orloff also notes that women's citizenship may require very different forms of engagement with the state than does men's in "Gender and the Social Rights of Citizenship," *American Sociological Review*, 58, 3 (June 1993), pp. 308–9.

29 Gordon, *Heroes of Their Own Lives* and, especially, "Family Violence, Feminism and Social Control," in *Women, the State and Welfare*, ed. Linda Gordon (Madison: University of Wisconsin Press, 1990).

30 Sodomy statutes were ruled unconstitutional by the Supreme Court's decision in *Lawrence v. Texas* 539 U.S. 558 (2003); same-sex marriage (or something akin to it) is legal in only a handful of states as of December 2008.

31 Indeed, Bill Baird noted that one of his goals in challenging laws against the use of contraceptives was to open the way to testing anti-sodomy laws. Talk at Smith College, Northampton, MA, November 2007.

32 *In re Marriage Cases* S147999, Supreme Court of California, May 2008.

33 See, e.g. Toni Morrison, "Introduction: Friday on the Potomac," in *Race-ing Justice, En-gendering Power*, ed. Toni Morrison (New York: Pantheon, 1992) and Nell Irvin Painter, "Hill, Thomas, and the Use of Racial Stereotype," in *Race-ing Justice, En-gendering Power*.

34 Deborah Rhode, *Justice and Gender: Sex Discrimination and the Law* (Cambridge, MA: Harvard University Press, 1989), pp. 231–32.

35 The words and phrases are from a variety of Court cases, cited in Rhode, *Justice and Gender*, p. 235.

36 On this point, see Kimberlé Crenshaw, "Whose Story Is It, Anyway? Feminist and Antiracist Appropriations of Anita Hill," in Morrison, ed., *Race-ing Justice, En-gendering Power*.

37 See, e.g. Nancy Fraser, "Sex, Lies and the Public Sphere: Some Reflections on the Confirmation of Clarence Thomas," *Critical Inquiry* 18 (Spring 1992), pp. 595–612.

38 See A. Leon Higginbotham, Jr., "An Open Letter to Justice Clarence Thomas from a Federal Judicial Colleague," in Morrison, ed., *Race-ing Justice, En-gendering Power*.

39 See, e.g., Patricia Hill Collins, *Black Feminist Theory* (Cambridge: Unwin Hyman, 1990); Martha Fineman, "Images of Mothers in Poverty Discourses"; Wahneema Lubiano, "Black Ladies, Welfare Queens, and State Minstrels: Ideological War by Narrative Means," in *Race-ing Justice, En-gendering Power*, and Hancock, *The Politics of Disgust*.

40 For more on issues of "care" and dependency, see Chapters 4 and 11.

6 GENDER, RESISTANCE, AND CITIZENSHIP

1 Women did not get the vote in the US until 1920, and southern Black women were not effectively enfranchised until the Voting Rights Act of 1964. In Argentina, democratic guarantees had been abolished by the military juntas.

2 See, for example, Carole Pateman, *The Sexual Contract* (Stanford, CA: Stanford University Press, 1988), esp. Chapters 2–4; Pateman, "Feminist Critiques of the Public/Private Dichotomy," in *The Disorder of Women* (Stanford, CA: Stanford University Press, 1989), pp. 118–40; Anne Philips, *Engendering Democracy* (University Park, PA: Pennsylvania State University Press, 1991); and Cynthia Enloe, *Bananas,*

Beaches, and Bases: Making Feminist Sense of International Politics (Berkeley: University of California Press, 1989); and *The Curious Feminist: Searching for Women in the New Age of Empire* (Berkeley: University of California Press, 2004).

3 See, for example, Robert Ingalls, "Lynching and Establishment Violence in Tampa, 1858–1935," *The Journal of Southern History* LIII, 4 (November 1987), pp. 613–44; and Donald L. Grant, *The Anti-Lynching Movement: 1883–1932* (San Francisco: R. and E. Research Associates, 1975), especially Chapter 1.

4 Cited in Bettina Aptheker, "Woman Suffrage and the Crusade against Lynching, 1890–1920," in *Woman's Legacy: Essays on Race, Sex, and Class in American History* (Amherst, MA: University of Massachusetts Press, 1982), p. 60.

5 Robert L. Zangrando, *The NAACP Crusade Against Lynching, 1909–1950* (Philadelphia, PA: Temple University Press, 1980), p. 5.

6 Jane Addams, "Respect for Law," *The Independent*, January 3, 1901, in "Lynching and Rape: An Exchange of Views," by Jane Addams and Ida B. Wells, edited and with an Introduction by Bettina Aptheker, Occasional Paper No. 25 (New York: American Institute for Marxist Studies, 1977), p. 23.

7 Ibid., p. 26.

8 Ida B. Wells, *Crusade for Justice: The Autobiography of Ida B. Wells*, edited by Alfreda M. Duster (Chicago: University of Chicago Press, 1970), p. 71; see also Paula Giddings, *When and Where I Enter: The Impact of Black Women on Race and Sex in America* (New York: William Morrow and Co., Inc., 1984), pp. 26–31; and Giddings, *Ida: A Sword Among Lions: Ida B. Wells and the Campaign Against Lynching* (New York: Amistad, 2008).

9 Wells, *Crusade for Justice*, pp. 47–50.

10 Wells, "Lynching and the Excuse for It," *The Independent*, May 16, 1901, cited in Aptheker, ed., "Lynching and Rape," p. 34. It would be wrong to completely dichotomize the views of Addams and Wells. They both opposed lynching; and the woman-centered analyses they each sometimes expressed contributed to the development of twentieth-century feminism. Furthermore, Wells used the new statistical social science methodology, developed by Jane Addams and her associates at Hull House, to argue her case. We are grateful to Marjorie Murphy for bringing these points to our attention in her comments at the Social Science History Association, Chicago, IL, November 1992.

11 Terrell, "Lynching from a Negro's Point of View," reprinted in *Quest for Equality: The Life and Writings of Mary Eliza Church Terrell, 1863–1954*, edited by Beverly Washington Jones. In the series, *Black Women in United States History* (Brooklyn, NY: Carlson Publishing, Inc., 1990), Vol. 13, pp. 167–68, 177.

12 Ironically, Clarence Thomas' claim, during his confirmation hearings, that he was the victim of a "high tech lynching" drew upon this analysis of the myth of the black rapist while, at the same time, ignoring the powerful role of black women in opposing lynching. See, for example Nelly Y. McKay, "Remembering Anita Hill and Clarence Thomas: What Really Happened When One Black Woman Spoke Out," in *Race-ing Justice, En-gendering Power*, ed. Toni Morrison (New York: Pantheon, 1992), pp. 284–89; Kimberlé Crenshaw, "Whose Story Is It, Anyway? Feminist and Antiracist Appropriations of Anita Hill," in ibid., pp. 402–40; and Nancy Fraser, "Sex, Lies, and the Public Sphere: Some Reflections on the Confirmation of Clarence Thomas," *Critical Inquiry* 18 (Spring 1992), pp. 595–612.

13 Wells, "Lynching and the Excuse for It," p. 32.

14 "Lynch Law in all Its Phases," reprinted in *Ida B. Wells Barnett: An Exploratory Study of an American Black Woman, 1893–1930*, ed. Mildred I. Thompson, in the series, *Black Women in United States History* (Brooklyn, NY: Carlson Publishing, Inc., 1990), Vol. 15, p. 177.

15 Wells, *Crusade for Justice*, p. 71.

16 Giddings, *When and Where I Enter*, p. 86. The power of the myth of black female "looseness," even in the black community, was well illustrated by an incident recounted by Wells in her autobiography. When Wells was a school teacher in Memphis, a black minister at a social gathering compared the morals of southern black women unfavorably with those of their northern sisters. Wells, born and raised in the south, was outraged, and insisted that the minister recant his remark from the pulpit the following Sunday. The incident was testimony to Wells' perception of the destructive force of the myth of black wantonness even within the black community. See Wells, *Crusade for Justice*, pp. 42–45. See also Paula Giddings' discussion of Wells' anger at many of her black male friends for not coming to her defense after *she* was so slandered, asking in an editorial, "Is mine a race of cowards?" Giddings, *Ida: A Sword Among Lions*, p. 312, citing Wells from *Indianapolis Freeman* 21 July 1894.

17 Aptheker, "Woman Suffrage," p. 62; see also Giddings, *Ida: A Sword Among Lions*, *passim*.

18 Giddings, *Ida: A Sword Among Lions*, Chapter 11.

19 Ingalls, pp. 643–44; see also Aptheker, "Woman Suffrage," p. 72. Similar arguments about the impact of economic factors have been made about the struggle for integration in the South in the 1950s and 1960s, evidenced perhaps most notably in Atlanta's motto: "The city that's too busy to hate."

20 Wells, "Lynch Law," p. 184.

21 Mark Osiel, "The Making of Human Rights Policy in Argentina: The Impact of Ideas and Interests on a Legal Conflict," *Journal of Latin American Studies* 18 (1986), pp. 139–40, citing *Nunca Más: The Report of the Argentine National Commission on the Disappeared* (New York: Farrar, Straus and Giroux, in association with the Index on Censorship, London, 1986), pp. 299–322.

22 Marysa Navarro, "The Personal Is Political: Las Madres de Plaza de Mayo," in *Power and Popular Protest: Latin American Social Movements*, ed. Susan Eckstein (Berkeley: University of California Press, 1989), p. 250. See also Temma Kaplan, *Taking Back the Streets: Women, Youth and Direct Democracy* (Berkeley: University of California Press, 2004); Marjorie Agosín, *Ashes of Revolt: Essays on Human Rights* (Fredonia, NY: White Pine Press, 1996); Matilde Mellibovsky, *Circle of Love Over Death* (Willimantic, CT: Curbstone Press, 1997); and Marguerite Guzman Bouvard, *Revolutionizing Motherhood: The Madres of the Plaza de Mayo* (Wilmington, DE: Scholarly Resources, 1994).

23 Navarro, "The Personal Is Political," p. 251; and sources cited above, note 22.

24 See Evelyn P. Stevens, "Marianismo: The Other Face of Machismo in Latin America," in *Female and Male in Latin America*, ed. Ann Pescatello (Pittsburgh: University of Pittsburgh Press, 1973).

25 Marjorie Agosín, "Metaphors of Female Political Ideology: The Cases of Chile and Argentina," *Women's Studies International Forum* 10 (1987), pp. 571–75.

26 Ximena Bunster-Burotto, "Surviving Beyond Fear: Women and Torture in Latin America," in *Women and Change in Latin America*, eds. June Nash and Helen Safa (South Hadley, MA: Bergin and Garvey, 1986); Alicia Partnoy, *The Little School: Tales of Disappearance and Survival in Argentina* (Pittsburgh: Cleis Press, 1986); and Kaplan, *Taking Back the Streets*, especially Chapters 1, 4.

27 See, among others, Kaplan, *Taking Back the Streets*, Chapters 4 and 5; Bouvard, *Revolutionizing Motherhood*, Chapter 9; and Georgina Waylen, *Engendering Transitions: Women's Mobilization, Institutions, and Gender Outcomes* (Oxford: Oxford University Press, 2007), pp. 55–61, 70; and Michelle D. Bonner, *Sustaining Human Rights: Women and Argentine Human Rights Organizations* (University Park, PA: Pennsylvania State University Press, 2007).

28 See Georgina Waylen's formulation of this criticism in "Rethinking Women's Political Participation and Protest: Chile 1970–90," *Political Studies* 40, 2 (1992), pp. 299–314, citing Susan Bordo, "Feminism, Postmodernism and Gender Scepticism," and Nancy Fraser and Linda J. Nicholson, "Social Criticism without Philosophy," both in Nicholson, ed., *Feminism/Postmodernism* (London: Routledge, 1990).

29 Elshtain, "Mothers Against the Authoritarian State," paper prepared for the Convention of the IPSA, Buenos Aires (July 1991), p. 6.

30 Navarro, "The Personal Is Political," p. 257.

31 María del Carmen Feijóo, "The Challenge of Constructing Civilian Peace: Women and Democracy in Argentina," in *The Women's Movement in Latin America: Feminism and the Transition to Democracy*, ed. Jane S. Jaquette (Boulder, CO: Westview Press, 1991), pp. 89, 92–93. Of course, these debates are reminiscent of debates in the US feminist movement over "maternalist" politics. See, for example, Sara Ruddick, "Maternal Thinking," *Feminist Studies* 6, 2 (Summer 1980), pp. 342–67; Jean Elshtain, "Reflections on War and Political Discourse," *Political Theory* 13, 1 (February 1985), pp. 38–57; and Mary Dietz, "Citizenship with a Feminist Face: The Problem with Maternal Thinking," ibid., pp. 19–37, and "Context Is All: Feminism and Theories of Citizenship," *Daedalus* 116 (Fall 1987), pp. 1–24.

32 "Historia de las Madres II," *Madres de Plaza de Mayo*, 3 (Feb. 1985), quoted in Rossi, "Cómo Pensar a las Madres de Plaza de Mayo?" *Nuevo Texto Crítico* 4 (Año II), p. 149. See also Temma Kaplan, "Female Consciousness and Collective Action: The Case of Barcelona, 1910–18," *Signs* 7, 3 (1982), pp. 545–66; "Community and Resistance in Women's Political Cultures," *Dialectical Anthropology* 15 (1990), pp. 259–67; *Crazy for Democracy: Women in Grassroots Movements* (New York: Routledge, 1997) and *Taking Back the Streets*. Marguerite Bouvard argues, in fact, that the Madres and similar groups created new, transformative, models of political practice. See *Revolutionizing Motherhood*, especially Chapter 9.

33 Schirmer notes that the Madres are like women who joined bread riots in past centuries, engaging in the "defiant transformation of the powerless victim into the political actor," thereby "dramatiz[ing] powerlessness and help[ing] to demystify the powerful." See Jennifer G. Schirmer, "'Those Who Die for Life Cannot Be Called Dead:' Women and Human Rights Protest in Latin America," *Feminist Review* 32 (Summer 1989), p. 4; also Rossi, p. 151; Laura Beatriz Gingold and Inés Vázquez, "Madres de Plaza de Mayo: Madres de una nueva práctica política?" *Nueva sociedad* 93 (January–February 1988), pp. 114–22; and Jo Fisher, *Mothers of the Disappeared* (Boston: South End Press, 1989), pp. xii, 86, 91. See also Chapter 3, above.

34 Feijóo, "The Challenge of Constructing Civilian Peace," p. 84.

35 Temma Kaplan makes a similar argument in *Taking Back the Streets*; see, especially, "Prologue" and "Epilogue." See also the extensive, and comparative, discussion in Waylen, *Engendering Transitions*.

36 Louise A. Tilly and Patricia Gurin, "Introduction: Women, Politics, and Change," in Louise A. Tilly and Patricia Gurin, eds., *Women, Politics and Change* (New York: Russell Sage, 1990), p. 8; see also Temma Kaplan, "Female Consciousness and Collective Action: The Case of Barcelona, 1910–1918," *Signs* 7 (1982), pp. 545–566 and Kaplan, *Crazy for Democracy*.

37 Tilly and Gurin, "Introduction: Women, Politics and Change," p. 28.

38 Paula Baker, "The Domestication of Politics: Women and American Political Society, 1780–1920" in Linda Gordon, ed., *Women, the State, and Welfare* (Madison: University of Wisconsin Press, 1990), pp. 55–91; and Suzanne Lebsock, "Women and American Politics, 1880–1920," in Tilly and Gurin, eds., *Women, Politics, and Change*, pp. 35–62.

39 Beatriz Schmukler has noted, for example, that silent marches around a public plaza—a practice created and introduced by the Madres—have now become a relatively "normal" feature of political protest life in Argentina, and been adopted by other groups even outside of Buenos Aires. Schmukler, "Women in Social Democratization in the 1980's in Argentina," unpublished paper as a Tinker Fellow, Amherst, MA (1991), p. 13; and personal communication, April 1991. See also Temma Kaplan, *Taking Back the Streets*; Georgina Waylen, *Engendering Transitions*; and Velma García, *Mothers and the Mexican Antinuclear Power Movement* (Tucson: University of Arizona Press, 1999).

40 For further discussion of this point, see Martha Ackelsberg and Mary Lyndon Shanley, "De la Resistencia a la Reconstrucción? Las Madres de Plaza de Mayo, el Maternalismo y la Transición a la Democracia en Argentina," *Doxa* III, 7 (Otoño 1992), pp. 56–61; Waylen, *Engendering Transitions*; and Kaplan, *Taking Back the Streets*. For further discussion of the relationship between public/private and "the political," see below, Chapters 10, 12.

41 See, for example, Wells, *Autobiography*, pp. 222, 291, 311, 362. See also Giddings, *Ida: A Sword Among Lions*.

42 See Teresa Brennan and Carole Pateman, "'Mere Auxiliaries to the Commonwealth': Women and the Origins of Liberalism," *Political Studies* 27, 2 (1979), pp. 183–200. On the relationship of "protection" and citizenship, see also Michael Walzer, *Obligations: Essays on Disobedience, War and Citizenship* (Cambridge, MA: Harvard University Press, 1970); and Judith Shklar, *American Citizenship: The Quest for Inclusion* (Cambridge, MA: Harvard University Press, 1991).

43 See Cheryl Walker, *Women and Resistance in South Africa* (London: Onyx Books, 1982), pp. 6–7, 11, 28, 39, 126–30; also Richard E. Lapchick and Stephanie Urdang, *Oppression and Resistance: The Struggle of Women in Southern Africa* (Westport, CT: Greenwood Press, 1982), p. 140; CIIR and Vukani Makhosikazi Collective, *South African Women on the Move* (London: Zed Books, 1985), p. 235; Hilda Bernstein, *For Their Triumphs and for Their Tears: Women and Apartheid in South Africa* (London: International Defence and Aid Fund for South Africa, 1985); and Temma Kaplan, *Crazy for Democracy*.

44 See Susan Schechter, *Women and Male Violence: The Visions and Struggles of the Battered Women's Movement* (Boston: South End Press, 1982) and Jean Grossholtz, "Battered Women's Shelters and the Political Economy of Sexual Violence," in I. Diamond, ed., *Families, Politics, and Public Policy* (New York: Longman, 1983), pp. 59–69. See also "Privacy, Publicity, and Power," Chapter 5, above.

7 RETHINKING ANARCHISM/RETHINKING POWER

1 This formulation of the issues owes much to conversations and writing with Irene Diamond.

2 Colin Ward, *Anarchy in Action* (London: Freedom Press, 1988).

3 See, for example, John P. Clark, "What Is Anarchism?," in *Anarchism*, Nomos XIX, ed. J. Roland Pennock and John W. Chapman (New York: New York University Press, 1978), especially p. 17; Peggy Kornegger, "Anarchism: The Feminist Connection," *The Second Wave* 4, 1 (Spring 1975), pp. 26–37; Carol Ehrlich, "Socialism, Anarchism, and Feminism," *The Second Wave* 5, 1 (Spring/Summer 1977), pp. 29–35, and "The Unhappy Marriage of Marxism and Feminism: Can It Be Saved?" in *Women and Revolution*, ed. Lydia Sargent (Boston: South End Press, 1981), especially pp. 114, 116, 131; Marsha Hewitt, "Emma Goldman: The Case for Anarcho-Feminism," *Our Generation* 17, 1 (Fall/Winter 1985–86), pp. 167–75, and "Is Sexism Genetic?" *Our Generation* 16, 2 (Spring 1984), pp. 13–14; and L. Susan Brown, "Anarchism, Existentialism, Feminism, and Ambiguity," *Our Generation* 19, 2 (Spring/Summer 1988), pp. 1–18.

4 I have developed these arguments more fully in *The Possibility of Anarchism: The Theory and Practice of Non-Authoritarian Organization*, PhD dissertation, Department of Politics, Princeton University, 1976; in *Free Women of Spain: Anarchism and the Struggle for the Emancipation of Women* (Bloomington: Indiana University Press, 1991; Oakland, CA: AK Press, 2005), especially Chapter 1; (with Kathryn Pyne Addelson) in "Anarchist Alternatives to Competition," in *Competition: A Feminist Taboo?* eds. Valerie Miner and Helen E. Longino (New York: The Feminist Press, 1987), pp. 221–33; and (with Kathryn Pyne Addelson and Shawn Pyne), "Anarchism and Feminism," in *Impure Thoughts: Essays on Philosophy, Feminism, and Ethics*, ed. Kathryn Pyne Addelson (Philadelphia, PA: Temple University Press, 1991), pp. 159–87.

5 *Anarchy in Action*, Chapter 4.

6 See, for example, Peter Kropotkin's attempt to develop an alternative to social-Darwinist understandings of evolutionary theory that emphasized cooperation rather than competition in *Mutual Aid* (London: William Heinemann, 1902) and *Fields, Factories and Workshops Tomorrow*, introduced and edited by Colin Ward (New York: Harper and Row, 1974); also Myrna Breitbart, "Peter Kropotkin: Anarchist Geographer," in *Geography, Ideology and Social Concern*, ed. David Stoddart (New York: Oxford University Press, 1982), pp. 134–53; David Miller, "The Neglected (II) Kropotkin," *Government and Opposition* 18 (Summer 1983), pp. 119–38; and William M. Dugger, "Veblen and Kropotkin on Human Evolution," *Journal of Economic Issues* XVIII, 4 (December 1984), pp. 971–85.

7 On this point, see Ackelsberg and Addelson, "Anarchist Alternatives"; also Kropotkin, "Expropriation" (pp. 160–209) and "Must We Occupy Ourselves with an Examination of the Ideal of a Future System?" (pp. 46–117), both in *Peter Kropotkin: Selected Writings on Anarchism and Revolution*, ed. Martin A. Miller (Cambridge, MA: MIT Press, 1970).

8 "Federalism, Socialism, and Anti-Theologism," p. 145; see also "Representative Government and Universal Suffrage," p. 221; and "The Program of the Alliance," pp. 245–46, all in *Bakunin on Anarchism*, ed. Sam Dolgoff (Montreal: Black Rose Books, 1980).

9 "Must We Occupy Ourselves?" p. 62. See also Pierre-Joseph Proudhon, *Du principe fédératif et de la nécessité de reconstituer le Parti de la Révolution* (Paris: E. Dentu, Libraire-Editeur, 1863), p. 42.

10 See my *Free Women of Spain*, pp. 18–20.

11 Bakunin, *God and the State*, with a New Introduction and Index of Persons by Paul Avrich (New York: Dover, 1970), pp. 31–32; and "Letters on Patriotism," in *Oeuvres* (Paris: Stock, 1895), Vol. I, pp. 222–224; and Kropotkin, "The State: Its Historic Role," in *Selected Writings*, p. 252.

12 José Prat, *A las mujeres*, Conferencia leída en el "Centro Obrero" de Sabadell y en el "Centro Fraternal de Cultura" de Barcelona, October 18 and 24, 1903 (Barcelona: Biblioteca Editorial Salud, 1923), pp. 14–15. See also Mariano Gallardo, "Tendencias del instinto sexual humano," *Estudios* 136 (December 1934), and "Influencia de las instituciones sociales sobre el carácter humano," *Estudios* 137 (January 1935), p. 63.

13 "The Tragedy of Woman's Emancipation," in Goldman, *Anarchism and Other Essays* (New York: Dover, 1969), p. 224.

14 I discuss these arguments at some length in *The Possibility of Anarchism*, Chapter 1.

15 I discuss the concept of "natural authority" in *The Possibility of Anarchism*, pp. 42–54. For Bakunin's views see *God and the State*, pp. 28–35; "Federalism, Socialism, and Anti-Theologism," p. 129, and "The Paris Commune and the Idea of the State," pp. 261–62, both in *Bakunin on Anarchism*. For Kropotkin, "Law and Authority," especially pp. 202–3; "Modern Science and Anarchism," especially pp. 146, 149,

152, 179; and "Anarchism: Its Philosophy and Ideal," especially pp. 120–21, 141, all in Roger Baldwin, ed., *Kropotkin's Revolutionary Pamphlets* (New York: Dover, 1969). For more contemporary anarchist perspectives, see Richard T. De George, "Anarchism and Authority," in J. Roland Pennock and John Chapman, eds., *Anarchism*, NOMOS XIX. (New York: New York University Press, 1978), especially, pp. 98–100; Alan Ritter, "The Anarchist Justification of Authority," in Pennock and Chapman, eds., *Anarchism*, pp. 130–40; and Clark, "What Is Anarchism?" especially pp. 8ff.

16 "The Unhappy Marriage," pp. 114, 116.

17 Ibid., p. 131. See also "An Anarcha-Feminist Looks at Power Relationships," *Quest* 5, 4 (1982), pp. 76–83.

18 Hewitt, "Is Sexism Genetic?" pp. 13–14, and "Emma Goldman," p. 169.

19 "Anarchism, Existentialism, Feminism," p. 18.

20 See, for example, Ann Bookman and Sandra Morgen, eds., *Women and the Politics of Empowerment* (Philadelphia, PA: Temple University Press, 1988). My own work on the Spanish anarchist organization, Mujeres Libres, focuses on their goal of *capacitación*, which I translated "empowerment." Barbara Cruikshank criticizes the concept (and the strategy) of empowerment in *The Will to Empower: Democratic Citizens and Other Subjects* (Ithaca, NY: Cornell University Press, 1999).

21 See Jones, *Compassionate Authority: Democracy and the Representation of Women* (New York: Routledge, 1993), pp. 46, 69, 157.

22 Ibid., p. 70.

23 Ibid., pp. 157, 159, 160; see also pp. 230–31 and 245 and Jones, "Citizenship in a Woman-Friendly Polity," *Signs* 15 (1990), pp. 781–812.

24 I have discussed these questions in "Identity Politics, Political Identities: Reclaiming Politics," *Frontiers: A Journal of Women's Studies* XVI, 1 (Fall 1996), pp. 87–100; see also María C. Lugones and Elizabeth V. Spelman, "Have We Got a Theory for You!" *Women's Studies International Forum* 6, 6 (1983), pp. 573–81; Gloria Anzaldúa, *Borderlands/La Frontera: The New Mestiza* (San Francisco: Spinsters/Aunt Lute, 1987).

25 Laclau and Mouffe, *Hegemony and Socialist Strategy: Towards a Radical Democratic Politics* (London: Verso, 1985), p. 159; see also Mouffe, "The Sex/Gender System and the Discursive Construction of Women's Subordination," in Sakari Hänninen and Laena Paldán, eds., *Rethinking Ideology: A Marxist Debate*, International Socialism-Discussion 3 (Berlin: Argument-Verlag, 1983), p. 142.

26 Laclau and Mouffe, *Hegemony and Socialist Strategy*, p. 169. Frances Fox Piven makes a related argument about the contingent nature of protest and resistance in *Challenging Authority: How Ordinary People Change America* (Lanham, MD: Rowman and Littlefield, 2006), although the political implications she draws are somewhat different.

27 See Bernice Johnson Reagon, "Coalition Politics: Turning the Century," in Barbara Smith, ed., *Home Girls: A Black Feminist Anthology* (New York: Kitchen Table, 1983), pp. 356–68; also Judith Butler, *Gender Trouble* (New York: Routledge, 1990), p. 148; Lee Quinby, "Ecofeminism and the Politics of Resistance," in *Reweaving the World: The Emergence of Ecofeminism*, eds. I. Diamond and G. Orenstein (San Francisco: Sierra Club Books, 1990), p. 123; and Jana Sawicki, "Identity Politics and Sexual Freedom," ibid., pp. 185–7. I have explored these issues in some detail in "Identity Politics, Political Identities."

28 See Ackelsberg, *Free Women of Spain*, especially pp. 18–33; and Clark, "What Is Anarchism?"

29 Stenstad, "Anarchic Thinking," *Hypatia* 3, 2 (Summer 1988), pp. 96, 99.

30 Carole Pateman offers a powerful contemporary articulation of this position in *The Problem of Political Obligation: A Critique of Liberal Theory* (Berkeley: University of

California Press, 1985) (originally published by John Wiley, 1979), especially Chapter 7. See also Robert Paul Wolff, *In Defense of Anarchism* (New York: Harper and Row, 1970).

31 Isaac Balbus, *Marxism and Domination* (Princeton, NJ: Princeton University Press, 1982), p. 333. See also Jean Elshtain, "Feminism, Family, and Community," *Dissent* (Fall 1982), pp. 442–49, and "Reclaiming the Socialist-Feminist Citizen," *Socialist Review* 74 (1984), pp. 1–27; Kathy E. Ferguson, *The Feminist Case Against Bureaucracy* (Philadelphia, PA: Temple University Press, 1984); Irene Diamond, "American Feminism and the Language of Control," in *Feminism and Foucault*, ed. Irene Diamond and Lee Quinby (Boston: Northeastern University Press, 1988), pp.193–206, and *Fertile Ground* (Boston: Beacon Press, 1994); and Gwendolyn Mink, *The Wages of Motherhood* (Ithaca, NY: Cornell University Press, 1995). I explore these and related issues in more detail in Chapter 4, above.

32 See Susan Moller Okin, *Justice, Gender, and the Family* (New York: Basic Books, 1989); Frances Olsen, "The Myth of State Intervention in the Family," *University of Michigan Journal of Law Reform* 835 (1985); Margaret Burnham, "An Impossible Marriage: Slave Law and Family Law," *Law and Inequality* 5, pp. 187–225; Maxine Baca Zinn, "Family, Race, and Poverty in the Eighties," *Signs* 14, 4 (Summer 1989), pp. 856–74; Butler, *Gender Trouble*; Martha Ackelsberg, "Jewish Family Ethics in a Post-Halakhic Age," in *Imagining the Jewish Future: Essays and Responses*, ed. David A. Teutsch (Albany: State University of New York Press, 1992), pp. 149–164; Martha Ackelsberg and Judith Plaskow, "Beyond Same-Sex Marriage," in *Righteous Indignation: A Jewish Call for Justice*, ed. Rabbi Or N. Rose, Jo Ellen Green Kaiser and Margie Klein (Woodstock, VT: Jewish Lights, 2008), pp. 195–205; and Chapters 4 and 5 above.

33 See, especially, Barbara Nelson, "The Origins of the Two-Channel Welfare State: Workman's Compensation and Mothers' Aid," in Linda Gordon, ed., *Women, the State and Welfare* (Madison: University of Wisconsin Press, 1990); Gwendolyn Mink, "The Lady and the Tramp: Gender, Race, and the Origins of the American Welfare State," in Gordon, ed., *Women, the State, and Welfare*, and "Welfare Reform in Historical Perspective," in *Whose Welfare?* (Ithaca, NY: Cornell University Press, 1999); and Linda Gordon, *Pitied But Not Entitled* (New York: Basic Books, 1994).

34 See, for example, Frances Fox Piven and Richard A. Cloward, *The New Class War* (New York: Pantheon, 1982), Zillah Eisenstein, "The Patriarchal Relations of the Reagan State," *Signs* 10, 2 (Winter 1984), pp. 329–37, and "The Sexual Politics of the New Right," *Signs* 7, 3 (Spring 1982), pp. 567–88; Ida Susser, "Working Class Women, Social Protest, and Changing Ideologies" and Sandra Morgen, "'It's the Whole Power of the City Against Us,'" both in Bookman and Morgen, eds., *Women and the Politics of Empowerment*; Linda Gordon, "Family Violence, Feminism, and Social Control," *Feminist Studies* 12, 3 (Fall 1986), pp. 453–78; and Kathryn Kish Sklar, "The Historical Foundations of Women's Power in the Creation of the American Welfare State, 1830–1930," in *Mothers of a New World*, eds. Seth Koven and Sonya Michel (New York: Routledge 1993), pp. 43–93.

35 I have explored these and related issues in some detail in "Review Article: Feminist Analyses of Public Policy," *Comparative Politics* (July 1992), pp. 477–93. Frances Fox Piven makes a similar argument about the complexities of oppression and resistance in *Challenging Authority*. See also Chapter 4, above, and sources cited there.

36 Again, the literature here is almost too vast to cite. Piven and Cloward have written of these issues most directly in *Poor People's Movements: How They Succeed, Why They Fail* (New York: Pantheon, 1977), in *The Politics of Turmoil* (New York: Pantheon, 1972), especially Part Two, in "Normalizing Collective Protest," in *Frontiers in Social Movement Theory*, ed. Aldon D. Morris and Carol McClurg Mueller (New Haven,

CT: Yale University Press, 1992), pp. 311–12, and (Piven) in *Challenging Authority*. See also Laclau and Mouffe, *Hegemony and Socialist Strategy*, pp. 152–3, 169. On class consciousness, see E.P. Thompson, *The Making of the English Working Class* (New York: Vintage, 1966), and Aldon Morris' discussion of it in "Political Consciousness and Collective Action," in Morris and Mueller, eds., *Frontiers in Social Movement Theory*, pp. 352–3; and Jane Mansbridge and Aldon Morris, eds., *Oppositional Consciousness: The Subjective Roots of Social Protest* (Chicago: University of Chicago Press, 2001). There has also been extensive discussion among feminist historians about what constitutes "resistance" by women. For an early example see "Politics and Culture in Women's History: A Symposium," *Feminist Studies* 6, (1980), pp. 26–64.

37 Kathryn Addelson, Shawn Pyne, and I developed this argument more fully in "Anarchism and Feminism." We drew there, also, on W.E.B. DuBois' analysis of the "doubled" nature of black consciousness under racism in *The Souls of Black Folk* (Chicago: A.C. McClurg, 1953). Such doubled consciousness is also the focus of some of Simone de Beauvoir's discussion in *The Second Sex*, translated and edited by H.M. Parshley (New York: Bantam Books, 1961), and may be found, as well, in Patricia Hill Collins, *Black Feminist Thought* and Lani Guinier and Gerald Torres, *The Miner's Canary: Enlisting Race, Resisting Power, Transforming Democracy* (Cambridge, MA: Harvard University Press, 2002), especially Chapters 3 and 5.

38 See, for example, Emma Goldman, "Woman Suffrage," in *Anarchism and Other Essays*, p. 211.

39 See *Free Women of Spain*, especially Chapter V.

40 Many examples of this sort of empowerment are to be found in Bookman and Morgen, eds., *Women and the Politics of Empowerment*. See also Sara Evans and Harry Boyte, *Free Spaces* (New York: Harper and Row, 1986); Bettina Aptheker, *Tapestries of Life: Women's Work, Women's Consciousness, and the Meaning of Daily Experience* (Amherst: University of Massachusetts Press, 1990), especially Chapter V; and Cathy J. Cohen, Kathleen B. Jones and Joan C. Tronto, "Women Transforming U.S. Politics: Sites of Power/Resistance," in *Women Transforming Politics*, ed. Cathy J. Cohen, Kathleen B. Jones and Joan C. Tronto (New York: New York University Press, 1997), pp. 1–14. Of the classical anarchist theorists, Kropotkin is, perhaps, the most eloquent on this point. See, especially, "The Spirit of Revolt" and "The Commune of Paris," both in *Selected Writings*.

41 On this point, see, especially, Jacquelyn Dowd Hall, "Disorderly Women: Gender and Labor Militancy in the Appalachian South," *Journal of American History* (September 1986), pp. 354–62; Jacquelyn Dowd Hall, Nancy Hewitt, Ardis Cameron, and Martha Ackelsberg, "Disorderly Women: Gender, Politics and Theory," roundtable presentation, Berkshire Conference of Women Historians, Wellesley College, June 1987; Amrita Basu, *Two Faces of Protest: Contrasting Modes of Women's Activism in India* (Berkeley: University of California, 1992); and Ackelsberg, *Free Women of Spain*, especially pp. 171–72. See also above, Chapter 6. For a view reflecting the position that such behavior is, simply, "disorderly," see Edward C. Banfield, "Rioting Mainly for Fun and Profit," in *The Unheavenly City Revisited* (Boston: Little, Brown, 1974).

42 *Hegemony and Socialist Strategy*, p. 153. See also Anna Yeatman's discussion of new social movements as engaging in symbolic challenges, opening up "public spaces of openly-contested representations," *Postmodern Revisionings of the Political* (New York: Routledge, 1994), pp. 114–15.

43 Laclau and Mouffe, *Hegemony and Socialist Strategy*, pp. 153–54.

44 Ibid., pp. 155, 159–60. Temma Kaplan makes a similar argument about the power of the language of democracy to stir people to resistance in *Crazy for Democracy: Women in Grassroots Movements* (New York: Routledge, 1997) and in *Taking Back the*

Streets: Women, Youth and Direct Democracy (Berkeley and Los Angeles: University of California Press, 2004). See also Guinier and Torres, *The Miner's Canary*.

45 See, especially, *The Politics of Turmoil* and "Normalizing Collective Protest," pp. 319–22; and Piven, *Challenging Authority*, especially Chapters 2, 5, 6.

46 On this point, see also Chapter 3 above; also Yeatman, *Postmodern Revisionings*.

47 See, for example, Donna Haraway, "A Manifesto for Cyborgs," in Linda Nicholson, ed., *Feminism/Postmodernism* (New York: Routledge, 1990), p. 199; Butler, *Gender Trouble*, p. 148; Biddy Martin and Chandra Talpade Mohanty, "Feminist Politics: What's Home Got to Do With It?" in Teresa de Lauretis, ed., *Feminist Studies, Critical Studies* (Bloomington: Indiana University Press, 1986), p. 210; Shane Phelan, "(Be)Coming Out: Lesbian Identity and Politics," *Signs* 18, 4 (Summer 1993), pp. 778, 783–84; Arlene Stein, "Making It Perfectly Queer," *Socialist Review* 22, 1 (January–March 1992), p. 26; Barbara Epstein, *Political Protest and Cultural Revolution: Nonviolent Direct Action in the 1970s and 1980s* (Berkeley and Los Angeles: University of California Press, 1991), p. 260–61; Anna Yeatman, *Postmodern Revisionings of the Political*; and my "Identity Politics, Political Identities," especially pp. 95–98.

48 Epstein, *Political Protest*, p. 269; see also pp. 109, 116, 123, 159.

49 Ibid., p. 269.

50 See, especially, Amy Gutman, "Communitarian Critics of Liberalism," *Philosophy and Public Affairs* 14, 3 (Summer 1985) and Susan Moller Okin, "Is Multiculturalism Bad for Women?" in *Is Multiculturalism Bad for Women?*, ed. Susan Moller Okin (Princeton: Princeton University Press, 1999). See also Jane Mansbridge, *Beyond Adversary Democracy* (New York: Basic Books, 1980), p. 10; Kathleen P. Iannello, *Decisions Without Hierarchy: Feminist Interventions in Organization Theory and Practice* (New York: Routledge, 1992), pp. 28–9. For a related study, see Helen Brown, *Women Organising* (London and New York: Routledge, 1992).

51 See, among others, Floya Anthias and Nira Yuval-Davis, "Contextualizing Feminism: Gender, Ethnic and Class Divisions," in Yuval-Davis and Anthias, eds., *Woman–Nation–State* (New York: St. Martin's, 1989); Nira Yuval Davis, Kalpana Kannabiran, and Ulrike Vieten, eds., *The Situated Politics of Belonging* (London: Sage, 2006); Nira Yuval-Davis, *Gender and Nation* (London: Sage, 1997); Young, "The Ideal of Community and the Politics of Difference," *Social Theory and Practice* 12, 1 (Spring 1986), pp. 1–26, and *Justice and the Politics of Difference* (Princeton, NJ: Princeton University Press, 1992); Audre Lorde, *Sister Outsider* (Trumansburg: The Crossing Press, 1983); Patricia Hill Collins, *Black Feminist Thought* (Boston: Unwin Hyman, 1990) and *Fighting Words: Black Women and the Search for Justice* (Minneapolis: University of Minnesota Press, 1998); Gloria Anzaldúa, ed., *Haciendo Caras: Making Face, Making Soul* (San Francisco: Aunt Lute, 1990); Cherríe Moraga and Gloria Anzaldúa, eds., *This Bridge Called My Back: Writings by Radical Women of Color* (Watertown: Persephone Press, 1981); Elizabeth V. Spelman, *Inessential Woman* (Boston: Beacon Press, 1990); and Okin, ed., *Is Multiculturalism Bad for Women?*

52 On this point, see also Anna Yeatman, *Postmodern Revisionings of the Political*, especially pp. 114–22.

53 Shane Phelan makes a similar argument about "local politics" in *Getting Specific: Postmodern Lesbian Politics* (Minneapolis: University of Minnesota Press, 1994), especially pp. 145–47.

54 Phelan, "Coyote Politics: Trickster Tales and Feminist Futures," *Hypatia* 11, 3 (Summer 1996), pp. 130–49.

55 Lugones, "Purity, Impurity, and Separation," *Signs* 19, 2 (Winter 1994) pp. 458–79, especially pp. 459–69.

56 Anzaldúa, *Borderlands/La Frontera*, Preface, and p. 195. While agreeing with Anzaldúa and others that it is important not to freeze identities, Cristina Beltrán argues

that Anzaldúa's use of the metaphor of "borderlands" may, in fact, contribute to the reification of the "hybrid" identity itself. See Beltrán, "Patrolling Borders: Hybrids, Hierarchies and the Challenge of Mestizaje," *Political Research Quarterly* 57, 4 (Dec. 2004), pp. 595–607.

8 EXCLUSION OR INCLUSION?

1 *Citizenship and Identity* (London: Sage Publications, 1999), p. 2.

2 For an exploration of some of these issues in relation to understandings of power and of strategies for change, see previous chapter. For an overview of these debates in the British context, see Nira Yuval-Davis, "The Citizenship Debate: Women, Ethnic Processes and the State," *Feminist Review*, 39 (Winter 1991) and "Belonging and the Politics of Belonging," *Patterns of Prejudice* 40, 3 (2006), pp. 197–214; and also Isin and Wood, *Citizenship and Identity*, especially Chapters 1, 2, and 7.

3 On the US context, see Judith Shklar, *American Citizenship: The Quest for Inclusion*, The Tanner Lectures on Human Values (Cambridge, MA: Harvard University Press, 1991).

4 See Jürgen Habermas, "Three Normative Models of Democracy," in *Democracy and Difference: Contesting the Boundaries of the Political*, ed. Seyla Benhabib (Princeton, NJ: Princeton University Press, 1996), pp. 21–30; and Nancy Fraser, "Rethinking the Public Sphere: A Contribution to the Critique of Actually Existing Democracy," in *Habermas and the Public Sphere*, ed. Craig Calhoun (Cambridge, MA: The MIT Press, 1992), pp. 109–42.

5 See, for example, Fraser, "Rethinking the Public Sphere," especially pp. 115–19, and Fraser, "What's Critical About Critical Theory?" in *Unruly Practices: Power, Discourse and Gender in Contemporary Social Theory* (Minneapolis: University of Minnesota Press, 1989), pp. 113–43; Seyla Benhabib, "Models of Public Space: Hannah Arendt, the Liberal Tradition, and Jürgen Habermas," in *Habermas and the Public Sphere*, ed. Craig Calhoun (Cambridge, MA: The MIT Press, 1992), pp. 93–95; Mary P. Ryan, "Gender and Public Access," in *Habermas and the Public Sphere*, ed. Craig Calhoun (Cambridge, MA: MIT Press, 1992), pp. 265–67; Holloway Sparks, "Dissident Citizenship: Democratic Theory, Political Courage, and Activist Women," *Hypatia* 12, 4 (Fall 1997), pp. 74–110; and Iris Marion Young, "Communication and the Other: Beyond Deliberative Democracy," in *Democracy and Difference: Contesting the Boundaries of the Political*, ed. Seyla Benhabib (Princeton, NJ: Princeton University Press, 1996), pp. 120–35.

6 Gwendolyn Mink has made this argument quite forcefully in pointing out the gender-, class-, and race-based understandings of citizenship that developed in and through the history of welfare provision in the US. See Mink, *The Wages of Motherhood: Inequality in the Welfare State, 1917–1942* (Ithaca, NY: Cornell University Press, 1995). For a brief overview of the exclusions and perversions of citizenship in the US, see Ackelsberg, "Citizenship," in *Poverty in the United States: An Encyclopedia of History, Politics and Policy*, eds. Gwendolyn Mink and Alice O'Connor (Santa Barbara, CA: ABC-CLIO, 2004), Vol. I, pp. 175–79.

Judith Shklar notes the powerful ways the realities of slavery framed claims to egalitarian citizenship in the US in *American Citizenship*. Uma Narayan directs our attention to the exclusionary aspects of citizenship in "Towards a Feminist Vision of Citizenship: Rethinking the Implications of Dignity, Political Participation, and Nationality," in Mary Lyndon Shanley and Uma Narayan, eds., *Reconstructing Political Theory: Feminist Perspectives* (Cambridge: Polity, 1997), pp. 48–67; and Engin Isin focuses on citizenship as "a generalized form of otherness," in *Being Political: Genealogies of Citizenship* (Minneapolis: University of Minnesota Press, 2002).

7 Sylvia Walby, "Is Citizenship Gendered?" *Sociology* 28, 2 (1994), p. 391.

8 T.H. Marshall, "Citizenship and Social Class," in *Citizenship and Social Class and Other Essays* (Cambridge: Cambridge University Press, 1950), p. 11.

9 The sources on these struggles are almost too numerous to mention. In addition to Marshall, another classic is Karl Marx, "On the Jewish Question," in *Karl Marx: Early Writings*, translated and edited by T.B. Bottomore (New York: McGraw-Hill, 1964), pp. 3–40. Helpful contemporary interpreters include Michael Walzer, *Obligations: Essays on Disobedience, War and Citizenship* (Cambridge, MA: Harvard University Press, 1970); Philip Green, "Social Equality and Political Equality" and "Prolegomena to Any Future Theory of Social Equality," both in *Retrieving Democracy* (Totowa, NJ: Rowman and Allanheld, 1985); Bryan S. Turner, "Outline of a Theory of Citizenship," *Sociology* 24, 2 (May 1990), pp. 189–217; Yuval-Davis, "The Citizenship Debate"; Linda Gordon, *Women, the State, and Welfare* (Madison: University of Wisconsin Press, 1990); Gwendolyn Mink, *The Wages of Motherhood* and *Welfare's End* (Ithaca, NY: Cornell University Press, 1998); Wendy Sarvasy, "Social Citizenship from a Feminist Perspective" *Hypatia*, 12, 4 (Fall 1997), pp. 54–73; and Elizabeth Bussiere, *(Dis)Entitling the Poor: The Warren Court, Welfare Rights, and the American Political Tradition* (University Park, PA: The Pennsylvania State University Press, 1997).

If anything, of course, what limited "rights" were once recognized in the US have been even further diminished and denied, viz. the destruction of welfare entitlement through the Personal Responsibility and Work Opportunity Act of 1996.

10 On citizenship as practice, see Isin and Wood, *Identity and Citizenship* and Temma Kaplan, *Taking Back the Streets: Women, Youth and Direct Democracy* (Berkeley and Los Angeles: University of California Press, 2004), especially "Prologue" and "Epilogue." Citizenship also has other meanings, in particular as nationality; and as what Shklar terms "ideal republican citizenship." See Shklar, *American Citizenship*, esp. pp. 2–14; on citizenship as nationality, see Narayan, "Towards a Feminist Vision"; and Ruth Lister, "Dialectics of Citizenship," *Hypatia* 12, 4 (Fall 1997), especially pp. 10–17.

11 "Citizenship and Social Class," pp. 28–29.

12 "Dialectics of Citizenship," p. 24.

13 "Models of Public Space," p. 85.

14 Benhabib, "Models of Public Space," p. 86. It is not surprising, then, that Harry Boyte, Jane Mansbridge and Benjamin Barber, to give just three examples, all use the language of "public sphere" or "free spaces" (albeit critically) to make arguments about what used to be termed "participatory democracy." See Boyte, "The Pragmatic Ends of Popular Politics," in *Habermas and the Public Sphere*, ed. Craig Calhoun (Cambridge, MA: MIT Press,1992), pp. 340–55; Boyte, "Beyond Deliberation: Citizenship as Public Work," *The Good Society* 5, 2 (Spring 1995), pp. 15–19; Jane Mansbridge, "Reconstructing Democracy," in *Revisioning the Political: Feminist Reconstructions of Traditional Concepts in Western Political Theory*, eds. Nancy J. Hirschmann and Christine DiStefano (Boulder, CO: Westview Press, 1996), pp. 117–38 and "Using Power/Fighting Power: The Polity," in *Democracy and Difference: Contesting the Boundaries of the Political*, ed. Seyla Benhabib (Princeton, NJ: Princeton University Press, 1996), pp. 46–66; Benjamin Barber, "An American Civic Forum," *The Good Society* 5, 2 (Spring 1995), pp. 10–14 and Barber, "Foundationalism and Democracy," in Benhabib, ed., *Democracy and Difference*, pp. 348–59.

15 Phillips, "Dealing with Difference: A Politics of Ideas, or a Politics of Presence?" in Benhabib, ed., *Democracy and Difference*, p. 143. Note also Nancy Fraser's comment that "something like Habermas' idea of the public sphere is indispensable to critical social theory and democratic political practice," in "Rethinking the Public Sphere:

A Contribution to the Critique of Actually Existing Democracy," in Calhoun, ed., *Habermas and the Public Sphere*, p. 111. For an exploration of some of the dilemmas of "identity politics" for contemporary democracy, see Isin and Wood, *Citizenship and Identity*; Martha Ackelsberg, "Identity Politics, Political Identities: Thoughts Toward a Multicultural Politics," *Frontiers: A Journal of Women's Studies* XVI, 1 (1996), pp. 87–100 and Chapter 7 above.

16 See Mink, *The Wages of Motherhood*; Seth Koven and Sonya Michel, eds., *Mothers of the New World: Maternalist Politics and the Origins of Welfare States* (New York: Routledge, 1993); Linda Kerber, *Women of the Republic: Intellect and Ideology in Revolutionary America* (Chapel Hill: University of North Carolina Press, 1980); Mary Beth Norton, *Liberty's Daughters: The Revolutionary Experiences of American Women, 1750–1800* (Ithaca, NY: Cornell University Press, 1996); and Molly Ladd-Taylor, *Mother Work: Women, Child Welfare, and the State, 1890–1930* (Urbana: University of Illinois Press, 1994).

17 Nancy Fraser, "What's Critical About Critical Theory?" in *Unruly Practices: Power, Discourse and Gender in Contemporary Social Theory* (Minneapolis: University of Minnesota Press, 1989), especially pp. 123–29; and Fraser, "Struggle Over Needs: Outline of a Socialist-Feminist Critical Theory of Late Capitalist Political Culture," in *Unruly Practices*, pp. 166–71. For a discussion of other aspects of the public/private binary, see Chapter 5 above.

18 One of the clearest early arguments for this position can be found in John Stuart Mill, *The Subordination of Women*, edited, with Introduction, by Susan Okin (Indianapolis: Hackett Publishing Company, 1988; originally published 1869). See also Shklar, *American Citizenship*, especially Chapter 2: "Earning" – although she argues that the emphasis on earnings/independence in the US context is a particular consequence of the legacy/specter of chattel slavery. On the issue of bearing arms, see Walzer, *Obligations*, especially pp. 77–98.

19 See especially Alice Kessler-Harris, "The Wage Conceived: Value and Need as Measures of a Woman's Worth," in *A Woman's Wage: Historical Meanings and Social Consequences* (Lexington: University Press of Kentucky, 1990), pp. 6–32; and Nancy Fraser, "Women, Welfare, and the Politics of Need Interpretation," in *Unruly Practices: Power, Discourse and Gender in Contemporary Social Theory*, especially pp. 147–51.

20 Bonnie Thornton Dill, "Fictive Kin, Paper Sons, and *Compadrazgo*: Women of Color and the Struggle for Family Survival," in Maxine Baca Zinn and Bonnie Thornton Dill, eds., *Women of Color in U.S. Society* (Philadelphia, PA: Temple University Press, 1994), p. 166; see also George J. Sanchez, "'Go After the Women': Americanization and the Mexican Immigrant Woman, 1915–29," in Vicki L. Ruiz and Ellen Carol Dubois, eds., *Unequal Sisters: A Multicultural Reader in U.S. Women's History*, 2nd edition (New York: Routledge, 1994), pp. 284–97; Gwendolyn Mink, *The Wages of Motherhood*; Nancy Fraser and Linda Gordon, "Decoding 'Dependency': Inscriptions of Power in a Keyword of the US Welfare State," in Mary Lyndon Shanley and Uma Narayan, eds., *Reconstructing Political Theory* (Cambridge: Polity Press, 1997), especially pp. 33–39; and Chapter 4 above.

21 See Aileen Kraditor, *The Ideas of the Woman Suffrage Movement: 1890–1920* (New York: Columbia University Press 1965); Linda Gordon, *Pitied But Not Entitled: Single Mothers and the History of Welfare* (Cambridge, MA: Harvard University Press, 1994); Barbara Nelson, "Women's Poverty and Women's Citizenship: Some Political Consequences of Economic Marginality," *Signs* 10, 2 (Winter 1984), pp. 209–31; and Nelson, "The Origins of the Two-Channel Welfare State: Workmen's Compensation and Mothers' Aid," in Linda Gordon, ed., *Women, the State and Welfare* (Madison: University of Wisconsin Press, 1990), pp. 123–51.

22 Fraser and Gordon, "Decoding 'Dependency'"; Sara Ruddick, *Maternal Thinking* (Boston: Beacon Press 1989); and above, Chapter 4. Nancy Hirschmann's effort at

a relational and contextual refiguring of "freedom" makes a similar point; see Hirschmann, "Revisioning Freedom: Relationship, Context, and the Politics of Empowerment," in Hirschmann and Distefano, eds., *Revisioning the Political*, pp. 51–74, and Hirschmann, *The Subject of Liberty: Toward a Feminist Theory of Freedom* (Princeton, NJ: Princeton University Press, 2003); on privacy see also Carole Pateman, "Feminist Critiques of the Public/Private Dichotomy," in *The Disorder of Women* (Stanford, CA: Stanford University Press, 1989); Zillah Eisenstein, "Equalizing Privacy and Specifying Equality," in Hirschmann and Distefano, eds., *Revisioning the Political*, pp. 181–92; Anita J. Allen, "Privacy at Home: The Twofold Problem," in Hirschmann and Distefano, eds., *Revisioning the Political*, pp. 193–212; Anne Phillips, *Engendering Democracy* (University Park, PA: The Pennsylvania State University Press, 1991), especially Chapter 4; Patricia Boland, *Privacy and the Politics of Intimate Life* (Ithaca, NY: Cornell University Press, 1996); and Chapter 5 above.

23 For an overview of this literature, see Christine Distefano, "Autonomy in the Light of Difference," in Hirschmann and Distefano, eds., *Revisioning the Political*, pp. 95–116; also Joan Tronto, *Moral Boundaries: A Political Argument for an Ethic of Care* (New York: Routledge, 1993); Emily K. Abel, *Hearts of Wisdom: American Women Caring for Kin, 1850–1940* (Cambridge, MA: Harvard University Press, 2000). Gwendolyn Mink argues, in *Welfare's End* (Ithaca, NY: Cornell University Press, 1998), that one way to overcome this devaluing is by *paying* women for caretaking. Evelyn Nakano Glenn explores the consequences of these divisions even within the context of *paid* work in "From Servitude to Service Work: Historical Continuities in the Racial Division of Paid Reproductive Labor," *Signs* 18, 1 (1992), pp. 1–43. See also Chapter 11, below.

24 *The Sexual Contract* (Stanford, CA: Stanford University Press, 1989), p. 135.

25 Ibid., p. 131.

26 "What's Critical About Critical Theory?" p. 124.

27 Alice Hearst, in conversation with the author, explored the notion of privatizing relations of dependency in the family; see also Fraser and Gordon, "Decoding 'Dependency,'" especially pp. 36–39; and Martha Fineman, *The Neutered Mother, the Sexual Family and Other Twentieth Century Tragedies* (New York: Routledge, 1995).

28 Marshall, "Citizenship and Social Class," p. 29.

29 Ibid., pp. 32–33.

30 Pateman, *The Sexual Contract*, p. 151. See also Fraser and Gordon, "Decoding 'Dependency'," p. 30. Judith Shklar, too, notes that the identification of paid work with independence in the American political ethos required an obfuscation of the dependency entailed in the wage-earning relationship; see *American Citzenship*, p. 94.

31 *American Citizenship*, pp. 92, 98.

32 Foner, "Workers and Slavery," in Paul Buhle and Alan Dawley, eds., *Working for Democracy* (Urbana: University of Illinois Press, 1985), p. 22.

33 Amy Bridges, "Becoming American: The Working Classes in the United States before the Civil War," in Ira Katznelson and Aristide Zolberg, eds., *Working Class Formation* (Princeton, NJ: Princeton University Press, 1986), p. 175.

34 See, on this point, Martin Shefter, "Trade Unions and Political Machines: The Organization and Disorganization of the American Working Classes in the Late 19th Century," in Ira Katznelson and Aristide Zolberg, eds., *Working Class Formation* (Princeton, NJ: Princeton University Press, 1986), pp. 197–276; and Sean Wilentz, *Chants Democratic: New York City and the Rise of the American Working Class, 1788–1850* (New York: Oxford, 1984).

35 Elizabeth Bussiere, *(Dis)Entitling the Poor: The Warren Court, Welfare Rights, and the American Political Tradition* (University Park, PA: The Pennsylvania State University Press, 1997), especially pp. 24–33.

36 "Trade Unions and Political Machines," p. 273; see also Bussiere, *(Dis)Entitling the Poor*, especially Chapter 2.

37 On this point, see Gwendolyn Mink, "The Lady and the Tramp," in Linda Gordon, ed., *Women, the State, and Welfare*, p. 96; and Uma Narayan, "Towards a Feminist Vision of Citizenship," in *Reconstructing Political Theory*, pp. 60–64.

38 Mary Jo Buhle, "Women's Labor and Politics," in Buhle and Dawley, eds., *Working for Democracy*, p. 33; see also Susan Estabrook Kennedy, *If All We Did Was to Weep at Home: A History of White Working-Class Women in America* (Bloomington: Indiana University Press, 1979), especially Chapter 4.

39 Kennedy, *If All We Did Was to Weep at Home*, p. 88; Elizabeth Bussiere makes brief reference to this issue in relation to Jacksonian workingmen in *(Dis)Entitling the Poor*, pp. 45–46.

40 Shefter, "Trade Unions and Political Machines"; and Katznelson, *City Trenches: Urban Politics and the Patterning of Class in the United States* (New York: Pantheon, 1981).

41 Nancy Fraser, "What's Critical About Critical Theory?," p. 126; she draws on Pateman, *The Sexual Contract* and "Feminist Critiques of the Public/Private Dichotomy"; see also Anne Phillips, *Engendering Democracy*; Ruth Lister, "Dialectics of Citizenship," *Hypatia* 12, 4 (Fall 1997), p. 8; Iris Marion Young, "Communication and the Other: Beyond Deliberative Democracy," in *Democracy and Difference: Contesting the Boundaries of the Political*, ed. Seyla Benhabib (Princeton, NJ: Princeton University Press, 1996), p. 132; and Holloway Sparks, "Dissident Citizenship: Democratic Theory, Political Courage, and Activist Women," *Hypatia* 12, 4 (Fall 1997), p. 75.

42 Lebsock, "Women and American Politics, 1880–1920," in *Women, Politics and Change*, eds. Louise A. Tilly and Patricia Gurin (New York: Russell Sage Foundation, 1990), p. 46; see also Mary Ryan, "Gender and Public Access: Women's Politics in Nineteenth-Century America," in Calhoun, ed., *Habermas and the Public Sphere*, pp. 259–88; and Ryan, *Cradle of the Middle Class: The Family in Oneida County, New York, 1790–1865* (Cambridge and New York: Cambridge University Press, 1981); Nancy Hewitt, *Women's Activism and Social Change: Rochester, NY, 1822–1872* (Ithaca, NY: Cornell University Press 1984); Kathryn Kish Sklar, "The Historical Foundations of Women's Power in the Creation of the American Welfare State, 1830–1930," in Seth Koven and Sonya Michel, eds., *Mothers of a New World* (New York: Routledge,1990), pp. 43–93; and Linda Gordon, *Heroes of Their Own Lives: The Politics and History of Family Violence* (New York: Viking, 1988).

43 See J. Stanley Lemons, *The Woman Citizen: Social Feminism in the 1920's* (Urbana: University of Illinois Press, 1973); Kathryn Kish Sklar, "The Historical Foundations of Women's Power"; and *Florence Kelley and the Nation's Work* (New Haven, CT: Yale University Press, 1995); Jane Addams, *Twenty Years at Hall House* (New York: Macmillan, 1910) and *The Second Twenty Years at Hull House: Sept. 1909–Sept. 1929* (New York: Macmillan, 1930); and Wendy Sarvasy, "Social Citizenship from a Feminist Perspective," *Hypatia* 12, 4 (Fall 1997), pp. 54–73.

44 Darlene Clark Hine, "The Housewives' League of Detroit: Black Women and Economic Nationalism," in Nancy Hewitt and Suzanne Lebsock, eds., *Visible Women: New Essays on American Activism* (Urbana: University of Illinois Press, 1993), pp. 223–45; Deborah Gray White, "The Cost of Club Work, The Price of Black Feminism," in Hewitt and Lebsock, eds., *Visible Women*, pp. 247–69; Elsa Barkley-Brown, "Womanist Consciousness: Maggie Lena Walker and the Independent Order of St. Luke," in Vicki L. Ruiz and Ellen Carol Dubois, eds., *Unequal Sisters: A Multicultural Reader in U.S. Women's History*, 2nd edition (New York: Routledge, 1994), pp. 268–83; Mary Church Terrell, "First Presidential Address to the National Association of Colored Women" (1897), reprinted in Beverly Washington Jones, ed., *Quest for Equality: The Life and Writings of Mary Eliza Church Terrell, 1863–1954*. In

the series, *Black Women in United States History* (Brooklyn, NY: Carlson Publishing, Inc., 1990), Vol. 13, pp. 133–38; and Terrell, "Lynching from a Negro's Point of View" (1904), reprinted in *Quest for Equality*, Vol. 13, pp. 167–77; Josephine St. Pierre Ruffin, "Presidential Address to the First National Conference of the Colored Women of America" (1895), reprinted in *Black Women in White America: A Documentary History*, ed. Gerda Lerner (New York: Vintage, 1973), pp. 441–43; Paula Giddings, *When and Where I Enter: The Impact of Black Women on Race and Sex in America* (New York: William Morrow and Co., Inc., 1984) and *Ida: A Sword Among Lions* (New York: Amistad, 2008); Ida B. Wells, *Crusade for Justice: The Autobiography of Ida B. Wells*, ed. Alfreda M. Duster (Chicago: University of Chicago Press, 1970); Ida B. Wells-Barnett, "Lynch Law in all Its Phases" (1893), available at www.blackpast.org/?q=1893-ida-b-wells-lynch-law-all-its-phases, accessed October 13, 2008. For a further discussion of black women's anti-lynching activism see also above, Chapter 6.

45 "Social Citizenship from a Feminist Perspective."

46 Baker, "The Domestication of Politics: Women and American Political Society, 1780–1920," in Linda Gordon, ed., *Women, the State and Welfare*, especially pp. 76–77; and Chafe, "Women's History and Political History: Some Thoughts on Progressivism and the New Deal," in *Visible Women*, pp. 101–18.

47 Baker, "The Domestication of Politics," p. 70; see also Suzanne Marilley, *Woman Suffrage and the Origins of Liberal Feminism in the United States, 1820–1920* (Cambridge, MA: Harvard University Press, 1996). Significantly, although these problems did become a focus of *social* policy, they soon became part of the administrative-bureaucratic apparatus—relatively removed from any popular control—a process which Habermas describes as a characteristic of the modern state, and which James Morone views as a manifestation of the paradoxical nature of the "democratic wish." See Morone, *The Democratic Wish: Popular Participation and the Limits of American Government* (New York: Basic Books, 1990).

48 Vivien Hart refers to some of these reformers as "reluctant maternalists" in her study of struggles for the minimum wage in the US and Britain, though her focus is on the constitutional constraints which profoundly affected their rhetoric and strategy; see Hart, *Bound By Our Constitution: Women, Workers, and the Minimum Wage* (Princeton, NJ: Princeton University Press, 1994), especially Chapters 4–6. Gwendolyn Mink makes the argument about building notions of dependence into welfare provision in, e.g., *The Wages of Motherhood*. Most feminist scholarship has focused on the administrative side: the ways understandings of gender and race infused both the construction and the administration of state welfare programs.

49 "Struggle Over Needs: Outline of a Socialist-Feminist Critical Theory of Late Capitalist Political Culture," in *Unruly Practices: Power, Discourse and Gender in Contemporary Social Theory* (Minneapolis: University of Minnesota Press, 1989), p. 183.

50 Ernesto Laclau and Chantal Mouffe, *Hegemony and Socialist Strategy: Towards a Radical Democratic Politics* (London: Verso, 1995), pp. 155, 159–60; see also Chapter 7, above.

51 "Citizenship and Social Class," p. 29.

52 Benhabib, "Models of Public Space: Hannah Arendt, the Liberal Tradition, and Jürgen Habermas," in Calhoun, ed., *Habermas and the Public Sphere*, pp. 93–94; James Morone highlights a parallel problem in *The Democratic Wish*.

53 Mary Ryan, "Gender and Public Access," in Calhoun, ed., *Habermas and the Public Sphere*, pp. 267, 283–84; see also Holloway Sparks, "Dissident Citizenship: Democratic Theory, Political Courage, and Activist Women," *Hypatia* 12, 4 (Fall 1997), pp. 74–110; and Ruth Lister, "Dialectics of Citizenship," *Hypatia* 12, 4 (Fall 1997), pp. 8–9 and Lister, "Inclusive Citizenship: Realizing the Potential," *Citizenship Studies* 11, 1 (February 2007), pp. 49–61. Engin Isin and Patricia Wood argue for

a multi-focal and multi-faceted understanding of the practices of citizenship in *Citizenship and Identity.*

54 Nancy Fraser, "Rethinking the Public Sphere: A Contribution to the Critique of Actually Existing Democracy," in Calhoun, ed., *Habermas and the Public Sphere,* pp. 119, 124.

55 Mansbridge, "Reconstructing Democracy," in Hirschmann and DiStefano, eds., *Revisioning the Political,* pp. 117–38; see also "Using Power/Fighting Power: The Polity," in Benhabib, ed., *Democracy and Difference,* pp. 46–66.

56 Shane Phelan, "All the Comforts of Home: The Genealogy of Community," in Hirschmann and DiStefano, eds., *Revisioning the Political,* p. 248; see also Susan Bickford, "Anti-Anti-Identity Politics: Feminism, Democracy, and the Complexities of Citizenship," *Hypatia* 12, 4 (Fall 1997), p. 124; all of these draw on insights first articulated by Bernice Johnson Reagon in "Coalition Politics: Turning the Century," in *Home Girls: A Black Feminist Anthology,* ed. Barbara Smith (Brooklyn, NY: Kitchen Table/Women of Color Press, 1983), pp. 356–68.

57 See also Anne Phillips, *Engendering Democracy* (University Park, PA: The Pennsylvania State University Press, 1991), p. 118; Benjamin Barber, "Foundationalism and Democracy," in Benhabib, ed., *Democracy and Difference,* pp. 348–59; Mansbridge, "Using Power/Fighting Power"; Susan Bickford, "Anti-Anti-Identity Politics"; and Harry Boyte, "The Growth of Citizen Politics," *Dissent* (Fall 1990), pp. 513–18.

9 BROADENING THE STUDY OF WOMEN'S PARTICIPATION

1 I am grateful to Janet Flammang, Carol Hardy-Fanta, Cathy Cohen, Susan J. Carroll, and other participants in the conference on "Research on Women and American Politics: Agenda-Setting for the 21st Century" for engaging conversations and helpful comments on earlier drafts of this chapter. I have added some references to recent studies and more current events; but, otherwise, this chapter appears with only minor revisions from its original publication in 2003.

2 See, for example, Joyce Gelb and Marian Lief Palley, *Women and Public Policies* (Princeton, NJ: Princeton University Press, 1987); Mary Katzenstein, *Faithful and Fearless: Moving Feminist Protest Inside the Church and Military* (Princeton, NJ: Princeton University Press, 1998); and Frances Fox Piven, *Challenging Authority: How Ordinary People Change America* (Lanham, MD: Rowman and Littlefield, 2006).

3 I have in mind here such activities as Margaret Sanger's birth control clinics in the early years of the twentieth century in the US; the children's aid programs and mothers' support groups that volunteer clubwomen established in both the US and Western Europe at roughly the same time, and which served as "models" for later government programs; the battered women's shelter movement; and many others. I discuss this phenomenon in more detail below.

4 See, for example, Michelle Zimbalist Rosaldo, "Woman, Culture and Society: A Theoretical Overview," in *Woman, Culture and Society,* ed. Michelle Zimbalist Rosaldo and Louise Lamphere (Stanford, CA: Stanford University Press, 1974), pp. 14–42; Susan Bourque and Jean Grossholtz, "Politics as Unnatural Practice: Political Science Looks at Women's Participation," *Politics and Society* 4 (1974), pp. 225–66; *Capitalist Patriarchy and the Case for Socialist Feminism,* ed. Zillah Eisenstein (New York: Monthly Review Press, 1978); and Jean Elshtain, "Moral Woman and Immoral Man: A Consideration of the Public–Private Split and Its Ramifications," *Politics and Society* 4 (1974), pp. 453–73. Irene Diamond and I summarized some of the contours of this debate in "Gender and Political Life: New Directions in Political Science," in *Analyzing Gender: A Handbook of Social Science Research,* eds. Beth B. Hess and Myra Marx Ferree (Newbury Park, CA: Sage, 1987), especially pp. 505–07.

5 See, for example, Carole Pateman, *The Sexual Contract* (Stanford, CA: Stanford University Press, 1988) and Pateman, "Feminist Critiques of the Public/Private Dichotomy," in *The Disorder of Women* (Stanford, CA: Stanford University Press, 1989), pp. 118–40; Michelle Zimbalist Rosaldo, "The Use and Abuse of Anthropology," *Signs* 5 (1980), pp. 389–417 1980; Susan Moller Okin, *Justice, Gender, and the Family* (New York: Basic Books, 1989); Patricia Boling, *Privacy and the Politics of Intimate Life* (Ithaca, NY: Cornell University Press, 1996); Anne Phillips, *Engendering Democracy* (University Park, PA: Penn State University Press, 1991), especially Chapter 4; and above, Chapters 2, 5, 6 and 8.

6 Linda Gordon and Nancy Fraser, "A Genealogy of Dependency: Tracing a Keyword of the U.S. Welfare State," *Signs* 19 (1994), pp. 309–36; Barbara Nelson, "Women's Poverty and Women's Citizenship," *Signs* 10 (1984), pp. 209–31; Gwendolyn Mink, "The Lady and the Tramp: Gender, Race, and the Origins of the American Welfare State," in *Women, the State, and Welfare*, ed. Linda Gordon (Madison: University of Wisconsin Press, 1990), pp. 92–122; Mink, *The Wages of Motherhood* (Ithaca, NY: Cornell University Press, 1995); Mink, *Welfare's End* (Ithaca, NY: Cornell University Press, 1998); Mink, *Whose Welfare?* (Ithaca, NY: Cornell University Press, 2000). See also above, Chapter 4.

7 Pateman, *The Problem of Political Obligation* (New York: John Wiley, 1979) and Pateman, "Women and Consent," *Political Theory* 8 (1980), pp. 149–68, reprinted in *The Disorder of Women* (Stanford, CA: Stanford University Press, 1989), pp. 71–89.

8 Pateman, *The Sexual Contract* (Stanford, CA: Stanford University Press, 1988). On the complicated (and changing) relationship between economic self-support and citizenship in the United States, see also Judith Shklar, *American Citizenship* (Cambridge, MA: Harvard University Press, 1991). For a more extended discussion of these issues see Chapter 8, above.

9 "Women and Consent," p. 84; see also *The Sexual Contract*, pp. 183–88.

10 Irene Diamond and I summarized some of the contours of this debate in "Gender and Political Life," pp. 512–14; see also Mink, *The Wages of Motherhood* and *Welfare's End*; Linda Gordon, "Black and White Visions of Welfare: Women's Welfare Activism, 1890–1945," in *Unequal Sisters: A Multi-Cultural Reader in U.S. Women's History*, second edition, ed. Vicki L. Ruiz and Ellen Carol Dubois (New York: Routledge, 1994); Gordon, *Pitied But Not Entitled* (New York: Basic Books, 1994); Ackelsberg, "Review Essay: Feminist Analyses of Public Policy," *Comparative Politics* 24 (1992), pp. 477–93; and above, Chapters 4 and 5.

11 Piven, "Women and the State: Ideology, Power, and the Welfare State," *Socialist Review* 74 (1984), pp. 11–19; Frances Fox Piven and Richard Cloward, *Poor People's Movements* (New York: Pantheon, 1977) and *The New Class War* (New York: Pantheon, 1982); and Eisenstein, *Feminism and Sexual Equality: Crisis in Liberal America* (New York: Monthly Review Press, 1984).

12 Isaac Balbus, *Marxism and Domination* (Princeton, NJ: Princeton University Press, 1982); Irene Diamond, *Fertile Ground* (Boston: Beacon Press, 1994); Jean Elshtain, "Antigone's Daughters," *democracy* 2, 2 (April 1982), pp. 46–59; Elshtain, "Reclaiming the Socialist-Feminist Citizen," *Socialist Review* 74 (1984), pp. 21–27; Kathy E. Ferguson, *The Feminist Case Against Bureaucracy* (Philadelphia, PA: Temple University Press, 1984); see also Abramovitz, *Regulating the Lives of Women: Social Welfare Policy from Colonial Times to the Present* (Boston: South End Press, 1988).

13 See, for example, Jean Cohen, "Strategy or Identity: New Theoretical Paradigms and Contemporary Social Movements," *Social Research* 52 (1985), pp. 663–716, especially 712–16; this perspective is, of course, as critical to the work of Michel Foucault and his followers, as it is to Habermas, on whose analysis Cohen draws.

14 Chafe, "Women's History and Political History: Some Thoughts on Progressivism and the New Deal," in *Visible Women: New Essays on American Activism*, ed. Nancy A. Hewitt and Suzanne Lebsock (Urbana: University of Illinois Press, 1993), p. 102.

15 Abramovitz, *Under Attack, Fighting Back: Women and Welfare in the United States* (New York: Monthly Review Press, 2000); Linda Gordon, "Black and White Visions of Welfare"; *Pitied But Not Entitled*; Gordon and Nancy Fraser, "A Genealogy of Dependency"; Koven and Michel, "Womanly Duties: Maternalist Politics and the Origins of Welfare States in France, Germany, Great Britain, and the United States, 1880–1920," *American Historical Review* 95 (1990), pp. 1076–1108; Mink, "The Lady and the Tramp," *The Wages of Motherhood, Welfare's End*, and *Whose Welfare?* (Ithaca, NY: Cornell University Press, 2000); Barbara Nelson, "The Origins of the Two-Channel Welfare State," in *Women, the State and Welfare*, ed. Linda Gordon (Madison: University of Wisconsin Press, 1990), pp. 123–51 and "The Gender, Race, and Class Origins of Early Welfare Policy and the Welfare State," in *Women, Politics and Change*, eds. Louise Tilly and Patricia Gurin (New York: Russell Sage, 1990), pp. 413–35; Jill Quadagno, *The Color of Welfare: How Racism Undermined the War on Poverty* (New York: Oxford University Press, 1994); Wendy Sarvasy, "Beyond the Difference versus Equality Policy Debate: Postsuffrage Feminism, Citizenship, and the Quest for a Feminist Welfare State," *Signs* 17 (1992), pp. 329–62 and "Social Citizenship from a Feminist Perspective," *Hypatia* 12 (1997), pp. 54–73; Sklar, "The Historical Foundations of Women's Power in the Creation of the American Welfare State," in *Mothers of a New World*, ed. Seth Koven and Sonya Michel (New York: Routledge, 1993); and Theda Skocpol, *Protecting Soldiers and Mothers: The Political Origins of Social Policy in the United States* (Cambridge, MA: Harvard University Press, 1992).

16 Lebsock, "Women and American Politics: 1880–1920," in *Women, Politics and Change*, eds. Louise Tilly and Patricia Y. Gurin (New York: Russell Sage, 1990), pp. 35, 36.

17 Baker, "The Domestication of Politics: Women and American Political Society, 1780–1920," in *Women, the State, and Welfare*, ed. Linda Gordon, pp. 55–91; see also Nancy Hewitt, *Women's Activism and Social Change* (Ithaca, NY: Cornell University Press, 1984) and "In Pursuit of Power: The Political Economy of Women's Activism in Twentieth Century Tampa," in *Visible Women: New Essays on American Activism*, ed. Nancy Hewitt and Suzanne Lebsock (Urbana: University of Illinois Press, 1993), pp. 199–222.

18 See Cheryl Gilkes, "Building in Many Places: Multiple Commitments and Ideologies in Black Women's Community Work," in *Women and the Politics of Empowerment*, ed. Ann Bookman and Sandra Morgen (Philadelphia, PA: Temple University Press, 1988), pp. 53–76, and "'Holding Back the Ocean with a Broom,'" in *The Black Woman*, ed., LaFrances Rodgers-Rose (Beverly Hills, CA: Sage, 1980), pp. 217–31; Deborah Gray White, "The Cost of Club Work, The Price of Black Feminism," in *Visible Women*, pp. 247–69; Darlene Clark Hine, "The Housewives' League of Detroit: Black Women and Economic Nationalism," ibid., pp. 223–41; and the work of Mary Church Terrell and Ida B. Wells Barnett in anti-lynching struggles. On these latter, see Terrell, "Lynching from a Negro's Point of View" (1904), reprinted in *Quest for Equality: The Life and Writings of Mary Eliza Church Terrell, 1863–1954*, ed. Beverly Washington Jones, *Black Women in United States History* (Brooklyn, NY: Carlson Publishing, Inc., 1990), 13: 167–81; Ida B. Wells, *Crusade for Justice: The Autobiography of Ida B. Wells*, ed. Alfreda M. Duster (Chicago: University of Chicago Press, 1970); Paula Giddings, *Ida: A Sword Among Lions: Ida B. Wells and the Campaign Against Lynching* (New York: Amistad, 2008); Wells-Barnett, "Lynch Law in

all Its Phases" (1893), reprinted in *Ida B. Wells-Barnett: An Exploratory Study of an American Black Woman, 1893–1930*, ed. Mildred I. Thompson, *Black Women in United States History* (Brooklyn: Carlson Publishing, Inc., 1990), 15: 171–87; and "Lynching and the Excuse for It" (*The Independent*, May 16, 1901), in "Lynching and Rape: An Exchange of Views," by Jane Addams and Ida B. Wells, Edited and with an Introduction by Bettina Aptheker. Occasional Paper No. 25 (New York: American Institute for Marxist Studies, 1977), pp. 28–34.

19 Sarvasy, "Beyond the Difference versus Equality Policy Debate: Postsuffrage Feminism, Citizenship, and the Quest for a Feminist Welfare State," *Signs* 17, 2 (Winter 1992), pp. 329–62; and Sarvasy, *Social Citizenship and Feminist Welfare State Politics* (manuscript made available to the author). See also Lebsock, "Women and American Politics: 1880–1920," in Tilly and Gurin, eds., *Women, Politics and Change*, pp. 35–62; and Paula Baker, "The Domestication of Politics: Women and American Political Society, 1780–1920," in Gordon, ed., *Women, the State, and Welfare*, pp. 55–91; Gordon, "Introduction," *Women, the State and Welfare*, also *Heroes of Their Own Lives* (New York: Viking, 1988); Nancy Hewitt, "In Pursuit of Power: The Political Economy of Women's Activism in Twentieth Century Tampa," in Hewitt and Lebsock, eds., *Visible Women*, esp. pp. 208–17; and Hewitt, *Women's Activism and Social Change* (Ithaca, NY: Cornell University Press, 1984). There has been an enormous amount of feminist writing over the past decade that explores questions of citizenship, writing that addresses many questions related to the definition and "contents" of politics. See, among others, the special issue of *Hypatia* (Fall 1997) on citizenship; Nancy Fraser, *Unruly Practices: Power, Discourse and Gender in Contemporary Social Theory* (Minneapolis: University of Minnesota Press, 1989) and "Rethinking the Public Sphere: A Contribution to the Critique of Actually existing Democracy," in *Habermas and the Public Sphere*, ed. Craig Calhoun (Cambridge, MA: MIT Press, 1997), pp. 109–42; Mary E. Hawkesworth, "Democratization: Reflections on Gendered Dislocations in the Public Sphere," in *Gender, Globalization, and Democratization*, ed. Rita Mae Kelly, Jane H. Bayes, Mary E. Hawkesworth, Brigitte Young (Lanham, MD: Rowman & Littlefield, 2001), pp. 223–36; Ruth Lister, "Inclusive Citizenship: Realizing the Potential," in *Citizenship Studies* 11, 1 (February 2007), pp. 49–61; Lister, *Citizenship: Feminist Perspectives*, 2nd edn. (New York: NYU Press, 2003); Jane Mansbridge, "Reconstructing Democracy," in *Revisioning the Political: Feminist Reconstructions of Traditional Concepts in Western Political Theory*, ed. Nancy Hirschmann and Christine DiStefano (Boulder, CO: Westview Press, 1996), pp. 117–38; Chantal Mouffe, "Democracy, Power, and the 'Political,'" in *Democracy and Difference*, ed. Benhabib (Princeton, NJ: Princeton University Press, 1996), pp. 245–56; Anne Phillips, *Engendering Democracy* (University Park, PA: Penn State University Press, 1991); Ruth Rosen, *The World Split Open: How the Modern Women's Movement Changed America* (New York: Penguin Putnam, 2000); Iris Marion Young, *Inclusion and Democracy* (Oxford: Oxford University Press, 2000); Nira Yuval-Davis, "Intersectionality, Citizenship and Contemporary Politics of Belonging," *Critical Review of International Social and Political Philosophy* 10, 4 (December 2007), pp. 561–74; Yuval-Davis, "Belonging and the Politics of Belonging," *Patterns of Prejudice* 40, 3 (July 2006), pp. 197–214; *Gender and Nation* (Thousand Oaks, CA: Sage Publications, 1997); *Women and Citizenship in Europe: Borders, Rights and Duties*, edited by Anna Ward, Jeanne Gregory and Nira Yuval-Davis (Stoke-on-Trent: Trentham Books and EFSF, 1992); *The Situated Politics of Belonging*, ed. Nira Yuval-Davis, Kalpana Kannabiran, and Ulrike Vieten (London: SAGE, 2006) and Chapters 8 and 12 in this volume.

20 On this point, see Jacquelyn Dowd Hall, "Disorderly Women," *Journal of American History* (Sept. 1986), pp. 354–82; "Disorderly Women: Gender, Politics and

Theory," roundtable discussion with Jacquelyn Hall, Nancy Hewitt, Ardis Cameron, and Martha Ackelsberg, Berkshire Conference of Women Historians, Wellesley College, June 1987; Ackelsberg, *Free Women of Spain: Anarchism and the Struggle for the Emancipation of Women* (Bloomington: Indiana University Press, 1991), especially Conclusion; and also Edward C. Banfield, "Rioting Mainly for Fun and Profit," in *The Unheavenly City Revisited* (Boston: Little, Brown, 1970).

21 Katzenstein, *Faithful and Fearless: Moving Protest Inside the Church and Military* (Princeton, NJ: Princeton University Press, 1998); Cohen, *The Boundaries of Blackness: AIDS and the Breakdown of Black Politics* (Chicago: University of Chicago Press, 1999); Flammang, *Women's Political Voice: How Women Are Transforming the Practice and Study of Politics* (Philadelphia, PA: Temple University Press, 1997); Jo Freeman, *The Politics of Women's Liberation: A Case Study of an Emerging Social Movement and Its Relation to the Policy Process* (New York: David McKay, 1975); Gelb, *Feminism and Politics*; Gelb and Palley, *Women and Public Policies*; Hart, "Watch What We Do: Women Administrators and the Implementation of Minimum Wage Policy, Washington, D.C. 1918–23," panel presentation at the Eighth Berkshire Conference of Women Historians, Douglass College, June 1990 and *Bound by Our Constitution: Women, Workers, and the Minimum Wage* (Princeton, NJ: Princeton University Press, 1994); and Tobias, *Faces of Feminism: An Activist's Reflections on the Women's Movement* (Boulder, CO: Westview Press, 1997).

22 Some exceptions to this generalization include Marla Brettschneider, *Democratic Theorizing from the Margins* (Philadelphia, PA: Temple University Press, 2002); Cohen, *The Boundaries of Blackness*; Cathy Cohen, Kathleen Jones, and Joan Tronto, eds., *Women Transforming Politics* (New York: New York University Press, 1997); Flammang, *Women's Political Voice*; Carol Hardy-Fanta, *Latina Politics, Latino Politics: Gender, Culture and Political Participation in Boston* (Philadelphia, PA: Temple University Press, 1993); Nancy J. Hirschmann, *The Subject of Liberty: Toward a Feminist Theory of Freedom* (Princeton, NJ: Princeton University Press, 2003); and Holloway Sparks, "Dissident Citizenship."

23 For an exploration and critique of the importance and power of these approaches in political science, see Kristen Monroe, ed., *Perestroika! The Raucous Rebellion in Political Science*, (New Haven, CT: Yale University Press, 2005).

24 See, for example, Kristen Amundsen, *A New Look at the Silenced Majority* (Englewood Cliffs, NJ: Prentice-Hall, 1977); Karen Beckwith, *American Women and Political Participation* (New York: Greenwood, 1986) Sandra Baxter and Marjorie Lansing, *Women and Politics: The Visible Majority* (Ann Arbor: University of Michigan Press, 1983); and Anne Phillips, *Engendering Democracy*.

25 See, for example, *Women's Political Voice*, especially Chapters 3 and 4; see also Mary E. Hawkesworth, "Knowers, Knowing, Known: Feminist Theory and Claims to Truth," *Signs* 14, 3 (Spring 1989): 533–57; and Susan Heckman, "The Feminization of Epistemology: Gender and the Social Sciences," *Women and Politics* 7, 3 (Fall 1987): 65–83.

26 Myra Marx Ferree and Arthur J. Miller, "Mobilization and Meaning: Some Social-Psychological Contributions to Resource Mobilization Perspectives on Social Movements," *Sociological Inquiry*, 55 (1985), pp. 55.

27 See, for example, Eloise Buker, "Storytelling Power: Personal Narratives and Political Analysis," *Women and Politics* 7, 3 (Fall 1987), pp. 29–46; Kathy E. Ferguson, "Subject Centeredness in Feminist Discourse," in Kathleen B. Jones and Anna G. Jonasdottir, eds., *The Political Interests of Gender* (London: Sage, 1988), pp. 66–78; and Jane Flax, "Postmodernism and Gender Relations in Feminist Theory," *Signs* 12, 4 (Summer 1987), pp. 621–43. I am grateful to Janet Flammang for directing me to many of these sources. See also Cohen, Jones and Tronto, *Women Transforming*

Politics; Cohen, *The Boundaries of Blackness*; Marla Brettschneider, ed., *The Narrow Bridge: Jewish Perspectives on Multiculturalism* (New Brunswick, NJ: Rutgers University Press, 1996). A number of recent books join qualitative and quantitative methodologies; thus, Dara Strolovitch, *Affirmative Advocacy: Race, Class and Gender in Interest Group Politics* (Chicago: University of Chicago Press, 2007) draws on quantitative data to develop a model of social justice advocacy; R. Amy Elman, *Sexual Equality in an Integrated Europe* (New York: Palgrave Macmillan, 2007), attempts to measure degrees of overcoming sex discrimination; and Cathy Marie Johnson, Georgia Duerst-Lahti, and Noelle Norton, *Creating Gender: The Sexual Politics of Welfare Policy* (Boulder, CO: Lynne Rienner, 2007) use quantitative data to develop their argument about the construction of gender.

28 Kaplan, "Female Consciousness and Collective Action: The Case of Barcelona, 1910–18," *Signs* 5 (1980), pp. 545–66; also Kaplan, *Crazy for Democracy: Women in Grassroots Movements* (New York: Routledge, 1997).

29 Ruddick, *Maternal Thinking: Toward a Politics of Peace* (Boston: Beacon Press, 1989); Jean Elshtain, "Feminism, Family, and Community"; Elshtain, "Antigone's Daughters"; and Elshtain, *Power Trips and Other Journeys: Essays in Feminism as Civic Discourse* (Madison: University of Wisconsin Press, 1990); Elshtain, "Antigone's Daughters Reconsidered: Continuing Reflections on Women, Politics and Power," in *Life, World and Politics,* ed. S. White (Notre Dame, IN: University of Notre Dame Press, 1989), pp. 222–36 and "The Mothers of the Disappeared: Passion and Protest in Maternal Action," in *Representations of Motherhood,* ed. Donna Bassin, Margaret Honey, and Meryle Mohrer Kaplan (New Haven, CT: Yale University Press, 1994), pp. 75–92.

30 Dietz, "Context Is All: Feminism and Theories of Citizenship," *Daedalus* (Fall 1987), pp. 1–24 and "Citizenship with a Feminist Face: Problems with Maternal Thinking," *Political Theory* 13 (1985), pp. 19–37, both reprinted in *Turning Operations: Feminism, Arendt, and Politics* (New York: Routledge, 2002), Chs. 1 and 2; Hine, "The Housewives' League of Detroit: Black Women and Economic Nationalism," pp. 223–41, Deborah Gray White, "The Cost of Club Work, The Price of Black Feminism," pp. 247–69, and Hewitt, "In Pursuit of Power," all in *Visible Women,* Hewitt and Lebsock, eds.; Cheryl Townsend Gilkes, "Building in Many Places," in Bookman and Morgen, eds., *Women and the Politics of Empowerment*; Nancy Naples, *Grassroots Warriors: Activist Mothering, Community Work, and the War on Poverty* (New York: Routledge, 1998); and Sarvasy, "Social Citizenship." See also Annelise Orleck, *Storming Caesars Palace: How Black Mothers Fought Their Own War on Poverty* (Boston: Beacon Press, 2005); Rhonda Y. Williams, *The Politics of Public Housing: Black Women's Struggles Against Urban Inequality* (New York: Oxford University Press, 2004). See also below, Chapter 10.

31 Writings on the civil rights movement, and its rootedness in existing community networks, represent one counter to this perspective; do the same findings hold, for example, for the women who became active in the National Welfare Rights Organization? Other movements and organizations located primarily within the African American community? What about other ethnic/minority-based organizations? Some clues may be found in Kathleen Blee, ed., *No Middle Ground: Women and Radical Protest* (New York: NYU Press, 1998); Alexis Jetter, Annelise Orleck and Diana Taylor, eds., *The Politics of Motherhood: Activist Voices from Left and Right* (Hanover, NH: University Press of New England, 1997); Nancy Naples, *Community Activism and Feminist Politics: Organizing Across Race, Class, and Gender* (New York: Routledge, 1998); and Annelise Orleck, *Storming Caesars Palace,* among others.

32 "Female Consciousness and Collective Action," p. 564. See also Chapter 3, above.

33 Cockburn, "When Women Get Involved in Community Action," in Marjorie Mayo, ed., *Women in the Community* (London: Routledge and Kegan Paul, 1977), p. 67. See also Chapter 1 above, and sources cited there.

34 See, for example, Michael Parenti, "Power and Pluralism: The View from the Bottom," *Journal of Politics* 32, 3 (1970), pp. 501–30; Michael Lipsky, "Protest as a Political Resource," *American Political Science Review* 62, 3 (September 1968), pp. 1144–58; Piven and Cloward, *Poor People's Movements* and Piven, *Challenging Authority*.

35 On these points, see, for example, Manuel Castells, *The City and the Grassroots* (Berkeley: University of California Press, 1983), especially Chapters 6, 13, 15, 25–26; Saul Alinsky, *Reveille for Radicals* (Chicago: University of Chicago Press, 1947) and *Rules for Radicals* (New York: Random House, 1969); Ira Katznelson, *City Trenches* (New York: Pantheon, 1981); Peter Medoff and Holly Sklar, *Streets of Hope* (Boston: South End Press, 1994); Eve S. Weinbaum, *To Move a Mountain: Fighting the Global Economy in Appalachia* (New York: New Press/W.W. Norton, 2004); Archon Fung, ed., *Deepening Democracy: Institutional Innovations in Empowered Participatory Governance* (London and New York: Verso, 2003); and Fung, *Empowered Participation: Reinventing Urban Democracy* (Princeton, NJ: Princeton University Press, 2004).

36 On this point, of course, the classic text is Sara Evans, *Personal Politics: The Roots of Women's Liberation in the Civil Rights Movement and the New Left* (New York: Random House, 1979).

37 Nancy Naples' *Grassroots Warriors* provides some fascinating material for such an exploration. On the women of the welfare rights movement themselves, see Guida West, *The National Welfare Rights Movement: The Social Protest of Poor Women* (New York: Praeger, 1981); Susan Hertz, "The Politics of the Welfare Mothers Movement: A Case Study," *Signs* 2, 3 (Spring 1977), pp. 600–611; Jackie Pope, "Women in the Welfare Rights Struggle: The Brooklyn Welfare Action Council," in *Women and Social Protest*, eds., Guida West and Rhoda Lois Blumberg (New York: Oxford University Press, 1990), pp. 57–74; Premilla Nadasen, *Welfare Warriors: The Welfare Rights Movement in the United States* (New York: Routledge, 2005); and Felicia Kornbluh, *The Battle for Welfare Rights: Politics and Poverty in Modern America* (Philadelphia, PA: University of Pennsylvania Press, 2007). See also Annelise Orleck, *Storming Caesars Palace*.

38 In addition to sources cited above, see R. Amy Elman, *Sexual Equality in an Integrated Europe* and Anne Stevens, *Women, Power and Politics* (Houndmills and NY: Palgrave Macmillan, 2007), especially Chapters 6–9.

39 These questions, of course, are central to much of the work of Frances Fox Piven, most recently, *Challenging Authority*.

40 The studies, here, are almost too numerous to mention. Among the most influential, however, have been Michele Zimbalist Rosaldo and Louise Lamphere, eds., *Women, Culture and Society* (Stanford, CA: Stanford University Press, 1976); Sherry B. Ortner and Harriet Whitehead, eds., *Sexual Meanings: The Cultural Construction of Gender and Sexuality* (Cambridge: Cambridge University Press, 1981); Peggy Reeves Sanday, *Female Power and Male Dominance: On the Origins of Sexual Inequality* (Cambridge: Cambridge University Press, 1981). See also Deborah Rhode, ed., *Theoretical Perspectives on Sexual Difference* (New Haven, CT: Yale University Press, 1990); Judith Butler and Joan Scott, *Feminists Theorize the Political* (New York: Routledge, 1992); Scott, *Gender and the Politics of History*, rev. edn. (New York: Columbia University Press, 1999); Martha Minow, *Making All the Difference: Inclusion, Exclusion and American Law* (Cambridge, MA: Harvard University Press, 1990); and Alice Kessler-Harris, "The Debate over Equality for Women in the Workplace: Recognizing Differences," in Laurie Larwood, et al., eds., *Women and Work: An Annual Review,*

Vol. 1 (Beverly Hills, CA: Sage, 1985), pp. 141–61, and Kessler-Harris, "Equal Employment Opportunity versus Sears, Roebuck and Company: A Personal Account," in *Unequal Sisters*, 2nd edition, eds., Vicky L. Ruiz and Ellen Carol Dubois (New York: Routledge, 1994), pp. 545–59.

41 The citations here could easily fill a book. The classics include Audre Lorde, *Sister Outsider* (Trumansburg, NY: Crossing Press, 1984); Diane K. Lewis, "A Response to Inequality: Black Women, Racism, and Sexism," *Signs* 3, 2 (Winter 1977), pp. 339–61; Margaret A. Simons, "Racism and Feminism: A Schism in the Sisterhood," *Feminist Studies* 5, 2 (Summer 1979), pp. 389–410; Bonnie Thornton Dill, "Race, Class and Gender: Prospects for an All-Inclusive Sisterhood," *Feminist Studies* 9, 1 (Spring 1983), pp. 131–50; María C. Lugones and Elizabeth V. Spelman, "Have We Got A Theory for You! Feminist Theory, Cultural Imperialism, and the Demand for 'The Woman's Voice'," *Women's Studies International Forum* 6, 6 (1983), pp. 573–81; Gloria T. Hull, Patricia Bell Scott, and Barbara Smith, eds., *All the Women Are White, All the Blacks Are Men, But Some of us Are Brave* (Old Westbury: Feminist Press, 1982); Evelyn Torton Beck, *Nice Jewish Girls: A Lesbian Anthology*, revised and updated edn. (Boston: Beacon Press, 1989); Irena Klepfisz, *Dreams of an Insomniac: Jewish Feminist Essays, Speeches, and Diatribes* (Portland, OR: Eighth Mountain Press, 1990); Melanie Kaye/Kantrowitz, *The Issue Is Power: Essays on Women, Jews, Violence and Resistance* (San Francisco: Aunt Lute, 1992). Shane Phelan attempted to incorporate these perspectives into a politics of "specificity," in *Getting Specific: Postmodern Lesbian Politics* (Minneapolis: University of Minnesota Press, 1994). I have explored these issues at greater length in "Identity Politics, Political Identities: Toward a Multicultural Politics," *Frontiers* XVI, 1 (Fall 1995), pp. 87–100.

42 I have developed this argument at greater length in "Identity Politics, Political Identities." See also Shane Phelan, "Coyote Politics," paper presented at the 1994 Annual Meeting of the Western Political Science Association, Albuquerque, NM, March 1994, and *Getting Specific*; Lisa Albrecht and Rose M. Brewer, eds., *Bridges to Power: Women's Multicultural Alliances*, published in cooperation with the National Women's Studies Association (Philadelphia, PA: New Society Publishers, 1990); María Lugones, "Purity, Impurity, and Separation," *Signs* 19, 2 (Winter 1994), pp. 458–79; and Marla Brettschneider, "Introduction," in *The Narrow Bridge: Jewish Perspectives on Multiculturalism* (New Brunswick: Rutgers University Press, 1996); Tamar Carroll, "How Did Feminists Meet the Challenges of Working across Differences? Brooklyn's National Congress of Neighborhood Women, 1974–2006," in *Women and Social Movements in the U.S., 1600–2000*, eds., Kathryn Sklar and Thomas Dublin (Alexandria, VA: Alexander Street Press) available at *http://womhist.alexanderstreet.com* (accessed July 27, 2008); and Carroll, "Unlikely Allies: Forging a Multiracial, Class-based Women's Movement in 1970s Brooklyn," pp. 196–224; María Bevacqua, "Reconsidering Violence against Women: Coalition Politics in the Antirape Movement," pp. 163–77; and Premilla Nadasen, "'Welfare's a Green Problem': Cross-Race Coalitions in Welfare Rights Organizing," pp. 178–95, all in *Feminist Coalitions*, ed., Stephanie Gilmore (Urbana: University of Illinois Press, 2008). See also Chapter 10, below.

43 There is an extensive and growing literature on patterns and/or determinants of women's participation in politics. See, for example, Charles Payne, "'Men Led, But Women Organized': Movement Participation of Women in the Mississippi Delta," in *Women and Social Protest*, eds., West and Blumberg, pp. 156–65; Celene Krauss, "Blue-Collar Women and Toxic Waste Protests: The Process of Politicization," *Second Annual Women's Policy Research Conference Proceedings* (Washington, DC: Institute for Women's Policy Research, 1991), pp. 279–83; Nancy Romer, "Is Political Activism Still a 'Masculine' Endeavor?" *Psychology of Women Quarterly* 14 (1990), pp. 229–43;

Claire K. Fulenwider, "Feminist Ideology and the Political Attitudes and Participation of White and Minority Women," *Western Political Quarterly* 34, 1 (March 1981), pp. 17–30; Arthur Miller, Patricia Gurin, Gerald Gurin, and Oksana Malanchuk, "Group Consciousness and Political Participation," *American Journal of Political Science* 25 (August 1981), pp. 494–511; Susan B. Hansen, Linda M. Franz and Margaret Netemeyer-Mays, "Women's Political Participation and Policy Preferences," *Social Science Quarterly* 56, 4 (March 1976), pp. 576–90 Ethel Klein, "The Diffusion of Consciousness in the United States and Western Europe," in *The Women's Movements in the United States and Western Europe*, eds., Mary Fainsod Katzenstein and Carol McClurg Mueller (Philadelphia, PA: Temple University Press, 1987), pp. 23–43. See also Stevens, *Women, Power and Politics*; Charles Payne, *I've Got the Light of Freedom: The Organizing Tradition and the Mississippi Freedom Struggle* (Berkeley: University of California Press, 2007); and Tananarive Due and Patricia Stephens Due, *Freedom in the Family: A Mother–Daughter Memoir of the Fight for Civil Rights* (New York: One-World, 2003).

44 Sarvasy, "Beyond the Difference versus Equality Policy Debate: Postsuffrage Feminism, Citizenship, and the Quest for a Feminist Welfare State," *Signs* 17, 2 (Winter 1992), pp. 329–62; and "Social Citizenship from a Feminist Perspective," *Hypatia* 12 (Fall 1997), pp. 54–73.

45 To name just a few, Chafe, "Women's History and Political History"; Lebsock, "Women and American Politics: 1880–1920"; Paula Baker, "The Domestication of Politics"; Sklar, "The Historical Foundations of Women's Power."

46 *The Morning After: Sexual Politics at the End of the Cold War* (Berkeley: University of California Press, 1993), p. 39.

10 WOMEN'S COMMUNITY ACTIVISM

1 "Culture, Citizenship, and Democracy: Changing Discourses and Practices of the Latin American Left," in *Cultures of Politics, Politics of Cultures: Re-Visioning Latin American Social Movements*, eds. Sonia E. Alvarez, Evelina Dagnino, and Arturo Escobar (Boulder, CO: Westview Press, 1998), p. 45. Catherine Holland issues a similar call for attention to these issues, and makes a fascinating case for the linkages between citizenship and difference in US political theory and practice in *The Body Politic: Foundings, Citizenship, and Difference in the American Political Imagination* (New York: Routledge, 2001). Arlene Saxonhouse locates the problem in the Greek origins of political science in *Fear of Diversity: The Birth of Political Science in Ancient Greek Thought* (Chicago: University of Chicago Press, 1992).

2 NCNW has since become not only a national, but an international, organization, forming part of GROOTS (Grassroots Organizations Operating Together in Sisterhood), which was founded with NCNW help after the Nairobi conference in 1985. For a good overview of many of NCNW's activities, particularly in the area of diversity, see Tamar Carroll, ed., "How Did Working-Class Feminists Meet the Challenges of Working Across Differences? The National Congress of Neighborhood Women, 1974–2006 Introduction," in *How Did Working-Class Feminists Meet the Challenges of Working across Differences? The National Congress of Neighborhood Women, 1974–2006* (Albany, NY: State University of New York at Binghamton, Binghamton, NY, 2006), available at: www.alexanderstreet6.com/wasm.

3 Gwendolyn Mink, *The Wages of Motherhood* (Ithaca, NY: Cornell University Press, 1995); Judith Shklar, *American Citizenship: The Quest for Inclusion* (Cambridge, MA: Harvard University Press, 1991); Shane Phelan, *Sexual Strangers* (Philadelphia, PA: Temple University Press, 2001); Charles Mills, *The Racial Contract* (Ithaca, NY: Cornell University Press, 1997); Ruth Lister, *Citizenship: Feminist Perspectives*, 2nd edition

(New York: NYU Press, 2003), especially Chapter 2; Engin Isin, *Being Political: Genealogies of Citizenship* (Minneapolis: University of Minnesota Press, 2002). I have explored these issues in Chapter 8, above.

4 Barbara Nelson, "Women's Poverty and Women's Citizenship," *Signs* 10 (1984), pp. 209–31; Martha Ackelsberg, "Citizenship," in *Reader's Companion to U.S. Women's History*, eds. Wilma Mankiller, Gwendolyn Mink, Marysa Navarro, Barbara Smith, and Gloria Steinem (Boston: Houghton Mifflin, 1998), pp. 99–100; and Chapter 4, above.

5 In addition to the works cited above, see Nancy Hirschmann, "Revisioning Freedom: Relationship, Context, and the Politics of Empowerment," pp. 51–74 and Zillah Eisenstein, "Equalizing Privacy and Specifying Equality," pp. 181–92, both in Nancy Hirschmann and Christine DiStefano, eds., *Revisioning the Political: Feminist Reconstructions of Traditional Concepts in Western Political Theory* (Boulder, CO: Westview Press, 1996); Carole Pateman, "Feminist Critiques of the Public/Private Dichotomy," in *The Disorder of Women* (Stanford, CA: Stanford University Press, 1989); Anne Phillips, *Engendering Democracy* (University Park, PA: The Pennsylvania State University Press, 1991); and Patricia Boland, *Privacy and the Politics of Intimate Life* (Ithaca, NY: Cornell University Press, 1996). For a consideration of some of these issues in the context of debates about care and justice, see Julie White, *Democracy, Justice, and the Welfare State* (University Park, PA: Pennsylvania State University Press, 2000); Joan Tronto, *Moral Boundaries: A Political Argument for an Ethic of Care* (New York: Routledge, 1993); and Selma Sevenhuijsen, *Citizenship and the Ethics of Care: Feminist Considerations on Justice, Morality, and Politics* (New York: Routledge, 1998); and above, Chapter 4.

6 *The Sexual Contract*, p. 135.

7 The classic argument, here is, of course, that by T.H. Marshall, "Citizenship and Social Class," in *Citizenship and Social Class and Other Essays* (Cambridge: Cambridge University Press, 1950). For contemporary arguments that draw on his initial insight, see, for example, Sylvia Walby, "Is Citizenship Gendered?" *Sociology* 28, 2 (May 1994); Ruth Lister, "Dialectics of Feminist Citizenship," *Hypatia* 12, 4 (Fall 1997), pp. 6–26; Lister, *Citizenship: Feminist Perspectives* and "Inclusive Citizenship: Realizing the Potential," *Citizenship Studies* 11, 1 (February 2007), pp. 49–61; Nancy Fraser, "Rethinking the Public Sphere: A Contribution to the Critique of Actually Existing Democracy," in *Habermas and the Public Sphere*, ed. Craig Calhoun (Cambridge, MA: MIT Press, 1992); Anne Phillips, "Dealing with Difference: A Politics of Ideas, or a Politics of Presence?" in *Democracy and Difference: Contesting the Boundaries of the Political*, ed. Seyla Benhabib, (Princeton, NJ: Princeton University Press, 1996), pp. 139–52. Nancy Fraser and Axel Honneth engage in a related debate, focused around the usefulness of the concept of "recognition," in *Redistribution or Recognition? A Political-Philosophical Exchange* (London: Verso, 2003).

8 Seyla Benhabib, "Models of Public Space: Hannah Arendt, the Liberal Tradition, and Jürgen Habermas," in *Habermas and the Public Sphere*, ed. Craig Calhoun (Cambridge, MA: MIT Press, 1992). See also Benjamin R. Barber, *Strong Democracy: Participatory Politics for a New Age* (Berkeley: University of California Press, 1984) and *A Place for Us: How to Make Society Civil and Democracy Strong* (New York: Hill and Wang, 1998); Harry C. Boyte, "Beyond Deliberation: Citizenship as Public Work," *The Good Society* 5, 2 (1995), pp. 15–19; Boyte and Nancy N. Kari, *Building America: The Democratic Promise of Public Work* (Philadelphia, PA: Temple University Press, 1996); Philip Green, *Equality and Democracy* (New York: New Press, 1998); and Iris Young, *Justice and the Politics of Difference* (Princeton, NJ: Princeton University Press, 1990) and *Inclusion and Democracy* (New York: Oxford University Press, 2000). Mary Lyndon Shanley and I discussed Young's wariness of "distributive justice" in "Reflections on Iris Marion Young's *Justice and the Politics of Difference*," *Politics &*

Gender 4, 2 (June 2008), pp. 326–34. Joe Soss explores the ways public policies construct both clients and citizens, and the implications of that dichotomization for our democracy in "Making Clients and Citizens: Welfare Policy as a Source of Status, Belief, and Action," in Anne Schneider and Helen Ingram, eds., *Deserving and Entitled: Social Constructions and Public Policy* (Albany, NY: State University of New York Press, 2005). See also Soss, *Unwanted Claims: Politics, Participation and the U.S. Welfare System* (Ann Arbor: University of Michigan Press, 2000); Barbara Nelson, "Women's Poverty and Women's Citizenship"; Theda Skocpol, *Diminished Democracy: From Membership to Management in American Civic Life* (Norman, OK: University of Oklahoma Press, 2004); and Matthew Crenson and Benjamin Ginsburg, *Downsizing Democracy: How America Sidelined Its Citizens and Privatized Its Public* (Baltimore, MD: The Johns Hopkins University Press, 2004).

9 Phillips, "Dealing with Difference: A Politics of Ideas, or a Politics of Presence?" in S. Benhabib, ed., *Democracy and Difference*, p. 142. See also Iris Young, *Inclusion and Democracy*; Catherine Holland, *The Body Politic*; and Marla Brettschneider, *Democratic Theorizing from the Margins* (Philadelphia, PA: Temple University Press, 2002).

10 Philip Green's *Equality and Democracy* (New York: The New Press, 1998), Iris Young's *Inclusion and Democracy*, and Crenson and Ginsberg's *Downsizing Democracy* are among the important exceptions. For a study exploring specific factors affecting participation at the community level, especially that of women, see Amy Caiazza, "Women's Community Involvement: The Effects of Money, Safety, Parenthood, and Friends," IWPR Publication #C346 (Washington, DC: Institute for Women's Policy Research, Sept. 2001).

11 "Models of Public Space," pp. 93–94. There are significant similarities here with the work of James Morone, *The Democratic Wish: Popular Participation and the Limits of American Government* (New York: Basic Books, 1990).

12 See White, *Democracy, Justice and the Welfare State*, especially Chapters 6 and 7. I return to this constellation of factors in greater detail below.

13 Ryan, "Gender and Public Access," in Calhoun, ed., *Habermas and the Public Sphere*, pp. 267, 283–84; see also Holloway Sparks, "Dissident Citizenship," *Hypatia* 12, 4 (Fall 1997); Ruth Lister, "Dialectics of Citizenship," *Hypatia* 12, 4 (Fall 1997), pp. 6–26, especially pp. 8–9; Jacquelyn Dowd Hall, "Disorderly Women: Gender and Labor Militancy in the Appalachian South," *Journal of American History* 73 (1986), pp. 354–82; Michael Lipsky, "Protest as a Political Resource," *American Political Science Review* 62, 4 (1968), pp. 1144–58; and Frances Fox Piven and Richard A. Cloward, *Poor People's Movements: How They Succeed, Why They Fail* (New York: Pantheon, 1977) and Frances Fox Piven, *Challenging Authority: How Ordinary People Change America* (Lanham, MD: Rowman and Littlefield, 2006).

14 Fraser, "Rethinking the Public Sphere: A Contribution to the Critique of Actually Existing Democracy," in Calhoun, ed., *Habermas and the Public Sphere*, pp. 119, 124. She develops this line of critique further in her exchange with Honneth, *Redistribution or Recognition?*

15 Young, *Inclusion and Democracy*, p. 155. See also Barber, *A Place for Us*; Harry Boyte, "Beyond Deliberation: Citizenship as Public Work," and Boyte and Nancy N. Kari, *Building America*; and Boyte, *The Backyard Revolution* (Philadelphia, PA: Temple University Press, 1980).

16 See White, *Democracy, Justice and the Welfare State*, pp. 152, 169; also Holland, *The Body Politic*; Crenson and Ginsberg, *Downsizing Democracy*. Sheldon Wolin explored some of the earliest stages in the constriction of "the public" in the US in "The People's Two Bodies," *democracy* 1, 1 (January 1981); he revisited that argument in the aftermath of the Bush Administration's responses to 9/11 in "Inverted Totalitarianism," *The Nation* May 19, 2003.

17 Phelan, "All the Comforts of Home: The Genealogy of Community," in Nancy Hirschmann and Christine DiStefano, eds., *Revisioning the Political: Feminist Reconstructions of Traditional Concepts in Western Political Theory* (Boulder, CO: Westview Press, 1996), p. 248. See also Susan Bickford, "Anti-Anti-Identity Politics: Feminism, Democracy, and the Complexities of Citizenship," *Hypatia* 12, 4 (Fall 1997), p. 124.

18 This paragraph draws on Chapter 8, above.

19 See Naples, *Grassroots Warriors: Activist Mothering, Community Work, and the War on Poverty* (New York: Routledge, 1998). I am drawing here on my summary of Naples' discussion in Chapter 12, below.

20 Kaplan, "Female Consciousness and Collective Action: The Case of Barcelona, 1910–18," *Signs* 7 (Spring 1982), pp. 545–66. Kaplan takes up the idea again in *Crazy for Democracy: Women in Grassroots Movements* (New York: Routledge, 1997); and in *Taking Back the Streets: Women, Youth, and Direct Democracy* (Berkeley: University of California Press, 2004); see also Maxine Molyneux, "Mobilization without Emancipation? Women's Interests, the state, and Revolution in Nicaragua," *Feminist Studies* 11 (Summer 1985), pp. 227–54.

21 Sometimes, of course, that rejection is a self-consciously strategic move, as Temma Kaplan makes clear in her treatment of El Poder Femenino and other right-wing groups that mobilized women against the government of Salvador Allende. She notes that "these groups insist that they are not challenging the prevailing gender system" and, also, that they were not "political," but were simply trying to meet the needs of their families; but, in doing so, they undermined the legitimacy of the regime, and paved the road for the military coup. On the complexities of the women's activities see especially, *Taking Back the Streets*, pp. 46–47, 58, 60, 65–68.

22 See below, Chapter 12.

23 Miguel Díaz-Barriga, "Beyond the Domestic and the Public: *Colonas* Participation in Urban Movements in Mexico City," in *Cultures of Politics, Politics of Cultures*, p. 260.

24 Myrna Breitbart and I made a similar argument about the political significance of being drawn out of familiar spaces in Chapter 3, above. Note, as well, Julie White's related argument about the move from "essentializing" to "politicizing" needs, in *Democracy, Justice, and the Welfare State*, pp. 154ff.

25 I owe this particular framing to Julie White's discussion of needs and care in *Democracy, Justice and the Welfare State*, especially pp. 154 ff.

26 For arguments about a broader understanding of what constitutes politics see Chapters 1, 2, and 9. See also Marla Brettschneider, *Democratic Theorizing from the Margin*, especially Chapter 6.

27 Young, *Inclusion and Democracy*, p. 160. She draws, there, on Jürgen Habermas, *The Theory of Communicative Action* (Boston: Beacon Press, 1984); Jean Cohen and Andrew Arato, *Civil Society and Political Theory* (Cambridge, MA: MIT Press, 1992); and Michael Walzer, "The Idea of Civil Society," in Walzer, ed., *Toward a Global Civil Society* (Providence, RI: Berghahn Books, 1997).

28 Young, *Inclusion and Democracy*, pp. 162–63.

29 Joe Soss makes an interesting argument about the ways different social welfare schemes construct people as citizens or as clients in "Making Clients and Citizens: Welfare Policy as a Source of Status, Belief, and Action," in Anne Schneider and Helen Ingram, eds., *Deserving and Entitled: Social Constructions and Public Policy*. I am grateful to Peregrine Schwartz-Shea for calling this analysis to my attention. See also Barbara Nelson, "Women's Poverty and Women's Citizenship." A number of recent works discuss the increasing construction of *all* of us more as consumers/ clients than as active citizens. See especially Matthew Crenson and Benjamin Ginsberg, *Downsizing Democracy* and Theda Skocpol, *Diminished Democracy*.

30 Patricia Williams, "The Pain of Word Bondage," in *The Alchemy of Race and Rights* (Cambridge, MA: Harvard University Press, 1991), p. 152.

31 On this point, see my "Dependency or Mutuality," above, Chapter 4 in this volume; White, *Democracy, Justice and the Welfare State*; Soss, "Making Clients and Citizens"; and Nelson, "Women's Poverty and Women's Citizenship."

32 Naples, *Grassroots Warriors*, p. 199. See, in addition, Frances Fox Piven and Richard A. Cloward, *Regulating the Poor* (New York: Pantheon, 1970); Piven and Cloward, *Poor People's Movements: How They Succeed, Why They Fail* (New York: Pantheon, 1977); and Piven, *Challenging Authority*. Irene Diamond and I explored the complicated and ambiguous relationship between state policies and women's participation in "Gender and Political Life: New Directions in Political Science," in *Analyzing Gender: A Handbook of Social Science Research*, eds. Beth B. Hess and Myra Marx Ferree (Beverly Hills: Sage Publications, 1987), pp. 504–25. See also my "Review Article: Feminist Analyses of Public Policy," *Comparative Politics* (July 1992), pp. 477–93.

33 Nancy Naples, "Women's Community Activism: Exploring the Dynamics of Politicization and Diversity," in *Community Activism and Feminist Politics: Organizing Across Race, Class, and Gender*, ed. Nancy Naples (New York: Routledge, 1998), p. 343.

34 LaDoris Payne, interview with author, Northampton, MA, February 21, 2004.

35 *Inclusion and Democracy*, p. 156. See also Ann Shola Orloff, "Gender and the Social Rights of Citizenship: The Comparative Analysis of Gender Relations and Welfare States," *American Sociological Review* 58, 3 (June 1993), pp. 303–28; and White, *Democracy, Justice and the Welfare State*, especially pp. 156–65.

36 "National Congress of Neighborhood Women," n.d. [1982?], 2 pp. typescript. Located in Sophia Smith Collection, Smith College, Papers of the National Congress of Neighborhood Women (hereafter cited as NCNW Papers), Box 3, Folder 14.

37 National Congress of Neighborhood Women, "Report of Activities for 1980–81," prepared by Wanda Wooten, July 8, 1981, p. 1. NCNW Papers, Box 1, Folder 23.

38 "National Congress of Neighborhood Women: Principles," 2 pp. typescript, undated [Fall/Winter 1974?], NCNW Papers, Box 1, Folder 8. This understanding of "political involvement" would seem to provide an example of what Iris Young describes as a civil society association of the political sort.

39 Note the similarity with the perspective of the Spanish anarchist women's organization, Mujeres Libres, which I explored in *Free Women of Spain: Mujeres Libres and the Struggle for the Emancipation of Women* (Bloomington: Indiana University Press, 1991), especially Chapters 4 and 5; and, of course, the consciousness-raising feature of the early women's movement. The issue of recognizing women—and their leadership—came up repeatedly in virtually all the interviews I conducted with women active in NCNW—both those involved in the early years, and those still affiliated.

40 Mary Field Belenky, Lynne A. Bond, and Jacqueline S. Weinstock, "The National Congress of Neighborhood Women," in *A Tradition That Has No Name: Nurturing the Development of People, Families, and Communities* (New York: Basic Books, 1997), p. 206.

41 Jan Peterson, interview with author, Williamsburg, Brooklyn, August 21, 2002. Belenky, Bond, and Weinstock also give some hints in this direction in "The National Congress of Neighborhood Women."

42 Cited by María Giordano, in untitled paper on class and feminism. NCNW Papers, Box 118, Folder 5. Similar sentiments were expressed by many of the participants in the NCNW's "Sharing Strategies" conference that took place at Smith College, Northampton, MA, February 19–22, 2004.

43 "Consciousness Interview with [Ann Giordano], National Congress of Neighborhood Women," July 15, 1981. 14 pp. typescript, with hand-written corrections. Interviewer: lkg [Linda Grey?]. NCNW Papers, Box 109, Folder 2. She made

similar comments in a joint interview conducted by Mary Belenky with Maria Fava, Ann Giordano, Elaine Carpinelli, Sandy, and Jan. 3/26/92 Transcript in NCNW Papers, Box 8, Folder 4.

See also Terry Haywoode's comments in "Women Against Women: Middle-Class Bias in Feminist Literature," paper presented at the annual meetings of the Society for the Study of Social Problems, San Francisco, CA, Sept. 2, 1978. NCNW Papers, Box 118, Folder 4; and "Working-Class Women and Local Politics: Styles of Community Organizing," *Research in Politics and Society* 7 (1999), pp. 111–34.

44 Untitled paper by [María Giordano], NCNW Papers, Box 118, Folder 5. The pattern is an all-too-common one in many community organizations. See, for example, Ronald Lawson and Stephen E. Barton, "Sex Roles in Social Movements: A Case Study of the Tenant Movement in New York City," *Signs* V (Winter 1980), pp. 230–47.

45 María Giordano, untitled paper, NCNW, Box 118, Folder 5.

46 "National Congress of Neighborhood Women: Principles," 2 pp. typescript, undated [Fall/Winter 1974?], NCNW Papers, Box 1, Folder 8. The wording here is significant. They were not saying that women had to *learn* to be leaders; rather, that they needed to become more aware of the significance of what they were *already* doing, and to develop their skills to improve their ability to function effectively.

47 Interview with author, August 21, 2002, Brooklyn, NY.

48 Interview with author and Tamar Carroll, February 21, 2004, Northampton, MA.

49 "Consciousness interview with Ann Giordano," July 15, 1981. NCNW Papers, Box 109, Folder 2.

50 Interview with author, Camden, NJ, May 7, 2004. Along similar lines, Carol Judy (who has been involved with an NCNW-affiliated organization in East Tennessee for many years) spoke often about the importance of finding, and using, her voice. Interview with author and Tamar Carroll, February 21, 2004, Smith College; and during NCNW's "Sharing Strategies" conference, Smith College, February 19–22, 2004.

51 See White, *Democracy, Justice, and the Welfare State*, especially pp. 132, 135–36. I discuss below the connections between this notion of a democratic politics of care, and the ambiguous status of "leadership training" or "leadership development" in a democracy.

52 NCNW, interview by Mary Belenky with María Fava, Ann Giordano, Elaine Carpinelli, Sandy [Schiaparelli?] and Jan [Peterson], 3/26/92. NCNW Papers, Box 8, Folder 2. Note, too, in this context, the study by Amy Caiazza and Heidi Hartmann, indicating that parenthood (particularly having children aged between 5 and 17) tends to *increase* participation rates for both men and women, but especially for women, in community-based/civic organizations. Caiazza, "Women's Community Involvement."

53 James Weldon Johnson/Neighborhood Women, Manual #1: "Organizing Your Group: Finding, Keeping and Supporting Neighborhood Leaders," pp. 12–13. NCNW Papers, Box 109, Folder 13.

54 Jan Peterson, "How to Include Women Effectively in Your Efforts to Revitalize Neighborhoods," Memorandum for Neighborhood Leaders from National Congress of Neighborhood Women, 2–81, 2 pp. NCNW Papers, Box 109.

55 María Rivera Brown, interview with author, Camden, NJ, May 7, 2004.

56 "National Congress of Neighborhood Women," undated manuscript [1982?], 2 pp. NCNW papers, Box 3, Folder 14.

57 Interview with Jan Peterson and Bertha Gilkey, March 17, 1983. 8 pp. typescript. NCNW Papers, Box 108, Folder 2; emphasis mine.

58 On the meaning and importance of preparation (and *capacitación*) within the Spanish anarchist movement, see my *Free Women of Spain*, especially Chapter 5. In the US context, the Highlander Center in Tennessee has long been involved in mounting programs of education and training for would-be organizers and activists in a variety of popular movements. And, of course, the Civil Rights Movement had an important educational component, as well. For a discussion of the role of education in support of organizing among GE workers in East Tennessee, see Eve Weinbaum, "Transforming Democracy: Rural Women and Labor Resistance," in Cohen, et al., eds., *Women Transforming Politics*, pp. 324–39, especially pp. 331–33. I am grateful to both Rachel Roth and Joan Tronto for pressing me to address this issue, and for suggesting useful resources.

59 White, *Democracy, Justice and the Welfare State*, p. 136.

60 Group interview with Mary Belenky, March 26, 1992. NCNW Papers, Box 8. Interestingly, many theorists of discursive democracy—including White, Bickford, Phillips, Mansbridge, and Young—argue for the importance of *inclusion* (or, in Phillips' framing, the "politics of presence"; others have written of a politics of "recognition") to make that democracy more possible. Jan Peterson, Lisel Burns, and others involved in the creation of the Leadership Training program seemed to have a clear sense of that need *in practice*: perhaps this stemmed from their earlier experiences with the Civil Rights Movement?

61 "National Congress of Neighborhood Women: Principles," 2 pp. typescript, undated [Fall/Winter 1974?], NCNW Papers, Box 1, Folder 8. See also report of a task-force on developing a statement of goals, November 27, 1979, NCNW Papers, Box 1, Folder 11.

62 "A Dialogue on the Organization, Goals, and Needs of the National Congress of Neighborhood Women," transcript taped in June 1978 between two NCNW board members (Michaela Hickey and Inez Padilla) and NCNW Executive Director, Christine Noschese, pp. 1–2. 35 pp. typescript. NCNW Papers, Box 1, Folder 8.

63 "A Dialogue," p. 7.

64 "Guidelines for women's Leadership Support Groups," undated, 26 pp. typescript. NCNW Papers, Box 109, Folder 12.

65 I am grateful to Amrita Basu and Eileen McDonagh for this framing of the issue.

66 See reports of such workshops in NCNW Papers, Box 11, Folder 6.

67 "Policies on Support Groups and Political Issues," written by Lisel Burns and Jan Peterson, edited by Ann Giordano. 3pp. typescript, NCNW National Office, undated. NCNW Papers, Box 109, File 15.

68 "National Congress of Neighborhood Women," undated [1982], typescript, 2 pp., NCNW Papers, Box 3, Folder 14.

69 Interview by Mary Belenky with María Fava, Ann Giordano, Elaine Carpinelli, Sandy [Schiaparelli?], Jan [Peterson], March 26, 1992. NCNW Papers, Box 8.

70 On the college program, see Belenky et al., "The National Congress of Neighborhood Women," especially pp. 215–18; also Terry Haywoode, "College for Neighborhood Women: Innovation and Growth," in *Learning Our Way: Essays in Feminist Education*, eds. Charlotte Bunch and Sandra Pollack (Trumansburg, NY: Crossing Press, 1983); Terry Haywoode, "Neighborhood Women Keeping It Together," *City Limits* (April 1985), pp. 20–21; and Terry Haywoode and Laura Polla Scanlon, "World of Our Mothers: College for Neighborhood Women," *Women's Studies Quarterly*, XXI, 3 and 4 (1993), pp. 133–41. On the importance of *education* in the process of conscientization and politicization, see Ackelsberg, *Free Women of Spain, passim*; and Rina Benmayor and Rosa M. Torrruellas, "Education, Cultural Rights, and Citizenship," in Cohen et al., eds., *Women Transforming Politics*, especially pp. 197–201.

71 Interview with author, "Voices of Feminism Oral History Project," Northampton, MA, April 10–11, 2005.

72 I am reminded, here, of the song from Rodgers and Hammerstein's *South Pacific* about hatred and prejudice, that "You've Got to Be Carefully Taught." NCNW's programs recognized that, in the context of a society characterized by inequalities and prejudice, tolerance and a sense of commonality also have "got to be carefully taught."

73 It is, I am sure, not coincidental that Barack Obama's 2008 presidential campaign schooled its volunteer organizers in the importance of the "story of self"—which highlights both obstacles overcome and cultural resources—as an essential component of its strategy.

74 See, for example, Ida Susser, *Norman Street: Poverty and Politics in an Urban Neighborhood* (New York: Oxford University Press, 1982); *Metropolitan Avenue* (video); Tamar Carroll, "Unlikely Allies: Forging a Multi-Racial Class-Based Women's Movement in 1970s Brooklyn," in *Feminist Coalitions: Historical Perspectives on Second-Wave Feminism in the United States*, ed. Stephanie Gilmore (Champaign: University of Illinois Press, 2008), pp. 196–224; and sources cited above, notes 40, 70.

11 FAMILIES, CARE AND CITIZENSHIP

1 Ackelsberg, "'Sisters' or 'Comrades'? The Politics of Friends and Families," in *Families, Politics, and Public Policy: A Feminist Dialogue on Women and the State*, edited by Irene Diamond (New York: Longman, 1983), pp. 339–56. For overviews of some earlier feminist critiques of the family, see Susan Moller Okin, "Families and Feminist Theory: Some Past and Present Issues," in *Feminism and Families*, edited and with an introduction by Hilde Lindemann Nelson (New York: Routledge, 1997), especially pp. 15–22; Naomi Zack, "'The Family' and Radical Family Theory," in *Feminism and Families*, pp. 43–51; Linda Nicholson, "The Myth of the Traditional Family," in *Feminism and Families*, pp. 27–42; Cheshire Calhoun, "Family's Outlaws: Rethinking the Connections between Feminism, Lesbianism, and the Family," in *Feminism and Families*, especially pp. 131–32; and Calhoun, *Feminism, the Family, and the Politics of the Closet: Lesbian and Gay Displacement* (Oxford: Oxford University Press, 2000).

2 Ackelsberg, "Sisters or Comrades," p. 350.

3 Exceptions to this include Mary Dietz, "Context Is All: Reconsidering Feminism and Citizenship," *Daedalus* 116 (1987), pp. 1–24 and "Citizenship with a Feminist Face: The Problem with Maternal Thinking," *Political Theory* 13 (1985), pp. 19–37, both reprinted in *Turning Operations: Feminism, Arendt and Politics* (New York: Routledge, 2002); Katherine Side, "In the Shadow of the Family: Women's Friendships with Women," in *Feminism and Families*, pp. 182–91; Marilyn Friedman, *What Are Friends For? Feminist Perspectives on Personal Relationships and Moral Theory* (Ithaca, NY: Cornell University Press, 1993) and Sybil Schwarzenbach, "On Civic Friendship," *Ethics* 107, 1 (October 1996), pp. 97–128.

4 I am using the broad definition of the work of care proposed by Berenice Fisher and Joan Tronto in "Toward a Feminist Theory of Caring," in *Circles of Care: Work and Identity in Women's Lives*, eds. Emily Abel and Martha Nelson (Albany, NY: State University of New York Press, 1990), p. 40, cited in Tronto, "Care as a Political Concept," in *Revisioning the Political: Feminist Reconstructions of Traditional Concepts in Western Political Theory*, eds. Nancy Hirschmann and Christine DiStefano (Boulder, CO: Westview Press, 1996), p. 142: "care is 'a *species activity that includes everything that we do to maintain, continue, and repair our 'world,' so that we can live in it as well as possible.* That world includes our bodies, our selves, and our environment, all of which we seek to interweave in a complex, life-sustaining web."

5 Okin, "Families and Feminist Theory," p. 24.

6 See, for example, Marilyn Friedman, "Welfare Cuts and the Ascendance of Market Patriarchy," *Hypatia* 3, 2 (Summer 1988), pp. 145–49; Saskia Sassen, *Cities in a World Economy*, 3rd edn. (Thousand Oaks, CA: Pine Forge Press, 2006), especially Chapter 6; and Sassen, *The Global City: New York, London, Tokyo*, 2nd edn. (Princeton, NJ: Princeton University Press, 2001), especially Chapters 8 and 9.

7 A similar set of questions was raised by Joan Tronto in "Care as a Political Concept," especially pp. 143, 147–51.

8 Calhoun, "Family's Outlaws," pp. 146, 138.

9 Nicholson, "The Myth of the Traditional Family," p. 40. On this point see also Stephanie Coontz, *The Way We Never Were: American Families and the Nostalgia Trap* (New York: Basic Books, 2000), especially Chapters 1, 4, and 6. Joan Tronto makes a related argument about how paying *political* attention to care might challenge some of the ways we engage in "othering," in "Care as a Political Concept," pp. 146–47. For some possible starting points for such a broadened conversation, see Anna Marie Smith, *Welfare Reform and Sexual Regulation* (New York: Cambridge University Press, 2007), especially Chapter 4.

10 See Mary Midgely and Judith Hughes, "Are Families Out of Date?" in *Feminism and Families*, p. 63.

11 See especially Nancy Folbre, *Valuing Children: Rethinking the Economics of the Family* (Cambridge, MA: Harvard University Press, 2008) and *The Invisible Heart: Economics and Family Values* (New York: The New Press, 2001); Okin, "Families and Feminist Theory"; Ann Shola Orloff, "Gender and the Social Rights of Citizenship," *American Sociological Review* 58, 3 (June 1993), pp. 303–28; Iris Marion Young, "Mothers, Citizenship and Independence: A Critique of Pure Family Values," *Ethics* 105, 3 (April 1995), pp. 535–56; Young, "House and Home: Variations on a Theme," in *Intersecting Voices: Dilemmas of Gender, Political Philosophy, and Policy* (Princeton, NJ: Princeton University Press, 1997), pp. 134–64; Eva Feder Kittay, "Taking Dependency Seriously: The Family and Medical Leave Act Considered in the Light of the Social Organization of Dependency Work and Gender Equality," *Hypatia* 10, 1 (Winter 1995), pp. 8–29; and Kittay, "Dependency, Equality, and Welfare," *Feminist Studies* 24, 1 (Spring 1998), pp. 32–43.

12 One exception—at least in terms of attention to the issue, and which makes a connection between the work of care and mothers' ability to work—is Michael Winerip, "Filling a Gap in Child Care, a Few Families at a Time," *The New York Times*, Sunday, November 30, 2008, Westchester and the Region, p. 5.

13 Ann Shola Orloff, "Gender and the Social Rights of Citizenship," p. 313.

14 On this point, see especially Susan Moller Okin, *Justice, Gender and the Family* (New York: Basic Books, 1989) and Okin, "Feminism, Women's Human Rights, and Cultural Differences," *Hypatia* 13, 2 (Spring 1998), pp. 32–52; Carole Pateman, "The Patriarchal Welfare State," in *Democracy and the State*, ed. Amy Gutmann (Princeton, NJ: Princeton University Press, 1988), pp. 231–60; Pateman, "Feminist Critiques of the Public/Private Dichotomy," in *The Disorder of Women* (Stanford, CA: Stanford University Press, 1989), pp. 118–40; and Pateman, *The Sexual Contract* (Stanford, CA: Stanford University Press, 1988). Joan Tronto explores several dimensions of this claim in "Care as a Political Concept," especially pp. 142–47.

15 Cited in Orloff, "Gender and the Social Rights of Citizenship," p. 313.

16 Ibid., p. 312.

17 Ibid., p. 321. See also Linda Gordon, ed., *Women, the State, and Welfare* (Madison: University of Wisconsin Press, 1990); and Gwendolyn Mink, *The Wages of Motherhood* (Ithaca, NY: Cornell University Press, 1996).

18 Wendy Sarvasy, "Social Citizenship from a Feminist Perspective," *Hypatia* 12, 4 (Fall 1997), pp. 54–73; Sarvasy, "From Man and Philanthropic Service to Feminist Social Citizenship," *Social Politics* 1, 3 (1994), pp. 306–25; and Sarvasy and Birte Siim, "Gender, Transitions to Democracy, and Citizenship," *Social Politics* 1, 3 (1994), pp. 249–55. For an interesting discussion of earlier social feminists in relation to local activists under CAP programs in the 1960s and 1970s, see Nancy Naples, "Toward a Multiracial Feminist Social-Democratic Praxis: Lessons from Grassroots Warriors in the U.S. War on Poverty," *Social Politics* 5, 3 (Fall 1998), p. 304.

19 "Gender and the Social Rights of Citizenship," p. 321.

20 The call for access to the labor market, of course, was not limited to socialist feminists. Many liberal feminists adopted a similar strategy, albeit for somewhat different reasons.

21 See, for example, Dorothy Dinnerstein, *The Mermaid and the Minotaur: Sexual Arrangements and Human Malaise* (New York: Harper and Row, 1976); Nancy Chodorow, *The Reproduction of Mothering: Psychoanalysis and the Sociology of Gender* (Berkeley: University of California Press, 1978); Pat Mainardi, "The Politics of Housework," in *Notes from the Second Year*, eds. S. Firestone and A. Koedt (New York: Radical Feminism, 1970), pp. 28–31; and Isaac Balbus, *Marxism and Domination: A Neo-Hegelian, Feminist, Psychoanalytic Theory of Sexual, Political and Technological Liberation* (Princeton, NJ: Princeton University Press, 1982). Yvonne Hirdman recently argued that, even in the supposed feminist "utopia" of Sweden, the labor market is very sex-segregated. Nevertheless, the wage gap between men and women has been reduced, and women can manage to raise children (without men to help) because of public policy that articulated, and institutionalized, the goal of gender equality as a communal/public good. "In Between – Gender Equality in Sweden," paper delivered at "What Is Feminist Politics Now?" conference sponsored by the Institute for Research on Women and Gender, Columbia University, Sept. 20, 2008.

22 The approach, as Hirdman has argued, that allowed for the "success" of the Swedish approach.

23 More recent arguments—especially by Nancy Folbre—have again raised broader questions of a *social* responsibility for raising children. See *The Invisible Heart: Economics and Family Values* (New York: The New Press, 2001), especially Chapter 5; and Folbre, *Valuing Children: Rethinking the Economics of the Family* (Cambridge, MA: Harvard University Press, 2008).

24 Jet Bussemaker's analysis of the ways these rationales have developed in the Netherlands has many parallels to the US case. See Bussemaker, "Rationales of Care in Contemporary Welfare States: The Case of Childcare in the Netherlands," *Social Politics* 5, 1 (Spring 1998), especially pp. 73, 90–91.

25 Of course, expectations about women's work are clearly class-differentiated. Middle- to upper-class women are suspect if they *do* work (when they don't "have" to because they have a husband to support them); while poor women are suspect and punished if they do *not*. See Chapter 4 above.

26 See especially Gwendolyn Mink, "The Lady and the Tramp (II): Feminist Welfare Politics, Poor Single Mothers, and the Challenge of Welfare Justice," *Feminist Studies* 24, 1 (Spring 1998), pp. 55–64, and "Aren't Poor Single Mothers Women? Feminists, Welfare Reform, and Welfare Justice," in *Whose Welfare?* ed. Mink (Ithaca, NY: Cornell University Press, 1999), pp. 171–88; Eva Feder Kittay, "Dependency, Equality, and Welfare," *Feminist Studies* 24, 1 (Spring 1998), pp. 32–43, and Kittay, "Welfare, Dependency, and a Public Ethic of Care," in *Whose Welfare?* pp. 189–213; and Felicia Kornbluh, "The Goals of the National Welfare Rights Movement: Why We Need Them Thirty Years Later," *Feminist Studies* 24, 1 (Spring 1998), p.

73 and Kornbluh, *The Battle for Welfare Rights: Politics and Poverty in Modern America* (Philadelphia, PA: University of Pennsylvania Press, 2007).

27 See Mink, "The Lady and the Tramp (II): Feminist Welfare Politics, Poor Single Mothers, and the Challenge of Welfare Justice"; "Aren't Poor Single Mothers Women?"; and *Welfare's End*, revised edn. (Ithaca, NY: Cornell University Press, 2002).

28 Piven, "Welfare and Work," in *Whose Welfare?* ed. Gwendolyn Mink (Ithaca, NY: Cornell University Press, 1999), pp. 83–99; see also Frances Fox Piven and Richard A. Cloward, *Regulating the Poor: The Functions of Public Welfare*, rev. edn. (New York: Pantheon, 1993).

29 Friedman, "Welfare Cuts and the Ascendance of Market Patriarchy," *Hypatia* 3, 2 (Summer 1988), pp. 147, 148.

30 On this point, see also Sonya Michel, "Childcare and Welfare (In)Justice," *Feminist Studies* 24, 1 (Spring 1998), pp. 44–54.

31 "Gender and the Social Rights of Citizenship," p. 316.

32 For a cogent framing of the contemporary care crisis see Ruth Rosen, "The Care Crisis," *The Nation* (March 12, 2007), available at www.thenation.com/doc/20070312/rosen.

33 See, for example, Joan Tronto, *Moral Boundaries: A Political Argument for an Ethic of Care* (New York: Routledge, 1993) and "Care as a Political Concept," especially pp. 149–50; Eva Feder Kittay, "Taking Dependency Seriously," "Dependency, Equality, and Welfare," and "Welfare, Dependency, and a Public Ethic of Care"; Emily Abel, *Hearts of Wisdom: American Women Caring for Kin, 1850–1940* (Cambridge, MA: Harvard University Press, 2000); Iris Marion Young, "Mothers, Citizenship, and Independence: A Critique of Pure Family Values," *Ethics* 105 (April 1995), pp. 535–56; and above, Chapter 4.

34 Susan Moller Okin, "Families and Feminist Theory," p. 23. Young makes a similar critique in "Mothers, Citizenship and Independence," pp. 543–44.

35 Kittay, "Taking Dependency Seriously," p. 18.

36 For one attempt at raising the question of care in a contemporary *political* context, see Traci Levy, "At the Intersection of Intimacy and Care: Redefining 'Family' through the Lens of a Public Ethic of Care," *Politics and Gender* 1, 1 (March 2005), pp. 65–95.

37 Joan Tronto, "Care as a Basis for Radical Political Judgments," *Hypatia* 10, 2 (Spring 1995), p. 146. See also Tronto, "Care as the Work of Citizens: A Modest Proposal," in *Women and Citizenship*, ed. Marilyn Friedman (New York: Oxford University Press, 2005), pp. 130–45; and Iris Young's related discussion, "Mothers, Citizenship, and Independence: A Critique of Pure Family Values," *Ethics* 105 (April 1995), pp. 535–56.

38 Martha Minow and Mary Lyndon Shanley, "Relational Rights and Responsibilities: Revisioning the Family in Liberal Political Theory and Law," *Hypatia* 11, 1 (Winter 1996), pp. 22, 23.

39 Tronto, "Care as a Political Concept," p. 149.

40 Narayan, "Colonialism and Its Others: Considerations On Rights and Care Discourses," *Hypatia* 10, 2 (Spring 1995), pp. 134–35; see also Uday Mehta, *Liberalism and Empire: A Study in Nineteenth-Century British Liberal Thought* (Chicago: University of Chicago Press, 1999).

41 Williams, "The Pain of Word Bondage," in *The Alchemy of Race and Rights* (Cambridge, MA: Harvard University Press, 1991), p. 151. See also "On Being the Object of Property," in ibid., pp. 217–36.

42 Narayan, "Colonialism and Its Others," pp. 138, 139. See also Tronto, "Care as a Political Concept," pp. 147–50.

43 Virginia Held, "The Meshing of Care and Justice," *Hypatia* 10, 2 (Spring 1995), p. 131.
44 Sybil Schwarzenbach, "On Civic Friendship," *Ethics* 107, 1 (October 1996), pp. 98, 122–23, n. 47.
45 Naples, "Toward a Multiracial, Feminist Social-Democratic Praxis," pp. 288, 306.
46 Orleck, *Storming Caesars Palace: How Black Mothers Fought Their Own War on Poverty* (Boston: Beacon Press, 2005). And see Chapter 10, above.
47 See, for example, Young's critique of Galston in "Mothers, Citizenship, and Independence."
48 Young, "Mothers, Citizenship and Independence," pp. 552, 551.
49 Ibid., p. 553.
50 Cheshire Calhoun, "Family's Outlaws," p. 147.
51 Karen Struening, "Feminist Challenges to the New Familialism: Lifestyle Experimentation and the Freedom of Intimate Association," *Hypatia* 11, 1 (Winter 1996), p. 138; and Levy, "At the Intersection of Intimacy and Care: Redefining 'Family' through the Lens of a Public Ethic of Care," *Politics and Gender* 1, 1 (March 2005), pp. 65–95.
52 See especially Mink, "Aren't Poor Single Mothers Women?"; related arguments about the effective denial of citizenship rights to women are reflected in Young, "Mothers, Citizenship and Independence," especially pp. 553 and 554; and Anna Marie Smith, *Welfare Reform and Sexual Regulation*. For potential connections, see also Jyl Josephson, "Citizenship, Same-Sex Marriage, and Feminist Critiques of Marriage," *Perspectives on Politics* 3, 2 (June 2005), pp. 269–84; and Nancy Polikoff, *Beyond (Straight and Gay) Marriage: Valuing All Families Under the Law* (Boston: Beacon Press, 2008), especially Chapters 3, 7, 9.

12 DEMOCRACY AND (IN)EQUALITY

† Author's note: This chapter was originally written and published as a review essay in *Feminist Studies*. I have revised it for this volume, but am struck by the degree to which, even though the political-economic context has changed considerably between 2001 and 2008, many of the questions it raised about both activism in the face of retrenchment and about the relationship between struggles for democracy and efforts to attend to cultural, ethnic, and gender differences remain central concerns for students of social change.
1 Mary Louise Pratt, "Where To? What Next," in *Cultures of Politics, Politics of Cultures: Re-visioning Latin American Social Movements*, eds. Sonia E. Alvarez, Evelina Dagnino, and Arturo Escobar (Boulder, CO: Westview Press, 1998), p. 434.
2 Dagnino, "Culture, Citizenship, and Democracy: Changing Discourses and Practices of the Latin American Left," ibid., p. 45.
3 Two scholars who have framed these issues most dramatically (though from somewhat differing perspectives) are Nancy Hartsock, "Foucault on Power: A Theory for Women?" in *Feminism/Postmodernism*, ed. Linda Nicholson (New York: Routledge, 1990), pp. 157–75; and Shane Phelan, *Getting Specific* (Minnesota: University of Minnesota Press, 1994), especially Chapter 8; "All the Comforts of Home: The Genealogy of Community," pp. 235–50 in Nancy Hirschmann and Christine DiStefano, eds., *Revisioning the Political: Feminist Reconstructions of Traditional Concepts in Western Political Theory* (Boulder, CO: Westview Press, 1996); and *Sexual Strangers: Gays, Lesbians and Dilemmas of Citizenship* (Philadelphia, PA: Temple University Press, 2001). See also Ernesto Laclau and Chantal Mouffe, *Hegemony and Socialist Strategy: Towards a Radical Democratic Politics* (London: Verso, 1995); and Engin Isin and Patricia Wood, *Citizenship and Identity* (London: Sage Publications, 1999), especially Chapters 1 and 2.

4 See, for example, Seyla Benhabib, ed., *Democracy and Difference: Contesting the Boundaries of the Political* (Princeton, NJ: Princeton University Press, 1996), especially essays by Benhabib, Iris Young, Jane Mansbridge, and Anne Phillips; Nancy Fraser, *Unruly Practices: Power, Discourse and Gender in Contemporary Social Theory* (Minneapolis: University of Minnesota Press, 1989) and "Rethinking the Public Sphere: A Contribution to the Critique of Actually Existing Democracy," in *Habermas and the Public Sphere*, ed. Craig Calhoun (Cambridge, MA: the MIT Press, 1992), and essays by Benhabib, Harry Boyte, and Mary Ryan, in that same volume. I have explored these issues in Chapter 8, above.

5 T.H. Marshall, "Citizenship and Social Class," in *Citizenship and Social Class and Other Essays* (Cambridge: Cambridge University Press, 1950).

6 See, for example, Gwendolyn Mink, *The Wages of Motherhood: Inequality in the Welfare State, 1917–1942* (Ithaca, NY: Cornell University Press, 1995) and especially Mink, *Welfare's End* (Ithaca, NY: Cornell University Press, 1998; revised edn., 2002); also Linda Gordon, *Pitied But Not Entitled* (New York: Basic Books, 1994); Gordon and Nancy Fraser, "Decoding 'Dependency': Inscriptions of Power in a Keyword of the US Welfare State," in Mary Lyndon Shanley and Uma Narayan, eds., *Reconstructing Political Theory: Feminist Perspectives* (Cambridge: Polity Press, 1997), pp. 25–47; and Chapter 4 above.

7 Martin Shefter's discussion of the 1974 New York City fiscal crisis now seems prescient in this regard; see "The New York City Fiscal Crisis: The Politics of Inflation and Retrenchment," *The Public Interest*, Summer 1977. Also, *Political Crisis/ Fiscal Crisis: The Collapse and Revival of New York City* (New York: Columbia University Press, 1992). As I complete the editing of this volume, the US is in the midst of what everyone now seems to agree is the "most serious financial crisis since the Great Depression." The Bush Administration has requested—and Congress has authorized—unprecedented power to use taxpayer funds to rescue banks and businesses. The Secretary of the Treasury attempted (although not quite successfully) to avoid all democratic checks on his use of the funds—on the grounds that he must be able to act quickly in an emergency. Where this will all lead, we do not know.

8 Fraser, "The Struggle over Needs: Outline of a Socialist-Feminist Critical Theory of Late Capitalist Political Culture," pp. 161–87, in *Unruly Practices: Power, Discourse, and Gender in Contemporary Social Theory* (Minneapolis: University of Minnesota Press, 1989), quotation, p. 171; see also "Women, Welfare, and the Politics of Need Interpretation," ibid., pp. 144–60.

9 Naples, *Grassroots Warriors: Activist Mothering, Community Work, and the War on Poverty* (New York: Routledge, 1998), p. 3.

10 Ibid., p. 114. For another study of a similar moment, see Annelise Orleck, *Storming Caesars Palace: How Black Mothers Fought Their Own War on Poverty* (Boston: Beacon Press, 2005).

11 Kaplan, "Female Consciousness and Collective Action: The Case of Barcelona, 1910–18," *Signs: A Journal of Women and Society* 7, 3 (1982), pp. 545–66; also above, Chapters 3 and 10.

12 Naples, *Grassroots Warriors*, p. 181.

13 *Grassroots Warriors*, p. 199.

14 Ibid., p. 195.

15 Annelise Orleck makes a similar assertion at the conclusion of her study of welfare activists in Las Vegas, "'If It Wasn't for You, I'd Have Shoes for My Children': The Political Education of Las Vegas Welfare Mothers," in *The Politics of Motherhood: Activist Voices from Left to Right*, eds., Alexis Jetter, Annelise Orleck and Diana Taylor (Hanover, NH: Universtiy Press of New England, 1997), p. 116. See also

Orleck, *Storming Caesars Palace* and multiple contributors to Gwendolyn Mink, ed., *Whose Welfare?* (Ithaca, NY: Cornell University Press, 1999).

16 Scitz, "Class, Gender and Resistance in the Appalachian Coalfields," in *Community Activism and Feminist Politics*, pp. 233–34. Eve S. Weinbaum explores similar phenomena in *To Move a Mountain: Fighting the Global Economy in Appalachia* (New York: Norton, 2004).

17 Roberta Feldman, Susan Stall, and Patricia Wright, "'The Community Needs to Be Built by Us': Women Organizing in Chicago Public Housing," in Naples, ed., *Community Activism and Feminist Politics*, p. 272. See also Mary Pardo, "Creating Community: Mexican American Women in Eastside Los Angeles," pp. 275–300, in *Community Activism and Feminist Politics*; and Pardo, "Mexican-American Grassroots Women Activists," *Frontiers* 11 (1990), pp. 1–7.

18 Naples, "Introduction: Women's Community Activism and Feminist Activist Research."

19 Pardo, "Creating Community," p. 276.

20 Wittner, "Reconceptualizing Agency in Domestic Violence Court," p. 84. Note the parallel with Linda Gordon's discussions of the ways women used social service agencies to try to improve their situations, even if that meant subjecting themselves and their families to greater levels of social "control." See "Family Violence, Feminism, and Social Control," pp. 178–98 in Gordon, ed., *Women, the State, and Welfare* (Madison: University of Wisconsin Press, 1990).

21 Kendrick, "Producing the Battered Woman: Shelter Politics and the Power of the Feminist Voice," p. 155.

22 Naples, "Women's Community Activism: Exploring the Dynamics of Politicization and Diversity," p. 343. See also above, Chapters 9 and 10.

23 Kathleen Blee, "Introduction: Women on the Left/Women on the Right," in *No Middle Ground: Women and Radical Protest*, ed. Kathleen Blee (New York: New York University Press, 1998), p. 3. See also Blee, *Women of the Klan: Racism and Gender in the 1920s* (Berkeley: University of California Press, 1991) and *Inside Organized Racism: Women in the Hate Movement* (Berkeley: University of California Press, 2002).

24 Ibid., p. 3.

25 Belinda Robnett, "African American Women in the Civil Rights Movement: Spontaneity and Emotion in Social Movement Theory," in *No Middle Ground*, p. 67.

26 Beth Roy, "Goody Two-shoes and the Hell-Raisers: Women's Activism, Women's Reputations in Little Rock," in *No Middle Ground*, p. 115.

27 "From Housewives to Activists: Women and the Division of Political Labor in the Boston Anti-Busing Movement," in *No Middle Ground*, pp. 251–88, citation, p. 253.

28 "'We're Fighting Millionaires!': The Clash of Gender and Class in Appalachian Women's Union Organizing," *No Middle Ground*, p. 303.

29 *The Politics of Motherhood: Activist Voices from Left to Right*, eds., Alexis Jetter, Annelise Orleck and Diana Taylor.

30 Orleck, "Introduction: Tradition Unbound: Radical Mothers in International Perspective," in *The Politics of Motherhood*, p. 5. For an early framing of motherhood as *institution* see Adrienne Rich, *Of Woman Born: Motherhood as Experience and Institution* (New York: Norton, 1976).

31 Diana Taylor, "Making a Spectacle: The Mothers of the Plaza de Mayo," in *The Politics of Motherhood*, pp. 192–93.

32 "Motherhood and the Politics of Women's Resistance: Israeli Women Organizing for Peace," in *The Politics of Motherhood*, p. 145.

33 Rena Hammami, "Palestinian Motherhood and Political Activism on the West Bank and Gaza Strip," in *The Politics of Motherhood*, p. 164.

34 Kaplan, "Naked Mothers and Maternal Sexuality: Some Reactions to the Aba Women's War," in *The Politics of Motherhood*, p. 220.

35 Claudia Koonz, "Motherhood and the Politics of the Far Right," in *The Politics of Motherhood*. I am struck here by the parallels to an argument Susan Ostrander made some years ago, in a rather different context, on the compromises between gender and class identity made by upper-class women in the US. See Susan A. Ostrander, *Women of the Upper Class* (Philadelphia, PA: Temple University Press, 1984).

36 Hirsch, "Feminism at the Maternal Divide: A Diary," in *The Politics of Motherhood*, p. 353.

37 Ruddick, "Rethinking 'Maternal Politics'", pp. 368, 380. Jean Elshtain has made some similar comments in "Is There a Feminist Tradition on War and Peace?" in *Real Politics: At the Center of Everyday Life* (Baltimore, MD: The Johns Hopkins University Press, 1997), pp. 303–17.

38 Temma Kaplan, *Crazy for Democracy: Women in Grassroots Movements* (New York: Routledge, 1997), p. 3.

39 On that "third space," see, for example, Iris Young, *Inclusion and Democracy* (New York: Oxford University Press, 2000), especially Chapter 5.

40 "Mobilization without Emancipation? Women's Interests, the state, and Revolution in Nicaragua," *Feminist Studies* 11, 2 (Summer 1985), pp. 227–53.

41 Kaplan, *Crazy for Democracy*, p. 186.

42 Many feminist (and other) observers of welfare states have noted women's special relationship to them—whether as those who effectively act as the "coordinators" of its services, or as the "reserve army of the welfare system." See Laura Balbo, "Crazy Quilts: Rethinking the Welfare State Debate from a Woman's Point of View," in Ann Showstack Sassoon, *Women and the State: The Shifting Boundaries of Public and Private* (London: Hutchinson, 1987), pp. 45–71; Helga Hernes, "Women and the Welfare State: The Transition from Private to Public Dependence," ibid., pp. 72–92; Michael Walzer, "Socializing the Welfare State," in *Democracy and the Welfare State*, ed. Amy Gutman (Princeton, NJ: Princeton University Press, 1988), p. 23; Carole Pateman, "The Patriarchal Welfare State," ibid., pp. 231–60; Cynthia Cockburn, *The Local State* (London: Pluto Press, 1977); and Ida Susser, "Working Class Women, Social Protest, and Changing Ideologies," in Ann Bookman and Sandra Morgen, eds., *Women and the Politics of Empowerment* (Philadelphia, PA: Temple University Press, 1988).

43 Kaplan, *Crazy for Democracy*, p. 188. One of the fascinating aspects of Barack Obama's presidential campaign—in addition to his successful melding of grassroots and electoral political strategies—is the campaign's effort to *maintain* those networks, so as to be able to call on them over the long term. What this will mean for democratic politics in the US remains to be seen.

44 "Introduction: The Cultural and the Political in Latin American Social Movements," in *Cultures of Politics, Politics of Cultures: Re-Visioning Latin American Social Movements*, eds. Sonia E. Alvarez, Evelina Dagnino, and Arturo Escobar (Boulder, CO: Westview Press, 1998), p. 23.

45 Evelina Dagnino, "Culture, Citizenship, and Democracy: Changing Discourses and Practices of the Latin American Left," in *Cultures of Politics, Politics of Cultures*, p. 37.

46 Dagnino, "Culture, Citizenship and Democracy," p. 50. On the relationship among culture, politics and citizenship see also Isin and Wood, *Identity and Citizenship*.

47 Verónica Schild, "New Subjects of Rights? Women's Movements and the Construction of Citizenship in the 'New Democracies,'" in *Cultures of Politics, Politics of Cultures*, p. 95.

48 Sonia Alvarez, "Latin American Feminisms 'Go Global': Trends of the 1990s and Challenges for the New Millenium," in *Cultures of Politics, Politics of Cultures*, pp. 293–

324; and Elizabeth Jelin, "Toward a Culture of Participation and Citizenship: Challenges for a More Equitable World," in *Cultures of Politics, Politics of Cultures*, pp. 405–14. See also Amrita Basu, "Introduction," *The Challenge of Local Feminisms: Women's Movements in a Global Perspective*, ed. Amrita Basu (Boulder, CO: Westview Press, 1995).

49 George Yúdice, "The Globalization of Culture and the New Civil Society," in *Cultures of Politics, Politics of Cultures*, p. 373.

50 Melucci, "Third World or Planetary Conflicts?" in *Cultures of Politics, Politics of Cultures*, p. 426.

51 Slater, "Rethinking the Spatialities of Social Movements: Questions of (B)orders, Culture, and Politics in Global Times," in *Cultures of Politics, Politics of Cultures*, p. 386. Note the comment of Carolyn Howe to the same effect, "Gender, Race, and Community Activism: Competing Strategies in the Struggle for Public Education," in *Community Activism and Feminist Politics*, p. 251. For discussions about the process of depoliticization in the contemporary US see Matthew Crenson and Benjamin Ginsburg, *Downsizing Democracy: How America Sidelined Its Citizens and Privatized Its Public* (Baltimore, ND: Johns Hopkins University Press, 2002); and Theda Skocpol, *Diminished Democracy: From Membership to Management in American Civic Life* (Norman: University of Oklahoma Press, 2003).

52 Kay B. Warren, "Indigenous Movements as a Challenge to the Unified Social Movement Paradigm for Guatemala," in *Cultures of Politics, Politics of Cultures*, pp. 179–82. For another perspective on the potential dangers of Pan-Latino identity in the US context see Cristina Beltrán, "Patrolling Borders: Hybrids, Hierarchies and the Challenge of *Mestizaje*," *Political Research Quarterly* 57, 4 (Dec. 2004), pp. 595–607.

53 Grueso, Rosero and Escobar, "The Process of Black Community Organizing in the Southern Pacific Coast Region of Colombia," in *Cultures of Politics, Politics of Cultures*, pp. 196–219.

54 As Alvarez, Dagnino and Escobar put it in their "Introduction: The Cultural and the Political in Latin American Social Movements," p. 21.

55 Baierle, "The Explosion of Experience: The Emergence of a New Ethical-Political Principle in Popular Movements in Porto Alegre, Brazil," in *Cultures of Politics, Politics of Cultures*, pp. 123, 135.

56 Slater, "Rethinking the Spatialities of Social Movements," p. 384.

57 Miguel Díaz Barriga, "Beyond the Domestic and the Public: *Colonos* Participation in Urban Movements in Mexico City," in *Cultures of Politics, Politics of Cultures*, p. 260.

58 Jelin, "Toward a Culture of Participation and Citizenship," p. 413.

59 Melucci, "Third World or Planetary Conflicts?" pp. 426, 429.

60 Schattschneider, *The Semi-Sovereign People* (New York: Holt Rinehart, 1960); Peter Bachrach and Morton Baratz, "Two Faces of Power," *American Political Science Review* LVI (1962), pp. 947–52; and "Decisions and Non-Decisions: An Analytical Framework," *American Political Science Review* LVII (1963), pp. 641–51.

61 *Poor People's Movements: How They Succeed, Why They Fail* (New York: Random House, 1977); *Challenging Authority: How Ordinary People Change America* (Lanham, MD: Rowman and Littlefield, 2006).

62 Feminist historians have been recovering the stories of many such projects. See, for example, Seth Koven and Sonya Michel, eds., *Mothers of a New World: Maternalist Politics and the Origins of Welfare States* (New York: Routledge, 1993); Kathryn Kish Sklar, *Florence Kelly and the Nation's Work* (New Haven: Yale University Press, 1995); Suzanne Lebsock, "Women and American Politics, 1880–1920," pp. 35–62, in Louise A. Tilly and Patricia Gurin, eds., *Women, Politics and Change* (New York: Russell Sage Foundation, 1990); Vivien Hart, *Bound By Our Constitution: Women,*

Workers, and the Minimum Wage (Princeton, NJ: Princeton University Press, 1994); and Kathryn Kish Sklar, Anja Schuler, and Susan Strasser, eds., *Social Justice Feminists in the United States and Germany: A Dialogue in Documents, 1885–1933* (Ithaca, NY: Cornell University Press, 1998).

63 Kaplan, *Crazy for Democracy*, p. 189.

INDEX